THE LONELY SEA AND THE SKY

Sir Francis Chichester was born in Barnstaple in 1901 and educated at Marlborough College.

His life was packed with adventure and excitement. At 18 he emigrated to New Zealand with £10 in his pocket. He worked as a stoker, sheep-herder, horse-wrangler, lumberjack, coal-miner, gold-prospector and salesman. As a flier and sailor his exploits are legendary. In 1931 he made the world's first solo long-distance seaplane flight and the first east-west solo crossing of the Tasman Sea. In 1960 he won the first solo sailing race across the Atlantic and in 1966–7 accomplished the first single-handed solo circumnavigation of the world. His voyage captured everyone's imagination and on his return he was knighted by Queen Elizabeth II.

Among Sir Francis' many books are *The Lonely Sea and the Sky*, *Along the Clipper Way*, *Gipsy Moth Circles the World*, and *Alone Across the Atlantic*.

Sir Francis Chichester died in 1972

Francis Chichester

The Lonely Sea
and the Sky

Pan Books London and Sydney

First published 1964 by Hodder and Stoughton Ltd
Published 1967 by Pan Books Ltd
This new edition published 1985 by Pan Books Ltd,
Cavaye Place, London SW10 9PG
9 8 7 6
© Francis Chichester 1964
Maps © Hodder and Stoughton Ltd, 1964
ISBN 0 330 29079 7
Printed and bound in Great Britain by
Richard Clay (The Chaucer Press) Ltd,
Bungay, Suffolk

To
Sheila, my wife,
with my admiration, respect
and gratitude,
as well as my love

AUTHOR'S NOTE

If this book has any literary merit it is greatly due to John Anderson who selected the more interesting parts of my long story. I wrote far too much, for one reason; little voyages have been sweet to me – on a bicycle or a horse, on foot, skis or skates, but there is no room for bicycles in a biography.

Here is that great poem, *Sea Fever*,* because it gives in only twelve lines the key to my life-time search for romance and adventure.

I must go down to the seas again, to the lonely sea and the sky,
And all I ask is a tall ship and a star to steer her by,
And the wheel's kick and the wind's song and the white sails shaking,
And a grey mist on the sea's face and a grey dawn breaking.

I must go down to the seas again, for the call of the running tide
Is a wild call and a clear call that may not be denied;
And all I ask is a windy day with the white clouds flying,
And the flung spray and the blown spume, and the sea-gulls crying.

I must go down to the seas again, to the vagrant gipsy life,
To the gull's way and the whale's way where the wind's like a whetted knife;
And all I ask is a merry yarn from a laughing fellow-rover,
And quiet sleep and a sweet dream when the long trick's over.

> With thanks to the greatest of sea-poets,
> John Masefield, the Poet Laureate.

FRANCIS CHICHESTER

* Reprinted by permission of the Society of Authors and Dr John Masefield, OM; also The Macmillan Company (New York).

INTRODUCTION

We know nothing of the boyhood of Ulysses, and it has always seemed to me a great loss that he did not write the story of his early life after he had got back from his travels. Perhaps he could not; perhaps Tennyson was right, and he set off again 'to sail beyond the sunset', leaving himself no time for recollection in tranquillity. But still, it is a pity.

Autobiography is an intensely difficult task, and whatever satisfaction the writing of his own life may give the man who writes it, his readers will be satisfied seldom. If you are interested in a man, you want to know as much as you can about him, not only what he did, but what made him want to do it, what formed him, moulded him into the kind of man he is. Of what formed Ulysses, we know nothing; at the other extreme, in that lovely chapter of autobiography by W. H. Hudson, *Far away and long ago*, we read on with excitement to find suddenly that we have got to the last page and that Hudson is still about five years old. In so far as a man can succeed in making a rounded whole of a life that he has not yet finished living, I think Francis Chichester has succeeded in this book. His boyhood, his young manhood, achievement in maturity, all are there, credible, interesting always, and the more moving because the record is unadorned. How Homer would have loved a story Chichester tells of one of his early adventures in his North Devon woods. It is best to hear him *tell* it, in his quiet, unemphatic voice, rich in quarter-tones:

Once I fell from a crow's nest in an oak tree. First I was falling through branches, hitting one and then another, and then for the last twenty feet or so, dropping clear. I hit the ground with a terrific whang, and everything went black. I was in great pain, and wondered what damage had been done. I didn't move a millimetre from my position when I landed, just stayed dead still for what seemed a long time,

9

although, perhaps, it was only about a quarter of an hour. Gradually, the shock went away, and I tried to move my legs and body. To my astonishment, nothing was broken, and in a few minutes I was moving about without much pain. Since then I have tried this technique time after time with success – relaxing completely after a fall, or a big shock.

After his remarkable single-handed crossing of the Atlantic in 1962, Chichester began contemplating a book on the record of his life. I rather pressed him to it. I had been a good deal mixed up in the planning of his Transatlantic voyage, and I had edited his logs to produce a book. It seemed to me that Chichester is one of the really great men of our time – great in a *personal* way that is rare in this period of mass parties, mass achievement, and competing nationalisms. Chichester is in the line of great individualists who have enriched human history, in which, perhaps, our English race is (or was) particularly rich – Martin Frobisher, Richard Burton, Charles Doughty, Waterton, Shackleton and their peers. So I pressed him to write some record of his life, before he became too deeply involved in the next adventure.

His response to this was both flattering and vexatious. He said Yes, he would write the book I wanted him to write, but only if I would take his manuscript as he poured out memories of his life and put it into order for him. Now no man could feel other than proud at such a request, but to me it was vexing, and a severe practical problem too, because my association with Chichester has been solely related to the sea, and while we can talk the same language, as it were, here, his immense achievement in the air would have to be history rather than living experience. However, after some argument, I took it on. This book is the outcome of our partnership.

I must make it clear that I have been throughout a most junior partner. I am by trade a carpenter in words (a joiner, perhaps, if I am feeling arrogant), and like any good carpenter I respect my material. This book is in no sense 'ghosted' – a horrible term for a horrible form of literary faking. Everything in this book is Chichester's own: all that I have done is to cut and tighten here and there, as a documentary film may be cut and tautened by its editor, and occasionally do the mortice-work for joining things together. I have added nothing, commented on nothing: Chichester speaks for himself.

And I think that what he has to say is infinitely worth listening to. In an age when human society is inevitably becoming more and more highly organized, when great projects like the development of nuclear energy require the whole resources of the community, it is good to be reminded that one man's vision can still be the driving-force towards wholly individual achievement. Chichester is a single-hander, content to depend on himself, to get out of difficulties by himself. A superficial judgement would be that this is a selfish, or at least self-centred, attitude to life, but that would be a complete misunderstanding of Chichester's complex character. In the best sense, he is one of the least selfish men I have ever come across: he has undertaken whatever project he has set himself with no particular thought of gain, with no demands on others, and with a deep humility of conviction that in setting out to accomplish some hazardous purpose *by himself* he is fulfilling what he came into the world to do, and thereby performing a service. And in this, I think, he is quite right. His obvious services to the rest of us – his work on navigation for the RAF, for instance – have been great, but to my mind they are secondary to his demonstration of man's continuing ability to fend for himself – '*to strive, to seek, to find, and not to yield*'.

J. R. L. ANDERSON

CONTENTS

ILLUSTRATIONS IN PHOTOGRAVURE

Cover photograph of *Gipsy Moth IV* by Ian Yeomans

LINE ILLUSTRATIONS

Maps by A. Spark

*'From death before we are ready to die,
good Lord deliver us.'*

F.C.

PART ONE

CHAPTER ONE

THE BEGINNING OF THINGS

MY first adventure was the snake bite. I was eleven, and I had been out in the woods in the spring. There was a sheltered valley with a stream, the Yeo, running down it, which led from my Aunt Rosalie's lake at Arlington; a lush little valley with huge clumps of a broad-leaved plant like a giant rhubarb. I saw a snake twisting through the undergrowth beside a ride through the wood where it had been sunning itself. I caught it by the tail, got out my handkerchief and stowed it in that, then fastened the four corners together and set off for home, about three miles away. Half-way across a big hillside field I saw a beetle in the grass, and thought it would be nice for the snake to have a feed. I took it out and put it on the grass, but it paid no attention to the beetle. Holding it by its neck, I touched its mouth with the beetle, but still it paid no attention; instead, coiled itself up and, bending its head back, hissed at me. I moved my hand to put it back in the handkerchief and it struck my second finger. This stung like six wasp stings, and I danced about sucking the finger, which quickly swelled tight and went blue. I put the viper back in the handkerchief and set off for home. (I wonder why it did not bite me again?)

I was alternately running and walking. My arm was swelling and painful, particularly in the armpit. I got very frightened and, being intensely religious then, knelt down on the grass track through the wood at the top of the hill and prayed that I would not die. It was a lovely spring day and dappled sunlight was coming through the trees. When I reached the road in the valley at the back of our house, I met a farmer on horseback and told him I had been bitten by a snake; I undid the handkerchief and showed it to him. He got down from his horse and killed it with his heel, for which I was sorry.

When I reached home and told my father what had happened he said, 'What a thing to do, bringing the snake home; it might have bitten your sister.' (He was very fond of my sister.) He then told me to get on my bicycle and set off for the Infirmary in Barnstaple, four and a half miles away. By the time I reached Barnstaple, I was getting lightheaded, and lost my way in the town, although I knew it all perfectly well. I remember sitting on a bench in a waiting-room. I was very hazy by this time, but I can still see the semi-oval white gauze-covered frame being put over my face, and still recall the dreadful feeling of suffocation when the chloroform poured on the mask began to take effect. I think that was the worst of the whole affair. I saw my father, who had harnessed the buggy and followed me, standing by my bed. There was a very sharp pain, presumably as they started slicing open my finger, and then I passed out.

I heard afterwards that they had sent my father back to fetch the snake, so that they could use some of the poison as an antidote, but then decided not to do so, and waited until some stuff came down from London on a train. This arrived in the evening, and it rippled round inside me as they squirted syringefuls of it into the skin of my stomach. Afterwards my father told me that they did not know until next morning if I was going to survive.

This was my first experience of publicity. The adventure was reported in the local paper, and I seemed to have a stream of visitors in the hospital. They included Nancy Platt and my cousin Margaret, whom I adored.

      •   •   •

I do not know if I was born with a passion for spending all day alone in the wildest parts of the countryside. I suspect it was due to circumstances, such as the start of my school life. When I was seven I was sent off to school at Ellerslie, about seven miles away. My parents used to drive me there in the family buggy. During my first term the senior boys of the school were having a game, which was to prevent some of them from entering the building. I was standing on the concrete floor of the washplace at the time, with a row of basins round two sides of the room, and above the basins a row of oblong windows, hinged at the top, which pushed outwards. Through one of these windows appeared the head and shoulders of my brother, trying to get into the building. I picked up a handful of sawdust from a box on the floor and threw it in his face. It was a silly, thoughtless thing to do, but certainly not done from malice, only excitement. A bit of this sawdust went into his eye, and I can remember his bending over the basin and bathing it.

As a result of this I was 'put in Coventry' for three weeks, and for the whole of that time not a single boy in the school spoke to me. My brother, who was four and a half years older than me, was one of the senior boys. I do not know if he had any part in the 'Coventry' punishment, but he never spoke to me during the period of it. It seems hard to believe that senior boys would do such a thing to a seven-year-old new boy, just because of a stupid joke which went wrong. I can assume only that I must have been very objectionable, perhaps precocious; I don't know.

This episode turned me into a rebel against my fellows; every boy was an enemy unless he proved himself to be a friend. I seemed to have to fight for everything, and the school appeared as tough as a prison. To make matters worse, I was often in trouble with the headmaster. My first term I was up for a beating seven times. The headmaster, who was a big, powerful man, sent one up to one's dormitory at a fixed time. Here, one waited beside one's bed. Being kept waiting was the worst part, and I couldn't stop myself from trembling. He made us strip off our trousers, and beat us on the bare bottom. But not always. Sometimes he made us strip off and bend over, and then didn't beat us. Outside the windows of that dormitory there were creeping plants like Cape Gooseberries with bobble-shaped fruit dangling in the wind. Waiting there, I used to see the sparrows flitting amongst this creeper, and this stayed in my memory as a picture of misery. After a year or so my parents took me away from this school; but not because of the tough conditions, only because I was always ill there, which was a nuisance.

I made no friends at that school, and I had none at home. I had two sisters, but the older, Barbara, was five years younger than me, and we hadn't much in common in the way of adventure. I gradually drifted into the habit of setting off on my own into an escape world of excitement and adventure.

By the time I was transferred to another preparatory school, the Old Ride, at Branksome, Bournemouth, I must have been a thorough savage, a rebel against everybody, including my parents. But I loved the Old Ride. I liked the boys, I liked the masters and I liked the place itself with its strong, pine smell, and the sandy soil covered with pine needles. In summer we used to go down to the sea through a chine in the cliff, and bathe every morning. The salty water and the hot sunshine made one feel so languorous that it was difficult to struggle up the chine. I usually found time to scan some of the silvery-sided leaves looking for puss moth caterpillars, with their tapered green bodies and huge, dark-faced heads with two horns. We would be quite content to get a little brown egg or two on the underside of a leaf, and rear the caterpillars ourselves, until they made cocoons in a piece of pine bark. The headmaster, S. A. Phillips, with his stubby, round figure, walrus moustache (off which he would suck drops of soup) and big round spectacles which he pushed up his forehead, made his mistakes, but who doesn't? Perhaps one of the worst that I got involved in was when our dormitory was caught after Lights Out with everybody visiting some other boy in his bed. There was the most frightful hullabaloo about this, and we were brought up for questioning one at a time for week after week, and finally all flogged. We were told we were very lucky not to get the sack, and I believe that if we had not all been involved, we would have. No one mentioned the word homosexuality, and I would not have known what it meant if it had been mentioned. And as we used to visit every other bed in turn, I am quite sure that I must have known if any of the boys were interested in this vice. I don't think any of them knew anything about it, and that we merely used to go and swop yarns, and the whole spice of the matter was that it was forbidden to talk after Lights Out. Later, I nearly got expelled from my public school for the same offence when I was caught handing back a piece of indiarubber that I had borrowed from another boy, and which was suspected of being a note. At that time I still did not know what homosexuality was, and was not in the least interested. Maybe this was unusual at a public school. My view is that only one or two boys went in for it, though the masters seemed to think that every boy in the school was at it.

One of the first excitements at the Old Ride was a visit from HMS *Eclipse*, a cruiser training ship for Osborne cadets. We played cricket against them and, after dark, they turned their searchlight on to the school from where they were anchored in Bournemouth Bay, and I thought this was thrilling. From my dormitory window I could see the Old Harry rocks at Swanage, and I wonder what I would have thought if a fortune-teller had told me that fifty years later I should be navigating *Stormvogel* in the dark to an anchorage near these rocks so that a new main halliard could be rove during the Fastnet race.

One of the masters was a young parson called Copleston, who was a tremendous favourite with us. He came to stay at my home one holiday. My mother liked him, but I don't think my father did, and the visit was not a great success. Another great favourite as a master was a brother of Beverley Nichols; later he introduced me to Beverley at Marlborough. There was another young master who could not control boys, and I got involved in an episode which made me squirm with shame afterwards. We were out for a walk and crossing an open heathland on a hot summer's day. We were teasing this master, who was very well dressed (it was a Sunday), and wearing a bowler hat. While one boy distracted him in front, I tipped the hat over his eyes, whereupon he lashed out with his stick and hit the wrong boy, which caused tremendous joy amongst the rest of us. At that moment two of my cousins, who happened to be staying at a house near by, although I did not know it,

23

arrived on the scene, also out for a walk. They called me over and gave me a good dressing down. Years later, I thought how awful this must have been for the master, who was really an extremely nice chap.

Then we had a German woman who taught music. She had a sharp nose and straggly, thin hair, and disliked me very much. She let me know this on every possible occasion. One day I said that my mother wanted me to learn music. *I* didn't, however. How could I be fond of music at that time, when I had to spend every singing lesson without uttering a word? I could not get out the sound I wanted to, and as a result had to stand up with the others and mouth the words without uttering a sound. With the possibility of my taking music lessons, Fraulein was as sweet as honey to me; but I don't know what the outcome would have been next term if the war had not intervened. She disappeared without trace. The school boiler stoker was called back to the Navy, and during one of his leaves he visited us, and held forth to an admiring group of boys telling us how the *Hood* and another great battleship were about to be launched and would blow the Kiel Canal gates up. Copleston, whom we called 'Pebbles', was a great one for Secret Service, and our walks along the cliff tops were made exciting by the thought of all the submarines near us at sea, and the spies round us on land.

Somehow, I became captain of the cricket XI, although really I was never much good at cricket, and also I was captain of the school. One of my friends of today, Air Commodore Allen Wheeler, who is now one of the brains of aircraft design, was a junior at the Old Ride at that time. He told me recently that he had been entered in a swimming race at the end of one term, and that I said to him 'You have got to win – or else . . .'; and that he was so frightened that he went ahead and won. I expect I was still somewhat of a bully, and wonder if my experiences at Ellerslie were any excuse.

I was also Number One in the drill squad which the school became as soon as the First World War broke out. This was the last time I 'took a parade', if you could call it that, until the middle of the Second World War when I was sent down to the

24

Empire Flying School and had to take the parade as Duty Officer. I was scared stiff. Thirty years between parades is quite a long while, but we must have been hot stuff at the Old Ride, because I succeeded in foozling my way through the ordeal.

CHAPTER TWO

SHADES OF THE PRISON HOUSE

MARLBOROUGH COLLEGE was a fearsome shock after the Old Ride; it seemed like entering a prison. 'A' House, which was stuffed with small boys newly arrived, was grim; the iron discipline was prison-like; and the food, no doubt made worse by the war, was terrible. The diet was 150 years out of date. We used to say that the roast meat was horseflesh; no doubt all boys say that sort of thing, but the reek of it turned one's stomach. However, we felt half starved, and would have eaten anything. This feeling of starvation was certainly due to vitamin deficiency. From one term to the next we never had any fresh fruit or uncooked salad, or vegetables. There was no excuse for this, because we could easily have grown these things ourselves in the college meadows; it was just sheer ignorance (or lack of enterprise) on the part of the management. It was no wonder that we had a general outbreak of boils at one time.

Marlborough Downs are exceptionally cold. (I have read somewhere that this is the coldest place in England.) There was some heating in the form rooms, but none in the dormitories. The huge upper school room where 200 senior boys lived during the day when they weren't in actual classes, had only two open fires. Only the biggest boys were allowed to warm themselves at these fires. I decided that the occasional periods of warm-up available during the day only made one suffer more, so I wore nothing but a cotton shirt under my coat, discarded my waistcoat, and slept under a sheet only at night. I aimed to get used to the conditions like the Tierra del Fuegan natives of a century ago, except that I didn't sleep inside a dead whale I was eating.

The usual punishment was a beating; for instance, if late for early-morning school, or if one failed to turn up at the fixed target for an afternoon's run. Most of the discipline was in the hands of the senior boys. Their sole form of punishment was beating, and this was so copiously applied for any infringement of an extensive and complicated social code that it amounted to licensed bullying. At certain stages of their career, boys could fasten one button of their coats, put one hand in a trouser pocket, and things of that sort. Upper School was ruled by four prefects, who sat in state at a table in front of the fire. One of them would carry notes round to the boys he was going to beat; this was during prep when we were all at our desks, and as soon as prep finished, all the 200 boys made a wild rush to encircle the prefect's desk. The chairs were pushed away, the victim bent over the desk, and he was beaten as hard as the prefect could possibly manage by taking a running jump and using a very long cane.

We were allowed to buy milk and cereals, etc., to eat in Upper School during the afternoon, if we had the spare pocket-money. The sour milk and other refuse was dumped in an evil-smelling, huge iron bin on wheels. I remember one boy who was unpopular being dumped head first in this bin by a number of bigger boys.

My dormitory prefect was Edmonds and once, after he had beaten me (unfairly as I thought), his bed and bedding were completely missing the following night. Naturally, I knew that he would suspect me, so I had taken elaborate precautions to have nothing whatever to do with it, and had merely suggested the different steps to be taken for the project to be carried out successfully. It had to be carefully organized so that everybody had an equal share in it (except me, of course) so that no one person could be victimized. Edmonds did not beat me again after this.

Marlborough was a better place in the summer term. Cricket was not compulsory and one was allowed to go off on one's own in the afternoon play period. I usually bicycled

26

somewhere by myself. We were allowed to go within ten miles of Marlborough. This enabled me to reach Upavon, where I used to lie in the grass on the edge of the airfield watching aircraft doing their 'circuits and bumps'; they would take off with their wheels a few feet over my head. On a fine sunny day bicycling along the hot, dusty road, army lorries would be passing in a steady procession. Sometimes I would find a nice patch in a wood, and lie there for an hour or two under the trees, reading, or watching the birds. Sometimes I would lie on the banks of a river watching the fish. These periods of comparative freedom were a great joy.

I was crazy about Rugby football, and had a burning ambition to get into the First XV. I used to wait with impatient, anxious hope for the team to be pinned on the games board. I had read with great interest the tour of the New Zealand 'All Blacks' who won every match except the one against Cardiff during a tour of Britain. They had a new idea of playing only seven forwards instead of eight, thereby gaining an extra back, which tends to make the game much faster, provided that the forwards can hold the opposition. This seemed to me good tactics, and I suggested to the captain of the XV that it should be tried. He, too, thought it was a good idea, and changed the disposition of the team. Unfortunately, I was the eighth forward, and was therefore sacked; my place in the team went to my friend Paterson as an extra back. I would have played for the school XV against Wellington College (before the changeover to seven forwards), but I was ill in the sanatorium at that time. So I not only missed my First XV colours, but also the privilege of wearing blue shorts, which was accorded only to those who had played in the First XV against one of the major public schools, Wellington or Rugby. I once captained the Second XV in a match, but felt that I had failed because I had not reached my objective, the First XV. Considering that I had to play without my spectacles, and once ran in the opposite direction because the football, kicked into the air, passed out of my range of sight, I now think that that particular ambition was a stupid one.

When I first went to Marlborough I was a dedicated cadet

of the Officers Training Corps, and when I went to the summer camp at Tidworth Pennings my first year there, I was the youngest boy of 2,000 from various public schools. The NCO of my tent was the same chap Edmonds whom I thought rather an ass. Evidently other people did too, because the Eton men raided our tent one day, took it to bits and distributed every item of bedding and kit all round the camp. In one way I sympathized with them, but on the other hand, as the youngest boy, it fell to me to go and collect all this stuff and put it together again.

I used to take the field days very seriously, and even wore two pairs of spectacles so that I could shoot off my blank cartridges more accurately at the 'enemy'. One of the attractions of the first camp was a mock dog-fight between two aircraft. The wings were doped with stuff which made them semi-transparent. The other demonstration which excited me was shooting off mortar shells at an 'enemy' trench (unmanned).

The masters were a mixed lot, but there was one man, the housemaster in the junior 'A' House, a man called Adams, whom I admired enormously. He was severe, because it was the code, but he took a humane interest in his boys. Later he joined up in the army, and was killed in Flanders. He had sent back word that his books should be distributed among a few boys whom he named, of whom I was one. I have never been more sad over the death of anyone than I was about this man; he was a fine man, and in the absolute prime of life.

There was something mean and niggardly about our existence at Marlborough; we seemed to be mentally, morally and physically constipated. The whole emphasis was on what you must *not* do, and I consider that I am only now beginning to shake off the deeply-rooted inhibition which had gripped me by the time I left. One instance of the effect of this is that until recently I would shake with fear if I had to get up and speak to more than half a dozen people, because the terror of doing or saying anything which would not be approved of by a mob code was so rooted in me.

On the credit side, I did make some good friends at Marlborough. By the time I was a sixth former, and entitled to a study, three of us became almost inseparable. One was John Paterson, the son of a clergyman at East Bergholt in Essex. He was good looking, dressed well and was good at games. The second of our triumvirate was M. E. Rowe, whom I christened 'The Mole', because of his sharp, twitchy nose, shaggy eyebrows from under which he peered hard at you, and his untidy forelock (although perhaps that is unusual in a mole). He became a QC. Paterson joined the army, and was killed in Malaya in the Second World War. Both these friends became prefects, but not me. I was regarded as too much of a rebel, I think.

Another friend I made was Fred Smyth, who came not far from my home in North Devon. Fred also was good at games. I was very fond of his mother, and used to walk over every Sunday afternoon to their place at Stoke Rivers to have tea with them. Fred's mother made some wonderful rock cakes. The walk was six miles each way, but I used to look forward to it all the week. They were all 'horsey' people, and Fred became a first flight point-to-pointer. I used to be keen on birds-nesting. To add to my collection of birds' eggs was the nominal motive, but I think what really attracted me was the sport of climbing difficult trees after finding one with a nest in it. I used to go out for the whole day, roaming through the woods, which grew on the slopes of our Devon valleys. I could travel all day without ever emerging for more than a few yards from woodland, and it was part of the fun never to be seen by anybody. A buzzard's nest at the top of a tall tree, with no branches at all for the bottom twenty or thirty feet, was always a challenge. I don't think I ever took more than one egg from a nest; it was just a trophy that I was after.

Towards the end of my time at Marlborough, a new idea was introduced into the school, of having the senior boys specialize in some subject. I chose mathematics. All day I worked at maths of one kind or another. I found it a great strain trying to keep interested hour after hour, day after day, week after week. I had a letter in 1962 from a Marlborough boy who said he had been following with interest my sailing voyages. 'I found your name carved on the desk I am sitting at. It looks as if you must have spent as many boring hours here as I have.' (I wrote back and said that I did not remember being a carver-of-desks. Could it have been a forgery?)

There were thirty boys in this maths specialist form, and I was only eleventh in the form. I looked round one day at the ten boys above me, most of whom were far cleverer than I was, or could ever hope to be. I thought to myself, "What a knock-kneed, pigeon-breasted anaemic bespectacled, weedy crowd they are!' (I must have been in a liverish mood because I was bespectacled myself.) I thought, 'I can never hope to be as good as these chaps, and would I want to be, anyway? There must be something wrong with this set-up. Real life is flowing past, and leaving me behind.' I told my housemaster that I was leaving at the end of term.

That was the last term of 1918, and the college caught the Spanish influenza epidemic. There were so many boys down with it that we were lying in rows on the floor of the sanatorium. I think most of us were pretty ill, but only a few died. I was at my worst when the Armistice was signed on 11 November, and I could hear the crowds shouting and cheering outside. I could not even lift myself on one elbow or move on my mattress.

When I got home and told my father that I had left Marlborough, he was furious; justifiably so. I had treated him badly, and I do not know why I had not asked his permission to leave. Perhaps I wanted to be absolutely certain of leaving, and felt that he would not consent. I was due to go to the university and stay there until I was twenty-five, preparing for the Indian Civil Service. I felt that this was all wrong, and that I would not be living a proper life.

CHAPTER THREE

FARMHAND

I HAD read some old novels of my father's about Australia by Ralph Boldrewood. Two of them were *Miner's Right* and *The Squatter's Dream*, and there was another about bush-rangers. I thought that this would be the right life for me, and I said that I wanted to emigrate to Australia. At that time our neighbours the Royles had a pheasant shoot on the Youlston property, and I took part as a beater. There was a sergeant of the New Zealand Army there on leave, and he asked me what I intended doing. When I told him, he said, 'Why don't you come to New Zealand? I will get you a job.' This meant that if I went to New Zealand I would know one person, whereas if I went to Australia I would know no one. That turned the scales in favour of New Zealand, and I now sought for a passage. But passages to New Zealand were very hard to get. All the ships were booked up for a long time to come.

My father answered an advertisement for a boy on a farm in Leicestershire. The job was mine, and I took the train for Coalville, where I worked for seven months for J. G. de Ville. I was paid five shillings a week, and during that seven months de Ville gave me a pair of boots and one half day off to go to the Leicestershire Horse Show between milkings. It was a hard life, especially in winter, getting up in the dark to feed and milk the cows, and working all day on such jobs as spreading manure. In the evenings came more milking, and more feeding of calves. I was lonely, and fell back on my dreams. I looked forward every night to getting to sleep, and had wonderful dreams of warm-hearted, friendly people, lovable people, and comfortable living, with nice things to touch and eat. I often dreamed of my cousin Margaret, whom I adored.

I caught ringworm from the calves and could not get rid of the ugly sores, but summer came, and life was better. There was a wonderfully fine spell in June. The sun on the young grass, the smell of new-mown hay, with hard work from dawn to dusk induced a feeling of bodily fitness, of lustiness, with a kind of hazy, half-drugged stupor in the brain. De Ville had a daughter, Dorothy, by his first wife living with him. She was kind-hearted and amiable and I was madly in love with her. But I knew nothing; I was an oaf who didn't know what to do, or what to say, and I just had to suffer in silence. De Ville's second wife, who was part of the household, was not much older. She was a good-looking brunette who kept a tight hold on household affairs.

There was a railway cutting through one part of the farm, where the mainline expresses thundered past without being visible. Whenever I heard them I used to feel lonely with a great home-sickness, but precisely for what I did not know. One day while I was hoeing turnips, the airship R34 passed overhead on, I think, its maiden flight; it looked huge, new and shiny, and it went by slowly. De Ville not being near, I stopped hoeing turnips to watch it until it was out of sight. This was the first aircraft to make the double crossing of the Atlantic. I wonder what I would have said if I had been told by a fortune-teller then that I would be the first holder of the Johnston Memorial Trophy, founded in memory of the navigator of the last airship to be built in England, the R101, which crashed in France.

One of the more pleasant jobs on the farm was to drive the milk churns to the station. De Ville had an ex-stallion which had been retired late in life. (I think it was rather like de Ville himself, a tough character, but a hard goer.) One day on the way back from the station I was sitting on the box seat of a flat-bottomed dray to which the stallion was harnessed. I had eleven seventeen-gallon churns, all empty, standing on the dray. There was an 'improver' working on a near-by farm, who had also delivered milk in a float with a frisky, fast mare. We started to race home. I was in the lead when we came to a right-angled turn with a large, round stone at the corner of the footpath to keep vehicles off. I was driving with the reins in one hand only, too cocky to use a second hand for turning the corner, and the nearside back wheel went over the boulder.

The horse was going as fast as it could trot; I flew through the air, and looked up to the sky to see the milk churns around me like the great bear constellation coming to earth. The churns and I landed together, while the horse set off home at full gallop. It went clean through two five-bar gates on the farm, and ended up snorting in de Ville's garden. When I arrived, which was definitely in second place, although I had run as fast as I could over the two-mile track, de Ville was waiting for me. He knocked me down in the dining-room and held a chair over my head while he straddled my body. I listened to Dorothy sobbing in the next room out of sight, while wondering if the chair was going to come down or not. There wasn't anything that I could do that I could think of, and I was quite calm. I think this had an influence on him, and the chair did not descend. Then he gave me an hour to get out of the house with all my belongings. When I left it was midday, and I had already been working or busy about the farm for seven hours.

I tried to get trains across country to North Devon. I suppose that I should have taken a train to London, and then another one from there to North Devon, but I did not think of this, and no one suggested it. By midnight I had reached Burton-on-Trent, and was pacing up and down the platform nursing my wrist, which had been bitten by a dog of de Ville's during all the fracas. There was a rabies scare at the time and when my wrist began to throb I got frightened. I made inquiries, and was directed to a doctor's house in Burton. I rang the bell but could not make anyone hear. Then I saw a chink of light from a curtained window, and peeped through to see a number of people sitting round a roulette table. I knocked on the window, and they all jumped up and dispersed like a covey of frightened partridges. The doctor came to the door, and very sedately attended to my wrist, dressed it, and said that he thought it would be all right. He sent me away without charging me anything. When I got back to the station, I was immediately grabbed by two plain-clothes detectives who asked me where I had been. It flashed through my mind that they knew the doctor was running a gambling establishment (then strictly illegal), and wanted me to give evidence against him. The doctor having befriended me, I refused to say where I had been or why. At last I convinced them that I was only a passenger to Devon and then they told me that there had been some thefts at the station, and that they thought that I was one of the thieves.

About dawn I was approaching Exeter where I had to change trains. Unable to keep awake any longer I slept through Exeter and had to work my way back from Cornwall. I did not get home until 2 o'clock in the afternoon. By that time I was tired, and perhaps not as diplomatic as I ought to have been when my father was furious at my turning up suddenly without notice. There was decidedly no fatted calf awaiting a returning prodigal.

I tried to get a job in a garage. I bicycled to Exeter and back one day (ninety miles) and interviewed six garage owners, but without success. A few weeks later my father obtained a passage for me in the steerage of a ship going to New Zealand. My brother insisted on travelling down in the train to Plymouth with me to see me off, but he had just deeply offended me by laughing at my wish to have a revolver to take with me to New Zealand. This spoilt the start of the voyage for me.

Looking back, I think that I may not have been fair to my father. I have been told that he was ordered by my grandfather to enter the Church on the old principle of one son each for the Army, the Navy and the Church, but my father himself told me that he had wanted to enter the Church. I think, however, that he was unsuited for it, and that if he had been in some other profession, he would have made his mark. He was continually fighting against his possibly unconscious wishes and using up his nervous energy in a tremendous effort to do the right thing. In the end he became a puritan of the severest kind. One day he reprimanded one of the villagers for being drunk, and this man retorted that it was all very well for the likes of him to talk, because he could keep drink in his house, and have it at any time, whereas a poor man could not afford to do so. The logic of this seems a bit shaky, but it impressed my father so much that he never drank alcohol again, except in the sacramental wine.

In the house he seemed to be disapproving of everything I did, and waiting to squash any enthusiasm. Occasionally he was friendly, and on a bicycle ride or a walk he could be a wonderfully good companion. My happiest memory of him is of one day when we were out for a walk together and he wanted to hold me by the ankles over the side of a bridge so that I could take an egg from a water wagtail's nest. I wouldn't let him, and I still remember with regret the whimsical look of disappointment on his face. Building up his collection of birds' eggs was one of his great hobbies. At that moment he was a fellow human being for me.

CHAPTER FOUR

NEW ZEALAND 1919

THE *Bremen*, a German ship captured during the war, was lying in Plymouth Sound when I joined her. The steerage quarters were pretty rough, with bunks rigged up in every inch of space. The food was poor to start with, and the cooking made it worse.

But I was eighteen, and off on my own to New Zealand. My father had given me £10 in sovereigns and because of the deep distrust of my fellows, inculcated in me during my religion-dominated upbringing, I always kept this gold against my belly in a leather money belt. It was December; we had the expected rough weather crossing the Bay of Biscay, and I went through the normal agonies of sea-sickness. After this, the romance of the voyage took charge and I would stand in the bows at night, with the quiet roar of the bow wave in my ears, and watch the stars weaving to and fro above the mast. The deck throbbed, and the rigging shook at the end of each roll, but it was quiet for an instant before the ship started each roll back.

The steerage passengers were an odd collection. The English ones nearly all seemed to have quirks of behaviour, or queer ideas of some sort; the New Zealanders were more

35

balanced and practical. I think the one I liked best was a New Zealand blacksmith going home. One night a boxing match was arranged, and my opponent was a tall, broad-shouldered man with an exceptionally long reach. It was difficult to get inside his long guard, but the fact that I was getting into rather a mess, with a lot of blood over me, was not a proper indication of the state of the fight. I had not yet got his measure, and was most disappointed when the referee stopped the fight. I mention this boxing match because I think it had an important effect later in the voyage.

We reached Durban for Hogmanay, and the coal trimmers' shovels beat a terrific din over the still harbour at midnight. I swam in the surf behind shark-proof iron railings. There was a fresh breeze driving the spray off the combers in sheets, and the sea was so salt it stung my nostrils. The hot burning sun was a novelty. We drove about in rickshaws, and everything seemed romantic and exciting.

The chief trimmer on one watch had been my second in the boxing match, and when he was brought back to the ship handcuffed I talked the native policeman into freeing him and letting me take him aboard. He had been drunk, of course. Next day he deserted and therefore the watch was one man short. I volunteered to sign on, and was duly accredited a member of my first trade union, the Firemen's Union. My six mates of the watch were a tough lot. They were London-Irish. I was told that the Liverpool-Irish trimmers were the toughest in the world, but it was hard to believe that they were any tougher than these London-Irish. Most of them had been torpedoed at least once, and one man described how the engineer had stood at the top of the gangway, with a revolver threatening to shoot anyone who left his post after the torpedo had struck the ship in the side. The *Bremen* had hot stokeholds; particularly one double hold with a row of furnaces both fore and aft. When shifting clinkers in this hold I had furnace heat from both sides. I was soon exhausted, and working I felt at the end of my tether. But we were short-handed, and in stormy seas after leaving Durban we were on watch ten hours a day – four hours on, eight off, followed by six hours on and six off.

After each watch time was needed to wash our bodies grimed with coal black; also we had to eat. Although the food seemed plentiful after the severe English rationing, we were always ravenous. Looking back, I think that again this was probably due to lack of some vitamins in the diet.

Nearly every day there were fights over the food, sometimes with knives drawn. I never had a fight, and I attribute this to the boxing match early in the voyage which had been keenly watched by both trimmers and stokers. Besides the crew wanting as big a share as possible of any food going, there were also the cockroaches and weevils. I tried various dodges to keep the cockroaches off the plate and mug in my locker. My best catch from one biscuit was three weevils and two maggots.

I was not the only person exhausted. In the watch after ours, a big Swedish trimmer said that he could not go on watch. There had to be a full complement below and one of our watch had to take his trick for him. A second time one of our trimmers did his trick for him, but when he declared a third time that he was unfit to work, our watch was not having any more of it. They dragged him out of his bunk, and beat him up with their fists. They seized him by his legs, and dragged him along the alleyway to dump him down the ash chute into the hold. These chutes were shafts, just big enough to haul up a sack of ashes from the stokehold for dumping over the side of the ship. The man looked a ghastly sight being dragged along with his head bumping on the steel floor, and his face covered in blood. I had a feeling of shame that I did not come to his rescue, but I knew that if I intervened they would tell me to do his trick for him myself, and I was at the end of my endurance. Perhaps my mates were better psychologists than I; the Swede suddenly jumped to his feet, and thrusting his attackers aside ran down to the hold. I was told later that he worked harder than anybody else on his watch.

Years later when I was on a passage from Kobe to London in a P & O steamer after I had crashed in Japan in my seaplane, one of the engineers there turned out to have been seventh engineer in the *Bremen*. He told me the subsequent history of my trimmer watch. Of the seven who started the voyage, only three got back to England. One had deserted in Durban; one disappeared in very suspicious circumstances on the passage between New Zealand and Australia; one had been killed by a blow on the head from one of the long clinker slicing bars; and a fourth had been hanged for murder.

I got my discharge in Wellington, New Zealand, and drew £9 in wages for the three weeks' work. My ticket was endorsed 'Very good' for sobriety and two other virtues.

Ned Holmes, my New Zealand soldier friend, got me a job at ten shillings a week with the manager of a farm outside Masterton, belonging to his father. Old Maxwell, the manager, was a big chubby-cheeked man, with a bushy moustache, and was considered a great man with sheep. I lived with the family, which consisted of Maxwell, his wife, and their daughter, a sweet little thing of about seventeen, called Olive, whose name somehow exactly fitted her face.

Old Maxwell gave me the sack after three weeks; he said that with my bad sight I would not be able to spot the ewes when they were cast on their backs in the spring, when heavy with lamb, and unable to get up unaided. As a matter of fact, my visual accuracy with spectacles is not too bad; for instance I once shot two hares with two shots of a .22 rifle, the first was 145 yards off and the second, which bobbed up when it heard the shot, 95 yards away. Also, I shot five rabbits on the run one morning with a rifle, so I was not sure about Maxwell's reason for getting rid of me.

I got a new job on a sheep station thirty-eight miles from Masterton. There was no town or township (village) nearer than Masterton, and there were just two of us to look after a farm of 2,000 acres, with 3,000 sheep and about 200 head of cattle. I was in the saddle most of the day, riding round the hills attending to the sheep. When we were mustering a paddock, of which there were three, we would start off from the station house by moonlight at three in the morning. We worked the sheep steadily off the hilltops and down to the bottom of the paddock, where the dogs would keep them cornered while we inspected them. There were pens for drafting or sorting them.

Except for the shearing, the two of us, Arthur the boss and I the roustabout, did all the work on the station; dagging, which was shearing back legs and tails with hand shears, dipping, ear marking and cutting the ram lambs to turn them into wethers. It was the custom for shepherds to toast the lamb's testicles over a fire and eat them, but this was not for me. It was, however, my job as under-shepherd to kill and dress the hoggets which we ate. I shall never forget how my knees trembled when I killed my first sheep and the blood spurted out in beats as I cut its throat. I think that few mature people would eat beef or lamb if they had to kill the animals first.

Arthur, my boss, was an excellent shepherd, and could work his dogs easily a mile away. Two thousand acres is a sizeable slice of country – three square miles – but the surface area is more in that part of New Zealand because, being geologically a young country, the hills are steep. The ground we were on was blue papa (volcanic mud), and the storm streams cut steep gulleys out of it. Along the banks of the creeks grew clumps of lawyer vine, a kind of bramble but with hooked thorns of a vicious kind.

We did all our own cooking, and Arthur baked the bread. I tried one baking, but it was too hard to eat. Every other Sunday it was my turn to wash the kitchen floor. Arthur was a tidy man and washed up after every meal. Once he was supposed to be away on holiday, but couldn't bear to be parted from the farm, and came back before he was due. I remember the look of disapproval on his face when I came in to find him washing up an accumulation of six days' dirty dishes which I had piled up in his absence.

I loved the riding. One day I rode forty-five miles to a dance and home again next day. Arthur was annoyed and said it was not fair on a horse out at grass. Perhaps not if I had ridden at a canter as the New Zealanders did, but forty-five miles is not too far for a horse trotting in English style.

Nothing can be more stupid and obstinate than a sheep, and sometimes I found trying to move 500 stupid, obstinate, glassy-eyed sheep hard to bear. Once I was sent out with a blackhorse to a neighbouring sheep station to skin some dead sheep, and bring them back for dog food (the sheep carcasses were hung in trees out of reach of the dogs, which didn't seem to mind about the maggots). While being driven across country, the leading sheep of a mob had jumped down across a small stream below the track and landed on its knees. Before it got up, the sheep behind jumped on top of it. The sheep went on jumping until there were 500 piled up dead.

There came a time when I asked for a rise from fifteen shillings to twenty-five shillings a week. The visiting owner had a long discussion with Arthur about this, and then came over and offered me twenty shillings a week. This was not my style and I walked off the farm. I went to visit my blacksmith friend whom I had met on the *Bremen*, and he got me a job on a farm near Taihape at £2 10s. a week. They asked me if I could milk, and I said 'no'. This was untrue, because I had milked fifteen cows day and night while looking after de Ville's farm when he was away. But I hated the smell of milk, it rotted my boots, and I had no desire to be a milkman. I used to lie in my bunk in the morning listening to the other chaps getting the cows in, and I started work the easy way at 8 o'clock.

This farm belonged to three brothers called Williams, and their brother-in-law. Two of the Williams brothers and I totalled twelve feet round the chest, I being the smallest with forty inches. They were powerful men, and magnificent horsemen. We had eighty horses on the place, and used to break them in periodically. Sunday morning's amusement was to put me on one and see how long it took before I was thrown. Once the bucking bust the saddle girth, and I shot through the air in a great arc with the saddle still between my legs.

This farmland had not long been reclaimed from virgin bush. It had been felled, and a year later burnt. Trunks of two to three feet in diameter had survived the fire and still lay on the ground, unburnt. We used to muster cattle at full gallop round the steep sides of the hills, taking the logs as we went. I have seldom been more scared, but it was exciting.

There was a sawmill on the farm, and I used to work there for weeks at a time. I had a fine job, 'fiddling', which meant working away by myself with a seven-foot cross-cut saw, slicing the trees into twelve- or fourteen-foot lengths so that they could be handled and moved up to the sawbench. On spring mornings I was bursting with vitality and fitness. The grass, as we rode down to the mill, would be glittering with dew, the sun shining, the tuis and bell birds singing their endless, bell-like notes. There was the smell from sawdust and the burning bark slabs fed to the engine which drove the saw. Our smallest meal of the day, breakfast, usually consisted of a large plate (really large) of porridge, with plenty of milk and sugar, followed by a pound steak with three eggs on it, followed by two full rounds cut from a big loaf of bread, with plenty of butter and jam.

Another interesting job was shearing. After some practice, I was able to shear at the rate of seventy-five sheep a day. It was hard work, and I had to tie a handkerchief round my forehead to keep the sweat from running on to my spectacles, where it left a deposit of salt and spoilt my vision. My seventy-five sheep a day was a paltry quantity compared with what the experts could do – the Australian champion had shorn over 400 sheep in a day, using blade shears. The shearing machine, like the clipper used by a barber at the back of your neck, but engine driven, required a good deal of manual dexterity. I wonder if I could shear a big ram successfully today? Here's how: First, sit him on his tail and shear back forelocks and cheeks to the back of his head. Holding him between your knees, push the cutters down his chest, and then split the fleece open down to his tummy. Next shear his forelegs to the shoulder, and his hind legs to the rump. Take care! Don't forget he is a valuable ram. Then, over on to his side, with his neck against one leg and his tail against the other, and use long sweeping strokes from rump to neck until all that side is shorn. This is the most awkward position for control when he struggles. Over on to the other side, and repeat the last process, and there is the fleece lying on the floor. A boy would pick up the fleece, fold it carefully and take it to the sorting table, where he would spread it out. On our farm there were only four machines at work, but on a big station with twenty shearers the activity was prodigious. After the day's work our chaps used to pop into the big round tank of warm water used to cool the shearing engine.

Although I enjoyed much of the work, I could not feel settled. I was lonely, though I did not understand why, and I felt that I was in the wrong job. I wanted to be an author. (Just, say, a mixture of Conrad, Kipling and Somerset Maugham.) I left the farm, and took a room in a country town fifty miles to the south. It was a place of antimacassars (crocheted mats to keep hair oil off the chair) and of doilies (crocheted mats to keep plates off the table). I struggled hard to produce a masterpiece. But I knew nothing of life and nothing of writing. I bought an American book on *How to Write Short Stories* but my brain was hazy after manual toil. A dreary sense of failure crept over me.

I had only one interesting adventure at this place. I was bathing in the river when a flood spate came down. There must have been a deluge from a thunderstorm in the hills, and because the country was new, with the hills stripped of their timber by the settlers, the water rushed down and flooded violently. I have seen a river which I had crossed on foot without getting wet become a raging torrent half an hour later, with a thundery rumble from great boulders pounding along the river bed. The spate swept me off my feet and carried me away. I swam to the river bank, and grabbed at the boulders. The flood tore my grasp and rolled me over and over. I felt panic. My signet ring, with a cornelian stone, was torn off my finger. I resisted panic, which I knew was a killer, and kept swimming, not trying to buck the flood. At last I got into an eddy, and was able to seize a boulder and pull myself out of the water.

CHAPTER FIVE

GOLD AND COAL

FEELING rather a failure, I packed my things, and crossing from North Island to South Island by steamer, I set off for the

42

west coast. This meant crossing the Southern Alps by stage coach, with five horses. We made our way slowly up the mountain range to the pass, sometimes walking to ease the horses. The glacier-fed rivers were full of milky blue-grey water.

At Greymouth, on the west coast, I joined my second trade union, the Timber Workers. I got a job at a new mill that was being set up in the bush. To reach it, I travelled on the company's bush railway, running ten miles into the virgin forest. I worked in the gang extending this railway farther into the forest to get timber out. I liked the bush-whacking such as felling trees up to three feet in diameter with an axe. Even digging the cuttings, and laying the track, had interest, but it was made dreary because nobody had any incentive and the gang slacked shamelessly. Most of the soil round about was gold-bearing, and I used to amuse myself by panning off some of the dirt in a shovel. Every shovelful would produce a few colours of gold.

My mates were a suspicious, dull crowd. They could not make me out, and treated me as if I were an enemy spy. We used to assemble in one of the wooden huts which each of us had to live and sleep in and would swop yarns by the light of the log fire at night, but no one became friendly to me. It was a dreary life, and when I got news of a gold strike in the bush, I packed my swag (that is to say, stuffed my blankets and belongings into a bag which I humped on my shoulders) and made off.

Ten miles along a track through the bush brought me to a road of sorts, and I kept on walking until I got to the Blackwater Gold Mine at the terminus of another road. The Blackwater was a warm quartz reef more than half a mile below the surface. From here I took off into virgin forest following a blazed trail. I was given directions which would take me to the strike. A blazed trail through dense forests, with a small nick on a tree every fifty or a hundred yards, may be easy to follow if you blazed it yourself, or if you first follow it with someone who knows it. I was trailing up a small creek trying to spot a blaze which would indicate where I had to leave the creek, but I could not find any blaze, and finally mistook a deer track for the right trail. I followed this for some time, but an hour or so later I had to admit that I was well and truly bushed.

Panic came in a big wave. It was a new overwhelming panic which paralysed my brain. I wanted to tear wildly through the bush. I knew that I had to fight this panic, so I set my whole mind to fighting it, and finally I had control. Then I unpacked my swag and, feeling intensely alone and lonely, rolled up in my blanket and went to sleep. This was beside another stream, which ran over a rusty-coloured bottom, apparently full of new-chum gold which glittered more than the real stuff. It was hard to believe that I was not lying beside immense wealth, though I reasoned that real gold would have worked through the gravel to rock bottom.

When I awoke at dawn I lay still, pondering, until I had worked over all my movements. If I could get a direction, I ought to be able to hit off the valley from which I had started, even though it was merely a thin streak running into a vast area of solid forest. I had no compass and it was impossible to see farther than a few yards. I decided to try to get a bearing from the sun. The only hope for this was to climb to the top of a hill. This west-coast bush was a rain forest, created by the Westerlies sweeping in from the ocean and emptying their moisture as continuous rain for weeks on end as they lifted over the Alps. In places the forest was so dense that, without a slasher, it would take four hours to move a mile through it. From the ground I could not get the least sign of the sun through the dense growth overhead.

The surface of the hill that I knew I must climb was covered in moss a foot deep. My feet slipped on the roots under the moss, and I had to scramble over rotting tree trunks which lay all over the place. When I got to the top I climbed a tree with difficulty. But when I got near the top I could see that I was going to be no better off, because the leaves were too dense to see through, and the branches too frail to support my weight if I tried to get up higher. I climbed down, and started thinking again. I told myself that it was panic which usually killed someone who was lost, and I made up my mind that I ought to be able to find the stream where I had first gone wrong. I plotted all my movements in my head, and decided where that stream should lie. I set off in that direction. If I didn't find the stream within a certain time, I determined to follow a creek downstream until I came to the coast. That might take me three weeks, but I was bound to arrive there in the end if I could get food.

I set off, and within an hour located my lost stream. This was a sound lesson not to go off on such jaunts without a compass. In good daylight I followed the trail, and in due course reached the prospectors' log hut built of young trees with the ends sticking out at the corners. According to bush hospitality I moved into the hut and slept there without anybody asking any questions. I might have been there for years. In the end, I broached the subject of the reef. What I was told merely confirmed the opinion I had already formed; any idea of my pegging out a claim was fatuous. First because they had already pegged off claims for six miles along the line of the reef, and secondly, because the only way of finding a reef underfoot was to keep prodding through the moss with a long iron spear until quartz, which gave off a different note from other rock, was stabbed. It was then necessary to dig down and quarry a lump of this quartz, crush it, and assay it for gold. It would have taken me weeks to find their claim pegs; it was most unlikely that the reef would 'live' for anything like six miles; and if it did it was even more unlikely that there would be another outcrop which I could find. Finally, I had no tools. I was not unduly depressed; I had been to a gold strike, and enjoyed the adventure of getting there.

Years later I heard that the finders of this reef had turned down an offer of £50,000 for it. They set up a stamping plant themselves to mill the reef, but found that it did not 'live' down, that it petered out a few feet below the surface.

I came away richer in experience, and with two pieces of gold-bearing quartz in which the gold could be seen by the aid of a magnifying glass.

When I got back to the sawmill I was sacked for leaving

without permission. I humped my swag again, and set off back through the bush. I kept going until I reached the Paparoa Coal Mine where I asked for and got a job.

This coal mine was quite different from what I thought a coal mine would be like. Instead of going down in a cage, we climbed 2,000 feet before entering the mountain by way of a long drive or tunnel. The coal came from near the surface at the top. It was a thick twenty-four-foot seam of soft coal, which could be used only for steaming purposes. There were a few soft lumps, but most of it came out like powdered lead pencil which blackened face and hands.

At first I thought it was like working in Hell with the fires and lights out. I had to get used to bending to avoid the beams. I was continually banging them with the top of my forehead as I walked along.

The miners were a human lot, much more so than the bush workers. It was like being back in a public school, except that the surroundings were of coal and rock, the food was better, and rats ran over one's legs while eating lunch sitting on the floor of the mine. My comrades liked me, which was a big help; they thought I was a steward who had run away from a ship, which would explain my odd behaviour and speech. I didn't fancy having my Christian name Francis bellowed down the mine, so I called myself George, and as they could not pronounce Chichester, I shortened that to Chester. They liked my brand of humour, and I kept them amused. We had a strike meeting one day – I was now a due-paying member of my third trade union, the Miners – and I got up to speak in favour of the strike. I was hotly on their side; there is nothing like sitting seven hours on a box marooned in a pool of water flooding a drive into the coal seam, working a hand pump in pitch darkness, to make you feel communistic. And if there is no hope of getting out of the rut, why not pull the rest of the world down to your level? However, when I got on my feet to speak, I could not help seeing the funny side of the situation. I started to make the meeting laugh, and finally it broke up in a good-humoured scramble. Rather to my disappointment, there was no strike. Perhaps I can interpolate here that I

46

think that most strikes are due to a longing for a break from the deadly monotony of a repetitive job.

There were one or two tough characters in the pit, among them an ex-docker from Sydney Harbour, a lean long-legged Communist, who was annoyed one day because a deputy ticked him off. He pushed over a race of boxes on the main jig. A 'race' was six trucks, each holding three-quarters of a ton, and they left the seam by way of a long tunnel, inclined at an angle of one in two and a half. The race was attached to one end of a wire rope, half a mile long, and when pushed over the edge at the top, pulled up a race of empty boxes on the other end of the rope. This Bolshie pushed over the boxes without attaching them to the rope. They made a fantastic sight as they gathered speed with a comet's tail of sparks streaming from the wheels on the iron rails. When the speed became too great, they jumped the rails, crashed to the side of the tunnel, brought the timbering down from the sides and the roof, and effectively closed the mine with all of us inside it. Fortunately there was a separate water drain, and we managed to escape by crawling through this head first.

One of the people who suffered from this escapade was me, because I was one of the gang of shiftworkers given the job of repairing the damage. First, we had to erect sets of props of green timber, each fourteen feet high, and then raise a similar bar to straddle the top. These slippery props and bars were fourteen inches in diameter, and being green timber each required five men to handle. On an incline of one in two and a half and in the faint glimmer from safety lamps, this was no joke. At the top of each set, we had to erect another set of two props ten to twelve feet high and a bar, and, worse still, we had to get a third set up on top again to reach the roof, over thirty feet above the rails. The timber had to reach right up to the roof. On this job one man had his back damaged, and was away from work for eight month , another had his leg broken; I was lucky and got away with one finger squashed.

There was nearly always a dash of excitement about this coal mining. The coal was worked by driving a network of tunnels to divide the seam into pillars. Two of the best miners would get out as much coal as possible from each pillar. The tonnage which a pair of good miners would shift from one of these pillars in a day was fantastic. For a while I was trucking for a pair, Jim Devlin and Jim Hallinan. All I had to do was to push the full boxes singly along a short lead, and jig them down a slope with a wire rope to the next level, where another trucker took them over. Each full box was replaced with an empty one. The fact that I would have sweat streaming off me the whole day while doing only this job indicates, I think, how much coal those two men could shift. As the pillar got worked out, they had to slow down, through having to spend so much time 'listening', the idea being to get as much coal out as possible before the roof caved in. Experienced miners could tell when this was about to happen by the faint whisper which the rock made before it parted from the roof. Sometimes I too could hear this whisper, but usually they could hear what was complete silence to me.

For a time I drove the pony taking up full races along the level below. That was sport. I would call to the pony, or give it a friendly slap with my hand, and it would start off at a gallop. As the last box flashed past I took a flying leap for it, jumped on the back with a foot on each buffer, and buried my face in the coal to avoid being brained when passing under the bars of the roof. To stop the race I reached down with one arm and jabbed a sprag (an iron bar like a belaying pin) into the rear wheel of the truck. As soon as the pony felt the slow-ing down of the race of boxes it would stop galloping. Every now and then the train would be derailed, and the trucks would have to be manoeuvred back on to the rails. It took a knack to lift and shift one of these trucks, with fourteen hundredweight of coal in it, back on to the line. On my first derailment I called in my giant miner friends to help me – that a trucker had called in some miners to help replace a truck on the lines provided the pit with a laugh for weeks. I soon got the knack of doing it on my own.

This was a fire-damp mine, and it was eerie to lift one's safety lamp to the roof and see the light go dim in the gas. We used to go and smoke in an air-duct tunnel. After I left,

I heard that one of my friends, killed in an explosion there, was found with matches and cigarettes beside him, and it was assumed he had done it once too often. I was also told that one of my two Jims was killed by a fall of stone and the other invalided out with a damaged back.

I was still keen on boxing. I was the middleweight representative of the mine, and the two Jims, my mining pair, Devlin and Hallinan, were my sparring partners. I was entered for the west coast boxing competition at Westport, and my trainers took time off to escort me down to the ring. They rubbed me over with Elliman's embrocation before the fight (I'm not sure why), but they were as keen on my winning as I was. Unfortunately this ended in an anticlimax, because all my opponents withdrew at the last moment.

Some of the conditions at the mine were primitive. One Sunday I had an abscess in a back tooth and I went to the doctor at the big pit down the road. He used no pain-killer or such-like nonsense, and set to work to pull out the tooth. Having crushed off the top, he tried to get the roots out. I remember his stopping after about half an hour, and having a long drink of water. However, the roots got the better of him, and he had to give up the struggle. Next day I took the day off and went to a dentist in Greymouth, the biggest town on the west coast. He said, 'Come back in three weeks and maybe I'll be able to see what has happened.'

After a hard day's work in the mine, my legs trembled walking down the 2,000 feet of mountainside. It was hard to pass the pub at the bottom. I used to have a pint of beer – it makes my mouth water now to think of it. Heavens, what nectar! After two or three days it became two pints, and gradually built up to six pints. Usually something then happened. One day, I fell naked on the fire in my hut. This isn't quite as bad as it sounds: each of us had an individual hut and on going to work, left the fire banked up under two four-gallon kerosene tins full of water. If done expertly, the fire would just be breaking through the soft coal by the time we got back, and the water would be just on the boil. I had half an old barrel in which I used to wash. I had stumbled in this tub, fallen and sat bang on the fire. Next day, no pint.

It seemed a healthy life; our appetites were prodigious. I never heard of any of the miners in our pit having lung trouble like the gold miners, who suffered from the fine stone dust solidifying in their lungs. I felt extremely lusty. One of the drawbacks of that community life was the scarcity of female society. In fact, for me, there was none.

I was now in my twenty-first year. My twentieth birthday had been celebrated at the coal mine and perhaps it was memorable. I invited my friends among the miners, truckers and shift workers of the pit to my little wooden hut. I had a ten-gallon keg of beer to start with. There was whisky, but the miners mostly preferred beer. There were not many of us, but after midnight we had exhausted the keg, and I sent out for a second one. Either the publican, rousted out at 2 o'clock in the morning, recognized that it would be dangerous to refuse, or else he was a good sport. Perhaps both. Before the end of the party one of my guests, a huge miner, got d.t's and went berserk. We had been playing poker and two-up and my guests got over-excited about some move in the poker game. In order to throw him out we had two men on each leg and two on each of his arms, and he was tossing us about as if we were pears on a fruit branch. It was an eye-opener to me – the incredible strength that can be latent in a human being. I made a note that if a man when mad (if only temporarily) can call up such strength, it must be possible for me to do the same if I used the right will-power – if I could find out how.

One day I looked at one of my comrades who was drunk, and said to myself, 'My God! That's me in twenty years' time.' I depended entirely on what I could earn, and although this mining was well paid I could not save. There was the constant thirst for one thing, and sometimes five gambling schools would be in full swing at the same time. I decided that I must make a break.

I had an offer to join Dibbs Jones on a gold-prospecting expedition into the mountains. It was called 'fossicking'. This coincided with a day when I felt it was a poor life disappearing into a hole in the ground just after the sun had risen on a fine spring morning. I went off fossicking with Dibbs into the bush.

We were eight hours from the nearest other human being, an eight hours' foot-slog through the bush, carrying all our food and gear. Dibbs went to an abandoned hut, built by some gold diggers years before. Dibb's speciality was crevices, and we set to work washing the pay dirt in the river. We shovelled the gravel into long boxes with 'riffles', small pieces of wood across them, which stopped the heavy gold when the pay dirt was washed through the box by the river. When we got down to rock bottom we worked into the crevice with a pick to find the gold which had sunk there. Dibbs was said to be able to smell gold, but, if so, his scent was not strong. Once, however, I thought he had smelt some out. I had been off to the store to get food. I used to go off for the stores by myself for several reasons: one being that I could hump much more than Dibbs. I made the eight-hour trip with 100 lb. on my back with only one halt. Really it was better not to stop; with that load it was hard to get going again. I packed the stores into a sugar sack, with straps made of green flax leaves from the bottom corners of the sack to pass over the shoulder blades to a point in the middle of the sack. Success depended on getting the load high up on one's shoulders. Although I could pack so much more than Dibbs, he was more skilful with a shovel and could produce twice as much pay dirt for panning off as I could. The last reason for my going was that Dibbs went on the bend when he reached 'civilization' and once was away for ten days.

One day, when I got back with stores, feeling hot and exhausted, I came into the hut to find Dibbs sitting by the door. I was annoyed that he was not out working in the river while I had been struggling through the bush. 'Oh, I don't have to go into the river to get gold,' he said jauntily. He had found a tin of gold which had been cached underneath the hut. All the gold and the colours were rusty, so that it must have been there for a long time. Unless he had dumped it there himself, I thought that he must have smelt it.

I had my first experience of solitude while Dibbs was away on his ten-day binge. The bush was lovely, but seemed sad and lonely. The beautiful silvery notes dropped one by one by the bell birds and tuis became the most monotonous and lonely sound after I had been alone for a few days. My thinking got slower, until it seemed to be done word by word with long periods between. Solitude had a strong effect on me at twenty. I think I needed more to do. During the day, digging in the river there was the urge of gambling fever, the gnawing hope of striking it rich. It was at night, after cooking the meal, that loneliness took charge. Once I heard a kiwi call.

We were short of stores, and while Dibbs was away so long I got very hungry. One day I went into the bush and shot a kaka (a native New Zealand bird of the parrot species). By scratching a stone on the edge of a tin matchbox to imitate their harsh squawk I attracted a dozen of these birds down to a tree. They flew in and out of the tree and round it, making a frightful din. Now I am sorry I shot that interesting bird, but then I was glad. It was good to eat and I was hungry.

We cooked in our big iron camp oven. In order to bake 'damper', which is unleavened bread, we used to hang the oven high above the log fire and pile hot ashes on the lid.

During six months we won enough gold to pay for our food. The biggest nugget we found was 9 dwt. or $\frac{3}{8}$ oz. Afterwards I made a ring out of it for a girl friend.

CHAPTER SIX

HUNTING A FORTUNE

WHEN I left England I had made up my mind that I would not return until I had saved £20,000. Gold digging showed no sign of bringing me closer to this target. One day in the pub a man said to me, 'Why don't you become a book agent?' 'What's that?' 'A man who calls from house to house selling books. A lot of money can be made at it, but you have to do it in Sydney.'

So once more I set off for Australia. On the way through Christchurch I called on the editor of *The Christchurch Press* to try to sell him my story of the gold strike. He said that he was always getting such things and wasn't interested. He did, however, buy a snapshot of a gold dredge which I had taken, and for which he paid me five shillings.

When I told him what I was going to do he said, 'Why not sell the *Weekly Press*?' So bang went my second attempt to reach Australia. I went north to Wellington, and started canvassing from door to door for yearly subscriptions to the *Weekly Press*. The arrangement had been that I was to get a commission and travelling expenses but his accounts department must have been surprised when I immediately started earning £400 a year in commission and they 'reneged' on the expenses. That was not my style, so I quit.

Then I was offered a job selling a book-keeping system to farmers. Five guineas covered the cost of a ledger and two years' making up of income tax returns from it. I was sent out with the sales manager to learn the job, and I was eager and impatient to start. When my opportunity came, I went through my sales talk to a farmer and at the end he had agreed to take on the system and said, 'What about a cheque for you?' 'Oh,' I said, 'you've already signed it and it's in my pocket.'

This was a tough job, and only one other salesman besides myself, out of sixty-one, stuck it for a year, which was the target I had set myself. I found that if I could visit five farms in a day, I was fairly sure of making two sales, but if I could go to as many farms as I liked I would make no sales at all. To get round the country I bought a motor-bicycle. I had looked forward for a long time to having one. (I used to be keen on ordinary bicycling, and when at school used to bicycle home sometimes, sleeping under a haystack, or trying to sleep while listening to a nightingale singing in a near-by bush.) This motor-bike had a clutch but no gear-box, and could be started only by running it along the road. I set off from Wellington, and the first obstacle to climb was the Rimutaka Range. I climbed seven miles up these hills, until I reached a sharp corner which was protected from the wind by a high palisading on each side. The wind funnelled down that gulley in gale blasts, and some cars had been blown over the side. At this corner the wind stalled me. I could not restart the motor-bicycle by running up the steep hill; when I started it downhill, and then turned to head uphill, the engine stalled as soon as I let in the clutch. I was a hot man before I gave up, and coasted back to the bottom to start afresh. Next time I came up with a run, and knowing the hill better, I got round the corner and over the summit. When I reached the Up Country in the middle of North Island, where I was due to start work, most of the roads were still unmetalled. The surface was volcanic clay, and became so greasy after a shower of rain that the back wheel skidded to one side or the other and the motor-bike would not stay on the road.

I turned up in Taihape again, and bought an old Ford five-seater, with a hood. I paid £120 for it. It was worth £60, but I was new to business. I added a bicycle and a tent to my gear, and set off in the car. My technique was to drive to a new territory, and pitch camp there. I got so used to this that within twenty-five minutes of stopping the car, I could be lying on my folding camp-bed ready to sleep after unpacking the gear, driving tent pegs in all round, erecting the poles and rigging the tent, laying out my gear and the camp-bed inside, and getting undressed. Next morning I would set off on the bicycle. I found that this limited the number of farmers I could see to an average of five a day, which was what I wanted. I set out with my mind made up to get two sales out of the five, and I nearly always got them.

I gradually worked up the centre of North Island, until I approached Rotorua, the famous thermal district. I finished one day's work some miles south of Rotorua and had to pitch camp in the dark. The countryside was covered in manuka scrub, also called 'ti-tree'. This grows nearly as dense as bamboo, and frequently it is only possible to pass through it by slashing a track. I had trouble finding an open space for my tent, but at last I did, and was soon asleep in the usual way. During the night I was several times woken up by a strange noise, a kind of bubbling, rumbling noise. I looked out of the tent, and could see nothing strange, so went to sleep again. In the morning I found that I had pitched camp on a dried lake of volcanic mud, and the noises I had heard during the night came from pools of boiling mud about five feet away from the tent pegs. This blue-grey mud slowly formed into bubbles up to a foot in diameter, which kept on increasing until they burst with a loud plop. Other noises were rumbles underneath, and hisses of escaping steam.

I used Rotorua for my base while working the outlying district every day. I found it a fascinating place. Quite apart from the usual tourist attractions, it had a strange – indeed, unique – atmosphere. I don't mean the nauseating smell of sulphur, which was ever present, but the eeriness. Now I understood why people went back to live on the slopes of Vesuvius after their villages and the people in them had been destroyed. Rotorua could be destroyed any day by a giant eruption, but not only do the people not worry about this; it seems to add a spice to life there. The soil of pumice and volcanic sand is exotic; there are hot and cold rivers, boiling mud, geysers, and earthquakes. The cold lakes and rivers grow some of the biggest trout in the world.

I stayed in a rambling old wooden hotel of one storey called Brent's (all the buildings have to be, or should be, of wood because of the earthquakes). One day we left our lunch there, and rushed off to the edge of the lake. The owner of a little wooden bungalow wanted a supply of water for his detached wooden wash-house at the back, and proceeded to sink an artesian well through the middle of the floor. When we arrived a geyser had blown the roof off the wash-house, and was playing sixty feet into the air through it.

Once I went pheasant shooting (or perhaps it would be fairer to say trying to shoot a pheasant) over the site of the Tarawera village which had been overwhelmed by the great eruption in the nineteenth century. It was now an arid flat plain, with a few clumps of manuka. It was queer to think of the village, perhaps still intact, several hundred feet below our feet.

In Rotorua I became friendly with a man named Harold Goodwin. He was a queer cuss, very quiet spoken; he really ought to have been a Maori chief because he was so adept at grunting. We used to laugh at his views on women. The girls thought them a great joke. He was like a public schoolboy in the way he regarded women as either a nuisance, or a useless hindrance to enjoyment of life. But Harold had the laugh later: he made one of the happiest marriages I know to an adoring wife, and thirty years later he sailed from England to New Zealand in a yacht crewed by himself and his two daughters. He was an excellent companion for me, and we went on many little expeditions together. Later he was indirectly responsible for my life's being changed.

In the First World War he had joined the New Zealand Navy and had commanded a torpedo boat patrolling the English Channel, until he got TB and was invalided out. In Rotorua he was an architect, and a most ingenious one. Among the things he had devised was a folding canvas canoe, then a new idea. To try this out we set off to the Bay of Plenty and launched the canoe in an estuary. That wasn't enough for him, and we had to proceed across the bar out to the open sea. We survived and later we motored up to the Bay of Islands and he introduced me to sailing. We rented a seventeen-foot half-decked yacht from a Maori. As we were hard up, we could not afford a dinghy. Each evening we sailed the boat as close inshore as possible; one of us dropped off to wade ashore, and the other sailed the boat out and anchored it, before swimming ashore. In the morning we reversed the process.

One day we were fishing in the middle of the Bay of Islands in twenty fathoms. Even in this volcanic country I was intensely surprised when suddenly the bottom of the sea came up alongside us, a great grey-brown bank. This could be a serious matter. Fortunately, it moved away slowly, and we were relieved to find that it was only a whale. We had good sport fishing but it was not entirely on one side. Once when Harold bent down to pick up a fish lying on the deck it seized him by the finger and bit him to the bone. As he was alternately dancing his arm about madly and sucking his finger, he could not see how funny it was. I could. Harold flung his hand back so violently that the fish shot off back to the sea.

After that we could not get the anchor free. We tacked and gybed and sailed in all directions, but nothing would shift that anchor. We put a four-gallon kerosene tin down the cable in the hopes that it would work the anchor free, but no luck. Finally we had to cut the cable. Now we had no anchor, and no dinghy. We set off for Russell, which used to be the capital of New Zealand, and was then a small township on the east side of the bay. As we approached the long wooden jetty night was falling, and the wind dropped until we were barely moving. Presently we could see people hurrying down the jetty until it seemed that the entire population of Russell was collecting there. As soon as we were within hail, somebody sang out, 'Is that you, James MacDougall?' The only answer to this was, 'No'. The figures began drifting along the jetty the other way, and by the time we made it there was no one to take a line from us. They had thought we were the first boat of the Auckland to Bay of Islands annual 200-mile race. That was my first experience of an ocean race.

Once after a day's selling I found myself ten miles from my tent and car by road, but only a mile away across country. All that I had to do was to cross two valleys, and to climb a steep ridge between them. This I set out to do carrying the bicycle on my back. The creek had cut deeply into the soft volcanic soil of the valleys, so that I had some precipitous cliffs to negotiate. The ridge had not long ago been virgin forest, and scorched trunks lay all over it. In addition, it was steep on both sides. I did succeed in completing the traverse, but next morning I woke up with a bad attack of jaundice. A doctor told me that I must give up drinking whisky for life or it would kill me. Fortunately I didn't take his advice.

I had sworn to stick out my selling job for a year, and when I came to the end of the year I thought I would do one more week for some pocket money to have a spree. When I turned out the next day, the first of my extra week, I not only failed to make a sale, but realized that I could not have made another one for £1,000.

During that year I had earned £700, and saved £400. I determined to go to Australia, sold my spare gear and booked a passage. This was in Wellington, and Harold had come down. He said, 'Come and meet my brother Geoffrey,' and we went into the bar of the Cecil Hotel for a drink. Geoffrey Goodwin was a man about seven years older than me, taller and very strong. He had amazingly strong wrists, covered in ginger hair. He had a freckled face, and looked somewhat like Chairman Khrushchev, with his baldish, roundish cranium and upper eyelids hooding the outer corners of his eyes, which indicated his shrewdness. He said to me, 'What are you going to do?' And when I told him he said, 'Why don't you join me in a little business I've started and become a land agent?'

'What is a land agent?'

'Oh, he sells land and houses and things.'

'All right,' I said. Bang went my third attempt to reach Australia, and I became a partner of Goodwin and Chichester, Land Agents. My savings of the previous year went into a half share of the furniture and assets.

My life seemed to split in two during the next seven-year period, between twenty-one and twenty-eight. The business half was a great success; I invested everything I owned – the money I had saved during the previous year – in Geoffrey's business at the start of it, and in seven years I was able to set off for the return visit to England which I had determined not to make until I had saved £20,000. This was book value and it was all tied up in property, but it did pay for my later flights.

The other half of my life, my love life, was an equally disastrous failure. I took a bed-sitting room in a house high up the hillside above the Terrace in Wellington. From this room I had a marvellous view, looking out over the harbour. A strip of the city lay below, and only a few hundred yards away were the wharves with liners and cargo ships constantly docking and leaving. At night the twinkling lights of the buoys and ships in the harbour seen in the clear atmosphere of that place were breathtaking. But my loneliness sitting there every evening was terrible. People ask me, 'Aren't you lonely forty days in a yacht by yourself crossing the Atlantic?' But alone in the Atlantic is like a warm friendly party compared with the loneliness I felt in Wellington. New Zealand society was in sharply defined layers, and I had difficulty in distinguishing their fine differences. People all seemed much the same to me. There were strong elements in the social build-up of Scottish Presbyterianism, of

Irish pub life, of English provincial, suburban, Methodist and Chapel communities. For a man and a woman to live together unmarried would have been a black social crime. The pubs all had to close at 6 o'clock in the evening, to force workers back to their wives; with the result that there was a wild rush to close offices at 5 o'clock and to drink fast and furiously till 6 o'clock if one wanted to meet and talk with one's acquaintances. After that, for a bachelor, or at least for me, there was nothing to do but sit in my bed-sitting room and read or work.

I began a wretched series of love affairs. Unfortunately I never met anyone who had both a fascinating and intriguing personality, as well as the quality of arousing passionate love. A hurricane affair with one woman would perhaps set me hungrily searching for another with a personality and charming companionship. Once I had three love affairs going at the same time. I don't think my friends, whom I slowly acquired, would have been aware of these affairs. If my name was linked with any girl, it was most likely that it was only a platonic friendship. I fell madly in love with a tall blonde – not my type at all. She was friendly, but kept her love and passion in cold storage. I was so riddled with unrequited love that on one occasion I motored forty miles at night to stare in the dark at the window of the room she was sleeping in. Then I motored back again to start work in the morning. Another time I was sitting in my office, which was then at the top of a seven-storey building in Wellington, and from my desk I could see, at a wharf below, a ship tied up in which she was about to go to England via Sydney. Unable to concentrate on my job, I rushed down town and bought a ticket to Sydney, 1,400 miles to the west, and kept in my cabin till the ship had sailed. My loved one made a frightful fuss when she discovered that I was on board. What was so maddening about this affair was that I knew all the time that we were not suited to each other. One night in Sydney I went to a theatre alone, and suddenly after a joke on the stage heard my friend's laugh from the circle above. It was a distinctive laugh, a ringing melody; it may have been too loud, but it slashed my heart in two that night. What a brutal thing modern love can be; how I wished I had been living in the

Stone Age so that I could have grabbed her by the hair and dragged her off, or been killed in the process by a rival.

One night I was out courting and had an interesting adventure. I motored out to the coast and was among the sand-dunes close to the beach. Suddenly my friend, or shall I say *mon amie*, said, 'Look! over there.' It was a dark overcast night but I could see on the crest of a sand-dune silhouetted dense black against a less black sky a man creeping on all fours. I watched his position changing as he approached at an angle along the crest, though I could not see any movement. Then he disappeared, and I knew that he was coming down from the crest towards us. It was a thrilling excitement as he stalked us. There was no one within miles, not a sound of him could be heard above the subdued roar of the Pacific breakers and the rustle of the near-by dune grass in the light breeze. He had completely disappeared, and I had no idea whether he carried a gun or a knife. I took off my spectacles and passed them to my companion to hold. Suddenly she squeezed my arm and whispered, 'There.' I turned my head half-left, and stared into the dark with my short sight. 'There.' Then I saw a black form. It was stationary. I could see no movement but suddenly it was nearer, close. When I thought the distance down to six feet I sprang! He was off like a streak, away, over a low dune, towards the beach. There was a steep hard bank down to the beach. He went down it at full speed and fell at the bottom. I jumped on to his body, pinned down his spread-eagled arms with my knees, and seized his throat with both hands. I had him. He stopped struggling. Then the whole thing struck me as grotesquely comic, and I wanted to laugh. I loosed my hold and said, 'Now, explain.' He told some cock-and-bull story about hunting for his girl who had gone off with another man. There was nothing I could think of doing. I suppose that if he had been going to murder me I could not legally defend myself until I had been killed. So I let him go. I should be surprised if he stalked anybody else for a good while, however, and, after all, he had provided a great thrill. I had found being hunted can be more thrilling than being the hunter.

I fell in love with a young girl, and this ended disastrously.

She was a sweet, charming brunette. I was passionately in love, and when she steadfastly resisted everything else, I asked her to marry me. Before we were married I knew, or felt, with a dreadful sinking feeling, that it was a blunder; but I was fettered by some terrible code of honour and we got married. I was only twenty-three at the time, and three years later my personality seemed to have changed completely. I was leading a tremendously active life, while she retreated farther and farther into a narrow circle of domesticity. Sometimes I would get into my car and drive all night, mostly over primitive potholed roads, to reach Rotorua, 350 miles to the north, next morning. Then I would go off on some shooting or camping escapade with Harold Goodwin. Finally my wife and I parted, and she went off with our son George to live with her family.

All this period I was homesick and lonely and unhappy without knowing why. I had left England soon after leaving school without having any girl friends. And I had no chance to mix with any grown up social set. When I watch Giles, now sixteen, who is at Westminster School, and the lively, bright, active, press-on set of girls and boys in equal numbers with which he mixes, when I see the number of problems, serious and frivolous, which they tackle with no inhibition, I realize what a restricted, inhibited youth I had.

My business career was just as successful as my other life was disastrous. Geoffrey Goodwin already had a ghastly old-fashioned office at Lower Hutt. It was really a shop with the bottom half of the wide shop window painted bright green, and clear plate glass above. For these undesirable premises he paid a rent of ten shillings a week. He had acquired the local agency of the State Fire Insurance Department, the only nationalized concern I have found to compare with private enterprise for efficiency. There were 1,500 houses on the books, and our commission on the premiums paid for an office girl.

When I started work I found that I had not the slightest idea of how a house was built, nor what it was made of. Our first need was to get an agency for more houses to sell, so I started hunting round Lower Hutt (which was like a small suburb) calling on houseowners, to ask if they wanted to sell their houses. One of my first victims asked me what I reckoned his house was worth; I guessed a figure – £5,000 – and he burst out laughing; the house was worth about £1,500. However, it was not long before I could value a house to within £10 of its building cost.

With Geoff's shrewdness and my press-on vitality, we soon began to make a success of the job. At the start customers looking for a house or land did not come to us but went to the old-established firms in the township across the bridge on the other side of the Hutt River. However, on the way from the railway station they had to pass our office. I soon got to know the expression on a buyer's face and used to dart out and waylay him. Success depended on summing up a man's character and taste so well that one knew better than he did himself what was the best sort of house for him. This may sound smug, and naturally we had our failures, but it was surprising how many successes we had, too. I found quickly that even if one could tell what was the most suitable property after a minute or two's talk, it would be inviting failure to take the customer straight to it. I always showed him the second-best property, which I didn't think quite right for him.

After three years we moved on to the Main Street across the cantilever bridge with a framework of squared, unpainted timber baulks above the roadway. We bought the baker's shop with his dwelling place behind the shop and the baker's oven. We had the wooden shop and five-roomed house jacked up, moved and re-settled on concrete piles, so that we could build three new shop fronts facing the High Street. It was a corner lot, and we hid the old weatherboard wooden side of the dwelling with stucco on expanded wire netting. We made the corner shop into our new office.

All this time I was working immensely hard. One night, after midnight, I was sitting alone in the office working at the accounts (I did all the book-keeping myself), there was no sound in the township, and I must have been concentrating on what I was doing to the exclusion of all else. Suddenly, I became aware of a mouse burrowing into my thigh against my skin; it had run right up my leg inside my trousers without disturbing me. I pinned it against my groin from outside with one hand,

and with difficulty, as gently as I could, caught it with my other hand. As it had showed such trust in a human creature, I reciprocated as best I could; I left the office with it, and walked 200 yards to a fine garden which I thought a good place for a mouse and there let it go.

One day we bought a fifty-acre property at an auction sale. This was thirty miles from Wellington, the capital city, and we named it 'The Plateau'. It was a flat rectangle of land, deserted, with plenty of evergreen native trees dotted about; there were also some man-planted exotics, cypresses, firs and the like which gave it a parklike appearance. A stream running from end to end had cut its way down to a lower level leaving a sheer gravel cliff 100 feet high in places. Before leaving the property this little stream meandered round a razor-back ridge covered with tiny-leaved native birch trees. The saddleback of the ridge was sharp enough to sit astride it. It was a fascinating spot, and I used to love the days we spent there, walking about and planning its development. We ate our picnic lunch beside the stream to the tune of the cicadas zizzing in the heat. It was a social crime to chop this heavenly spot into small bits for weekend cottages, but if we had not done so, somebody else would have. We built a half-mile road through it, cut it into fifty allotments and made a financial success of it.

I advocated giving up our agency work, and selling only our own property. Finally Geoffrey agreed to this; I think he got bored with hearing me plug away at the theme that 'you cannot broke and deal at the same time'. We sold the goodwill of our land agency business with a lease of the shop we owned, and moved into offices in Wellington. Next we bought a property at Silverstream, about ten miles from Wellington, and started developing that. It was 1,100 acres.

CHAPTER SEVEN

LEARNING TO FLY

WE developed this property in two ways. First, we planted it with pine-trees. Geoffrey was an enthusiastic tree-grower, and believed in forestry as a profitable investment. I like trees, too, so we got cracking. I raised the first 40,000 trees in my back yard from seed collected from pine cones; it was fun watching the little pine-needle seedlings emerge with the seeds on their backs. The beds were protected from the sun's heat by scrim (a kind of sacking) stretched across wooden frames. We planted out these experimental seedlings on a hill in rows six feet apart, with nine feet between seedlings. They took well, so we started a nursery of our own, and soon had several planting gangs at work. We planted a million trees, and Geoffrey's son has been milling them for the past ten years. I am proud of having raised a crop of timber in my lifetime from seed planted in my own garden. New Zealand is a wonderful tree-growing country; our pines used to put on six feet in height a year, and, once they got started, an inch in diameter. We built miles of road, and at one time had three teams of surveyors at work. We had to sell off small lots of land as sites for week-end cottages in order to pay for the whole scheme. We bought another property alongside, and cut that up as well. We built up a sales force of thirty salesmen, selling only our own land. Geoffrey was himself a wonderful salesman, but I found that I could not sell my own property. I became shy and inhibited about it, which I never did when I was selling things belonging to other people. The only trouble was that Geoffrey was always selling ideas to me. We bought the Miller Chair Company which supplied seats for theatres and cinemas. I never could get really interested in this. We didn't know enough about it, and lost money through it. However, we now owned three private companies operating in land which were doing well. By the time I was twenty-six my income was £10,000 a year. Then Geoffrey sold me the idea of an aviation company, and we formed the Goodwin-Chichester Aviation Company Limited. My first flight made me wildly excited and enthusiastic. We took the New Zealand agency for A. V. Roe, bought two Avro Avians, and began a joy-riding tour of New Zealand.

This was good fun; first we had to scout around for a field suitable for landing and taking off passengers; then we advertised. Our aim was to fly around as many passengers as we could in the few hours when they flocked out to the field. We had four of the best pilots in New Zealand, but their experience had been with heavier military planes in the First World War, and they found the light Avian landing on grass fields too fragile for the job. We were lucky that we only lost ten shillings a head on the 6,000 passengers we carried. Under-carriages were the chief weakness in the planes, and sometimes farm fences seemed to be in the wrong place. One day I got exasperated at one of our crashes, and determined to learn how to fly myself, to find out what it was all about.

I went down to the New Zealand Air Force station at Christchurch and had some lessons there in an Avro 504K. This plane had a rotary engine, which means that the propeller and the engine went round together. You could not throttle back the engine; you just cut out the ignition when coming in to land, and cut it in again hopefully if you made a bad landing and wanted to take off quickly. The engine used castor oil which stank to high heaven, and sprinkled the pilot's face copiously. I struggled away trying to learn, but was a hopelessly bad pupil. By December 1928 I had had eighteen hours fifty minutes of dual instruction, and still could not fly. I think this was partly because of trying to mix flying with an intensely active business life. Geoffrey and I were running five private companies at full blast, besides our partnership, and I was ruthlessly trying to make money for twelve hours a day or more.

In the spring of 1929, ten years and three months after I had landed in New Zealand, I decided that the time had come for me to go to England for a visit. I wanted to fly back from London to Sydney, and thought that the best chance of achieving this was to obtain the safest and most reliable aeroplane. With this in view, I first visited the United States, and spent two months looking at any possible makes of aircraft. I had demonstration flights in an American Eagle with a 180 h.p. Hispano engine, a Ryan six-place Brougham, with a Wright 300 h.p., a Whirlwind six-place Kuntzer Aircoach with three 90 h.p. Le Blonds, a Curtis Robin three-place, with a Curtis 180 h.p Challenger, a Curtis Fledgling two-place trainer, and a Fairchild seven-place plane with a Pratt and Whitney Wasp.

Three other types I never tried out because in each case the aeroplane crashed between the time of my making an appointment and reaching the airfield. None of the types I flew in was really suitable, and my visit was aeronautically a flop. However, I made a good friend in Charlie Blackwell, and thoroughly enjoyed staying with him in Santa Barbara. There I survived a game of bridge with three millionaires, used the same bath as had Prince George (later Duke of Kent) during a visit to California, and was introduced by Charlie to his tailor in London who made the best dress clothes in the world.

At the end of July I arrived in London, and began learning to fly again. At first I had some instruction at Stag Lane, but I could see that I was not going to get on very fast there, and switched to Brooklands, where Duncan Davies and Ted Jones took me in hand. It was not until August 13th that I first went solo for five minutes, and that was after twenty-four hours of dual. I was a slow pupil, but perhaps not quite as bad as it sounds, because only five and a half hours of that dual instruction was in England. On August 28th I secured my 'A' flying licence, which permitted me to fly an aircraft alone. What about navigation? Suppose I couldn't navigate across country? The first time I ventured away from the aeodrome was most exciting. At first everything was a jumble; then I picked out a railway line, the Thames, the Staines reservoir. With the aid of the map I found Byfleet. Flying at a snail's pace, I recognized other landmarks shown on the map. Thrill, excitement, joy! If I could do that much the first day, competence must be a matter only of practice and experience. On September 8th I bought a Gipsy I Moth which weighed 880 lb. unloaded. I had left New Zealand with the idea of a bigger and better machine, but money worries were troubling me. Almost as soon as I had left New Zealand the 1929 slump had hit us hard. Everything I had was invested in land, and we had big overdrafts to finance our land purchases. The bank got jittery, and wanted us to reduce them. But our customers, like us, were hit by the slump, and although we had a lot of money owing to us for land we had sold in small lots, it was hard to collect it. The Moth was all I could afford, but I was lucky to get it. It turned out to be a wonderful little aeroplane with its Gipsy motor, and Handley Page slots. Three days after buying it I flew to Liverpool, where an actress friend of mine was playing in a show. I did no good in that direction so turned round and flew to North Devon to visit my parents.

The aeroplane was so new that it had not yet been fitted with a compass. I was 'flying by Bradshaw', following the railway lines across country, and I wondered if I could fly by the sun. The sky was overcast, with ten-tenths at 1,000 feet. I climbed up into the cloud, and proceeded until I had passed through a 9,000-feet layer of it to emerge at 10,000 feet in brilliant sunshine over a snowy-white field of cloud. Not only had I no compass, but no blind-flying instruments at all. I reckoned that if I got into trouble I could force the plane into a spin, that it was bound to spin round the vertical axis, and that therefore I should be sure to emerge vertically from the cloud. After flying along for half an hour by the sun, I climbed down through the 9,000-feet layer of cloud. I then wanted to find out how accurately I had carried out this manoeuvre, and I used a sound principle of navigation. I fixed my position by the easiest method available – I flew round a railway station low down, and read the name off the platform. By some extraordinary fluke I was right on course. I probably uttered for the first time the navigator's famous cry 'Spot on!'

This visit was not a great success. I had been away more than ten years and I arrived back thinking (privately) that I had a tremendous achievement behind me in building up a business and turning my £10 into £20,000. My family not only never mentioned this, but showed me plainly that I was an outsider as far as they were concerned. I had a New Zealand twang, and no doubt talked too much and too loudly. For my part, I disapproved of the air of decay creeping into the house where I had been born, the weeds sprouting from between the paving stones of the stable yard, and the difficulty my family was finding in attending to their own housework efficiently after having been used to having it all done for them. I believe that what upset my family most was the odd matter of a wreath. While I had been away in New Zealand my great aunt Jinny, of whom

I had been tremendously fond, had died at the age of over ninety. When I first visited my family I brought down a wreath for her grave. It was big and rather exotic looking; perhaps more suitable for a cemetery in Wimbledon than for a Devon village where the wreaths are more likely to be made with a few daffodils or primroses. I think that this wreath upset my family more than anything else that I did; they thought I must be a frightful barbarian to produce such an unusual thing.

As a result I took to showing off more than I would otherwise have done. Also I was bursting with the joy of living, and the thrill of flying my own aeroplane. After taking my sister for a flight I made a bad landing on a rabbit burrow, bounced into the air to find an oak-tree dead ahead. I could not take off again and plonked down with a bang. One wheel hit the side of a cart track; daylight burst through the side of the fuselage, and the plane came to rest with a drooping wing. The damage to my cocky pride was worse, and I scratched my head hard. Then I thought of George Moore, the local carpenter who used to be my sparring partner when I was a boy. I rushed off for George, and we got busy with hammer and saw. We quickly replaced the fractured ribs, and added one or two extra. Eighteen hours later I was in the air again. The next day I took up Wilkey, who used to be our gardener, and when we landed he reminded me that it was my birthday, and that twenty-eight years ago he had ridden into Barnstaple to fetch a doctor to help me make my first landing in the world.

I went back to Brooklands in a 35-m.p.h. wind – with the help of my two sisters and Wilkey hanging on to the wings I just managed to taxi into position safely to take off. In the strong gusty wind at Brooklands my first shot at landing was a dud. I bumped, and went off again. The next time, I put the plane down well, and rolled to a halt. I started taxiing towards the hangars across wind, but a gust started lifting the windward wing. I saw the other wingtip dip slowly and gracefully to the ground. I watched, fascinated, as the tip slowly crumpled up. The windward wing rose equally slowly, up, up, up until the whole aeroplane was balanced on the crumpled wingtip. Then it took a leap into the air, and landed fair and square on its nose, with the tail pointing to heaven. I found myself in the undignified position of dangling in the safety-belt and looking down at the ground ten feet below me.

I spent fifty hours working on the repairs, under the supervision of the chief rigger. I learned a lot. Perhaps I should add that my rustic repairs to the longeron and compression struts caused the riggers much amusement. It was a novelty for them to have a pilot repair his own aircraft. Fitting and rigging the new wing and the new propeller was valuable experience for me.

After this I settled down to serious flying training. For hour after hour I practised landing into wind, across wind and down wind, and then in a confined space. I used to plant my handkerchief ten yards inside a fence and practise touching down on it. Then I would move it 150 yards from the fence, and practise ending my landing run on it. This last (without brakes) was the hardest manoeuvre of all, because of the variable wind. For half an hour a day I practised forced landings. I used to climb to 1,000 feet, cut the engine, pick the best field I could see, and land in it. At first I always overshot the field. I imagined that my motor really was dead, and that to undershoot would be fatal. Eventually my skill improved, so that I could just skim the trees or the fence, and drop into the field I had picked. I played this game with serious concentration, and one day I put up a 'black'; after I had rolled to a halt on the grass with my dead motor after my forced landing, I found myself staring at Windsor Castle a few hundred yards in front.

I also liked to put in half an hour a day on aerobatics. I used to do my loops over a long stretch of straight railway line, so that I could check each loop for accuracy as I flattened out.

On October 3rd my compass arrived and was adjusted. I began feeding navigation into my day's programme and checking up on petrol consumption at different speeds. On October 15th I took off and landed in moonlight. This gave me twenty-three minutes of intense enjoyment; I had a feeling of complete isolation and solitariness, and the thousands of lights below intensified the feeling of being completely cut off. I looped, and did a few stall turns for the same reason that a dog barks at something which scares him.

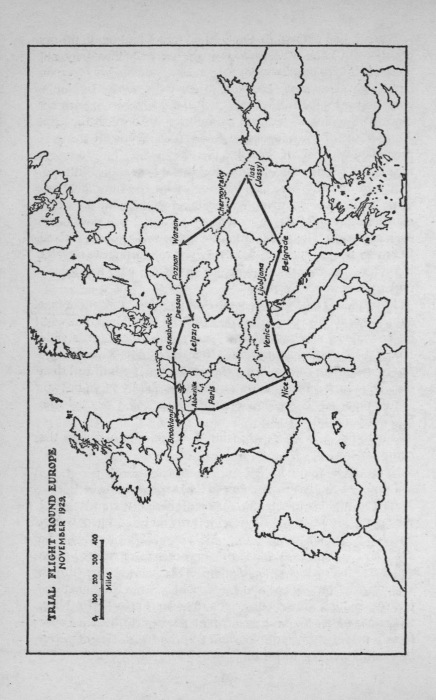

TRIAL FLIGHT ROUND EUROPE
NOVEMBER 1929.

0 100 200 300 400
Miles

Brooklands
Abbeville
Paris
Osnabrück
Dessau
Leipzig
Poznan
Warsaw
Chernovtsky
Tiasi
(Iassy)
Belgrade
Ljubljana
Venice
Nice

When I had arrived in England in July I had made up my mind to fly back to Australia single-handed. This may not seem much of a project today, but at that time only one person had flown alone from England to Australia, Bert Hinkler, a crack test pilot from Bunderberg, Australia. I gave myself six months in which to learn to fly sufficiently to make the trip. Time was now running out; and so was money; cash was getting desperately short. I cabled Geoffrey asking him to try to raise £400 for me while I went for a trial spin round Europe. The next difficulty was that I had to insure the aeroplane, because I still owed some money for it. November was the worst month in Europe for this kind of flying, and I was not an experienced pilot. However, Lamplugh, who was a good sport and friend to novice aviators, finally agreed to underwrite the risk if I would start by taking with me Joe King, who was an experienced commercial pilot.

That flight round Europe started on October 25th, and it was a sporting adventure from beginning to end. Joe King came with me to Paris. 'Let's go,' said Joe, and pushed the throttle wide open. I assumed that he wanted to take off himself, so I let go the controls. We were a long time leaving the ground, and then only just cleared the trees on St George's Hill by a foot or two.

'What on earth are you doing?' shouted Joe through the speaking tube.

'Nothing,' I said indignantly. 'I never even touched the controls.'

'Nor did I,' said he.

I don't think that manoeuvre can be repeated.

At first Joe kept asking me if I knew where I was, and where I was going. Crossing the Channel was my first flight over water, and I climbed up to 6,000 feet. Joe complained bitterly of the cold, so I landed at Abbeville in France, where we had some cognac. After this his worry diminished enough for him to sleep in the front cockpit until we reached Paris. Here he dropped off, and left me to continue on my own. I refuelled at Nice, where I landed on a deserted strip on the beach, thumbed a lift from a passing car into Nice, and returned with tins of petrol in a taxi. I went on to Milan.

Next day I was late in getting away from Venice for my hop to Ljubljana in Yugoslavia. As I flew over Trieste it was already twilight, and I could see that I would not reach Ljubljana before dark. However, I decided to risk that. But as soon as I climbed over the hilly country inland I ran into mist. If that persisted, I should be unable to see Ljubljana at all. I suddenly realized that I must land immediately, while I could still vaguely see the ground below. I was over a narrow valley, which was divided into hundreds of thin cultivated strips. I chose the best looking strip, came round in a steep turn, and landed on it. Unfortunately, it was too dark for me to realize that it was freshly ploughed land, and as the plane slowed I could sense the wheels sinking. Up came the tail, and the Moth went on to her nose. Once again I found myself dangling from my safety-belt ten feet from the ground. It was too dark to assess the damage, but next morning it turned out to be only a broken propeller. I spent an interesting ten days in Novi Vas pri Rakeku until a new propeller arrived.

The village mayor wanted to be taken for a flight, and as they had been so good to me I could not bear to refuse. I looked over all the flat land in the valley, and the best strip was only 15 yards wide and 200 yards long with a deep ditch on each side. Although the Gipsy Moth had no brakes, I took off from this strip with the mayor and landed him on it again.

I moved on to Belgrade, which I left in bad weather. For sixty miles I flew down the Danube with the hills on each side in thick cloud and mist. I was disappointed that the Danube was a dirty brown instead of the blue which Strauss had led me to expect. By the time I reached the Iron Gates I was flying in a huge tunnel with a cloud ceiling. After entering Rumania the cloud gradually lowered until I was dodging telephone poles in the mist. Finally, I had to land in a field where I was immediately surrounded by a running, shouting crowd of barefooted peasants. The difficulty was to explain in my bad German how fragile the aeroplane was, and that the people should keep their hands off it. In the end four soldiers, also barefooted, were produced, who mounted guard until the mist cleared sufficiently for me to take off again. I by-passed

Bucharest, and skirted the Transylvanian Alps, flying over clusters of oil derricks. I was headed for Iasi in the wide valley of the River Prut. Just before dark I crossed a wide range of hills to find the Prut Valley a dense sea of white fog with Iasi somewhere at the bottom.

An ice cold wave of fear passed through me, but it left me cool and clear-headed. I turned in a vertical bank, opened the throttle wide and set off to retrace my route at full speed. I had been flying over forest-covered hills where there was not enough flat ground to build a house on, but I remembered having seen a valley with some flat pasture thirty miles back. Night was falling when I arrived. I could still see the ground directly below me as I flew low. I chose a piece which seemed clear of obstructions, but I then had to turn twice, and find it blind, because it was too dark to see anything ahead. I flattened out, and landed nicely, then held my breath, waiting to hit a fence or run into a ditch. My luck was in; it was a perfect landing. This is one of the few occasions when I landed without anyone seeing the plane. I walked across pasture until I found a road, and waited there until a car came along loaded with fierce-looking peasants in sheepskin rig-outs. There was a tremendous babble of talk and argument, none of which I could understand, and then another car arrived with someone who spoke French. He explained that they had thought I was a Russian spy, and should be shot. I said, 'Tell them I have had nothing to eat all day, and would they please defer such frivolous debates until they have found me some dinner?' This changed the whole atmosphere; I was rushed to the village, and set before a mountain of goulash while for hours relays of noses were flattened against the window looking on to the one street of the village. I was offered a tiny, stuffy, dirty room, with a vast covering twelve inches thick stuffed with feathers to sleep under. Next morning I flew to Iasi with the mayor, Advocate Popovitch.

From Iasi I flew north to Czernowitz, later Czernauti and now Chernovtsky on the boundary of Moldavia and the Ukraine. Here I stayed the night as a guest of the Aerodrome Commandant, who had been one of the country's chief fighter

73

pilot aces in the First World War. I let him fly the Gipsy Moth by himself, which delighted him. He was the most hospitable host imaginable, and detailed his charming Russian girl friend to entertain me. She was a lovely creature. We only had a few words in German in common, but I think we were better off without being able to talk.

From Czernowitz I flew over hundreds of miles of dense forest, interlaced with streams and rivers and with few signs of people. I refuelled at Warsaw, and again at Poznan. I was making for Leipzig, but I ran into fog near the River Oder and landed in a huge stubble field at a place called Reppen. Here I was most grateful to be the guest of the Rittergutsbesitzer. Again I had had nothing to eat all day, and was most grateful for the meal with my host, who was the local squire.

This flying trip may sound simple, but in fact the negotiations and formalities at every landing I made were long and exhausting. Police, Customs, military, air force and civil aviation officials had to be satisfied after long questioning. Every time I landed my passport and permits, carnet, aircraft log books and journey log book, all had to be examined, interpreted, explained and stamped. In East Europe no one seemed to eat anything in the morning, and I was too anxious to get away to spend time hunting for food at any stopping place during the day. On top of this I nearly always had difficulty in obtaining suitable petrol and oil when I landed. Once I had to wait sixteen hours for petrol. Later, when I had grown wiser, I always carried a loaf of bread with me.

After Reppen I landed in a field in the Black Forest, and although I did take on some petrol there, I really did it for fun. A crowd of Germans surrounded me, and when I asked them not to handle the aeroplane because it was so easily damaged, they took offence. They thought that I was afraid of their damaging it purposely because of still hating the British as they had done in the war, whereas, they said, they now felt exceedingly friendly towards us. In due course I soothed them down, and we parted friends. I landed at Leipzig and from there flew on to the Junkers Works at Dessau, where I had a flight in a small all-metal Junkers monoplane. I thought it was heavy on the controls, and glided like a brick compared with the Gipsy Moth.

On leaving Leipzig I had an adventurous day. I landed in a field when I could not penetrate the fog near Munster. I waited an hour on the ground, and then tried again. I still could not get through to Munster, so I made for Osnabrück. Here, the area round the field was completely enveloped in fog. I cruised round for some time, and then landed in a field at Jeggen. I got someone to pinpoint the exact position of the airfield on my map and tried again. I flew low up a shallow valley, only to find it closed off by fog on the ground. I turned round to retrace my track down the valley, to find that meanwhile the fog had dropped on to the ground at the other end, and I was completely trapped. I was attacked by panic. There was no time; the fog was dropping everywhere to the ground; already I had not enough height to turn properly banked but had to slither round in horrible skidding flat turns. However, I saw a field which I thought suitable, and successfully found it again after sliding round in a horrible semicircle. I pulled off a good landing. That night I slept in the house of a small farmer who had fought against the New Zealanders at Dixmude. He was most hospitable, and I spent the night under the same roof as his father, mother, grandfather, grandmother, his children, my Gipsy Moth and five cows. The Gipsy Moth and the cows occupied the hall.

Next morning I found Osnabrück. The airfield officials knew I was coming and shot up red Very pistol lights in the mist as I approached.

After that I had no more adventures before returning to England. I recrossed the English Channel fifty feet above the water, grateful for no hazzards. I was sorry Joe King could not have seen it.

CHAPTER EIGHT

START FOR AUSTRALIA

I GOT back to England on November 20th to start a month of worry, work, suspense and fear. Now, this seems inevitable to me before the start of any big adventure, and it boils down to 'Can I start, or can't I?'

Geoffrey, my partner, had sent me £400, but I had already spent half of it. With it came a telegram, 'Advise selling plane. Expensive salvage Malay aerodromes. No more money possible.' The failure of any permit for the following countries could kill the flight – Egypt, Iraq, Persia, India, Straits Settlements, Timor, Dutch East Indies, etc. The Shell Company had agreed to lay down petrol supplies for me at 2s. 6d. a gallon throughout, but they could not do this until I knew where I could land. There was difficulty in finding out which airfields in the East Indies would be unusable. Eventually some of the petrol went into Northern Territory, Australia, by camel. I got my maps together, and cut them into long strips which I could handle easily by myself. These strips totalled over seventy feet.

I had difficulty in getting permission to fly along the north coast of Africa from Benghazi to Tobruk because the Arab rebellion against the Italians made it dangerous for any white man. The total inventory of difficulties was immense, but had this advantage, that it took my mind off the chief worry which was whether I had the flying skill to make the flight. I wanted to beat Hinkler's record. He had achieved the flight from London to Darwin, Australia, in fifteen and a half days. It was 12,000 miles by the route flown, so that he averaged 750 miles a day. It was not much use trying to beat his time by only a few hours, so I divided the distance as nearly as possible into 500-mile stages, and decided to attempt two stages a day. This would require twelve and a half hours' flying every day, with a halt for refuelling, probably in a fresh, strange country, in the middle of the day. In order to make the final landing of the day in daylight, I should have to start in the dark in the morning at about 2 o'clock. So I had to enlist the help of the Air Ministry to obtain permission from the various countries to fly over them at night without navigation lights, for to fit a Moth with the only navigation lights then available would be like fitting out a 5-ton yacht with a steamer's anchor.

On December 19th I worked hard all day. I flew over to De Havilland's at Stag Lane to have a cover fitted to the front cockpit, which was both streamlined and easy to open, so that I could get out my rubber boat in a hurry. Also, I had a hole cut in the back of the front cockpit seat, so that I could extract food from where I sat at the controls. I collected and stowed all my food and gear. I made telephone calls about last minute permits. Not until after dark did I take off from Brooklands to fly to Croydon Aerodrome, where I had to clear Customs, etc., before leaving the country. At Croydon an Air Ministry official immediately pounced on me to know why I was flying without navigation lights.

After refuelling with petrol and oil I cleared the Customs and collected my journey log-book, *carnet de passage*, licence, and my passport with endorsement for seventeen countries, and was ready to leave. Walking near a hangar I asked a stranger for some information. When we came under a light he said, 'Aren't you Chichester? Don't you know me? I'm Waller of Hooton. I shall always remember your turning up at Liverpool in a new machine without a compass and with that ridiculous map of yours.' He had just flown down himself in his own aeroplane. Had I been for any more flights since then? 'Yes, I made a flight round Europe.'

'Great heavens! But you've only just got your licence, haven't you? Perhaps you're going to fly home now,' he added, jokingly.

'Yes, as a matter of fact I am.'

I had not talked about my proposed trip for fear of failure and being laughed at.

'You're not really!' he said. 'When are you starting?'

'In six hours.'

He was silent for some time.

77

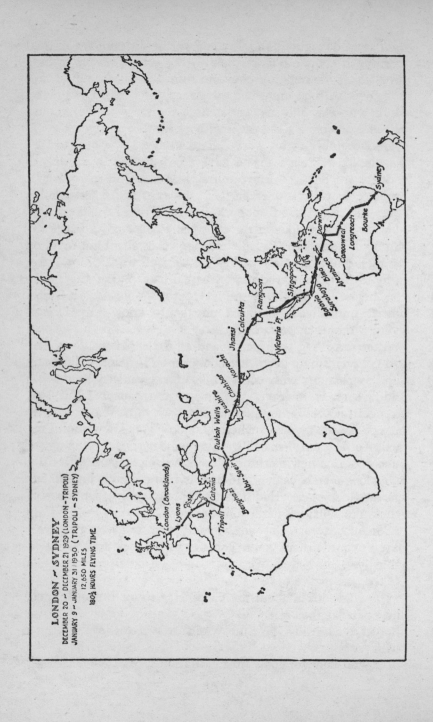

LONDON ~ SYDNEY
DECEMBER 20 ~ DECEMBER 21 1929 (LONDON~TRIPOLI)
JANUARY 9 ~ JANUARY 31 1930 (TRIPOLI ~ SYDNEY)
12,650 MILES
180½ HOURS FLYING TIME

London (Brooklands)
Lyons
Catania
Tripoli
Benghazi
Abu-Sueir
Rutbah Wells
Bushire
Chahbar
Karachi
Jhansi
Calcutta
Rangoon
Victoria Pt.
Singapore
Batavia
Soerabaia
Bima
Atemboea
Darwin
Camooweal
Longreach
Bourke
Sydney

I ate dinner in a panic. When the porter told me I was wanted on the telephone I got hot and cold with fear that it was something which would stop me. I gasped with relief when it turned out to be the Meteorological Office, telling me that I must not land at Grogak, Rembang, Bima, Reo or Larantoeka in the Dutch East Indies because they were flooded. I could not worry about that.

I was up at 1.30 and ate bacon and eggs.

At 3.15 I took off across the grass field. This was the first time I had taken off with a full load up. The aeroplane was carrying its own weight in payload. I thought this was the reason for the long and horribly bumpy take-off, but actually the ground, frozen hard, had ripped open a tyre and tube. As soon as I left the ground I felt the tremendous thrill of being off to Australia. The four exhaust stubs belched bluish flames against the night sky. I wobbled about at first both in yaw and pitch, for this was the first time I had steered a course at night. Luckily, I had moonlight at the start, and began to pick out the fields below. I could see the broad bands of hoar frost along the lee of the hedges. I kept on trying to fly steady and level. I had no blind-flying instruments, and the horizon was vague and indefinite. I set about trying to read the drift, another thing I had not had time to practise. Leaving the coast and flying off into the murky darkness was another exciting moment. The moonlight was cut off by a layer of cloud, and now the horizon had completely vanished. All I could see was a glint on a small patch of water directly beneath the aeroplane. I hoped to keep roughly level by means of the altimeter, and when I looked at it, the dial was rotating without stopping. I had nothing to judge the height by except the patch of sea underneath. If the waves were small I might be only a few feet above them; if large, I might be thousands of feet up.

I had expected to cross the Channel in about fifteen minutes, and when I was still over water after three-quarters of an hour I began to feel lost. The truth was that I was making a hash of my first night navigation. I had over-estimated the drift, and thought I had crossed the south coast at Folkestone.

When France did not show up as expected, I wondered if I was heading into the North Sea. If I had been able to study my map, and use a ruler and protractor, I would have seen quickly what was happening, but there was no light in the cockpit, and I did not like to stop looking out while I worked a torch with the map and instruments. Gradually, I reasoned that the North Sea was an impossibility and that I was headed south towards Dieppe.

At last, an hour after leaving England, a high, whitish cliff loomed up just ahead. I flew along beside the dim, ghostly white face for some five miles, determining the compass bearing of its direction. There was only one five-mile piece of coast running in this direction – I must be north-east of Dieppe. I worked out a fresh course for Paris from that spot, allowing ten degrees for drift; but the wind had dropped altogether, so I was set to the west of Paris. As a bleak, dismal, November grey crept into the sky, I was cold and cramped and attacked by an overpowering desire to sleep. I got a map fix, and worked out a fresh course for Lyons. Dawn broke, the earth was white with frost, the canals and patches of water covered with ice. Smoke drifted lazily above the chimney tops. After seven and a half hours in the air I landed at Lyons. It was a good landing, but the machine tried to slew round at the end of its run because of its flat tyre. I ran 300 yards in my big sheepskin boots, then had an enormous omelet with a bottle of red wine. The tyre was mended for me, and I got away after one and three-quarter hours on the ground.

Climbing with full load to 10,000 feet in order to cross the Alps seemed to take an age. I kept on looking at my watch, and wondering whether I could reach Pisa before dark. I flew over the Cenis Col with 3,000 feet to spare and it was a great relief to have crossed the Alps in smooth air; also to be flying faster on the long descent to Turin after the slow, tedious climb with full load. Everything went well until I ran into rough air at Genoa. Whizz! Whop! Bump! Each bump sent a shower of petrol into my face from the vent of the cockpit tank in front. I tried flying over the sea, but it was worse there. I was scared stiff that the wings would fold up. I bolted back to the mainland again, and was hurled this way and that as I climbed with throttle wide open at the steepest possible angle against the down-draught coming through a col in the hills. The slots clanked each time an extra strong bump stalled the aeroplane. I only just managed to clear the col. Then I flew down a valley parallel with the coast. At first I tried to climb in the hope of escaping the bumps, but each time I gained a few hundred feet a violent downwash of air forced me down again. I felt as hot as if I had just run a mile race.

Night fell, and at last the air became calm again. I plodded on to Pisa, where I could see the aerodrome a long way ahead splendidly lit with a searchlight signalling me. I flew up to it and cut my motor three times to let them know on the ground that I had arrived, and then shut off to land. Close to the ground I found that it was not an airfield, but bright lights illuminating a long, L-shaped hoarding, half a mile long at the corner of two streets. The searchlight was a powerful beam from a motor-car.

I soon recognized the airfield as a big black space, but there was not a single light showing except from some barracks at one end. My first shot at landing in the dark was a dud; I bumped and went round again. However, at my next shot I landed well and started to taxi in, but the wheels got bogged in the mud. A swarm of soldiers seemed to spring out of the ground and pushed the Gipsy Moth out of the mud, breaking one or two of the ribs in the leading edge.

I asked in French about the lights, and they said that they had expected me to circle for half an hour while they went to find the light operator. The Italians were extremely kind and helpful, but everything had to be discussed at great length. It took four and a half hours of solid talk and argument before I had refuelled, checked over the motor and satisfied the Air Force, Customs and police authorities. They lent me a camp-bed and I tried to sleep at 10 o'clock, but I was too tired. I had started tired, had put in a strenuous 20 hours, of which 12 had been spent flying 780 miles. I only had two and a half hours' sleep before getting into the air again at 1.45 AM. I took off in the dark with no lights on the airfield, so that I had landed and taken off from an airfield which I had never seen. It was a lovely, fine night when I reached Naples. The sky became overcast, and I was flitting along under the ceiling of a low, wide-roofed cavern. Vesuvius was a magnificent sight with dark, billowy smoke rolling slowly from the cone, and a million sparkling, twinkling lights clustering round the bay at the foot of the volcano. I flew over the Gulf of Salerno into pitch darkness. I could see nothing ahead or below. Presently, flashes of lightning from a black storm-cloud lit up the whole area. I was able to dodge this, but later flew into a rain-cloud. I could not see six feet ahead, and glided down until I could distinguish land by its utter blackness in comparison with the less black sea.

I was now flying beside a barren, mountainous country, apparently uninhabited, because there was not a single light visible anywhere. Daybreak was approaching, and as the tatty grey storm-clouds began to outline the mountains, sleepiness became an agony. I moved anything I could, waved my arms, jumped up and down in the seat, stamped my feet. If I jumped up I was asleep before I landed in the seat. I was primitive man looking at a stark, primeval scene, the black masses of towering mountains, the rugged grey precipices of rock dropping sheer into the sea and the dull surface of the sea flitting out of sight under threatening cloud. Each time I slept I heard separate motor explosions, usually about four, with an increasing interval of silence between them. Then silence, and I woke with a jolt, petrified with fear that the motor had stopped. The first few times this happened I felt certain the motor *had* stopped; it was worse when I realized that the motor was still firing steadily at 3,600 times a minute. I no longer had the fright which kept me awake for a few seconds. I took off my flying-helmet and stuck my head into the slip-stream. I tried watching the cliffs, but my eyes would not align properly; I saw double. At last day came; I had been flying for six hours. I was tempted to look for one of the three emergency landing-strips on the beach where it widened, for the desire for the aeroplane to roll to a standstill so that I could loll my head against the cockpit edge and go to sleep was overpowering. I had already passed the first of these landing-strips; when I came to the second it was half washed away. Then, at the toe of Italy, sleepiness abated, and I flew on for another age across the straits and on to Mount Etna, looking enormous and solid in her snow cap. I landed at Catania and was stuck there for three hours. Petrol and a Customs officer had to be fetched from the town. When I had everything ready I found my journey log-book was still in the town and I had to wait another hour for it to turn up.

I managed to get in fifteen minutes' sleep, which was a godsend. It was obvious now that I could not reach Africa before dark, so I asked carefully about night-landing facilities at Homs. I was assured that the airfield there had everything that could be desired in night-landing facilities. Then I flew over Malta. I thought of stopping there, but I had made up my mind to reach Africa in two days. I flew through a curtain of stinging hail, and a terrific flash of lightning near by made the aeroplane rock. After that, most of the 285-mile sea crossing was in fine weather. The sun set magnificently.

I was thrilled by my first sight of Africa, but surprised to see by the twinkling lights that the terrain sloped steeply up from the sea, whereas I had expected a broad, level sand desert. When I reached Homs it looked small, no more than a village, and there was no sign of an airfield. I thought I had made a mistake, and flew on for 6 to 8 miles to the next promontory of the coast. Looking back, I saw a large reddish light, stronger than any other. When I reached the headland there was not a light in sight ahead, so I returned to investigate the red light. I was disgusted to find that it was a big bonfire in a deserted area of the country. I did not realize that it was lit to indicate a landing-place. I decided to head for Tripoli, seventy miles to the west. If I did not find a landing-ground before that, I knew that Tripoli was an Italian air force base.

There were no lights visible along the coast. Presently I flew into cloud, and could see nothing. I did not like it, with no blind-flying instruments, and no altimeter. Later, I spotted a searchlight ahead, flashing at regular intervals. I thought it was an airfield signalling to me, and it cheered me up. After flying on another twenty miles I could see a magnificent cordon of light, and thought that the airfield was really well lighted up. I began to sing. Later the light appeared to be just as far away. When at last I arrived I found that the airfield was the harbour, and the searchlight was the lighthouse, on the Mole. I circled the town in the dark, but could not see any airfield. Then a starry light flashed ten miles to the west of the town, and I flew over to that. I could see no airfield boundary lights, and glided down close to the ground, when I found that a motor-car was switching its lights on and off, trying to overtake another one.

Then an unmistakable searchlight appeared in the sky to the east of the town. There were no boundary lights, just the one searchlight, which was lowered to the ground as I approached. It was pointing right at the hangars. If I landed along the beam, I should be heading right for the hangars, and I judged that there was only 200 yards between the light and the hangars. I could not be sure of a good landing in the dark after so long in the air. I circled the field, and could see a fine square of flat ground, surrounded by trees. I decided to land on this, short of the searchlight. I glided in steadily until suddenly, wonk! I was jolted forward and found myself held into the cockpit by my harness. The Gipsy Moth had tipped on to its nose. I had an empty feeling of utter failure; it was the end of my flight and my foolish dreams. I was aware of the dead silence which succeeded the motor roar, yet the rhythmic engine beat continued, not only in my brain but in every part of my body. I scrambled out of the cockpit, stepped on to one of the inter-wing struts and from there jumped to the ground. To my amazement I landed with a splash. 'Good God! I'm in the sea.' I listened but could hear no waves. The water only came to my ankles. I started towards the searchlight; a few steps and I floundered on to my knees. Then, stumbling forward, I touched a bank, and climbed up it (it was only a foot high). I felt like Puss in Boots in my long sheepskin boots. I stopped there, filled my pipe, but could not get the cigarette lighter to light.

The searchlight beam started moving, flickered round and

settled on the aeroplane. I could see waves in the fabric of the top and bottom wings, and a tear in the wing with the strut sticking through. 'Complete write-off,' I thought, and looked the other way. I tried to light my pipe. I was astonished to see the silhouette of a war dance on the wings of the Moth. Dozens of people dancing hard with their legs lifting like marionettes. Presently I heard the thumping of many feet. Then thirty soldiers came running to the ditch separating them from my bank. They rushed off to the side, found a crossing, then rushed up to me all talking to me at once, and pawing me as if unable to believe I was alive. I borrowed a match and set off with them for the searchlight. The commandant took me to a room in the empty mess and produced some wine. I kept on falling asleep as I drank. An orderly took me off to sleep in the room of a pilot away in the desert. Later I woke up and found myself groping along the wall, dreaming that I was flying, and suddenly all visibility vanished and I could do nothing but wait to crash.

Next morning I went out to find the Moth being wheeled in by a number of soldiers. The NCO in charge, Marzocchi, spoke French, and told me that the aeroplane was undamaged except for a front inter-wing strut and a broken propeller. I just did not believe him; but he was right. My amazement was only exceeded by my joy. I had landed in a dead flat salt pan, covered with four inches of water. It was so flat that coming in steadily I had not known I was down. The wheel-marks could be seen for thirty-five yards before the plane nosed over. This was due to my keeping the tail up in gliding trim.

I had been flying for twenty-six hours out of the forty hours since I left England, and flown 1,900 miles to Tripoli. Of the fourteen hours when I had not been flying I had had two and three-quarter hours' sleep, and the rest of the time had been very strenuously occupied working on the aeroplane and clearing formalities. On top of that I had had little sleep after the strenuous day before leaving Croydon. To put it bluntly, I could not achieve what I had set out to do. My only hope would have been to carry more petrol, and make a twelve and a half hour non-stop flight of 1,000 miles each day. The fatigue and time lost during the midday landing made my plan impossible to carry out.

CHAPTER NINE

TRIPOLI TO SYDNEY

WHILE I was waiting ten days for a new propeller to arrive, the Italian air force pilots were good to me. They amused me, and I think I amused them. There was Vallerani, for example, who, when he discovered that this was the third propeller I had smashed in four months, suggested a rubber one – perhaps a clever idea. Vallarani was in charge of the engineering section which carried out all the repairs on the aeroplane for me free of charge. There was Guidi, who looked like Adonis with a perfect modern tailor. I called him Topsy. He had a hair-net. I don't know who fascinated me more, the gorgeous Guidi or the ravishing beauties whose signed photographs covered his table and walls.

At last my new propeller arrived, and the Gipsy Moth was ready to fly. I dreaded this moment. The flight out from London to Africa had been almost beyond my powers, and my nerve was shaken. I had never flown in Africa in daylight, and was scared by all the stories I had heard about the air being so thin near the ground that an aeroplane would drop the last ten feet like a stone. The aerodrome officials did not like my going up, partly because there was a fresh wind blowing and the air was sand-laden, and partly because of all the crashes which had occurred since I arrived. The wreckage of Lasalle's aeroplane had been found along the coast, and the bodies brought to Tripoli. Lasalle had set out to fly from France to Indo-China. The Italians gave him a tremendous funeral in Tripoli. All the pilots were there; all the consuls; a large squad of soldiers, a troop of Fascists in their black shirts and tasselled caps, and a big band. The coffins were mounted on gun-carriages, and three Italian Romeos flew slowly up and down above the procession. The French consul asked me to represent British aviators, which I did, feeling sheepish because I only had one suit with me (with plus-four trousers), and every other civilian was dressed in a top hat and long tail coat. In the cathedral where the Bishop of Tripoli conducted an impressive service there was a field-gun, machine-guns, and crossed propellers, all covered with wreaths. One of the four censers caught alight, and after burning fiercely for a while exploded with a loud bang which added to the impressiveness.

There had been three other crashes in the same week; Jones-Williams and Jenkins killed on a flight to South Africa, Andre, a Swede, and one of their own Tripoli pilots in a Romeo looking for Lasalle. (The last two pilots had escaped alive).

My first view of Africa from the air was wonderful; the sea was bluer than I had ever seen it, and away to the south I had my first view of the desert looking like brown liquid which had overflowed from beyond the horizon. I sighed; I wondered if my Gipsy Moth was as strong as before the repairs. There was one way to find out; I started doing aerobatics. I went into one loop too slowly. The Moth stood on its tail and stuck there, then started sliding backwards. I imagined the elevators and rudder tearing off, and kept the controls steady. At last the Moth fell over slowly backwards. It was the worst loop I have ever done. I put the Moth into a spin, but she refused to come out of it, and went on spinning. I thought the controls must be jammed. But it was only my bad flying, and at last I coaxed her into a dive. Finally I had to land over the top of the hangars with only 275 yards between the hangars and an open ditch dug across the airfield. A month earlier I would have thought this a joke; but now my nerve was bad, and I was scared of the ten-foot drop I had heard about. I came in too fast, and overshot. I pretended that I had come down only to look at the airfield, and went around again. By now the whole aerodrome staff had turned out to watch the fun, which made me more nervous. At last I side-slipped between two hangars, with the hangar roofs above me at each wing tip, and landed safely. When the watchers ran out and swarmed round the Moth I thought they had come out to see what was wrong with me, and I felt a fool. When they told me they thought I had given a wonderful exhibition of stunting I burst out laughing. Perhaps that foozled loop *had* looked spectacular!

On January 9th, 1930, I was up before dawn, bursting with impatience to get started again. The night duty officer said he had not slept a wink, because he was worried about seeing me away safely. I was not properly sympathetic, having slept myself like a log. A mechanic and I pushed the Moth out of the hangar in the dark. I christened my fourth propeller by smashing on the boss a bottle of the best cognac I had been able to find (I felt that champagne was not strong enough). I started the motor, and waited impatiently. The duty pilot arrived at the double to say that I could not start because of a sand-storm at Syrte. I objected, but they refused to let me start, so I went back to my room and had another sleep. At 8.30 I asked them to get another report. Conditions at Syrte were improving, and they reluctantly let me leave. I was in the air fifteen minutes later.

It was thrilling to be setting off on the 12,000-mile flight alone, to be heading into unknown adventures. For the first 2,000 miles I should be flying over, or near, desert, nearly the whole way. On the coast, there were occasional patches of vineyard and olive grove beside the deep-blue fringe of the Mediterranean; otherwise, the brown desert stretched to the southern horizon. At El Agheila, 500 miles from Tripoli, I flew into a sand-storm with a fifty miles an hour wind from the south-east. The Moth sailed along through the murky sand-thickened air, drifting thirty-five degrees to port. The air grew thicker and thicker with sand, until I was down to 200 feet in order to keep a small patch of ground directly beneath the plane in view. I was fearful of its getting thick enough to kill all visibility, and I wondered how I should have got on at night if I had run into such a thing with no blind-flying instruments, because the air was bumpy. Fortunately the sand-storm lasted only for 100 miles, and I flew into the clear at Ghemines.

I landed at Benghazi after eight hours in the air to cover 570 miles, and I spent an interesting evening with Chaffy, the British consul, Andre, the Swedish pilot, and a local farmer named Bazzan. Andre had lost his aeroplane in an unusual way. He had landed in a sand-storm south of Ghemines, and was holding on to his plane in a gale to prevent its being blown over, when suddenly the sea broke through a sandbank and gradually submerged the aeroplane until Andre had to swim to dry land. Bazzan was an interesting man who had a farm near Benghazi. His farmhouse was square, and a man with a machine-gun kept watch all night at each corner. He said that the Italians had been bombing some Arabs some ten miles from Benghazi the day before. Unbelievable gruesome stories were told of what happened to pilots who fell into Arab hands. I wonder if Bazzan has survived the Second World War? In the morning Chaffy told me that my wife had died in New Zealand. This was a sad affair, which I could not understand, because although we had been separated for some years, I knew that she was perfectly well when I left New Zealand.

I left Benghazi at 6.35 with a good tail wind. After 350 miles I crossed into British territory at Es-Sollum. Although I was glad to have cleared the Italian territory after all the gruesome stories I had heard, and could now, presumably, survive a forced landing without being killed, the terrain immediately seemed less interesting. I had said that I would land at Mersa Matruh, which I reached at noon, but I reckoned that if I did I should be unable to reach the RAF airfield at Abu-Sueir, where a cousin of mine was stationed. I still had more than 300 miles to go, and I should be losing one and a quarter hours of daylight through flying east. By the time I reached the Nile Delta I had been flying for eight hours. The engine beat had drummed itself into every nerve of my body. I found myself squirming every few minutes to try to find a fresh part of my body to sit on. It had taken me an hour and twenty minutes to pump the contents of both the bottom petrol tanks up to the top tank between the upper pair of wings. While working the pump with my hand, I had to keep my feet absolutely steady on the rudder bar. My buttocks were sore and aching.

During the flight I had eaten dates, biscuits, cheese, sardines and tinned fruit, but by now I was too fatigued to eat anything. My brain was weary of so much country. It was like sitting on top of a mountain and watching the view for eight hours on end. From the air, the Nile Delta looked deadly dull, sliced up into countless tiny plots. I was glad when the desert reappeared, like a vast flow of lava invading the fertile delta. When close to Abu-Sueir I saw a tall column of black smoke rising from the airfield. Later, I learned that they were burning the debris of two planes which had collided there, killing four pilots. I landed after nine and a quarter hours in the air to cover 917 miles. When I taxied up to the hangars a small crowd of men stood motionless thirty yards away, as if I had arrived from Mars. This seemed strange after the Italian airfields. However, I clambered out of the cockpit, waddled over to them in my heavy flying-boots, and persuaded someone to look for my cousin.

My cousin Pat was a burly man who had been heavyweight champion of the RAF and was known as 'Firpo'. He had a gruff voice and a hug like a bear.

Next morning a telegram from Cairo arrived, ordering me to return there to clear Customs because I had not landed at Mersa Matruh. I had to sign that I had received this order. I detest having to turn back and retrace my route. I took off thinking, 'I'm damned if I'll go back,' and I set off towards Jerusalem along the trail of Moses when he fled from Egypt. (Later I was reprimanded for this, and ordered to apologize in person to the Egyptian Prime Minister the next time I visited Cairo.)

That morning before leaving, when I had checked over my motor, I found that the compression in No. 2 cylinder was bad. Evidently a valve seating there was defective. When I landed at Gaza to refuel before crossing the desert to Baghdad, I found that this cylinder was pretty bad. It would have to be fixed that night at the latest.

After leaving Gaza I made a mistake in navigation which

gave me a shock; when I reached the Dead Sea, with its still surface deeply bedded in hill land, I was eighteen miles too far south. A mistake like this could be serious when over the desert, and I could not puzzle out the cause of it. I flew on and picked out Ziza. There were only two or three shacks there, but I could see the scars made by aeroplane tail skids. I altered course to head into the desert. I looked for the wheel tracks of a convoy which had motored through, because I had been told that I would see these, and also some furrows ploughed in the sand here and there beside the track for guidance. Also, there were emergency landing-grounds spaced twenty miles apart along the route, and marked with the letters of the alphabet.

The track came down from Amman to the North, and I was to strike it twenty miles east of Ziza. I concentrated on watching the ground, but after twenty miles I had seen no sign of a track, and on looking round could see nothing in any direction but brown sand and desert, and a few hills far away on the northern horizon. Every mile I covered without spotting signs of anything I grew more anxious. Some thirty-three miles from Ziza I was wondering if I must turn back and start afresh, when I suddenly sighted a square building. I turned at once and flew over it. With no windows or doors, it was like a solid block of stone. I circled it, and found some tail skid marks in the sand but I could not find the letter C which should identify the first landing-ground. I found two wheel tracks, and began following them. I had to twist about to follow the faint tracks, and concentrated on keeping them in sight. The landing-ground D ought to have shown up seventy-three miles out, but there were no signs of it. After eighty-five miles and still no sign, I began to get worried. I had to determine the direction of those tracks. This was difficult, because the aeroplane was drifting hard to the left or north in the strong southerly wind, and the track was swinging from side to side through an arc of sixty degrees. I decided that we were flying in the direction of 110 degrees. 'Good Lord,' I thought, 'I should be headed eighty-four degrees. I'm probably headed for Mecca!'

I told myself that I must keep cool, for a desert was no place in which to lose one's head. I began reasoning things out as I flew along, and finally reckoned that I must be thirty miles south of the correct route. I ought to retrace my path and start afresh, but I hated turning back. I turned north, and headed across unmapped desert. I dropped down close to the ground and watched it so closely that I think I would have seen a rat on it. I crossed dry depressions, dry water-courses, dirty black hills and sandy mud, all dull, bare and lifeless.

I was excited and thrilled: this was the stuff that life was made of. My funny-looking map attempted only to map a strip within five to ten miles of the track, with bits of hills *hachured* in here and there. I doubted if the map would be any help to me. However, according to my mental dead-reckoning, I should arrive at some hills marked on the map with a watercourse running through them, with the track three or four miles on the other side. I flew up to some hills which answered the description. Then, suddenly, there was the track – quite different this time. Several wheel ruts showed clearly. I wanted another check; the landing ground D should be a few miles back. Sure enough the D turned up as expected. I turned right about, and set off for Baghdad singing a song about Antonio. I saw no sign of animal or plant life of any kind, until 200 miles from Ziza I came across an Arab caravan with a flock of sheep. I wondered how they could exist. I had an extraordinary sense of freedom and a feeling of well-being flying low over the desert.

I landed at Rutbah Wells after six and three-quarter hours in the air to cover 526 miles (without counting the diversion), a speed made good of only seventy-five miles an hour. Rutbah Wells was a romantic spot in the middle of the desert, a large square fort with buildings backed up inside to the high walls. There were camel caravans inside, and a squad of Iraqi infantry. Here the track which I had followed, and which they said was rarely used, joined the motor-coach route between Baghdad and Damascus. There was an Imperial Airways mechanic stationed at Rutbah, and I finally coaxed him to help me to grind the valve of my dud No. 2 cylinder.

We pushed the Moth through the barbed-wire entanglements into the fort, and drew her up to the window of the mechanic's room, so that he could fasten an electric inspection lamp to a blade of the propeller from a switch in his bedroom. We took off the manifold and piston head to find the exhaust valve badly pitted. I produced a new one which I thought would take less time to grind in. It began to freeze. We finished the grinding, and put the cylinder back, but the compression was worse than before. We tried to puzzle out what could be wrong. I was tempted to leave it, in the hopes that it would get right when the engine was warmed up next day; it was getting late, and I was very tired. However, I decided that we had better take it off again. The valves looked and seemed all right, and we fitted them back once more. We filled the cylinder head up with petrol and the valve seatings held the petrol, so they simply must be all right. This time the compression was excellent.

When I got to bed at last in an Iraqi officer's room I lay listening to some delightful music. I could distinguish flutes, quietly tinkling bells and some outlandish instruments that I had not heard before. When I was having breakfast at 5 o'clock next morning I asked the manager, Fraser, who had played this music last night. 'Music?' he said. 'There was no music here'.

It was wretchedly cold, and the motor would not start. The mechanic and I took turns at swinging the propeller, and got worn out at it. The motor would fire once, but had not enough power to overcome the friction of the frozen oil. It was not until 7.30 that it suddenly started with a roar, and I took off. Yesterday's unique feeling of isolation was now lost because the desert was crowded. In the first 100 miles I saw two motor-cars and several Arab caravans, with black tents and flocks of sheep.

At Baghdad the aerodrome manager, Phelps, was the most efficient I had come across. I told him that I would have been along three weeks earlier if he had been in charge of each of the airfields where I had refuelled. He had medical, Customs and police authorities waiting, who cleared me immediately;

he fed me, had the Moth refuelled with forty-three gallons of petrol and two gallons of oil, wrote his name on the fuselage, and got me into the air again within fifty minutes of my touching down. He had also procured me a weather report which forecast a thirty-five mile an hour favourable wind at 5,000 feet, so I climbed up straight away to that height.

The town of Bushire in Persia was already lighted up when I reached it. I found the airfield by spotting a hangar. A motor-car was moving slowly across the middle of the airfield, and as I flew over it low, to look at the surface, the car stopped and disgorged two or three women, who fled for their lives in different directions, leaving the car stranded. Had I been touching down as they thought I must surely have bowled over one of them.

When I landed and taxied towards the hangars I had been in the air for eight and three-quarter hours to cover a distance of 772 miles at a speed of eighty-eight mph. As I switched off the motor my 8s. 6d. alarm clock sounded. The Imperial Airways mechanic was intrigued, and asked for an explanation. I said that I used it to tell me when it was time to land, but I fear he thought I was joking. After a short snooze I went off to the shore for a bathe. The sea water was like soothing balm, after the beating my nerves had taken in the open cockpit from the roaring exhaust. It was a clear moonlight night, and I noticed two goats standing on the edge of a large log, solemnly watching me. They remained motionless so long that I became curious to know why. After drying myself by a run up and down the beach I dressed and went over to investigate. I found that the goats were two wheels and the under-carriage of a DH 9A aeroplane, lying on its back and dripping petrol. I filled my cigarette lighter from the petrol. I found out that a Persian military pilot had flown this aeroplane into the top of the wireless mast an hour before I arrived. He nearly pulled off an excellent landing afterwards, but ran out of flat land and somersaulted over a bank on to the sea-shore. The aeroplane was wrecked, but he escaped.

I was lent an old camp-bed and fell asleep listening to the same charming tune from my private orchestra. I slept comfortably till 5 o'clock when the camp-bed split in the middle, and dropped me on the floor with a bump.

I got into the air at 6.15 AM, and after 250 miles passed Qais Island, which Marco Polo visited in 1271. I refuelled at Jask at 1 o'clock after a 560-mile run. Then I flew on to Chahbar, where I landed after nine hours in the air to cover a distance of 740 miles at eighty-two mph. Hackett, in charge of the radio station, was the only European there, and he was very pleased to see the first European for several months. He told me how Alan Cobham had landed on his flight out to Australia when his mechanic was killed by a pot-shot from an Arab while crossing the desert.

I got away at 5.20 next morning for a six-hour flight to Karachi, a distance of 430 miles. This flight was uneventful, except that I saw a huge school of porpoises in the sea off the coast, which made me long enviously for the peace of the sea.

During the next five days I flew across India and down to Singapore. I was forty-two and a quarter hours in the air to cover 3,500 miles, an average speed of eighty-three and a half mph. Crossing India, I refuelled at Nasirabad, Jhansi, Allahabad and Calcutta. I spent the night at Jhansi, where I was lucky to find three R A F fighter planes on manoeuvres. I spent a delightful evening with the crews, and they provided me with a bath in a canvas camp bath, and a camp-bed in a tent. All this time the flying conditions were delightful. I enjoyed the flight, in spite of the motor, which was running increasingly rougher until it vibrated unpleasantly. This caused me to keep a constant look-out for a possible open space on which to land if the motor failed. At Calcutta an efficient mechanic called Woolland, working for the Aerial Survey Company, ground in the valves of the No. 2 cylinder which was causing most of the trouble. He, and some Indians helping him, worked all one afternoon and evening on the job. I was most grateful to have someone to do it for me. Fatigue was nagging at me again. It was not because of flying, but because of the unending negotiations and talk from the moment I landed up to the moment I took off again, apart from the few hours spent in sleeping. Each day my time on the ground was cut by about three-quarters of an hour because I was flying east.

After Calcutta, I flew along the coast to Akyab. Here I landed in sheepskin thigh boots, a Sidcote suit (like a boiler suit of three thicknesses) and fur gloves. An hour later I took off in shirt sleeves after a roasting on the ground.

I was beginning to find that the overloaded Moth required a much longer run for taking off in the hot air. I landed for the night on Rangoon race-course. Several horses were exercising there when I arrived, and I circled the course for ten minutes to give them time to get clear.

On leaving Rangoon at dawn, I flew over flat ground cut into tiny plots for forty miles. The smoke from each hut had drifted away in a straight level line. There were hundreds of lines of smoke, from one to five miles in length, all straight, level and the same thickness, so that they looked like grey lines joining the huts as far as one could see.

I had a scare at Victoria Point, the southernmost point of Burma. The landing-ground was a terrible spot, shut in by hills and bordered by dense jungle with palms. At the eastern end a hill seemed to overhang it. The Air Ministry notice had said it was 1,560 yards long, but in my first attempt to land I overshot badly. The second time, although I came in only a foot above the corner, it looked as if I was going to overshoot again. I thought that my judgement must be badly wrong to overshoot a 1,560-yard field. I side-slipped, and put the Moth down firmly with a bump. Even then I only just stopped short of the jungle, because the airfield sloped downhill there. I was told afterwards that the airfield would be 1,560 yards long when it had been enlarged, and the hill removed but that now it was 350 yards long. Next morning I was faced with taking off fully loaded, because there was no landing-ground between there and Singapore, ten hours' flying farther on. I was nervy and apprehensive, and I walked all over the field. If I used the longest possible run, I must take off straight towards the palm-covered hill. There was a narrow road winding through the jungle beside it, and I debated whether I could twist along the clearing made for the road.

Finally, I picked a shorter run across the field, where the trees at the end would be slightly easier to clear. I pushed the throttle wide open. The Gipsy Moth gathered speed so slowly that it seemed an age before even the tail skid began to lift from the ground. The plane just crawled across the field, and was still firmly sticking to the ground when I reached the wire fence at the end. At the last instant I yanked the nose up and hurtled over the fence in stalled condition. That was only one step. Straight ahead, a wall of palms. Again I kept the nose down till the last second in an attempt to get up more speed. I was wondering if she could clear them. I yanked her up again, and jumped the trees. Stalled, she just made it. This escape ruined the day's flying for me; it was just pure luck that I had got away.

I made a non-stop flight of ten hours to Singapore, and after an amusing evening in the mess of No. 205 Flying-Boat Squadron I took off next morning for Batavia. During the eighty-mile crossing to Sumatra I climbed above the clouds, which were then covering about seven-tenths of the sky. They were steadily growing thicker and higher. At 9 o'clock, when I reached Sumatra, the sun was scorching the side of my neck, so I pulled out a topi which Russell of Victoria Point had given me, but it blew overboard, and I had to watch it twirling down, down through the air. At first I was contented to be floating among the billowy white masses of cloud and sunshine, but when their tops were above me at 7,500 feet I thought that I had better not climb any higher and zigzagged down between them, finally shooting through into clear space beneath. The bottoms of these tall sugar-loaf clouds were flat, 2,000 feet above the land. It was like flying into hot steam. The map had the same symbols here as for the salt marshes in North Africa, but when I looked round for marshes I could see nothing but solid jungle to the horizon in every direction. There was no sign of life, and not even a single break for a river. Steam was drifting from patches of the dark green treetops. I could not imagine a more solitary place. A column of rain was pouring from the middle of each cloud, and soon it was like weaving through a forest of giant dirty-white mushrooms.

Occasionally the sun broke through, brightening a green patch of the forest tops. While traversing these I could see blue sky through a 7,000-foot-high chimney of blousy cloud.

I altered course and made for the foothills, where the map showed a railway line. I was sidling or crabbing across a fifty-mile wind, zig-zagging to dodge the rain columns. Gradually I was forced lower. The big rain-drops stung like hail. After flying over jungle for 200 miles, I came on a river with a narrow strip cleared along one bank, perhaps 100 yards wide, where a dozen native huts were squatting. They had dark thatch, and overhanging eaves. Close by, I came to a narrow cutting through the jungle, with a pipeline in the centre twisting through the forest as far as I could see. Suddenly I came on a town with a landing-ground, a railway and some roads which fixed it as Lahat. Here, the cloud came right down to the ground at the edge of hills, and I was forced to turn about and fly east to escape. Except for Lahat, during six hours' flying I had seen only one spot where I could possibly have put down the plane in an emergency.

I had been flying seven and a quarter hours when I reached the south-east coast of Sumatra. The storm-clouds were heavier, and there was one big black cloud ahead, but as it was not raining underneath, I held my course. As I got under the middle of the big cloud the bottom seemed to drop out; it was the heaviest rain I had ever known. I whirled round at once to get out, but I was still in the turn in a nearly vertical bank when visibility disappeared, and I was flying blind. As I was already accelerting in the turn, I could not regain a sense of direction or altitude. I sat tight, and checked each acceleration as smoothly as I could as soon as I identified it. If the speed increased till the struts screamed I eased up the nose. If the acceleration built up sideways I rolled to what I thought was level trim. If that put me upside down I looped. I tried not to overcorrect the control movements. I kept looking as nearly as possible in every direction; I knew that I was coming down, but I could not tell how. Suddenly, the sea appeared dead ahead – I was diving straight into it. I flattened out above the water, and tried to press on through the rain, but the visibility was so bad and the air so rough, that I turned back. I emerged abruptly from the wall of rain, flew five miles out to sea along the side of the storm, and got round it.

I could now see hills on the western corner of Java, and set course straight across the sea for them. Java was entirely different; the rain was normal, and every square inch of the ground was cultivated. I could see thousands of little squares of water where the rice fields were flooded. I landed after eight hours thirty-eight minutes in the air, for a 660-mile flight.

To my surprise I found that I was on a modern airport, and surrounded by a lot of handsome Dutchmen speaking perfect English.

CHAPTER TEN

AUSTRALIA

I MADE a mistake here; I decided to stay for a day to buy food, and to find out about landing-grounds ahead, etc. My time from Tripoli to here was the same as Hinkler had taken from Malta. However, I was not trying to beat Hinkler now, but only to satisfy myself. The mistake I made was that I got more tired staying than I would have if I had flown on next day. After official and business calls, many talks and interviews, laying in a fresh supply of stores, and servicing my motor, I was utterly exhausted with fatigue. I could not rest, the hotel seemed to be rustling and whispering with life, and the air was so wet and heavy that I expected to touch it. The city swarmed with people, and on one side of the street modern ferro-concrete buildings contrasted with hundreds of Malay women washing clothes in a dirty canal, and looking most seductive with their wet clothes clinging to their lovely bodies.

I wanted to find out about a landing-ground in Timor, the last island before crossing the Timor Sea to Australia. A Dutch air force pilot, representing the Dutch Government, said that Koepang was not to be used. A KLM pilot whom

I met said that it was excellent, and much the best airfield before crossing to Darwin. Later at Surabaya, I was told that Koepang was unusable. Farther on, at Bima, I was told that it was in first-class order, and that the other airfield I had intended to use was not usable. I was growing desperate about this when I was told that the Resident of Koepang himself was there, who settled the matter for me by saying that Koepang was bad in one place making it slightly dangerous for landing, whereas the other airfield, Atemboea, was in excellent order. All along the route I had the same difficulty in finding out about the next airfield.

Then there was difficulty about distances; no two maps of the East Indies seemed to agree. The best that I had been able to find had a scale of one inch to sixty-four miles. This gave the distance from Batavia to Semarang, for example, as 260 miles, whereas a map much used in Java and which I saw there gave it as 324 miles.

One hundred and twenty miles after leaving Batavia I came to Cheribon, and there achieved what must surely be one of the slowest flights on record. I found a heavy rain-storm blocking the route ahead, so flew south for ten miles to avoid it, only to find a bigger one ahead that stretched right to the mountains in the south. I returned to the coast and flew into the rain. It was like flying into a heavy shower-bath. I throttled back to sixty mph, and water began to trickle down my back. I turned round to fly back to Cheribon, but as soon as I got outside the rain I decided to have another shot. This time I got in farther, but was down to within a few feet of the ground and it was nervy work looking out for trees. The nearer I came to the centre of the storm, the more the plane was tossed about. The water stung my forehead like hail, streamed into my eyes, down my chest and back. I cursed myself for a fool, and turned back again. 'If only I can get out of this and find a landing-ground, nothing will budge me till this storm is finished,' I told myself. I got out and headed west, but thirty seconds later decided to have another attempt. I was flying round in a circle, wondering what was the best thing to do, when I saw a three-engined Dutch mail plane emerge from the middle of the black patch ahead. He was flying a few feet above the sea near the coast. 'Well,' I thought, disregarding the fact that he would be fully equipped with blind-flying instruments, 'if he can do it, I can.'

I thrust in again; it was more like entering a bath than a shower-bath. I was a few feet above the sea, bumped about badly, and missed the masts of a fishing-boat by inches. I turned left, and flew five miles out to sea. I could see nothing there, except a small patch of water a few feet vertically beneath the plane, and this was hard to distinguish, because both sea and rain were the same dirty colour. I made for land, and the bumps began again.

I plugged along till a sudden bump stalled the plane nearly dead, causing the slots to fly open with a loud clang. The plane dropped, and the stalled ailerons and elevators made the control-stick feel like a dead man's hand. The plane did not pick up flying speed until it cushioned, just above the surface of the water. I breathed again, but decided that I had had enough fooling. I turned about to make for the first landing-ground I could find.

It seemed easy flying back through the storm, which shows the difference between the first and second times of attempting anything. I passed between the masts of a junk drawn up on the beach, and another in the water fifty yards away. Half the Malays on the beach threw themselves on the sand, and the rest bolted up the beach. This cheered me up. I soon came to the emergency landing-ground I was looking for, circled it, and touched down. The ground felt soft, so I gave the motor a burst of full throttle to keep the tail down with the slip-stream. The landing finished well.

The glued fabric surface of the propeller was worn right through in some places, and the inside of the propeller blades had marks as if they had struck a cloud of stones. I wrung the water out of my flying-helmet, and made a hole to let the water out of the canvas pocket in the cockpit where I kept my papers and maps. A stream of Malays, like a column of ants, was winding towards me from the trees. Most wore coolie hats, some held banana leaves over their heads. I had a few sentences in Malay written down and tried these out. '*Saja minta satu orang djaga*,' etc. In a few minutes I had engaged a watchman, sent for a policeman, sent a telegram, and successfully made signs that I wanted to sleep. I set off with the policeman. I walked round the first few pools of water on the airfield, but soon got tired of that, and waded through them. We came to a big house, which seemed to be the policeman's. We entered a large room floored with hard mud, with a pigeon in a cage hung from one corner, a parrot in another corner, and two other birds I did not know. There was a big cane chair, and within thirty seconds I was asleep. An hour later I woke up, to find the room empty except for a very old man who was expert at spitting. I sensed a lot of life and activity behind a bamboo curtain. I asked for something to eat, and was given a bowl of rice, and some incredibly tough curried chicken for which I was grateful. The weather was clearing up, so I made a sign that I wanted to fly off again.

After I had presented some guilders, the policeman marshalled about 400 Malays clear of a take-off lane, and I took off. It had taken me an hour and twenty-two minutes to cover the fifty-seven miles between Cheribon and this place, Pemalang, which must surely be a record in slow flying.

I landed at Surabaya after six and a half hours in the air for a flight of only 420 miles for the day. The Gipsy Moth's wheels bogged down on the airfield, and she refused to move with full throttle; it required all hands from the hangar to pull her in. The morning's antics from the monsoon upset my plans. I did not reach Surabaya until 3.35, when it was too late to fly the next leg of 300 miles before dark. That cost me an extra day.

Next morning I flew 150 miles before I began dodging rainstorms. I think that if I had started earlier, perhaps before dawn, and landed in the middle of the day when these rainstorms were at their worst I should have been better off. And, of course, if I had flown over the route before, it would have all seemed much easier; but then the great romance of the unknown would have gone.

I spent the night at Bima, in Sumbawa, after a 450-mile

flight, taking six hours. The men of Bima mostly carried knives in their belts, and looked fighters, quite different from the Javanese. I made a social blunder by asking a big fat man in the crowd to help me with my fuelling, and the Dutch Resident told me that he was the Vizir of the Sultan of Sumbawa. I think he got square with me next morning by telling me that twenty warriors had guarded the Gipsy Moth all night, and that payment was wanted for them. The Resident fixed me up with a room in the Government rest-house, where I slept on a hard mattress under mosquito netting. In the evening I sat on the veranda, watching the house lizards, tjic-tjacs, stalking and chasing moths and large flying beetles on the ceilings. The lizards seemed a sporting lot, and willing to tackle beetles as large as themselves.

When I took off again, I scanned the slopes of the next island, Komodo, for sight of one of the giant lizards, or dragons, for which it is famous, but I had no luck. On the south coast of Flores I flew over a perfect miniature volcano, only 200 feet high, with a smouldering cone. From there I had a forty-four-mile water hop to Timor Island. The landing-ground was in a valley, running parallel with the coast, and it was like flying in the heat of an open furnace. I landed there after a 500-mile flight, which had taken me six and three-quarter hours. It was only 1 o'clock, and I had some lunch with the officer commanding a small squad of soldiers. He left me to sleep till 4 o'clock, when he had to call me three times before I stumbled off the bed, still half asleep. He drove me to the airfield and I started work on the motor. I wanted to check it thoroughly before the big water-crossing. The officer lent me some petrol lamps, but they attracted thousands of flying ants and bugs, which kept on walking over my eyes and into my ears, where it was difficult to dislodge them. I had taken the intake manifold off because of a crack in it, but found that the crack was only superficial. I finished the last nut five hours after I had started. I blew up my rubber boat, to make sure that it had no leaks, and arranged it so that I only had to pull a rope to yank it out of the front cockpit. I secured the mast, sail and oars to an inner tube, so that they would float if the plane sank.

I got to bed at midnight, and slept well, except for the same nightmare that I had had at Tripoli. I recorded this at the time in these words:

'I dreamed that I was flying, when suddenly my vision went completely, and I just had to sit tight until the plane crashed.'

I left Atemboea at 7.30, and flew along the coast for seventy miles before heading out to sea. I was out of sight of land in twelve minutes. I was excited, and elated to be crossing the famous Timor Sea. I had discussed many times the question of coming down in the sea and I was determined that if it did happen, I would glide down as usual, and kick the plane across its path at the last moment to pancake sideways. I aimed for Bathurst Island, north of Darwin, the nearest land to my take-off point. This reduced the water crossing to 320 miles.

The first 100 miles after leaving Timor the wind was coming in from the north-east, and I was drifting twenty degrees to starboard. This wind gradually died away to nothing for 100 miles, and then began coming in from the south-west, gradually increasing in strength, until I was drifting twenty-five degrees to port. I was lucky for the weather was perfect. In fact, the dreaded crossing which had brought disaster to planes and pilots, was the easiest flight of the whole voyage. I did not touch the control-stick during the three and a half hours over water. By then I felt a part of the machine, and could fly the aeroplane in ordinary conditions with the rudder only; I could even negotiate rough air with the rudder only. For level flight, I adjusted the tension on the elevator control with a spring, and to climb or come down I pumped a little petrol from the front or back tank up to the main tank in the top wing.

When I reached Bathurst Island the visibility was poor, and I flew along the coast for several miles to read off its bearing, and thus fixed my position. From Bathurst Island another fifty-mile water hop brought me into Darwin at 1.20. I had flown 500 miles in six hours and ten minutes.

I flew over the town before landing at the airfield, and could see some cars tearing along the road. When I taxied up to a few men standing on the airfield they looked at me as if I were a cobra. Then the Shell agent arrived, and introduced me to a tall elderly man in the group who refused to shake hands with me, 'No, Captain Chichester, my principles will not let me, until you have been passed by the medical authority.' Everyone called me 'Captain'. I was in a silly mood; I had reached my objective, Australia, and I said that if I was to be promoted to a rank, could I not be elevated to General straight away? I moved an adjournment to the nearest hotel, to try the local beer. Carried unanimously. I thought Darwin was a corner of Hell but I certainly felt at home there, and got on well with the inhabitants.

Next morning I took off at 6.45, circled, and picked up the railway which I followed for 300 miles through the bush. It was a good landmark, with the bush felled for a width of over twenty yards on each side. After the railway petered out at Daly Waters, I followed a telegraph line, just as easily because of the clearing through the bush, to Newcastle Waters, 425 miles from Darwin. At Newcastle Waters it was hot, bumpy, and the visibility was bad, because of a thick haze. Here I had to leave the telegraph line, and follow a track across the plain to the east. While I was circling to look for this track, I was tempted to land for a break after six hours' flying, but it was so hot in the air that each time I put my face out on the exhaust side of the aeroplane I felt scorched. I wondered if the upper wing, which gets blackened by the exhaust in ordinary weather, might catch fire. I decided that if it was so hot in the air, it must be grilling on the ground, so I turned down the idea of landing. Refuelling was not an inducement, because the description of Newcastle Waters read 'Petrol and oil can be obtained at Anthony Lagoon 178 miles away. Nearest town Camooweal 375 miles.' There were tracks leading in every direction. I chose the one that looked right, and followed it along the rim of a great expanse of flat country, which had nothing growing on it, and looked from the air like a vast dried-up lake.

The track consisted of two wheel marks. During the first fifty miles I met one or two drovers. I was flying low, because of the haze, and we saluted as if I, too, had been on a horse.

I passed the spot where the homestead of the Eva Downs Cattle Station should have been but could see no sign of it. (It had been burned down.) When I was due to arrive at Anthony Lagoon, the next cattle station by my reckoning, I came to a bore, a tall iron windmill for pumping water from an artesian well into a square water hole. There was a tin shed beside it. I thought that the shed was a store, shown on the map at Anthony Lagoon. There were tracks leading in every direction from it. I followed the most likely for a few miles, then decided that it was not the right one. I went back, and wasted twenty minutes circling at 100 feet above the ground in the thick haze, looking for the track. In the end, I was sure this could not be Anthony Lagoon, and I flew on in the same direction as before. A few miles farther on Anthony Lagoon showed up without doubt. There were several buildings on the edge of a permanent lagoon.

This was the homestead of another cattle station. I circled, and picked up the track for the next homestead, Brunette Downs. Once or twice I lost the track, and wasted time circling for it. When I reached Brunette Downs I had been told to land on a gravel patch north of the homestead, instead of on the landing-strip which was in bad condition. This required a cross-wind landing, which I thought dangerous. I had not only been flying for eight and three-quarter hours, but the last 240 miles had been in rough bumpy air close to the ground, requiring snatchy use of the control-stick, and it was difficult to make a smooth landing after that. I picked the best place on the gravel for landing into wind, but at the first approach overshot, and the second time bumped badly. The patch was not wide enough to land across it. The intense heat made me annoyed and irritable. I flew across to the landing-strip, and had a good look at it flying low. It seemed in good condition, and I made an easy landing on it. I drank all the water I had left, and lay on the ground under the shade of one wing. After twenty minutes a man strolled towards the aeroplane. At first I thought that he had an enormous black beard, but in fact it was a youth with a black flyproof net round his face, with a cloud of flies which at once transferred to me. I wished that he had brought some netting for me as well as the flies. I asked him a lot of questions, and he answered 'I don't know' to nearly every one of them. He did not know who the next neighbour was, he thought there was some petrol here, but if so, it was locked up. There was no one else there except himself, the manager was expected back, but he did not know when. Everything on the ground seemed maddeningly slow after long hours of flying.

The description I had of Brunette Downs read, 'Nearest railway station Dejarra, Queensland, 320 miles. Nearest town, Camooweal, 210 miles.' My top tank was nearly full of petrol so that I had just over three hours of flying left. That ought to be plenty to reach Camooweal. Now I had all the makings of a drama; I decided to fly on. I drank the juice of a tin of pineapple, and gave the rest of the fruit to a couple of blacks who had turned up. I emptied three quarts of oil into the motor, and took off again, muttering curses. I continued to follow the track by which I had arrived. It was not going in the right direction, but I thought that it would swing round later. After a while, when it did not, I turned, and headed south.

This was by far the most difficult country that I had come across for navigating – or ever have come across, for that matter. There were no distinctive landmarks at all. There were wheel tracks in places, but they could be most deceptive. For example, when an area became flooded, the tracks were obliterated, and the lorry or whatever had made the tracks, had to detour round the edge of the water. As the water receded, the lorry on its next visit would make tracks perhaps half a mile away from the last lot. The next lot might be half a mile away again. Tracks were apt to leave a water hole in all directions. I had two maps, one cut from a schoolroom map of Australia, and a large-scale strip map, a white print from a linen tracing covering the route from Darwin to Cunnamulla, which the Australian Civil Aviation Department had sent up to Darwin for me. These maps marked places in a grand manner, and where I expected to find a town of 5,000 people, there would be a house and one or two sheds. The strip map showed a great number of rivers, but in nine hours of flying I had not seen a single one. They were, in fact, dry watercourses, which held water only occasionally after heavy rain. From the air they looked like the rest of the country, which was all monotonously similar. The bush of evergreen gum-trees was sparse; the individual trees could have been counted from above. The general result of all this was that my target for each leg of the flight was a spot in a featureless landscape, and I would not be sure what the spot consisted of – whether it was a house, a house with sheds, or merely a bore. The haze shrouded everything, and cut down visibility to about a mile.

After flying five or six miles south without seeing another track, I decided that I had overshot, and turned north-east again. I picked up the track a few minutes later. There was one landmark between Brunette Downs and Camooweal – Alexandra, the homestead of a 12,000-square-mile cattle run. I duly located this, and passed over it at 5.05. They had just had rain here, the first for several years, and the mud colour of the ground I had been flying over was changing to a faint greenish tinge, where grass was beginning to sprout. I flew south-east, and picked up a bore with stockyards as shown on the map, eighteen miles from Alexandra. Tracks led from this bore in various directions, and I circled time after time before feeling sure that I had chosen the right one. I was burning petrol in a way I had not allowed for.

The terrain was changing, downs now alternated with stretches of red soil, with a few trees dotted about. I came on another bore, and an engine shed, but too soon, according to the map. The track ought to leave there in a south-easterly direction but, though I circled several times, the only sign of a track that I could see was one going due east. I flew along it for seven miles, but it did not deviate from east, and I concluded that it must be the wrong track. I turned, and headed south. Every minute hunting for the track seemed an age. How foolish I had been to leave Brunette Downs without refuelling! I flew on south for ten miles without crossing as much as a sheep track. I had lost the track, and I was in a nice fix. I had not enough petrol to return to the bore and start afresh. I turned east again, and decided that the track I had first followed from the bore must be the right one, and that it was going to turn south-east in due course, and that if I kept on heading east I must come across it. However, after flying east for twelve miles without any signs of the track and looking anxiously at the petrol gauge, I decided that I was too short of petrol to search any longer, and that I must head direct for where I reckoned Camooweal to be.

I was now flying close to the ground, forced down by the haze which had thickened, and the plane was being badly bumped about. The wind had freshened from SSE, and I was drifting between twenty and twenty-five degrees to port. The plane required careful flying, being tossed about close to the ground, and I was keeping an intent look-out, except for too frequent glances at the petrol gauge, now showing practically empty. I had not time or opportunity for working out what had gone wrong with the navigation. By then I no longer cared a damn about reaching Camooweal; if only I could see a building!

I had flown 100 miles since the water bore, and must land within another thirty miles, whether I saw anything or not. Approaching nightfall was cooling the air, but I felt so prickly with heat that I ripped off the scarf protecting my neck to let air blow down my back. Suddenly I streaked across a scar on the ground. I banked steeply, and turned back to it. It appeared to be a formed road, running north. It was puzzling; why had I not known about it? And why NS? I flew right down to have a good look. The odd thing was that it appeared to be unused. However, I stuck to it. I followed it south for a short distance, and came to a bore with an engine shed, and a sort of hut. I circled, looking for somewhere to land. There was a green patch beside the water hole; was it swampy? Everywhere else the ground was covered with stones and boulders. What about concealed tree stumps? There was a twenty-five to thirty mph wind blowing, and I had been in the air for eleven hours; I must expect a rough landing.

There was only a fifty-yard run of the green patch free of boulders, so I just had to make a good landing. I went round again, and put the plane down in the best landing I ever made.

It rolled to a standstill among the first stones. I at once turned off the petrol cock, struggled out of the cockpit, and shuffled with dragging feet into the shed. It was an open shed, built over a pumping engine, and the wind sighed mournfully through it. Another shed, six feet square, stood over a fireplace. This one was made from the sides of petrol tins, which creaked and clanked dismally in the wind. It was a bleak, solitary spot in the twilight. I felt the ashes, and fancied they had had heat in them, perhaps from a fire of two or three days before, and my heart bounded, until I realized that it might be due to the heat of the day. The flies were terrible; I had never seen so many flies before. They crawled ceaselessly over my eyeballs, filled up my ears, and each time I forgot and opened my mouth (which I did frequently, for my tongue felt swollen and stuck unpleasantly to the roof of my mouth) they flew in. They tickled my tongue horribly, and I had to blow them out. Next, I looked at the mudlike water in the square water hole. I stirred the soft bottom with a stick, but it made no difference to the colour. I was parched with thirst, but decided not to drink till I had boiled the water. At first I could not find the wonderful road, where I hoped that lorries or cars would be passing. At last I found where it sprang out of the plain from nothing. This was queer, and after walking along it for 100 yards without finding any signs of traffic whatever, I felt that it was too much to take in, dismissed the whole thing from my mind, and turned back. I collected some chips and twigs and a piece of paper from the cockpit to start a fire going, the effort making my knees tremble. I rested before fetching more chips, and two logs. Then I dipped a half-gallon tin of water out of the pool, and hung it over the fire.

I lifted the tail of the Gipsy Moth to move it to a more sheltered position, because the wind was strong, but I had lost the strength to move it that way, so I fished out some rope and, fastening it to the tail skid, I pulled the plane towards the shed with a series of jerks. It took me half an hour to shift the plane a distance which should have taken half a minute. At first, when I panted I swallowed flies. Mercifully, after dark they vanished. By the time that I had got the plane in the lee of the shed, I felt done. As I moved towards the fire the roaring in my ears ceased, and a black film seemed to cover my eyes until the fire faded away to a pin-point in the distance. I dropped on the ground and rested. I was exhausted and in a panic – at being lost – panic-struck so abjectly that I was disgusted with myself. I was lost, true; in bad country, true; I had no petrol, true; but compared with what might have been, I was well off. So I reasoned with myself, but it was no use.

I was so ashamed of this panic that at last I made a great effort, and determined to dismiss it from my mind until I had slept. I fetched wood for the fire, taking several rests on the way. I drank some of the Chianti I had brought from Tripoli, but it tasted nasty. I dragged out the rubber boat, pumped it half full, turned it upside down, flopped on it, and fell asleep at once. When I woke half the water had boiled away. I stood it in a corner, tilted it in the hope that the mud would settle, then half filled another can. It was only fifteen to twenty yards from the fire to the water hole, but I took spells all the way. I dipped in the top of my vacuum flask, and drank the boiled water as it cooled. It tasted like nectar. I finished it all, except for some mud and slime at the bottom. I could not eat anything. Now and then I heard a slight rustle among the wood chips beside me, so made an effort and fetched a torch to see if it was a snake. I could find nothing. I drank nearly half a gallon of water from the next lot when it was cool enough. Every few hours through the night I woke and drank again. In spite of this I was still thirsty in the morning. It was about 6 o'clock when dawn came, and I lay indolently on my back watching the sky, or rather the haze, change colour from dark to light grey.

I ran over all the data of the last flight, thinking over each item of evidence, and going through all the movements one by one, a mental dead reckoning. Had I overshot Camooweal? I imagined it an isolated blob of buildings in the centre of a featureless plain. Had I crossed to the north of the track from Alexandra to Camooweal? It seemed a likely thing to happen in the haze, flying low while I was distracted by the instrument board for a few seconds. I felt too tired to move until a buzz reminded me of the plague of flies. Then I jumped up, fetched the map from the plane, and began reckoning the details of last night's flight. I plotted all my movements carefully, one after the other. There was one discrepancy I could not understand. The water bore after Alexandra was shown on one of the maps, but I seemed to have reached it much sooner than I should have done. I had to let that pass. I made allowance for the drift on each of the courses flown, and in the end I reckoned that I was now ten miles west of Camooweal.

Then I thought of petrol. The gauge showed empty, but the plane was tail down. I shook the plane by one wing, and I could hear a splash in the tank. I decided to measure it exactly. I fished out a hat and a shirt, and buttoned the shirt over the hat, so that only a small aperture was left open in front. It was rather difficult to see wearing this affair, but it kept most of the flies away; they disliked entering the shaded opening. I walked round the water hole and studied all the tracks visible. There were a number of old motor vehicle tracks coming in from different directions from the east, but they all stopped at the water hole. There were cattle tracks from the south and southwest. The track of a shod horse cheered me up, but it was two or three days old. Suddenly I spotted the fresh tracks of a wagon, and got excited. I followed them gaily, but my enthusiasm was short-lived; after fifty yards I found that I had been following the tracks of my own aeroplane.

I took the tin in which I had boiled water the night before and wiped it clean with my handkerchief. I climbed on the wing and held the tin underneath the petrol cock until the tank had slowly drained into it. Measuring with a foot-rule, I found that I had three gallons left. This was good for thirty-six minutes' flying, say twenty miles out and back allowing for warming up, starting and taking off. The reasonable course of action would have been to wait on the ground where I was; the haze might clear which would make it possible to spot Camooweal ten or fifteen miles away, instead of groping about near the ground with visibility of a few hundred yards. Then I should be able to have a rest, which would result in my thinking more clearly, and perhaps getting some good fresh ideas. But I dreaded the prospect of a search being started for me. I made up my mind to try for Camooweal.

I warmed up for three minutes, and set off on a fifteen-minute flight to the east, determined to return to the water hole if nothing had showed up by then. Every second of this flight was exciting. There was a strong wind blowing from the south, and the dust haze was thick. The minutes fled as fast as they had travelled slowly the night before. In eleven minutes I thought I saw a man ahead, but it turned out to be a small horse which bolted. At fourteen and a half minutes, I came to a creek. I had a feeling of relaxation. I must return to the water hole. I decided to cross the creek and turn on the other side. I was just going into the bank for turning, when I caught the dull glint of light on an iron roof. It gave me a jolt. Then I saw another – five, six, seven. I cursed and swore as I tore round the place at full throttle, and finally landed. A truck drove up with the station book-keeper and a load of station hands and blacks. I thought that his Scots accent was the pleasantest sound I had ever heard.

This was Rocklands Homestead (3,400 square miles) four miles north of Camooweal, and I had been at Cattle Creek water hole, fifteen miles to the west, which probably would not have been visited for six weeks. The water hole where I had lost the track must have been an extra one, short of the one marked on the map. The perfectly formed road which had puzzled me was the work of a fire plough, I was told. This was my first serious exercise in mental dead reckoning. In 1943, during the war, one of my jobs at the Empire Central Flying School was to devise methods of teaching fighter pilots how to find a pin-point objective in enemy territory while jinking at zero feet. It had to be done by mental dead reckoning, because the pilot could not take his eyes off the ground ahead. It seemed easy after practice, and by using various tricks; it is the first time of doing anything which is difficult.

I was content with my two flights that day: fifteen miles to Rocklands, and four miles on to Camooweal. The remaining 1,380 miles to Sydney I flew off in three stages. To my surprise and uneasiness ten planes of the New South Wales Aero Club met me, and escorted me to Mascot Aerodrome, where I could see several thousand people on the airfield, waiting for me. I should like to be able to report that I made a perfect landing in front of such an audience, but the true story is that I was so nervous that I did it as badly as I possibly could—touching down with a bump and finishing in a series of rabbit hops.

It was a great surprise for me to find myself in the news. I had had no thought before the flight that any fame, or notoriety perhaps, would attach to making the flight. If I had not delayed at Tripoli I should have taken nineteen days over the flight from London to Darwin, three days more than Hinkler took.

PART TWO

CHAPTER ELEVEN

THE TASMAN SEA

THE fame which I ran into hit me like a shock. I had had no thought of it when I left England; I was trying only to achieve a private target which I had set myself. At first I liked being pointed out as a celebrity, while at the same time dreading it; then I began to think that I really must be a bit of a lad, and my head began to swell. I began to dislike *not* being pointed out to people. I feel ashamed of this period. I think I regained my balance within a year; I grew a beard and hid behind it. People could say anything they liked to me, and I just stood behind the scenes watching and enjoying it without being affected.

I was one of the few pilots who had first made the money needed to finance a flight. As soon as I returned to New Zealand, where the slump was now in full swing, I began looking for ways of replenishing the purse. First I wrote a book about the voyage called *Solo to Sydney*. I realized that the only hope of its having any success was to rush it out, and I dictated most of it. Reading it today makes me squirm; yet there were some fine reviews of it, and Christopher Beaumont wrote of it in the magazine *Airways*, 'One of the extraordinarily few classics of aviation literature, full of the art that conceals art.' My excuse for some of the corny passages was that I was still exhausted: *Solo to Sydney* records also that 'every night, almost without fail for nine weeks, I had the same nightmare between 3 and 4 o'clock. I was in the air flying, when my vision went completely and I waited in fearful darkness for the inevitable crash. Usually I woke to find myself clawing at the window or a wall trying to escape.' In view of what happened later I wonder if this was a sort of 'Experiment with Time' experience, or just a coincidence.

Gradually I made up my mind that there were two things I wanted to do; I wanted to complete a circumnavigation of the world in Gipsy Moth and I wanted to fly across from New Zealand to Australia. No one had flown across the Tasman Sea alone, and I had a great urge to be the first to do it. At that time only one solo ocean flight had been completed, Lindbergh's flight across the Atlantic. My problem was, How could I span the Tasman? My Moth was carrying sixty gallons with two extra tanks fitted, and taking off with a load equal to its own weight. The Tasman is two-thirds of the width of the Atlantic, and with 15 per cent extra for a safety margin – little enough – I needed over 100 gallons. I could not fit the tanks needed to carry this extra fuel. And 15 per cent extra range was not really enough, because the Tasman Sea is a dirty stretch for storms, which start suddenly, rolling across from east to west. How could I get across? I could not buy or borrow a plane with the necessary range, because there wasn't one in New Zealand.

One day I was looking at a globe while shaving and noticed two small islands in the North Tasman Sea. Norfolk Island was 481 miles from the northernmost tip of New Zealand, and Lord Howe Island, 561 miles from Norfolk, was 480 miles from Sydney. I was excited; instead of a blundering flight straight across, could I pick my way from island to island? I could not find anyone who knew if Lord Howe Island was inhabited, but an old encyclopedia told me that it was of 3,200 acres and 120 inhabitants. No aeroplane had been seen at either island, and according to the charts I managed to get, both appeared too hilly for even a level field. It was difficult to find out anything. A steamer visited the islands once a month from Sydney, taking a week on the outward trip, but I already knew better than to rely on some non-flier's idea of a field suitable for landing in: it might be a tennis-court sloping up hill with eighty-foot trees all round!

My next idea was, Why not turn the Moth into a seaplane, and alight on the sea? Lord Howe Island had a lagoon, and the idea of blowing in and settling on the lagoon of an untamed island caught my fancy. I decided to learn seaplane flying at

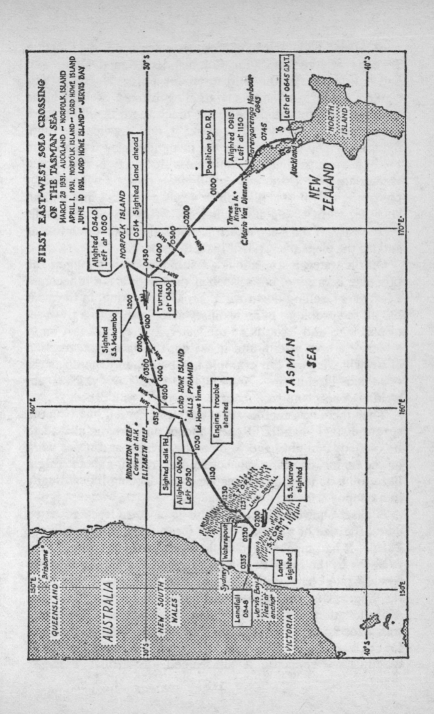

FIRST EAST-WEST SOLO CROSSING
OF THE TASMAN SEA
MARCH 28 1931: AUCKLAND ~ NORFOLK ISLAND
APRIL 1, 1931: NORFOLK ISLAND ~ LORD HOWE ISLAND
JUNE 10 1931: LORD HOWE ISLAND ~ JERVIS BAY

AUSTRALIA

QUEENSLAND

Brisbane

150°E.

NEW SOUTH WALES

Sydney

Jervis Bay

Landfall 0848

Jervis Bay: Fleet at anchor

VICTORIA

40°S.

NEW ZEALAND

NORTH ISLAND

Auckland

TASMAN SEA

Three Kings Is.
C. Maria Van Diemen

Parengarenga Harbour

170°E.

30°S.

40°S.

MIDDLETON REEF Covers at H.K.
ELIZABETH REEF

LORD HOWE ISLAND
BALLS PYRAMID

Sighted Balls Pd.

Alighted 0650 Left 0950

1050 Ld. Howe time

Engine trouble started

1130

1230

1255

Line squall

S.S. Kurow sighted

Waterspout

0200

S T O R M

0330

0335

Land sighted

NORFOLK ISLAND

Alighted 0540 Left at 1050

0514 Sighted land ahead

0430

Turned at 0430

0400

SUN

1200

Sighted S.S. Makambo

0100

0200

0300

0400

0500

SUN

Position by D.R.

Alighted 0915 Left at 1150

0745

0845

Left at 0645 G.M.T.

0100

0200

0500

SUN

160°E.

0505

0500

0400

0350

0300

SUN

once. Here I had a stroke of luck. New Zealand had a sporting Director of Aviation, Wing-Commander Grant-Dalton, who had enlisted me in the Territorial Air Force. He said, 'You can do a course of seaplane training instead of land-plane training.' I found seaplane flying much more thrilling; there was something wild and free about it, and it called for more flying skill. You must rely on your own judgement for choosing the best water to alight on, estimate wind and tide, and survey the surface for rocks or even small pieces of wood which might pierce the thin floats. A seaplane needs more skill in handling because, with its big floats, it loses flying speed and stalls more easily. If too steep a turn is made, the floats catch the air and tip the plane over, possibly on to its back.

On the water, a seaplane is a fast motor-boat as long as the propeller is turning, but as soon as the motor is cut it becomes a fast yacht, sailing down wind. Broadly speaking, in the air it has all the problems of an ordinary aeroplane, with a fresh set of problems and hazards on the water. It may drift fast on to a pier or a boat astern, and it has not the hardy construction of a yacht. A wing can crumple like paper, and the floats rip open like biscuit tins. At sea (at the time of which I am writing) a seaplane was about as seaworthy as a canoe.

Then there was another set of problems caused by flying the seaplane single-handed. Ropes, anchor and drogue all had to be carried, I might have to moor by myself, and usual work on the engine, checking valve clearances, refuelling, etc., might have to be done while the seaplane was dancing like a dinghy in a choppy sea.

A chart showed Norfolk Island as a squat rock of 8,500 acres, the size of a New Zealand sheep farm, dumped in the Pacific. It had no sheltered anchorage. A seaplane would have to alight in the open Pacific on the rollers pounding the 300-feet cliffs. A chart of Lord Howe Island, however, was more thrilling; perhaps it was responsible for the saying, 'To a man of imagination, a map is a window to adventure.' The island was 3,200 acres all told, shaped like a bow, with a coral reef for the bow-string. This coral was the southernmost reef in the world. How romantic it all seemed – 'Sugarloaf Passage',

'Smooth Water Lagoon', 'Coral Reef Awash here', 'Heavy Surf here', and 'Boat Passage at High Water'. I knew that I must fly there.

But here came another difficulty: how was I going to find these islands? Norfolk Island, approached from the northernmost tip of New Zealand, was a target only half a degree in width; there was no other land nearer than New Zealand, so that any shot at it must hit the bull's-eye. The smallest target of this sort so far aimed at was the Hawaii group from San Francisco, and that was seven degrees wide – fourteen times as wide as Norfolk Island. There were no radio aids then. Could a pin-point target of that size be found by dead reckoning? This would depend mainly on two things, the magnetic compass, and the drift caused by the wind. The compass was still an uncertain factor in a small aeroplane, and I had known a case of nine degrees of error developing in three weeks. As for wind, it turned out later that I could assess this accurately, but at the time it was not thought that a pilot flying alone could do so. What was known then was that a forty-mile wind undetected could put a Moth off course by thirty degrees. The only possible way of finding the island, I decided, was by using the sun. I should have to take shots at the sun with a sextant to measure the height of the sun above the horizon, and work out my position from that. 'Impossible,' said the experts, 'for a man flying a plane alone to use a sextant and work out sights.' 'If a sea navigator can navigate a steamer by the sun, I can navigate an aeroplane,' I said.

I started to teach myself astronomical navigation. By the time I had learnt enough to navigate a ship I realized that it would not do for an aeroplane. A ship could get its longitude six hours before its latitude by observations of the sun. A plane, however, required both latitude and longitude within an hour of each other, and this could not be done by the sun. I was downhearted by this discovery, and felt that I must devise a new system of navigation to overcome the obstacle.

The object in using a sextant is to measure the angle between the sun and the sea's horizon. I did not think a marine sextant would be suitable for this, because the plane might be too high, or clouds might intervene to hide the horizon. So I bought a sextant with an artificial horizon in the form of a built-in bubble level. I practised using this while motoring and running. I gained skill, but was worried to find silly mistakes creeping into my calculations, mistakes like writing down a number wrongly. About this time the Tasman Sea was flown solo from west to east by an Australian, Menzies, in the same plane in which Kingsford-Smith had just made his record flight from England to Australia. Menzies crashed in a flat swamp on the west coast of South Island, but he had flown the Tasman. At first this was a blow, but I soon got over it; I was firmly gripped by the idea of finding my island by my own system of navigation.

Then a fresh obstacle cropped up; new floats would cost £500, the slump had stopped all our land selling, and there was no £500 available. Perhaps I could earn the money by joy-riding? I took up a few hundred passengers, but it was not a success. They preferred flying in other planes. I discovered that people thought my plane was held together by bits of string and wire. However, I had some fun, and I had some valuable flying experience in taking up passengers. I had a great friend, Pat Maunsell, who had a farm outside Masterton. He let me fly from one of his fields, and helped me with the ground work. One day I forgot the power lines on the edge of the field when I was coming in to land with a passenger. The Moth went through the three power cables, carrying 11,000 volts, with no trouble at all. They made a grand flash and put out the town's lights. I said it was an Act of God, but was told 'not so', and that I must pay for the repairs. I seemed to be plagued by wires and such like in the air. There was a race-course bordering Pat's property, and one day I was checking the accuracy of my turns and banks by flying round it low down. I didn't notice that the starting ribbon was stretched across the track, and carried it away on one wing tip.

My passenger flying failed to bring in enough money for new floats and I lost sleep trying to think of ways to get money. One day I noticed an old discarded pair of floats in a corner of the hangar at the air base. They were the relics of a Moth which had been accidentally dropped twenty feet on to the deck of a cruiser. I thought that they would do if patched up, and asked the Government if it would sell them to me cheap. But it wouldn't.

About this time I had my first chance to try my hand with an ordinary sextant when flying alone. The result was 108 miles in error. I could hardly have been more depressed.

I found that I was charging obstacles like a goaded bull, and that was no way to get things done. So I threw everything out of my mind and took to a tent on the hills of our Silverstream property for a fortnight's hard bush-felling in the scorching heat of midsummer. I sweated away the poison of worry until I was bursting with vitality, and felt that I could achieve anything, tackle anyone. This was the life I loved, the true life, to return to camp with the mist of fatigue creeping over the brain and veiling any cares. Glowing and tingling after a bathe in a mountain stream; to hear the dull pop of a red hot stone in a camp fire, and feel the acrid manuka smoke biting one's nostrils; God! Why go back to that other life, to the terrible fatigue at dawn, to nerves wearing thin through sixteen hours of strain a day, to wondering each morning how much longer one's luck could hold? I could get no floats, had no money, my navigation was shaky, my plane, people said, was only a toy. Why not accept the inevitable, and stay here, living a life I loved?

But I felt that I *had* to make the flight, and could not escape it. I tried the Government again for a loan of the old floats, but the Ministry of Defence had just appointed a new official solely to seek economies in the slump. Autumn was drawing to a close, and soon the stormy Westerlies would set in across the Tasman. The head wind would put Norfolk Island out of range. However, I felt that the flight would come off, and went back to Auckland.

In the air, I tried out my new bubble sextant, and was 740 miles out. On hearing this, Grant-Dalton wrote me an official letter saying that I now ought to abandon the flight, that 'lost airman' publicity would set back aviation with the public, which still remembered Hood and Moncrieff, who had disappeared trying to fly the Tasman from Sydney. I wrote back that I was confident that I could make do with an ordinary sextant by flying lower, and using the sea horizon. Would the Government lend me the floats, or failing that, allow me to pay for them later? Grant-Dalton replied that I was doing good experimental work in navigation, and that he would recommend that the floats should be lent to me.

I became ill, and was sent to Auckland hospital. For some reason I could not walk, and I could cross a room only by crawling. The doctors could not find out what was wrong with me and after a week the illness passed, and I returned to the air base, where I found that the Government had relented, and was lending me the floats. I had such a strong presentiment that the flight would start on a certain day that I prepared navigation, working out the position of the sun for various times on that day. All this was at a time when the floats were still unmended, my Moth was still on wheels, had never been flown as a seaplane, and I would not know until she was launched whether she could carry enough petrol to reach Norfolk Island. I forgot all about the presentiment, and was amazed when, two days before the date, a wireless message arrived from Dr Kidson, head of the Met. Office, to say that a favourable wind was likely for the next few days and was I going to start? I showed the message to Squadron-Leader L. Isitt, the Commandant of the air base, and asked him if he would try to get me away to the extreme north of New Zealand on the Friday, ready for an early start on Saturday. Len Isitt, who was an experienced seaplane and flying-boat pilot, said, 'I don't like this flight of yours. I doubt if you can find your way alone by sextant; even if you can, suppose there is no sun? If you reach Norfolk Island there is nowhere to put down a seaplane; if you succeed in getting down, you won't be able to take off again, because of the swell. If there should, chance to be no swell, it would be impossible to take off a Moth loaded up like yours without a stiff wind.' Len had excellent judgement (as was shown by his becoming Chief of the New Zealand Air Staff in 1943 and Chairman of the New Zealand National Airways Corporation in 1963). But he was also a true sportsman, and having stated his official views he set to and made every possible effort to turn the Moth into a seaplane. He worked on the job himself, with the aircraftmen, until midnight on Thursday.

The Moth was ready for the water on Friday afternoon. A wading party wheeled her down the slipway on a trolley; she took to the water like a duckling, and took off into the air like a wild swan. Was I proud of her? After 34,000 miles as a landplane! But would she take the load: all my gear, boat, anchor, ropes, food, water, navigation instruments and books, besides fifty gallons of petrol? The experts said 'No'; the same model of plane and motor, with these same floats, had refused to leave the water at Samoa with only the pilot and petrol for eighty miles on board. My Moth thought nothing of the full load, and rose happily. I was jubilant.

'Don't forget,' said the CO gloomily, 'that you have ideal conditions at the moment. Strong breeze against you, tide with you, and choppy sea to break the suction of the water of the floats. I'd like to see you carry out a forty-eight hours' mooring test to make sure the floats don't leak; and also some long flights, to test your navigation farther.' It would certainly have been wise to do all this, but probably I would have had no flight if I had.

So we worked until midnight, stowing the gear, and fitting the tiny transmitting set which Partelow, the wireless operator, had built for me. Including the aerials stretching from wing tip to tail, it weighed only 23 lb. It was not of much value to me because there were no ships on the Tasman Sea if I put out an SOS, but Partelow wanted to experiment, and I thought that with careful organization of my work I could send a wireless message every hour. I could not receive any messages, but I liked the idea of doing a wireless operator's job as well as a pilot's and a navigator's.

Going to the hangar near midnight I took a short cut down a bank, and fell heavily on the gravel in the dark. I lay still for a few moments, thinking how a Roman senator, if he stumbled on the way to the Senate, regarded it as a bad omen, and went home. I wondered if fate was against me. But that was nonsense; any man was master of his own fate. The senator did right to stay at home because stumbling showed that his brain, nerve and muscle were not properly working together. I had had a good hint to take extra care next day.

I did not sleep well; seeming to wake every few minutes to hear the wind roaring about the house. Yet on being called at 4 o'clock I found it a calm and cloudless sky, with the planet Venus shining bright and steady. The hospitable Mrs Isitt cooked me some bacon and eggs to eat by candlelight, but they reminded me of my breakfast in the dark on the flight out from England, and weariness seemed to weigh down my spirits. I felt that I must be crazy to go through it all again voluntarily.

I sat in the cockpit while the seaplane was moved about on the concrete pad, so that Sid Wallingford, Len's second-in-command, could check the compass error. Suddenly I noticed that the time was 6.15 by the dashboard clock, and I had fixed 6 o'clock as the time for starting. I shouted to Sid that there was no time for any more checking; then I remembered having altered the clock to Greenwich time, so that there was still a quarter of an hour to go; but I refused to spend time for checking the compass error on any other bearing than that of Norfolk Island from New Zealand. I broke another bottle of brandy on the propeller, and then started the motor. I could get only 1,780 revs, forty less than I expected, and my spirits sank. I should never get off with a full load with a motor like that, but I said nothing to the CO about it. The seaplane was launched. I faced her into wind, and opened the throttle; to my surprise she left the water as easily as a sea bird. I climbed into the grey of dawn until I had enough height to turn. Then I fastened the wireless key to my leg with an elastic band, and began tapping out in Morse 'Can you hear me?' time after time. I circled the hangar, steeply banked in tight circles, watching the wireless operating-room while I kept on sending. No answer, the set must have failed. I ought to return, but no, I couldn't now. Suddenly a dazzling Aldis lamp flashed me 'OK.' I turned instantly towards the dawn, and made for the harbour entrance. The city of Auckland was sleeping in the cold grey light, with an occasional wisp of smoke slipping away from a chimney top. I thought of the people below lying comfortably in bed. It was 6.45 when I turned the harbour entrance and headed north. It would be sunset at Norfolk Island at 6.45 PM, so I had roughly twelve hours of daylight, with ten hours' flying to do. First I had three hours' flight to the northern tip of New Zealand, where I would fill up with petrol for the sea-crossing.

As the Moth had been a seaplane only for seventeen hours, I had to make the best use possible of this first flight. The big fifteen-foot long floats instead of the landing wheels spoilt the Moth's stability; as a land plane, I could trim her so finely that only moving my head backwards was needed to start her climbing slightly; now, she continually yawed as well as pitched. I could not leave the controls for ten seconds without her starting a steep dive or climb. I watched the grey-green sea looking coldly inhospitable below, where a long swell from the south-east could be seen unrolling smoothly. I waited for Cape Brett, and anxiously studied its effect on the swell. The waves radiated from the Cape like the spokes of a wheel, changing direction, and breaking on the rocks in the lee of the Cape in jagged lines of white surf. That meant I could not expect protection from the swell behind Norfolk Island.

A week before this I had worked out a fine system of navigation. I had found that I could follow an invisible curved path to the island by taking sextant shots of the sun every hour; this was based on the fact that measuring the height of the sun above the horizon with a sextant enabled one to calculate the distance of the seaplane from the spot vertically below the sun on the surface of the earth. Having calculated beforehand how far the seaplane would be from the point vertically beneath the sun (if on her right path) at that time, the actual sun sight when the time came would reveal if the seaplane was, say, five miles to one side or other of the invisible path. Unfortunately all this depended on leaving the north tip of New Zealand early in the morning, which in turn depended on flying up there the night before. Not starting from Auckland till the morning had ruined this carefully-computed system. As I flew along I thought up a replacement, and began afresh.

I estimated the time when I should arrive, and I computed the distance of the island from the sun position an hour before that time. Then I marked a spot on the chart about ninety miles to the left of the island which would be the same distance from the sun position at that time. This was my first target. By the height of the sun a sextant shot at the time would then tell me if I had reached the spot or not. As soon as I reached the spot I would turn and keep the sun abeam, which would bring me to the island. I had to aim well to one side of the island in case error in the dead reckoning, caused by a faulty compass reading, or undetected wind effect should put me on the wrong side of the island. And the island being out of sight, I must be certain that when I turned to the right I was turning towards it, and not away from it. This system was afterwards dubbed by one of my friends as 'my theory of the deliberate error'. I estimated that I should reach the turn-off spot at 4 o'clock (1600 hours) and computed for that time.

After 160 miles I flew over a deserted island of bare brown rock and had some trouble in locating it on the map. It gave me a shock to find that it was a third of the width of Norfolk Island. So far there had been no sign of any sun or a break in the grey-black clouds, but at 8.40 I spotted a shaft of light ahead, which cast a small circle of brightness on the dull sea. At 8.49 I struck the edge of the sunlight, and shot the sun four times before I was across. This was my last chance to check my astro-navigation. I worked out how far I was from the point under the sun and compared it with my position according to the chart. The observation was 140 miles out. For a second I felt panic. Then I found that I had forgotten to allow for the error in my watch. I felt desperate at thinking of all the blunders of this kind I could make. However, I recovered; the work required extraordinary concentration. It had been easy enough in a car driven at fifty mph by someone else; in the seaplane it was at first difficult to concentrate enough while attending to the five instrument readings, maintaining a compass course, reducing the sun sight, and solving the spherical triangle involved. The 90–100-mph wind of the propeller slipstream, which struck the top of my head just above the windshield, made concentrating difficult; so did the pulsating roar from the open exhausts.

While all these thoughts went through my head, the Moth flew on, and looking over the side I found that I was passing Parengarenga Harbour. I skimmed round, looking for a place called Te Hamua where my petrol was. There were no other buildings to be seen except a group of three or four wooden huts in a small clearing by the shore with a great stretch of stunted scrub all round. I flew low to inspect, and fowls scattered in all directions madly flapping. As I throttled back, I was glad to see one or two people waving to me. I was just about to alight, when the pebbles, shell and weed showed so clearly that I feared there was no water; I knew that this part of the harbour dried at low water, so I shied off, and went round again. I noticed a dark streak of deeper water in a channel farther out, and alighted on that. The floats settled with a sizzling swish, the seaplane swaying slightly in a way that was a sheer delight. I cut the motor, and as soon as the seaplane lost way it began to drift rapidly down wind. There was a snappish breeze, and I threw out the $3\frac{3}{4}$-lb. anchor with its 2-lb. chain, and paid out the full length of line. After watching for a while I realized that the anchor was not holding, and that the seaplane was drifting rapidly on to a lee shore. I looked round anxiously, but there was no sign of anyone. Then I looked at my watch, 9.30. I had been down a quarter of an hour already. I could not stay long. It was doubtful if the sun could be observed during the last hour before sunset, and I ought to have a reserve of time in case of a head wind. Also I needed some time up my sleeve for finding a place to moor on arrival. I ought to leave by 10 o'clock.

A man strolled on to the beach looking towards the plane. Then a boy followed, and they sauntered down to a dinghy which disappeared behind an anchored boat. This turned out to be a launch which moved away from its mooring, and swept round in a wide arc, dinghy in tow, to a point some 200 yards to windward of the seaplane. By the time the man and the boy had dropped into the dinghy they were 300 yards away; the seaplane was moving two yards to their one, and I anxiously watched the shore drawing nearer. At last I had to swing the prop, and as the plane moved forward I hauled in the dripping anchor line, precariously standing on a float behind the propeller blades. The launch moved away at full speed, and the two in the dinghy rowed like mad. Near the dinghy I switched off the motor and threw out the anchor. The rowers rested on their oars, staring speechless. They were Maoris.

'I want an anchor,' I bawled. No answer. 'Have you got an anchor?' No answer. 'I must have an anchor.' No answer. This went on until at last the man said, 'Py corry, he want te anchor, I tink, hey?' The boy agreed, and without saying anything else they set off leisurely for the launch, and after a long discussion on board the launch set off leisurely for the shore. My three-quarters of an hour ran out. At last the launch started again, just as I was forced to restart my motor and taxi back to the channel. When the dinghy arrived I persuaded them to make fast their anchor to mine, which they did after sweeping for my anchor line with an oar.

'I want the petrol,' I shouted.

'Hah?'

'Petrol! Where is my petrol?'

'Ho! Petrol!'

'Py corry!' said Hori senior to Hori junior, 'I tink he want his plurry petrol, hey?'

'He! He! He!' said the boy.

'Didn't you know I was landing here for petrol?'

'Ho, we think you not coming this soon.'

My request for him to get the petrol in a hurry was strongly worded. The Maori is a devilish fine fellow, friendly, good-natured, sporting and with perfect manners. The man in the boat said nothing, and rowed back to the launch. The launch returned to the shore. Men disappeared. It all seemed unreal; it was hard to connect this with a trans-Tasman flight already overdue to start. I was sick with impatience and anxiety, when suddenly I thought, "There's nothing I can do about it; why worry?" Peace descended upon me, as the Bible says. I fumbled below the seat for the jam and butter and loaf of bread given me by the Isitts, cut myself a thick slice, and began eating it, riding astride the fuselage behind the cockpit. I saw the launch put off again, hastily rammed the remainder of the bread and jam into my mouth, and scrambled forward on to the float. Well, the position was not really so hopeless after all. But the launch shot by, headed to the other side of the harbour, and none of the crew took the slightest notice of me.

It was 11 o'clock. At last the launch came back heading for the plane. It was 11.23. 'It's madness not to turn back now,' said Reason. 'You can be sure of a following wind,' said Instinct. The white bow waves increased in size. It really was petrol this time; the dinghy came down the anchor line, with three cases on board.

'Got a funnel?' I called out.

'No, we not got funnel. Hey, you make us present of this benzene case, hey?'

'All right, how about opening it first!'

'We not got a hammer, hey?'

I scrambled back to the fuselage-locker behind my cockpit for my collapsible funnel, then on to the wing-root, to ransack the front cockpit for the tools at the bottom of it. I passed over a big spanner, and my new screwdriver, which they belted into the wooden case to open it. After making a hole in the 4-gallon tin big enough to take his fist, he handed up the tin. I worked it up from the wing-root to the motor-cowling, then on to the top petrol tank between the two top wings. I clambered up after the tin, and stood, precariously balancing myself on the top of the motor of the bobbing seaplane, my right arm round a 30-lb. tin of petrol and my left hand holding the collapsible leather petrol-filter. And how that collapsible funnel could collapse! I got surges of petrol up my sleeves and down my legs, and when the seaplane pitched petrol shot into my cockpit. The Maori chose this moment for questioning me. It sounded as if they were questions he had been told to ask.

'You going far?'

'To Australia.'

'Ho, Australia, hey! You give me that benzene tin when it empty, hey? How many miles this Australia?'

'Fifteen hundred the way I am going.'

'Py corry! That th' phlurry long way to swim, I tink. What time you get there?'

'I'm only going to Norfolk Island today. That is to say,' I added looking up at the clouds, 'that's where I hope to get.'

'You give me that benzene tin when you finish him? Norfolk Island! You hear that? Ho! Ho! Ho! Norfolk Island; you hear that! How far is Norfolk Island?'

'About 500 miles from here.'

'Five hundred miles! Why! That's the phlurry long swim too, py corry!'

I filled up with 12 gallons so that I now had about ten hours' fuel. I had tanks for twelve hours, but knew that it would be hopeless to try rising with more than 50 gallons, ten hours. I made a deal with him for his anchor, and this took time, because I knew I should never get it if I tried to cut short the customary haggling. I asked him to hurry and lift the anchors, take off mine and bend on his, and he said they had a telegram on shore for me. I clutched my hair swearing till I cooled off. Then I laughed and suggested he go and fetch it. It must be the weather forecast I was expecting. Then a launch came up, with a white man in the bows waving a telegram. 'Forecast from Dr Kidson,' he read out. 'Weather expected fine; fresh to strong south-easterly breeze; seas moderate becoming rough.'

CHAPTER TWELVE

LANDFALL ON A PINPOINT

I OPENED the throttle wide, but the seaplane thrashed on and on through the water without a sign of leaving it. After more than a mile's run I had to stop because of the opposite shore ahead. As I turned and taxied down wind, I tried to think of a reason for the failure; at dawn, the seaplane had taken off in less favourable conditions; the motor was the same; were the floats leaking? They had been tested; when filled up with water scarcely a drop had leaked out, and if none could leak out none could leak in? (So I thought, but one float had been steadily filling all the time I was down on the water.) I turned into the wind for another attempt, but the seaplane bumped and porpoised with no sign of rising. I snatched at the control-stick and jerked up the seaplane's nose; she jumped out of the water, and settled back again with the waves dragging at the float heels; but she was not as deep in as before. I snatched again, and again she jumped, settled down after the jump, but this time held off the water. Slowly she gathered speed, overcame the heaviness of her stalled condition, and rose. I was away.

I headed for my imaginary point ninety miles to the left of Norfolk Island. Ahead, I could see an edge to the layer of black cloud with clear sky beyond. I slipped off my goggles and lifted the helmet flaps, so that I could stuff each ear with a plug of cotton wool, which muffled somewhat the roar from the open exhaust. At noon I flew over the edge of New Zealand; it was Spirit's Bay, where the Maoris believed there was a vast cavern through which all the spirits of the dead passed. I flew from under the cloud into clear sky. All my miserable anxieties and worries dropped away, and I was thrilled through and through. Over my left shoulder, the last of New Zealand receded rapidly. Ahead stretched the ocean, sparkling under the eye of the sun: no sport could touch this, it was worth almost any price. I seemed to expand with vitality and power and zest.

Although I could not rely on dead reckoning, I intended to work it up carefully. It was most important to determine the speed and direction of the wind. For example, a thirty-mile wind from the north-east would cause the seaplane to drift twenty-four miles to the side of its route during an hour. At the time pilots said that it was impossible to determine what the wind was over the sea when flying alone, because it was impossible to read the drift of the plane. I had devised a new way of doing it, however, by reversing the ordinary method. Instead of looking over the side, and trying to decide how much the plane was drifting by looking at the sea, I looked over the side, fixed a point in the water such as a fleck of white, and flew the plane so that this fleck left the side of the fuselage at an angle of, say, five degrees. In other words, I made the plane drift five degrees as it flew away from that speck. Then I looked back quickly at the compass, and if the compass reading showed that the plane was still on course, then the five degrees of drift must have been correct. If the compass showed that the plane was now off course, say, two and a half degrees, then I had judged the drift wrongly and I would try again. The next time I would make the plane drift seven and a half degrees, and if the compass showed that the plane was on course afterwards, then the correct drift was in fact seven and a half degrees. I reckoned that I could tell the drift to one and a quarter degrees by imagining a five-degree angle split into four. Of course, one drift was only part of the data needed, because lots of different winds could make a plane drift seven and a half degrees. I determined the drift on three different headings, and then plotted them on the chart for those headings. Whereas lots of winds could cause any one of the drifts, there was only one wind which could cause the different drifts on the different headings at the same time. I observed and plotted three drifts every half-hour, and used the mean of the two winds for the hour's flight.

The chart I used was one that I had drawn up myself, on Mercator's projection. I made it of a suitable scale, so that it would fit into a map case of aluminium which had a small flat surface and a roller at each side. I rolled the chart on as I flew along the route. There was not room in the cockpit to use an ordinary folded chart or map. The wind I was getting was an ideal tail wind, which seemed wonderful. I worked out how long it would take me to reach the 'turn off point' if this wind held. I made it 5 o'clock.

The flap I had got into before starting had now disappeared, and my brain was ticking over coolly and steadily. I knew that everything depended solely on accurate work. Conditions were perfect; the sun shone in a cloudless light-blue sky. The exhausts gave off a steady rolling roar. The needle of the revolution indicator might have been the hand of a clock, it kept so steady. The time for the sextant work on which everything depended was rapidly approaching.

At the end of the hour I observed the drift again three times, and after plotting the results found that the wind had drifted the seaplane twelve and a half degrees off course to the right. It altered course another ten degrees to the left to counteract this. This meant that the seaplane was in fact headed nearly 200 miles to the left of the island. It was difficult to convince myself that this was right. At 1.0 PM I had made good 103 miles in the past hour. Using the transmitting key strapped to my right leg, I tapped out a message in morse to the Auckland air base operator, who should be listening as the hour struck. 'Position by dead reckoning at 01.00 hours GMT 33° 15′ S., 171° 35′ E. Wind 24 mph from 162 degrees true.' I used exactly the same drill for the next hour, and at the end of it the wind was much the same though slightly stronger, and I had made good 105 miles in the hour. The wind had increased to 30 mph from 155 degrees true; it was giving me a great lift forward, but I could not help thinking of the mountainous seas such a wind must be raising round Norfolk Island. I had to try a sextant shot to find out how far I was from the turn-off point, and at the same time to check my dead reckoning. I trimmed the tail as delicately as I could to balance the plane, but she would not stabilize, and I had to use the control-stick the whole time while adjusting the sextant. I sighted the sextant to catch the sun above the top wing and a piece of horizon underneath it. To be quite sure that I was using a piece of horizon vertically below the sun, I had to wipe out the plane's balance from my mind, and concentrate only on the sextant. I had just got the sun and horizon together in the sextant, when terrific acceleration pressing my back made me drop the sextant. I grabbed the stick and eased the seaplane from its vertical nose dive into a normal dive, and then flattened it out. I reset the tail trimmer till the seaplane was bound to climb as soon as I left the control-stick alone. I tried again, and this time managed well enough, easing the control-stick forward with my left elbow whenever the seaplane climbed so steeply that the wing cut off the sun from view. I noted down the time to the nearest second, but when I turned to read the altimeter it showed 2,500 feet. Looking over the side I felt sure the height was not more than 400 feet. I must be mistaken. I had bought this altimeter especially for accuracy, and had been observing it every morning and night for six months. To prove whether it was right I dived down to the water surface. The altimeter still read 2,500 feet.

I tugged at the sextant to make sure that it was securely held by the lanyard round my neck. I still had the dashboard altimeter which had failed me over the English Channel. It would have to do after I had reset it at sea-level, although the height ought to be more accurately known for sextant work. I skimmed the surface, fascinated by the heaving sea. The seaplane was going fast enough to make each wave appear motionless as I passed, whether it was heaving up, leaping high, or with its top flicked into a white crest. It was like looking at the individual little pictures in a cinema film. The effect was to make the seaplane seem motionless, as if it were dead still over a dead sea. Glancing ahead, I was astounded to find that I was below the water-level, as if in a whirlpool with the rim of water above me; then I realized that in skimming the surface I was unconsciously rising to a huge swell, and dropping into the valley the other side. It was solitary down there, as if I were winging my way between this and another world. I was being hypnotized, and came to with a start.

I rose to 400 feet by the old altimeter, and took five shots at the sun. I had the results worked out and plotted twenty minutes later. They showed that I still had 230 miles to fly before turning off to the island.

I did not use log tables for working out the sight, for I had found that I always made mistakes when trying to use logs when flying alone: I would read a six-figure log in the table, glimpse a dashboard instrument while glancing from the tables to my notebook, my concentration would be broken, and I would record one of the six figures wrongly. Instead, I had a circular slide rule called a Bygrave position-line slide rule. This consisted of three cylinders revolving one inside the other, and they had over fifty feet of trig logs scaled off on them. This slide rule had to be used step by step, and I seldom made a mistake with it. When fully extended it was about nineteen inches long, and could just be used in the cockpit if held sideways.

At 3 o'clock I got four more shots at the sun, now dead ahead, and behind the petrol tank between the top wings. I had to use the sextant fast, setting the seaplane into a dive so as to get the sun above the tank with the horizon below the wing beside the motor, and immediately I had the sun touching the horizon in the sextant I jogged back the control to climb, while I recorded the sextant, watch and altimeter readings. My handling of the Moth was already becoming automatic – I was getting the feel of her as a seaplane. I worked fast at the computing, and made it 127 miles from the turn-off point.

My brain felt overstretched. With the two sets of drift readings, plotting them, and sending a wireless message every hour, I was being too hard-pressed. It would be no use getting an accurate position if I let the top tank run out of petrol, or something equally stupid. Suddenly I thought I could hear a muffled knocking in the motor; it must be that cursed No. 3 cylinder again. If the motor failed I must turn right about immediately to face into the wind before the seaplane hit the water. I knew that I must not let myself get hustled, and I decided to cut out the next set of drift observations, and think instead. I relaxed for a while, and then reviewed everything: fuel gauge, oil pressure, engine revs, height, compass, chart. I was getting near the turn-off point. With the big lift I'd had from the tail wind, I might be ready to turn off earlier than anticipated, so I must make a fresh set of calculations for 4 o'clock instead of 5 o'clock. And I had to hurry, for I could see some fleecy clouds ahead, though not thick, thank heaven.

I worked out in advance the sun's position, and how far I should be from it at 4 o'clock so that when the moment arrived I should have only to take the sights, and the results would tell me at once how far I was from where I expected to be. I was getting intensely excited, but it did me good by keying me up for the vital work ahead. At 4 o'clock I took four shots from between 100 and 150 feet up, turning the seaplane in a steep bank to the right, so as to catch the sun abeam between the wings. After each shot I turned on course again, while writing down the sextant and watch readings. I quickly plotted the result, which showed my dead reckoning to be nineteen miles out. There must have been a mistake somewhere: where? If there was one mistake, why wouldn't there be several? (My outboard air speed indicator was over-reading by five mph which had built up to twenty miles in the four hours of flying.)

But there was no time to worry about that; I had to put my faith in the sextant. According to that, I was only forty-five miles short of the turn-off point. I still had the same strong tail wind, and as a result I was travelling faster than I had expected. I cut the seaplane's speed back to sixty mph, so that I should have half an hour before reaching the turn-off point, and hurriedly computed the work for another sextant sight at the end of that half-hour. It would be the critical moment of the flight, for when I turned, it must be exactly towards the island.

The calculation gave me the true bearing of the island at the turn-off point, because it would then be at right-angles to the direction of the sun. The clouds were rapidly forming into dense cumulus, and I watched them anxiously. A few minutes before the end of the half-hour I realized that there would be no sun available for a shot. The clouds ahead were darker, and I could see no opening. Could I rely on the previous sight? No, I must have another, for a check. The whole enterprise depended on turning at the right moment. The clouds looked whiter away to the left. Close to the half-hour I turned left, away from the island instead of towards it, and opened up the throttle. After three or four miles I spotted a round patch of sunlight on the sea ahead, and slightly to the right. I opened the throttle wider still. I was so impatient that time seemed to stop while I raced for that sun-patch, yet it could not have been more than five miles away. The area of sunlight was small, and I set the seaplane circling in a steep bank. I used my feet on the rudder to fly it while I worked the sextant with both hands. After each shot I straightened out the seaplane, and flew out of the patch while reading the instrument. I got four shots in this way, while the seaplane was chasing its tail in a tight circle. I corrected them for the lapse of time since 4.30, and compared them with the figure already computed. They agreed. I was on the line! I had expected to be, and yet it was a great surprise, and immense relief. I turned round and headed for where the island should lie eighty-five miles away.

The moment I settled on this course, nearly at right-angles to the track from New Zealand, I had a feeling of despair. After flying in one direction for hour after hour over a markless, signless sea, my instinct revolted at suddenly changing direction in mid-ocean. My navigational system seemed only a flimsy brain fancy: I had been so long on the same heading that the island must lie ahead, not to the right. I was attacked by panic. Part of me urged, for God's sake, don't make this crazy turn! My muscles wanted to bring the seaplane back to its old course. 'Steady, steady, steady,' I told myself aloud. I had to trust my system, for I could not try anything else now, even if I wanted to.

The clouds were darkening, and hung above without a break. The wind was dropping; I was now drifting only fifteen degrees to the left. I allowed for that amount of drift. I felt that I had to get another sextant shot. I throttled back the motor again and again, watching the clouds as well as the horizon. Suddenly I picked out the shape of the sun through a thinning in the clouds, but it was covered almost at once. I adjusted the sextant to the angle I expected, removed the shades necessary for strong sunlight, and held it ready. Five miles went by, when suddenly I could see the rim of the sun through a wraith of black cloud. I got a good shot before the cloud closed over it again. This was ten seconds before 5 o'clock, so after all I used the calculation I had made before the start of the flight. I got the same result as before, that the seaplane was dead on the line to the island. Fair enough! I put the sextant away in its case for good. If the island wasn't there, it must have moved. The excitement was terrific. Every minute seemed a lifetime, as I scanned the horizon ahead. The wind was dropping with approaching nightfall, and the drift now was only ten degrees. The sea looked grey blue, cold and hostile. If I missed the island, what should I do? My brain was numb, and I could think of nothing. At 5.08 PM I ought to have sighted the island ten miles earlier. Well, I thought, this is a grand finish; risking everything on the cool working out of my own system. At 5.09 I thought I saw land away to the left, but it changed shape as I watched it, for it was a cloud on the horizon. At 5.12 the island ought to have been in sight fifteen miles earlier. Surely that was land to the left – two hill cones, above a narrow band of grey cloud with a dark-purple coast below? But it was only another cloud. Suddenly I relaxed, feeling that worrying was stupid when there was nothing I could do. The cloud lifted, and there was land. I felt like bursting with thrill and elation. My navigational system had proved right. I thought, 'I bet Cook wasn't as excited at discovering this island from the sea as I am at discovering it from the air.'

I studied the chart of Norfolk Island, and decided that Cascade Bay would be most sheltered from the SSE swell. The bay was scarcely an indentation of the coast, with a road carved out of the rock cliff and leading to a small jetty. At last I spotted some people; they were standing on the jetty. I closed the throttle, and glided down to inspect the surface. The propeller still beat the air like a plover's wing, but it seemed an eerie silence after the endless roar. The wind had now died right away. There was a swell breaking on the rocks, but the surface of the sea seemed calm. I was just thinking how marvellously lucky I had been with the weather, when there was a violent bump below the cliff top. I was left in the air above my seat, as the seaplane whizzed down. I grabbed at the dashboard with one hand and clung to the control-stick with the other, feeling hot and damp all over. I ought to have fastened my safety-belt, though I had been warned never to do so when alighting for risk of being dragged under water if anything went wrong. I flew on to the next bay, hoping that the air would be smoother there, but the cliffs looked even higher and more precipitous; there was no road, and the whole place looked deserted. I turned back to Cascade, and found a boat moving slowly through the water. I glided down, hanging on tightly for fear of another bump, which did not come. I was still gliding when the seaplane flopped unexpectedly into the water. A swell had risen under me while I was looking ahead at the trough. It could not have been easier. I switched off the engine. It was 5.40 PM, and I had made it in good time. Everything had gone right, and I had had tremendous good luck. The wind had been exactly right, and now had died away to a calm at the right moment.

The boat, like a big clumsy whaler, was bearing down fast on my frail Moth. A crew was driving it with powerful sweeps of great oars, and a big man stood in the stern, with a long steering oar. 'Hey there!' I shouted. 'Stand off, you're going to ram me!'

'All right, skipper, all right,' sang out the helmsman, who looked like Caligula, 'don't get excited, we won't hurt you.' They were very patient, considering that they must be some of the best boatmen in the world.

I wanted to refuel quickly, to be ready for an early start next morning. Petrol had to be fetched from the other side of the island, but the trip took only about ten minutes. When the petrol arrived, the fun began. Riding the swell, the Moth had a twisting pitch, which made it impossible to stand on the engine to fill the top tank. I sat astride the narrow engine cowling, holding a 4-gallon tin under one arm, and the collapsible funnel in my right hand, while I tried to fill the 20-gallon tank in the front cockpit. That funnel was a hellish instrument. As the seaplane pitched and tossed, the bottom of the funnel would fold up, the top fill, and petrol would spill on my leg. When I handled the second tin the petrol and sea water on my shoes, the floats and wings had made them all as slippery as wet ice. I slithered about with the tin in my arms, trying to get it up on to the top of the engine. I was soaked to the knees in salt water, and wet through with petrol in places below the waist. This petrol was strong stuff, because I found afterwards that it had burnt six inches of skin off my left leg.

I had a feeling of utter futility; the sea was calm now, but God help the seaplane and me too if it got rough. No wonder that no one had ever attempted to make a long-distance flight alone in a seaplane before! Then, 'Bah!' I thought, feeling savage, 'don't be weak! You're just not used to it.' I decided to leave the rest of the fuelling, and fixed on the engine and cockpit covers with the aid of my torch. At least I had covered the 718 miles before sunset.

I was invited to spend the night at Government House, which had been the Prison Governor's house when the island was a penal settlement. The walls were so thick that outside my room there was a sentry box cut out of the solid stone. It did not seem ten seconds before I was being knocked up at 4 AM. I groaned as I dressed wearily, in sticky cold clothes. I had some bacon and eggs, with a strong whisky and soda. Then I was asked to wait until dawn, for the administrator to arrive. He asked me to carry letters to his wife and to the Governor of New South Wales.

We set off in the secretary's car, picking up boatmen on the way. They lived in thick-walled, squat stone cottages, which once housed prison officers; before our knocking finished echoing, a door would open, and out would come a man, rubbing his eyes with one hand, and chasing elusive buttons with the other. These men were descendants of the Bounty mutineers who had come on to Norfolk Island from Pitcairn Island sixty-six years after Christian and Co. had landed at Pitcairn.

As soon as I got on board the seaplane, I tried out the compression by swinging the propeller. No. 4 cylinder was bad enough, but No. 3 had no compression at all. That meant that I should have to try to get off the water with a full load before starting on a eight-hour flight across the ocean with a defective motor. Possibly No. 3 would regain compression when warmed up. I finished my engine drill, checking the tappet clearances, inspecting the petrol filter, replinishing the oil, etc., then finished loading the petrol, and packed away my tools and gear. In the hope of a faint off-shore breeze, I taxied out to sea, to fly back into it. The seaplane ploughed through the water and bumped, but never approached take-off speed. Then there seemed to be a sea breeze, so I tried heading out to sea. At the end of a long run, hitting a succession of larger swells, the seaplane swerved to starboard, and I felt that I was beginning to capsize. I closed the throttle quickly, mopped the sea water off my face, and wiped my goggles clear of water and the evaporated salt. With the motor ticking over, I let the seaplane move on slowly seawards. The pounding must have been a terrific strain. Turning was oddly difficult; I thought that this was because of the lumpy sea, but really it was due to the starboard float's being half full of water, though I did not know about it at the time. I had to use bursts of motor at full throttle to turn, and then, with the floats settled in deep, the propeller time after time hit heavy spray, or nearly solid wave crests with a crack which made the seaplane quiver from end to end. It was nervy work, watching the rough water ahead, and closing the throttle every time I saw a curling crest in front of the propeller. I had to keep on wiping the spray from my goggles.

I reached down for the thick volume of *Raper's Log Tables* on the bottom of the cockpit, and sat on the books to get a better view. The seaplane felt heavy in the water, like a log of wood. She would get up speed on the crest of a swell, and perhaps shoot off it, only to strike the rise of the next swell. There the floats ploughed in deep, and the seaplane slowed down again. How about trying across the swell? I remembered the words of the seaplane training manual, 'A cross-wind take-off along the line of the swell is an extremely hazardous proceeding, and should not be attempted except by the most experienced seaplane pilot, and only then in cases of emergency."

But I should never get off into the swell, so I headed along the line of swell, and opened the throttle. The seaplane gained more speed than before, swayed and rocked, knocking the waves. It was much harder to control, made a big jump into the air, yawed to the right, and came down slightly across its course. A bigger jump, and a worse yaw made me realize that little more would be needed to sheer off the floats, or to capsize the plane. I was now well out to sea, picking up rough water of a deep-purple blue. It was solitary out there, and I had a feeling that my personality had split, and that I was watching myself futilely struggling. I was weary all through.

After one more try, I decided to make for Duncombe Bay, two and a half miles farther on from Cascade. Off Bird Rock, between the two bays, I had to nag at the controls the whole time, to get through the cross sea safely. Suddenly I heard a loud scream behind my head, and twisted round as if I had been stabbed! This was one place where I felt sure I was alone, and I was more startled because I had never before heard a noise above that of the engine roar. It was a large bird, with spread wings, outstretched neck and pointed bill, swooping at my head. (The bird was a shearwater, called 'mutton bird' by the islanders.) I ducked, but the bird swept on, turned, and then flew straight at the propeller. I watched anxiously, wondering if it could see the flying blades. It spun round when a few inches from them. Dozens of the birds appeared, whirling, screeching, and just missing me, while I cursed at them, knowing that the propeller would be smashed if it hit one. When at last I reached Duncombe, the water was smoother, and I decided to try once more before testing the bilges. Here the breeze was parallel with the cliffs, and to get the longest run as close under the cliffs as possible, where the water was calm, I threaded a way through craggy rocks to the far side of the bay. But these efforts to take off failed too. I switched off the motor, and wondered how I could test the bilges. I had no bilge pump, and if I removed the manholes, the floats would promptly be swamped by the waves. I dug out a rubber tube, and pushed one end down the pipe leading to the bottom of a float compartment. The other end I sucked, but there was no water in that bilge. From the fourth compartment I sucked a mouthful of water. I began sucking the water up three or four feet, and spitting it out. I was squatting in my socks, with one knee on the float, my feet awash, and waves lapping me to the waist. Now and then the floats submerged with a gurgle, and broke surface again like toy submarines, with water streaming away each side. The water was not really cold, but clammy. My mouth began to ache, my cheeks grew sore where they were drawn against my teeth, and soon my jaw muscles began to cramp. After half an hour's sucking, I reckoned that I had drawn up four gallons, and my jaws ached as if they had been hit with a pole. I no longer had the strength to spit the water out, but could only open my mouth, and let it fall out. Then my mouth jammed altogether with cramp. I could think of no other way of pumping the bilges, so replaced the cap on that bilge pipe, and left the rest unplumbed.

I started the motor and taxied inshore to calmer water. There was a rock ahead, and I put on some engine and full rudder to avoid it. The seaplane was slow to turn. The throttle was now nearly full open, and suddenly the seaplane was nearly on top of the rock – I found myself staring down at the black stone crown of it, some six feet above water, dead ahead. The seaplane had refused to turn, and my only hope was to do something drastic. I put on full opposite rudder and maximum engine. The seaplane lurched round, heeled over, and the wing-tip dipped into white water. I dared not slow the motor, but I eased the rudder amidships, and the seaplane dragged clear.

I thought, 'I may do it yet!' The next time I kept the seaplane on the surface, planing until I thought it was going as fast as it could, when I yanked the stick back hard, to pull her off suddenly. She jumped from the crest of the swell, and was in the air, but she had not enough speed to stay airborne, sank back and plunked into the sea. Again I tried, but this time as the seaplane hit the water, I saw a wire flicker like a rapier blade. One of the twelve inter-float bracing-wires had snapped. The question now was, Could I get back to Cascade? Each wave spread the floats apart like flat feet, and in the troubled sea off Bird Rock I was expecting them to break up every minute of the passage. I was surprised and relieved when I arrived.

CHAPTER THIRTEEN

WRECKED

THE next few days were spent in worrying efforts to get the wire stay replaced, and to take off. People were very kind to me. Mr Martin, a merchant, invited me to stay with his family – it was a most friendly, hospitable house. A man named Brent, who turned out to be a crack mechanic, gave me enormous help with the plane. Martin found some wire rope to make a new stay, and Brent fixed a shackle to take it. After he had fixed the shackle he started dismantling the motor. Holding the detached cylinder head, he said, 'You're lucky, aren't you? Look at this!' The exhaust and inlet valves had been changed over, and the metal seating of the exhaust valve had begun to unscrew and was already a third of the way out. 'It's a wonder it did not come right out and jam the valve port open or shut, in which case the motor would have broken up,' he said. It looked as if reaching the island was due to fate rather than to skill on my part.

Meanwhile I studied the floats. How had the water got in if they were watertight at Auckland? Martin helped me to fill up the eight float compartments one by one with fresh water. There was no sign of a leak – only a slight weep at one place; but that would not have let in ten gallons in a month. Brent and I examined them carefully, and finally decided that the only possible entry was under the inspection plates screwed into the top of each compartment. Some of the screw threads were worn, and we decided that the plates must have lifted when the floats were submerged. Brent fitted larger screws and we thought the trouble was fixed. But it wasn't. The *real* trouble, which eluded all the technicians who handled and examined these floats in New Zealand and later, was that after the floats had been dropped on the deck of the cruiser the keels had been replaced with stainless steel; and electrolytic action (which no one thought about in those days) corroded away the rivets and some of the thin duralumin skin of the float. When the floats

Francis Chichester

At Cascade Landing,
Norfolk Island,
30th March, 1931

Launching
The Mme. Elijah
at Cascade Pier,
Norfolk Island

At low tide

The seaplane sunk
by the gale in the
lagoon at
Lord Howe Island

The author rigging the fuselage during the rebuilding

Growing a beard while at Silverstream before the Tasman Sea flight

were in the water, the thin sides were pressed away from the keel, and the water flowed in. As soon as they came out of the water, the water inside pushed the sides of the float against the keel and stopped the leak.

Martin's stepson made me a bilge pump by reversing the valve in a bicycle pump, and he made me a new anchor in a borrowed forge. Martin collected a mail of 140 letters for me to take to Lord Howe Island and Australia.

When all this was done I tried to take off. It was a perfect, cloudless day, but there was not the slightest breeze, and still a swell from the south-east. I tried runs away from the island and towards the swell, but it was useless. I jettisoned an hour's petrol, my rubber dinghy and everything else I could possibly do without, and then the bracing wire fitting snapped. Brent repaired it on board the seaplane. Time after time I tried to take off, each time handling the sea plane more harshly, and I was amazed that it stood up to the bashing. The bracing wire snapped again. I needed a completely new idea. I went ashore and strolled about thinking; suddenly an idea came – the seaplane must be structurally rigid without the fore and aft bracing wires; why not see if one of these would fit in place of the actual wire which had snapped? Brent returned with me to the seaplane, and the wire fitted. It was then too late to start for Lord Howe Island, so I went off with Martin for something to eat.

I considered the other bays of the island for trying to take off. The only possible one seemed to be Emily Bay, on the south coast. It had a horrible coral reef, but there was water between reef and shore, and I thought that if I could get a run along the strip of water without the floats being ripped open on the coral, I could get off. The worst feature was a bend in the strip of water at its narrowest place where I should have to change course while taking off, but it seemed my only hope, and I decided to have a shot at it. The question was how to get the seaplane in to Emily Bay. It was a long way to taxi round with the propeller chopping spray all the time. I considered taking it across in a lorry, but there were many objections to this. 'Why not fly her over?' suggested one of the boatmen. Everyone applauded, and I realized that unless the seaplane flew soon people would lose interest in helping me. Hardly anyone had seen the seaplane fly.

I unloaded all my gear and syphoned all the petrol out of the lower tanks, filling ten 4-gallon tins with it. Empty, the seaplane took off at last. She left the crest with one swell, hit the next and sprang off about forty feet in the air. She looked like settling down again, but gathered speed before the floats touched. I climbed to 3,000 feet and made for the lagoon at Emily Bay. I circled the lagoon, studying it, and the longer I looked the less I liked it. Dark blobs of coral sprinkled it from end to end. 'If I look much longer,' I thought, 'I shall get stage fright.' I swooped down and put the seaplane on the surface at high speed and planed fast through where I judged the narrow neck to lie. As I passed the neck I let out the breath I had been holding.

I anchored off the little sand beach in Emily Bay, and Brent and I worked on the seaplane until the evening. I sorted my gear and left behind everything possible, including the rubber boat. I hated doing this, but it weighed 27 lb. with the oars and pump. On my way back to Martin's I suddenly remembered that my nautical almanac, which gave the position of the sun for every hour of the day, ran out on March 31st and that tomorrow was April 1st. There was no other nautical almanac on the island. I had to have one, because I had to rely on sun observations for finding Lord Howe Island. I decided to make a new almanac myself. I needed the sun's declination and right ascension for every hour, so I took the readings for several days beforehand, noted how they changed, and assessed the values for the corresponding times of tomorrow. The cable station checked my watch against Greenwich Time, and I promised to transmit a message every hour of the flight if I could get off.

In the morning, on waking, I walked out into the starlight to study the weather. I knew that I could get off that stretch of water only against a fresh breeze, and it had to be blowing straight up and down. Against a starlit sky I could see the fringe of a tree-top swaying. For the first time since I arrived there was a fresh breeze of fifteen to twenty miles an hour blowing. I turned my head till it was blowing equally on each cheek –

it was south-easterly, almost dead up and down the stretch of water. It was marvellous.

I had to get to the opposite end of the lagoon from where the seaplane was anchored in Emily Bay. In such a breeze it would have been impossible to taxi slowly down wind through the channel, so Martin had a dinghy carried overland to Emily Bay, and two boatmen towed the seaplane to the neck in the lagoon, and then let it drift down wind. We reached the end of the reef, and there we moored to an anchor by passing the rope over a float boom. Brent sat in the rubber boat astern, and held the loose end of the mooring rope. Standing on the float, I swung the propeller and then nipped back into the cockpit. Looking over the cockpit edge I found myself staring into the excited face of a swimmer, half out of water and balanced with his hands on the end of the float. The propeller blades, invisible to him, were cutting past his face, and if he swayed forward an inch he would be killed. I stabbed my finger at him and shrieked. He slipped back into the water with a sheepish expression – I think because of my screaming at him in front of the people, and not because he realized his narrow escape. I felt weak with the shock of having nearly killed him. I pulled myself together, and opened the throttle wide and signed to Brent to let go the rope. The seaplane shot forward and gathered speed quickly. I pressed back in the cockpit, my head as high as possible, darting quick looks from side to side at the reef, to shore, and ahead. I was not aware of the seaplane, or its controls at all. At the narrow neck, about to shut off for having failed, I found to my surprise that I had left the water, and was a few feet above it. I had not enough height to turn properly to avoid a hillock in front, and slithered round in a horrible flat skidding turn. I flew back to the lagoon in a wide sweep. I deeply regretted my rubber dinghy. I could have carried it easily! It seemed terrible to face the distance ahead without it, in this battered, strained plane. But no! I had escaped with the seaplane in one piece, and nothing would induce me to return. I dived, and flew along the lagoon, saluting the crowd. Then I headed west.

The sun was behind my right shoulder and during the flight

I could expect it to move round over the right wing, to ahead. To fit in with this I changed course ten degrees to the right, which should take me 100 miles to the right of Lord Howe Island. This would increase the flight to 600 miles, but it was the only scheme which would find me the island. Using the slide rule and my home-made nautical almanac I calculated what the bearing and distance of the sun-point would be from the island about an hour before I was due to arrive, and then selected the turn-off point along my present line of flight which would have the same bearing and distance from the sun-point as the island at that time. This imaginary turn-off point was my first objective.

I looked back for a last sight of Norfolk Island but was surprised to find it already hidden in a purple haze, although only fifteen miles away. I used the same navigation system as on the flight to Norfolk Island, taking three drift readings every half-hour, and plotting them. Forty minutes out I slipped the wireless key under a band round my leg to send a message to the cable station. I found the battery current meter needle dancing about madly before I switched on; I assumed that vibration had short-circuited it somewhere, and that the set was useless. But I had no means of checking whether it was working or not, and as I had promised to transmit, I did so.

At the end of the first hour I found that the wind had backed to E by N, and given me a lift of twenty miles. It looked as if I was going to have an easy flight, and I had to fight against drowsiness. I made the calculations necessary to check the compass error as soon as the sun was abeam. This was important, because I had not had an opportunity of checking the compass on this heading, and an error of ten degrees would put the seaplane 100 miles off its course in a 600-mile flight. The method I used for checking the compass was this: I calculated when the sun would be nearly abeam, and worked out how far I would be from an imaginary sun-point if I was on my right track; then, when the time came, I would take a sextant shot at the sun to find out my actual distance from that point. The difference between the two distances would tell me how far I was off the right track.

It was difficult to work; the seaplane was hard to control and could not be trimmed to fly level. If I took my hands off the controls for a second, it would go into a steep dive, or climb immediately. Besides the nuisance of having to nag continuously at the controls, this meant there was something wrong with the rigging – perhaps a float had been knocked out of trim. The speed indicator on the strut outboard showed that the speed had dropped to seventy-two mph. That suggested that perhaps the propeller might be damaged – that, at least, would explain the terrific vibration. A few months ago I would not have flown the plane in this condition over the safest route in the world, but now I just had to go on.

Glancing to the south I noticed a small black cloud on the horizon and as I watched, it changed shape. It was no cloud, but smoke, and I decided that it must be the steamer *Makambo* on her monthly visit to Norfolk Island. I rocked the seaplane's wings in salute, as excited as if I had seen a ship after being in the water for three days. I seized the wireless key, and tapped out an exuberant message that I could see her; as I finished, she belched out a big smoke, which warmed my heart as a signal that they had heard me on board, or seen the plane. I could not see the ship, for she was below the horizon from me. When plotting my drift observations it occurred to me that the slow old *Makambo* would be steaming a direct course from Lord Howe Island to Norfolk Island. I could see from the chart that she must have been thirty miles away when I joyfully waggled my wings in salute – I might as well have been at the North Pole for all the chance they had of seeing me. It was curious how plain the smoke was, whereas the island had been out of sight at half the distance.

Holding my log-book in my left hand with the little finger crooked round the control-stick, and my other elbow touching the side of the fuselage, I found it impossible to write. This drove home to me that the vibration was not only severe, but dangerous. The whole fuselage was shaking, with a quick short period, and the rigging wires, which should be taut, were vibrating heavily. Why? It was not the motor, because the exhausts were firing with a steady, even bark. I decided that it

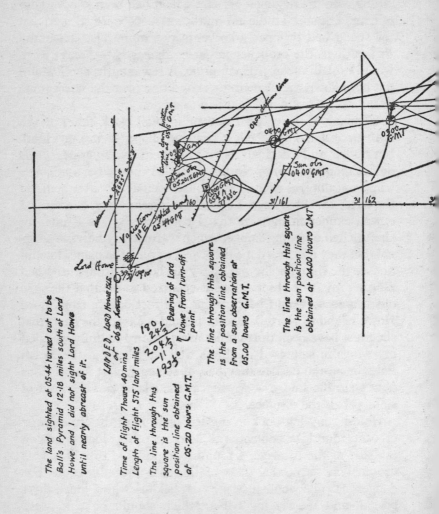

The land sighted at 05·44 turned out to be
Ball's Pyramid 12·18 miles south of Lord
Howe and I did not sight Lord Howe
until nearly abreast of it.

LANDED. LORD HOWE I5L5
at 06.30 hours

Time of flight 7 hours 40 mins
Length of Flight 575 land miles

The line through this
square is the sun
position line obtained
at 05.20 hours G.M.T.

180
24⅓
204⅓   Bearing of Lord
  1⅓   T Howe from turn-off
193⅔°   point

The line through this square
is the position line obtained
from a sun observation at
05.00 hours G.M.T.

The line through this square
is the sun position line
obtained at 04.00 hours GMT

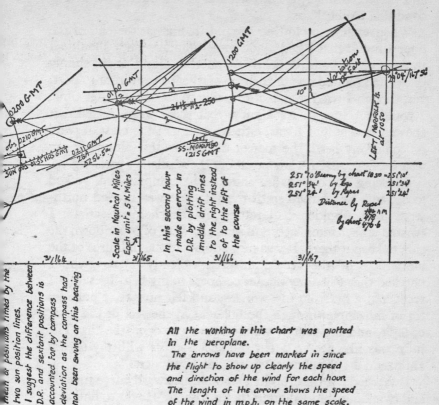

I suggest the difference between D.R. and sextant positions is accounted for by compass deviation as the compass had not been swung on this bearing

mean of positions timed by the two sun position lines.

Scale in Nautical Miles
Each unit = 5 N. Miles

In this second hour I made an error in D.R. by plotting middle drift lines to the right instead of to the left of the course

251°10' Bearing by chart 1850 = 251°10'
251° 34'   by Ezgo   251° 34'
251° 24.1' by Ropel   251° 24.1'
Distance by Ropel
                            478 n.m.
By chart 476.6

All the working in this chart was plotted in the aeroplane.

The arrows have been marked in since the flight to show up clearly the speed and direction of the wind for each hour. The length of the arrow shows the speed of the wind in m.p.h. on the same scale.

Round dots are positions arrived at by dead reckoning. Squares show positions arrived at by sun observation.

Francis Chichester
Pilot April 1st
1931

must be the propeller. I thanked heaven for a following wind and perfect weather; if the seaplane struck bumpy air in this condition God help us.

When I came to plotting three drift lines at the end of the hour I found that I had made some blunder. They should all three meet in a point, or nearly so, but they didn't. It was simply that I had plotted one of them to starboard instead of to port, yet, though I tried to detect this silly mistake time after time, I could not spot it. As I knew that there was a mistake, it showed how stupid I was, either because of the blast of wind on top of my head, the roar of the motor, the salt air, or my weariness, or perhaps anxiety about the seaplane's breaking up.

Glancing down, I had a shock. The compass had worked loose, and had turned until the seaplane was headed north-west. The vibration had rattled out the holding screws. I twisted it back into place, and rammed wads of paper down the side to keep it there. It was now subject to the full force of the vibration, and the needle shivered violently on its pivot. I checked that I had my pocket compass in my belt. Presently I recovered a bit from my worries, and felt hungry. I pulled a tin of pineapple through the hole cut in the seat of the front cockpit, and my mouth watered as I cut open the tin. The juice was like nectar. I cut the slices across with my sheath knife, and ate the chunks with a pair of dividers.

I watched the tin drop in a smooth backward curve turning and twinkling, and I plotted the third hour's flight to find that I had now flown 264 miles. When I needed to know the height to reduce the sextant reading accurately, I found that the needle of the dashboard altimeter was moving round the dial in endless jerks like a full-sized second hand on a clock. The vibration must have broken it. I felt despair – the wireless transmitter, the dashboard airspeed indicator, the compass seating, and now both altimeters broken. How long could the aircraft stand the strain?

As for that pig of an altimeter, it had always tried to fix me. This rage cheered me up a bit. To hell with it! I could judge the height above the water myself; I was getting pretty good at it now. I got three good sights.

During the fourth hour the wind backed about eighty degrees and was now almost a beam wind. At the end of the hour I was 337 miles on my way. I was nearly five hours out, and should reach the turn-off point six hours out. I had to get another sun observation at the end of this hour.

At five hours and ten minutes out I got three good shots of the sun. In computing this result it happened that I was using the bottom of the scale on one of the slide-rule cylinders, and I had to read it sideways, because there was not enough room to hold it in front of me in the cockpit. The result showed that I was twenty-six miles short of my dead reckoning position. The spectres of every mistake I had ever made rushed through my brain. Now I remembered that the strut speed indicator was over-reading by five miles an hour, which accounted for twenty-five miles in five hours. It had been stupid of me to forget it. So I had done only 391 miles, instead of 417. According to the sextant, I was 100 miles short of the turn-off point.

Looking ahead I could see dark grey rain-clouds squatting on the horizon – bad weather. That seemed more than I could bear. I felt empty of any courage. I tapped out a wireless message; although the transmitter might be useless, the routine act gave me support like an old friend. Before the end of the message I flew into stinging cold rain. There were still some gaps through which the sun shone, and I hurried through my drift observations and the plotting for the hour's flight. I glanced at the petrol gauge – three and a half hours left.

The plot showed that after six hours and ten minutes of flight I had made good 464 miles. I looked ahead for rays from the sun which I needed to check the distance flown for sure, but I could see none. I flew into a rain squall, and the heavy drops, striking my forehead, stung like hail. The squall only lasted about a mile, and on breaking through it I spotted a patch of wintry sunlight lying away to the right. I swung off course to the north and set off through spits of rain to chase the sun-patch. The seaplane was now plugging dead into wind, yet the sun-patch which had appeared close enough at the start seemed to keep its distance. Afraid of the gap's closing before I reached it, I opened the throttle, and sat tense waiting for an explosion from the propeller flying to bits, followed by a runaway roar from the motor. When this did not happen I gradually relaxed. The sun-patch did not seem any closer. Suddenly I realized why – on looking down I saw that the sun-patch was racing over the waves *against the wind* just as fast as the seaplane was flying. But I must have that sun. I pushed the throttle wide open. Several times I had a glimpse of the sun at the edge of the cloud, and at last I thought I was in position, and turned sharply to take the sight broadside on. But as I lifted the sextant, the shadows raced over the plane, and on again. Angry, I turned sharply, and set off again at full speed. Nothing else seemed to matter. I adjusted the sextant to what I estimated would be the right angle, and held it ready. I put the nose down, the speed rising until there was a shrill note in the rigging wires. I turned with a vertical bank, and got a single shot while still in the turn, pulling the seaplane out of its sideways dive just above the sea. The next moment I was in dull rain. I levelled off and flew on westwards. I was four and a half minutes late with my sun sight, but I made an allowance for the time difference, and compared the result with my pre-calculations for 5 PM. It put the position twenty-one miles short of the turn-off point.

What trust could I put in that last miserable sketchy sunshot? But there was no more sun. Fifteen minutes after the observation, I reckoned that I had reached the turn-off point. I turned, and headed SSW, changing course by nearly seventy degrees.

The clouds were steadily darkening and lowering. The seaplane was scudding over the rising, roughening sea, at a great pace, with the wind now nearly astern. A drift of fifteen degrees to port showed how the wind had increased. Fewer clouds were spilling rain, and that seemed an added threat. I stared at every dark, low-lying cloud on the horizon, each of which might be hiding the island, and I continually searched the stormy ceiling for a glimpse of the sun. At last I gave up hope of seeing the sun again. Immediately, as if it had been waiting for me to do that, it showed through a break in the clouds, dead ahead, and sun-rays slanted down. I opened the throttle and raced for it, leaning forward. I got three good sights while crossing the column of sunlight. I computed this observation entirely afresh, making heavy weather of it, my brain dopey with strain or fatigue. The result put the island dead ahead. I grasped the result slowly, and then my mood changed violently. I was puffed up with confidence and exultation. I closed the sextant and stowed it away with the other instruments. I looked at the sea, with the crests torn off in showers of spray. The drift had increased to twenty degrees – a forty-mile wind! With this rapid change in wind force, and the whole sky menacing, what was I running into? Six hours forty minutes. Where was the island? Had I, after all, miscalculated? I bitterly regretted my rubber boat.

Time seemed to go so slowly that I had to stare hard at the clock to convince myself that it had not stopped. All at once I got fed up with worrying, and I was stretching out my hand for something to eat when distinct, clean-cut land showed ahead and a few degrees to the left, a dagger of grey rock thrust through the surface. A hot flood of triumph and excitement swept through me. I could have smashed things with excitement. Then, good God! There was an enormous black bulk of land right alongside me. I stared astounded. It was little Lord Howe Island emerging from a dense squall cloud. It looked as big as Australia it was so close. What I had spotted was a rock off the south end of it.

I swung round and headed for the middle of the island. I recalled the warning of the Admiralty Sailing Directions that ships passing within a mile and a half of Lord Howe Island in a north-wester ran the risk of being dismasted by violent squalls of wind. I fastened the safety-belt, a weary effort. The island close up was quite different from my imaginary picture of it: it looked huge with two black trunks of mountains rising straight from the sea into a heavy roll of dark clouds. Above the lines of surf at the base were solidly packed palm-trees, and above them, almost sheer bare rock disappeared in the cloud. Only the lagoon was as I had pictured it, a stretch of bright colours, with patches of startling white sand on the bottom. I started circling to choose the best spot for alighting, but with a whizz the seaplane was suddenly hurled downwards at the lagoon. Cameras, sextant, protractors, pencils, chart, everything flurried round my head like a whirl of leaves. Only the safety-belt held me in the seat as I clutched frantically at the control-stick and instrument board. The seaplane fetched up with a bump that jarred me back into the seat. I dived straight down to the surface, taking only a glimpse at the water ahead for obstructions. The height of the waves showed me that there was depth enough, yet at the last moment I jibbed because I could see the lagoon bottom so clearly that I thought that there was no water there at all. The thought of another bump brought me to my senses in a fraction of a second, and I closed the throttle. The seaplane alighted like a duck, and at once began drifting astern at a great pace. I scrambled out of the cockpit and freed the anchor from the tangle of gear in the front cock-pit, heaved it overboard. The line wrenched at my arms and nearly tugged me overboard. I clung to the float strut with one hand with the line scouring through my other hand, until I could get a turn round the mooring ring. The anchor ripped and jerked along the lagoon bottom. The flight of 575 miles had taken me seven hours and forty minutes and I had one hour and forty minutes' petrol left.

I was relieved to see a launch coming. A second followed, and they began circling the plane. Men and women aboard stared as if a Dodo had arrived. I kept on bellowing, 'Where's the best place to moor?'; they kept on waving handerchiefs, pointing cameras and shouting things. There was one man I began to concentrate on; his voice was loud enough to be heard above the others; he was thickset and powerful looking, and did not get excited. It was agreed that I should moor in the boat pool, a deeper hole in the shallow lagoon, and I asked him to tow me there. 'Why not move across under power?' he asked. I explained that the seaplane would be blown over if I tried to taxi across that wind. He said nothing, but picked up my anchor line, and began towing aslant the wind. I was de-pressed and fearful of mooring out in this rough weather, but there was nothing else that I could do. I moored with a stout rope to two great anchors, and the launch took me ashore. As I arrived at a little wooden jetty, night had fallen. I had got in none too soon, though, curiously, I had never once during the flight been afraid of the risk of being caught by dark. P. J. Dignam, in charge of my petrol, was waiting for me. He asked me what time I left Norfolk Island and a string of other questions. I could not remember when I left Norfolk Island, and later I did not remember snapping at him, 'Don't ask so many questions!' which he declared I did. I had been hard at it since dawn and had seldom worked under greater mental strain. Dignam invited me to stay at his house.

I slept fitfully, waking to blasts of wind furiously flogging the tree-tops. At about 6 o'clock the most violent squall of all brought me wide awake; I expected the roof of the house to be stripped off. I lay in the dark for a while longer, and then got up to dress feeling as if my bones had been weary for a week. I went to call young Dignam, but found him already awake. I asked him to take me to the seaplane, and we moved off under a heavy grey sky before dawn. At the edge of the trees the stretch of water lay between us and the steep black hill.

'Isn't that where we moored the plane?' I asked him.

'Yes!'

'I don't see her,' I said. We walked on. 'Ah, there she is!' I said, but not yet certain. A little closer, I added, 'She looks queer to me.'

'She looks queer to me too,' said Dignam.

I could not make out why, but day was breaking fast. 'Sunk!' I said, though not yet believing it myself. At last we could see only too clearly; the tail of the seaplane was slanting above the surface, like a big fish diving into the water.

We dragged out a boat and rowed across. All the seaplane, except the tail and the float ends, was under water.

CHAPTER FOURTEEN

SALVAGE

THERE seemed nothing to do except to have breakfast. We went back to the house, and Mrs Dignam, whom everyone called 'Auntie', produced a delicious feast of salmon and kumeras (sweet potatoes).

'How is the seaplane, Captain?' she asked. 'Done for?'

'Completely, except for the floats,' I said, unable to decide which tasted better, the fish or the kumeras.

'Oh, dear, dear, dear! What a shame! And I did so want to see it rise from the water. Have some more fish, Captain?'

After breakfast young Dignam rallied a salvage party. I coaxed myself to turn out only by promising myself a week's sleep afterwards. Everyone else seemed keen, though, and three launches put off to the wreck. For the next hour or two I balanced precariously on the bottom of the fuselage, fixing rope to various bits of it. Sometimes I was waist deep in the water, while gusts of wind spat rain and spray into my face. The seaplane was now bumping upside down on the bottom, and I wanted to right it by pulling the tail over the nose. This seemed a simple thing to do, and I crawled up the bottom of the fuselage on hands and knees to secure a rope to the tail. But every time a pair of launches took the strain of the rope, the tail slewed round to one side or the other, and refused to come up. We paid out a long warp to the side of the hill to get a steadier pull on the tail, but still it refused to come up, and swivelled round in an exasperating way. In the end a stout rope broke with the pull, and it was a mystery how the seaplane could stand such a strain without breaking in half: the fuselage was only a three-ply skin, covering a slender frame of which the thickest piece was only an inch square of spruce. It was a miracle of engineering design.

We changed our tactics, and towed the seaplane by the tail, bumping and dragging it along the bottom, as far inshore as we could. We left it there, until we could get at it at low water. When we returned, it lay on greenish, slippery mud. The wings looked crushed and mangled. About thirty people, a quarter of the island's total population, were splashing through the shallow water round the seaplane. They included three handsomely-built girls in shorts, and all together formed the most amazingly efficient and enthusiastic salvage team. I had expected men who had never seen an aeroplane before to be bamboozled when asked to unscrew rigging-wire turn-buckles, or wing-root bolts, or to slack off control-cables, or airspeed indicator tubes. But it was the quickest and slickest salvage job I have ever conducted. One stream of people carried pieces to the shore, while another came back for more. The seaplane was dismantled in twenty minutes, and I was the only person who lost anything – some shackle-pins which I pocketed before realizing that there was a hole in my borrowed pair of shorts. We rolled the fuselage, stripped of its wings, on to its side, and then righted it, with the floats sitting on the mud. One party led this round the shore to the jetty, while the rest of us dumped all the bits and pieces in an old boat shed under a great old banyan tree. I went round to the jetty to dismantle the motor, thinking that parts of it ought to fetch something, if salvaged quickly before the salt water ate into the aluminium.

That night Phil Dignam asked me, 'What are you going to do about the plane, Skipper?'

'Salvage everything saleable, I suppose, and wait till the steamer calls.'

I had a feeling of resignation about the wreck which was suspiciously like relief, for the seaplane had not been in a fit state for the final hop to the mainland. Next morning I went up to the cargo shed, where two men named Kirby and Keith helped me to dismantle the motor. The zest with which they attacked the engine was astonishing. There were no motor-cars on the island, and the only tools were those for one or two roughish launch motors. We managed everything until we reached the crank-case. The propeller boss had to be drawn off the shaft before the crank-case could come away, and this required a special tool, which we lacked. Kirby walked off, and came back with a gadget he had made himself, of two iron strips and some long bolts. With this he drew off the propeller boss, and freed the crank-case. A gallon or two of Pacific Ocean ran out of the crank-case. I said, 'I vote we knock off now, and the rest can be left until tomorrow.'

'You ought to finish the job thoroughly now you've started it,' said Kirby. 'You ought to polish those valve seatings, and decarbonize the cylinder heads.'

'They won't hurt now if left for a few days,' I said.

'All right, then give them to me, and I'll do them.' He went off, carrying a sack full of pistons and valves. I went to buy some tobacco, irritated at being made to feel a slovenly workman. I could not buy any tobacco, because there would be no more until the steamer returned from Sydney in a month's time.

After starting off across the Tasman by aeroplane with such a flourish, the idea of creeping in to Sydney in a miserable steamer was humiliating. I felt that I would rather sail the rest of the way in a dinghy; it would not matter how long it took, or how I finished the passage, if only I could finish it as I had started – solo. In the middle of the night I was suddenly woken up by the thought, 'Why not rebuild the seaplane here?'

It seemed impossible, but in the morning, on my way to the cargo shed, I thought, 'Some people say that there is no such thing as an impossibility.' I started to inspect the relics afresh.

There had not been room in the shed for the fuselage, and it stood forlornly on the grass with the rudder occasionally flapping in the wind. It looked naked, stripped of its wings, motor and fittings. I went over it carefully. The plywood covering the fuselage was tacked and glued to the framework. This plywood was thin enough to break in your fingers, and the strength of the whole depended on the plywood's keeping the framework rigid. If salt water had destroyed the glue, the plane might as well be made of cardboard. As far as I could tell, by pricking it with the point of my knife, the glue was unweakened. Perhaps the careful varnishing and enamelling of the fuselage at Auckland had kept the water out of the wood. The plywood was somewhat cracked where I had climbed up it to the tail, but otherwise it seemed all right.

Then I turned to the fuselage itself. It was built like a latticed tower, and the four corner pieces, the longerons, were only inch-square lengths of spruce. These were all-important, because both the lower wings and all the float struts were secured to the bottom longerons, and as two of the middle fittings joining the float struts to them were torn in half, I feared that the frail wood must certainly be smashed. I climbed into the cockpit, and scraped away the silt. To my amazement I could find no sign of a break, though they were bruised – no doubt badly enough for an AID inspector to condemn them, but fortunately I would be acting for him on Lord Howe Island, and would be able to pass the longérons on his behalf. I decided that the fuselage would be used again, if every bolt, wire, fitting and tube were removed, cleaned of rust and salt and repainted.

Looking at the motor from a different viewpoint, I thought that we had got at it in time, and that it might be made to work again. That night I said to Phil Dignam, 'I believe I could make that seaplane fly again. It's a big job, and I should need some new gear.'

'What sort of gear?'

'I should need a new revolution indicator, an oil gauge, an airspeed indicator, a clock and the two magnetos. I should want four new wings and a pair of ailerons, and some new struts, bracing wires and fittings.'

'What about the money?'

'That is a hurdle; I haven't thought out that one yet.'

During the night I was woken up by an idea. Why not extract the spars from the broken wings, and send them to the mainland? The new wings could be built on to them and that should mean a big saving. It seemed a stupid idea, not worth waking up for, because the spars were sure to be fractured at the roots. But when I went up to the boat shed in the morning, I found every spar intact.

On the way back I met Kirby. He was about twenty-nine, my own age, and had been on the mainland for a time as a salesman. When I was selling land, I remembered that I could never sell to anyone with reddish hair. He asked me what I was going to do, and I told him I was going to try to rebuild the seaplane on the island, sending the spars to Sydney for the wings to be rebuilt there.

'Don't be feeble, man! Why not rebuild the wings yourself?' He had a rather throaty, slighty nasal voice.

'Hopeless,' I said. 'Obviously you can have no idea how intricate the inside of a wing is. There must be 4,000 different pieces of wood in those wings, a lot of them only half as thick as a pencil, and they all have to be tacked and glued in exactly the right place. There's the fabric covering to be sewn on, not to mention half a dozen coats of dope. There are no tools here, and no place to work in.' I walked off. The truth was that I myself knew nothing of wing building. Presently I was back in the boat shed, where I stripped each wing and re-examined it. I studied those wings for hours. Coming away I met another man, called Gower Wilson.

'What are you going to do with the plane?'

'Rebuild it here.'

'And get new wings, I suppose?'

'Oh, no. Rebuild the wings here, too.'

'Why, what do you know about wing construction? It looked to me pretty intricate, and besides there are no tools here, and there's no place to work in. It seems impossible to me.'

'Oh, that's nothing, I'll just watch how they come apart, and rebuild them the same way.'

'Well, I must congratulate you on the idea, at any rate.'

'It's not my idea, damn it, it's Kirby's.'

I set to work and made up a list of the material and replacements I should need. This made fourteen pages.

Then began a strange, but strangely happy period of my life. I stayed with the Dignams, and settled into life on the island, fishing, rat-hunting (a rat's tail earned a bounty of 3d.), and enjoying being a member of one of the friendliest communities I have ever met. As far as I could see the island was communistic in the Biblical rather than any political sense. Its income was derived from the sale of its produce, which was divided up equally. If anyone did extra work, the money he earned was deducted from his share of the community income. This island income was chiefly derived from selling palm seed of the Kentia palms growing there. The seed from these palms was the only kind that would germinate in cold countries. The island was owned by the New South Wales Government, which took orders for the seed, and instructed the islanders to ship the required number of bags of seed every time the steamer called. I began to find the island the most attractive spot imaginable. The islanders were happy, lovable people, the men interesting, and the girls charming, the island itself a paradise. The beach of white coral sand with the piled up line of sea debris marking high-water mark was a romantic spot in the white light of the full moon with the lagoon at hand. Sometimes at night the beauty would swell one's heart. The still air was pure, and strangely clear.

All the time I schemed about how to rebuild the seaplane. I had worked out my list of materials, and when the steamer came, sent it off to Sydney. I soon realized that unless I hurried, I should be caught by the gales and storms of late winter, and I gave up the idea of doing all the work myself. I found Roley Wilson, Gower Wilson's brother, and asked him if he would help me. Certainly. How much should I pay him? He would gladly do it for nothing. No, that would not be right; how much would he be paid if he was working for an islander? He replied, 'So much for ordinary work, and then again, so much more if working with a horse.' I said I thought that he should get as much for working with me as with a horse, and away he went. He was a great craftsman, a splendid fellow to work with. Roley started painting the floats. It was tricky work, because an arm inserted up to the shoulder completely filled a manhole, making it impossible to look into the float, so that the painting had to be done by touch. One morning he called to me, 'Hey, Chicko! Just look at the keel of this float! Someone has plugged the crack between the keel and the shell of the float with putty. I can dig it out with my knife.'

We thought this was a queer thing for anyone to do, but Roley picked out this putty as well as he could, and painted the seam with extra care to make sure of its being watertight. It was years before I found out that this 'putty' was simply the duralumin shell eaten away by electrolytic action. To think that I had before my eyes the source of such great trouble, and that I did not realize it!

The *Makambo* returned from Sydney with materials for me, and we began rebuilding the wings. Often I feared that I had taken on too much. Studying a blueprint sent by the Sydney branch of de Havillands, I read that each bay of the wing must be trammelled to fifteen-hundredths of an inch.

'Roley, what is a trammel?'

'Trammel?' said Roley. 'Isn't that what a bishop carries when preaching in a cathedral?'

'I think we shall get into an unholy mess with this blueprint. I think we had better keep one wing intact until we have rebuilt its mate.'

'That's just what I think, too,' said Roley.

Apart from the riblets of the leading edges and trailing edges, there were ten ribs for each of the four wings. Each of these was made of twenty-one pieces of spruce, no thicker than cardboard. Every piece must be in its right place, glued and tacked there, and the rib must fit tightly to the spars. We plugged away, and slowly the job yielded us its secrets. We acquired skill, and at the end of a week's work we knew something about building an aeroplane. We could plug and glue old screw holes, cut, glue and tack pieces of rib together; fit trailing edges; clean, screw, measure, saw, shave and shape like a pair of old factory hands. Each wing had two main spars, with a metal strut inside the wing between the two spars. It was a surprise to find each of these struts inside the wing full of sea water, although five weeks had already elapsed since the seaplane was wrecked. We finished the woodwork of the first wing and it looked pretty good to me. We painted it all over, every corner, stick and cranny, with waterproof Lionoil. Secondly, it must have a coat of dope-resisting paint, to prevent the cover from sticking to each rib. I had forty gallons of paint, but could not find this one. It was on the invoice so must be there. There was one tin not on the invoice; it was labelled 'Thinners'. So we slapped on a coat of thinners before laying the light brown linen fabric 14 ft by 10 ft on the frame. Should the cover be sewn on tight, or loose? Roley and I disagreed. 'If sewn on tight at the start,' I said, 'the dope would shrink it tighter, and would split it in half.' 'No, sew it on tight,' said Roley. By nightfall we still had not agreed, so we left it draped over the wing skeleton. Next morning I said, 'You know, Roley, you were right, sew it on tight.' 'That's funny,' he said, 'I was just thinking that you were right, and that it ought to go on loose.'

We split the difference, and next day Minnie offered to do

the sewing. She was a generous, warm-hearted creature who helped Auntie once a week, singing away at her work from morning till night. She was like a tall radiant sunflower that looks happily and generously at all comers until a slight touch contrary to its fancy makes it curl up its petals, angry or hurt. With next day's sun she joyfully uncurls them all again. Minnie sewed away in great style, until she came to a corner where I said the fabric must be turned in and sewn with just so many lock-stitches to the inch. Now Minnie was an expert, the island's wizard at converting chiffon, ninon, voile, georgette or what have you to the latest fashion. The fabric, she said, must be sewn with so-and-so stitches to the inch.

'But, Minnie,' I pleaded, while Roley, I could see in the corner of my eye, was barely suppressing his mirth, 'naturally so many lock-stitches would not be needed for a skirt.'

But no, my way was wrong, the stitch was wrong, the number of stitches was wrong. At last I said, 'Well, I've got to fly the thing, why not let me have it the way I want, even if it is the wrong way?'

'Now you've done it,' said Roley as she stalked off. However, with next day's sun she was as cheery as ever. Our tiff of yesterday was quite forgotten – but so was the sewing.

The curved surgical needles remained stuck in the fabric. I began to think I must have been posted as an impossible boss, and that we should have to do all the sewing ourselves, when Eileen, surprised to hear that we had no seamstress, enrolled on the spot. She was Gower's eldest daughter and what a jewel! She often suggested an improvement to de Havilland's written instructions, and it always turned out to be an improvement. There was a lot of sewing; there was 92 ft of it just around the edges of the wing, and tape had to be sewn over the top and bottom of the forty ribs, each $4\frac{1}{2}$ ft long, with a lock-stitch every 3 inches. During the night, after Eileen had finished sewing the first wing, I suddenly woke up to realize – to be told from within, I would say – that I had forgotten to lock the bracing wires inside the wing bay. Poor Eileen had to take the fabric half off again.

One morning Roley took me aside. 'Look here, Chicko,'

he said, 'I know another girl who would help with the sewing.'

'Who's that?'

'Ah, ha!' said he. I thought, 'So that's how the wind lies,' but I asked no more questions and he brought her along. Now there were four of us in our island plane factory, and the sheer pleasure of craftsmanship, of using hand and eye, was a revelation to me. It was hard but interesting work, that made one's appetite keen for everything. How craftsmen and artisans are to be envied.

We were ready to start doping, and life became more strenuous because of the hours I spent thinking at the end of the day's work. With no previous experience, I had to plan every operation in advance. I knew nothing about doping, and it would be serious if I spoiled a fabric wing cover. The wings had to have three coats of red dope, followed by five coats of aluminium dope. Besides a right way to dope and a right consistency of dope to use, the temperature must be 70° F. while the dope was put on. Did that mean it must be 70° all the time while the dope was drying? With winter approaching, it did not often reach 70°, even at midday with the doors closed. In the morning we would watch the thermometers: one read 4° higher than the other, and we promptly discarded the one with the lower reading. As soon as the thermometer reached 70°, coats, brushes, and dope began to fly in all directions.

The first wing was not a complete success. One panel, especially, was so baggy that I tried to take a tuck in the slack of it, doping another piece of fabric over the scar. The wing had a gaunt look, like a half starved mongrel with its ribs showing. Something had gone wrong.

A wireless message from Sydney solved the puzzle; the dope-resisting paint had been omitted. The fabric had stuck to every rib, instead of drawing tight over the whole wing like a drum skin. It was a relief to know that the mistake was not more serious, and as the fabric could not be taken off once it had been doped, we went ahead and finished it, making the best job we could. What arguments we had about doping that wing! Everybody helped – Frank, whose idea was to slap it on good and hearty, with the biggest brush he could find; Charlie Retmock who made me think of 'Gert' Jan Ridd in *Lorna Doone*, and who painted steadily and ponderously, as if the wing were a barn door; young Stan, the postmaster and Minnie's brother, who dashed it on with furious abandon and energy; young Tom, the island buck, who used small strokes with a flourish and who did not exceed the speed limit, even when no island damsel was framed in the doorway (it was queer how often one happened to pop in just when Tom *was* there). They had different views on how to dope, but they were all agreed on one point, that I was a poor hand at it.

'Here!' cried Frank, pointing to a rib I had taped the day before, 'you can't do that sort of work here, you know!'

'No, I say, Chicko,' Roley added, 'you can't go to Sydney and have them think that that is the sort of work we do at Lord Howe Island.'

'We wouldn't mind,' said Frank, 'if they knew that it was your work; but of course, after one look at you, they are bound to realize we have done all the important work on the plane.'

Frank had offered to do all the doping for me. He didn't want any pay, he said, but would like my old altimeter. I told him that it had never worked when I needed it, even before its bathe in the sea; but that seemed to make him keener to have it; perhaps he thought it would be a suitable alarm clock for him.

The doping was not the short job we had expected. We seldom had two hours in the morning or afternoon warm enough for it, and as we had to give each coat several hours to dry, we were lucky if we could give a wing one coat in a day. One morning a retired Australian architect called Giles visited our 'factory'. He was about seventy, tall and handsome with a short white beard. 'I should like to know why a young man like you wants to grow a beard,' he said.

I said, 'Growing a beard is like undertaking a flight. First you have the idea which you dare not reveal to a soul. You feel that there will be wide open spaces you cannot cover. If it fails, have you the courage to face the condescending pity which people have for failures? If it succeeds, have you the endurance to be pleasant to everyone who asks why you did it?'

'Well, anyway,' grunted Mr Giles, 'I don't agree with half the funny things people say about it.'

The *Makambo* was due to call again a few days later on her way to Sydney, so I thought that I had better put the motor together before she arrived. I went down to Kirby's to ask about the cylinder heads. 'Oh,' he said, 'the valves must first be thoroughly ground and the cylinders thoroughly cleaned. When I do a thing I like to do it properly.'

'Don't you think I ought to put the engine together again before the boat returns?' I said. 'It's not much good cleaning the cylinder heads until they shine only to discover after the *Makambo* has left that a new one is required. How about just a little grinding of the valves? After all they were perfect when I left Norfolk Island.'

He washed his hands of a job unless it was done properly, so I set to work grinding them myself at his bench. It was a job I disliked intensely.

Putting the engine together again was simple enough in one way. All the tinfuls of nuts, bolts, washers, screws and parts must be used up. If anything was left over, I nosed round the engine until a place was found for it. In the end, the engine seemed perfectly all right, except that it would not go. There was no spark in either magneto, so I packed them off to Australia on the *Makambo*.

We could not cover any more wings until the *Makambo* returned with the dope-resisting paint. Roley and I carried on rebuilding the wing and aileron frame. We finished the second wing in three days, the third and fourth in two days each. The steamer was soon back, and life became still more arduous. Repairing, covering and doping all went on at the same time. We were always jostling for room, though the islanders had lent me the only shed large enough to hold a spread wing, the seed-packing shed. There was only room there to work on one wing, and room in the cargo shed for the wing being covered.

I had been going about barefoot, but I gave it up because the sand had grown cold. It was the edge of winter, with the days shortening and rain squalls more frequent. As the warmth went out of the sunlight, the glow of my island life cooled. I had to think day and night. It was not a question of making as few mistakes as possible; I mustn't make any mistakes. All the time I felt the urgency of hurry; the stormy Westerlies were setting in, and they lessened the chance of obtaining a run of fine days necessary for assembling and launching the seaplane. Once the wings were attached to the fuselage they must stay out at the mercy of the weather, for there was no room to take them back under cover. Once the seaplane was on the lagoon, it must stay there until it left the island.

CHAPTER FIFTEEN

FRESH START

THE magnetos had returned with the dope-resisting paint, and one morning I set about fixing and timing them. I had not had much to do with motors, and this was another chore which scared me beforehand. However, after I had locked the doors, and, sitting on a petrol-case, had mastered the principles of the operation, it turned out to be easy. It was only a matter of marrying a cog wheel on the magneto to a cog wheel on the engine, so that a spark was produced when the piston was in a certain position. Then came the fun – we had to test the motor. I went off to find Ted Austic, the island's star cricketer. I had no trouble in coaxing him away from his task of building himself a house, and he sauntered along with a peaked cap on the back of his head and a vast curl in front overhanging his forehead. Hammering long spikes into lengths of wood he made a horse, a frame for the engine as used for sawing wood. I climbed up with a gallon tin of petrol, and balanced it on a rafter of the cargo shed. This represented the petrol tank in the top wing of the seaplane. A long rubber tube led the petrol from the tin on the rafter down to the carburettor. The engine horse stood on the edge of the pit inside the cargo shed, so that the revolving propeller should not strike the floor. I laid an earth-wire from each magneto to the metal of a screw-driver, and gave Roley the screwdriver to hold, and told him to earth the current if the pace grew too hot. 'Now listen, Chicko,' he said, 'are you sure this is all right? Everyone seems to have urgent business somewhere else suddenly.'

'If I yell "earth!" bang those screwdrivers down as if your life depended on it,' I said.

I pulled over the propeller with a distinct respect. At each fresh swing without the least sign of life, the less I liked it. It might catch on fire, or it might fly to pieces, it might explode. Suddenly, with a crackling roar, it started at full throttle! 'Earth!' I yelled, and jumped for the back of the stand. What-ever Roley did, it had no effect. The engine roared with enough pull to fly a plane at 90 mph. The wooden stand jumped and danced madly on the edge of the pit. 'Hang on, Roley!' I shouted. 'Hang on!', and one of us on each side of the engine, feet jammed against a niche in the concrete at the edge of the pit, leaning right back, we began a tug o' war with it. The roar reverberated from the roof, the blast tore at the roots of our hair, and the shed was full of whirling papers. The stand teetered and stuttered on the edge of the pit until I snatched the pipe off the carburettor, the petrol ran out of it, and the engine died.

After the engine had had its run, the compression was good, greatly to my relief. There had been none beforehand, and I was afraid that Kirby had been right saying that I had not ground the valves thoroughly. When I imparted the glad tidings to him, he turned up next morning and offered to help me again. I gratefully accepted. All the morning he worked away in the cargo shed, while Roley and I were in the other one. When we returned we found he had discovered the one thing on the fuselage that I had not dismantled. This was a down pipe, to lead away waste oil from the engine. It had no mechanical value. Kirby had spotted a dent in it, and had taken it off to straighten out the dent. He pointed out to me that a job should be done properly. When the dent was straightened out the part could not be replaced, because of the trestle supporting the fuselage. It had to be left till later, when the engine was lifted by block and tackle to a rafter for dropping back into position in the fuselage, which was then moved out of the shed and fixed on to the float chassis. Now both the fuselage and the float struts were in the way of that pipe. I lost more knuckle skin over it than over the rest of the seaplane, and it was only by replacing the dent as before that I finally got the pipe back at all.

Kirby also spotted the old lock-washers still on the propeller shaft's collar-bolts. 'Look here, Chick,' he said. 'You ought not to use those old washers! Surely you ordered new ones!' I had made up my mind to secure those collar-bolts myself, with the idea that if a wrongly done job meant a watery entrance to the next world, I should have the consolation that it was my own fault. But not wanting to hurt Kirby's feelings I said I had no other washers. I reckoned without his new determination to help me. He proceeded to screw home every nut on to an old washer, and I had to watch the whole operation, conscious of Roley's laughing with his back turned, and of the new washers weighing down my pocket like lead.

Roley and I decided that it was not fair to associate Kirby with our slipshod work, and asked him to undertake the sign-writing, of painting the registration letters ZK-AKK in 3-foot letters on the top and bottom of the wings. He could do the job in his own way, and be as efficient as he wished. He said, 'Certainly,' and took away our dope trestles and used the whole packing-shed to begin setting out the letters on the first wing. Roley and I were forced to abandon our doping, and went off to look for a job in the cargo shed until Kirby had finished. He made a thorough job of it, and afterwards Roley and I nearly succeeded in taking out the dents made by his elbows in the wing surface.

Often it seemed that we should never finish but at last the time came when we had rebuilt four wings and two ailerons, painted them first with oil, and then with dope-resisting paint, taped and covered them, doped serrated tape along the line of the ribs, applied seven coats of dope to the surfaces, fitted the automatic slots and replaced the fixtures and fittings, struts, rigging wires and aileron controls. At last the overhauled motor was back in place, the fuselage beautifully enamelled

171

inside and out, the floats carefully painted, ninety-six new screw threads through the manhole rims, the wings loosely assembled in pairs ready to fix to the fuselage, the bent float boom repaired, and the bruised longerons strengthened with steel fish plates.

The Gipsy Moth was ready at last for rigging again, and the ground outside the cargo shed had become an island meeting-place. Some volunteers carried the float undercarriage out, others carried out the fuselage with the engine attached, tediously secured by thirty-six bolts and twelve bracing wires to the float undercarriage. I sighed with relief when after an hour and a half we had the fuselage level and ready for rigging. The trouble we had had to get the seaplane level was explained when I happened to turn the spirit-level end for end. The bubble rushed to one end of it; the instrument itself was not level and I could not find an accurate level on the island. Now I was face to face with rigging. I had watched in awed silence a rigger performing this mystic ritual and I studied the book. The wings must be dihedrally rigged, three and a half degrees upwards, and this angle must be corrected to one sixth of a degree, measured with a variable inclinometer. In other words the wings must be cocked up.

'Roley,' I said. 'You will have to make an inclinometer.'

'All right,' he said, 'if you can draw one, I can make one.'

I marked an angle of three and a half degrees on a piece of wood 3 feet long, which Roley took home and planed until it was a long thin wedge. It was so accurately made that I could not find it the slightest degree out of true anywhere. We laid this along the wing spar with the rather dubious level on top of it, and cocked up the wing by adjusting the rigging screws until the bubble was at least in the centre of the level.

The leading edge of each wing had to be higher than the trailing edge, so that the wing made an angle of three and a half degrees with the horizontal fore and aft. After that we had to rig for 'stagger' – the upper wings had to be $3\frac{1}{2}$ inches ahead of the lower wings. At the end, it all appeared to have been so simple that I started looking round for something I felt sure must have been forgotten. No, by lunchtime next day the seaplane was finished. I thought she looked handsome, superb with her white enamelled body and floats, her bright aluminium wings with Kirby's jet-black lettering. My pride went flat on finding a large bolt in the cargo shed which had obviously been left out from somewhere. We ferreted round the seaplane but could not find any place lacking a bolt. In the middle of the night I was woken up with the solution; there had been a duplicate rudder bar in the front cockpit, so that the seaplane could be flown from there if necessary. I had dismantled this, because it would never be needed, and the bolt had come from there. The Gipsy Moth was in perfect order.

She was ready for launching, but I could not think how to launch her safely. There was a 6-foot drop from the edge of the bank down to the sand. There was not enough room to pass the seaplane between the bank and the side of the sheds to reach a steep wooden boat-launching slip in front of the sheds. I was scratching my head, when Gower passed. 'How much does it weigh?' he asked.

'Half a ton.'

'Why not carry it, then?'

'Gower, will you launch it for me?'

'My way might not be your way.'

'You can do it entirely your own way. I'll not interfere at all.'

'The boys might think . . .'

'I'll ask you in front of everybody to do the job for me.'

So Gower took it on. Under the floats he placed four beams, manned by four men each. He walked backwards in front of them, conducting them with a baton like an orchestra. He passed between the barbed-wire fence on the edge of the bank and the side of the shed, he had them drop the wings on one side till nearly touching the beach and hold the other wings high over the shed roof while the bearers shuffled along. It was a great strain for those on the beach side, and I followed behind, biting my thumbs. All the bearers held on, and finally dumped the seaplane in the water. Everyone cheered – it was a fine piece of work. I am sad to say that Gower, who was himself so amazingly efficient, was drowned some years later in a yacht which went down sailing from the island to Australia.

I went aboard at once for a trial flight, thinking that if I waited I should get nerves, imagining all the things which could be wrong with the seaplane. I taxied well out, faced into wind and opened the throttle. The seaplane left the water as easily as a fairy dancing off. There was a splutter, the engine choked, picked up again, spluttered for a few seconds, choked again, coughed out a few backfires, and then stopped dead. I closed the throttle to prevent the engine from bursting into life again unexpectedly, and concentrated on alighting. Fortunately I was still over the lagoon, and it was easy enough.

I anchored off the jetty, and, standing on a float, I tried not to drop any tools into the lagoon as I removed the carburettor. The jet was blocked by a small piece of skin. I had cleaned the salt water from the carburettor and then wiped it with a rag soaked in linseed oil to prevent further corrosion. This oil had dried in a thin skin, which the petrol had peeled off. There were enough pieces to choke the jet fifty times. 'Awkward for you if you had not found that until half-way to Australia,' said Gower. We cleaned every part as thoroughly as possible, but there were bends and passages into which one could not see. Gower said, 'I wonder if you have left one piece behind.'

Again the Gipsy Moth danced off the surface with thrilling ease. I flew low over the lagoon, first waggling the wings a little, and then more and more, until the plane was rocking from one wing tip to the other. Now I began hurdling. I put her through her paces, increasing the strain steadily. She had never been more fit, I thought. Then I jumped her up 200 feet, and trimmed the elevators for hands-off flying. I left the stick alone – she flew dead level. The rigging by our island plane factory was perfect first shot.

The least I could do was to offer my helpers a flight. I sent the boat for Auntie; she sent back word, 'Oh, she didn't think she would come.' The third time I sent the boat for her she turned up, groaning and sighing. 'Oh, Captin, do you think it's all right? Oh, Captin, are you sure I won't die?' During the flight she scarcely moved an inch. When we were back on the water she turned and said in a quiet voice, 'Oh Captin, that was a wonderful thing! And to think I should have missed it if you hadn't made me go up!'

Minnie arrived, full of chatter and giggles. Eileen was intent and quiet, as if unwilling to waste the enjoyment of one second. Gower told me exactly what type of windscreen would improve the excessive blast in the front cockpit, and had I seen the big school of bluies at the mouth of North Passage?

Frank surprised me most. Poor slow old Frank, I thought, will realize we have left the water just about when we settle on it again. To my surprise, we were barely in the air, when he coolly picked out his house half hidden by trees, and signalled me to fly there and circle it while he waved to his wife. Suddenly he gripped the cockpit edge and stared down. Curious to know why, I banked steeply. He was looking at his small garden. A horse, two calves, a lot of hens and ducks were steeplechasing through it. I tapped Frank on the shoulder and laughed, at which he shook his fist at me.

Next morning, with a stiff sou'east breeze in a lopping sea, I was still taking up passengers, but becoming more uneasy and peevish every trip. I must be flying badly, I thought, as the seaplane swerved to the right on alighting, and nearly capsized. I seemed to take longer to leave the water each time. I stopped flying to pump the bilges dry with my new specially made bilge pump, but there was scarcely any water in them. When Roley said to me, 'You know, Chicko, I can see water trickling off the bottom as you fly low over the shed; you must have water in the starboard float,' I pooh-poohed the idea. I had only just pumped all the bilges dry. The truth was that the fixed metal bilge pipe which led to the bottom of the compartment with the big leak had buckled and cracked when the float was dropped on the deck of the cruiser. When the bilge pump was attached to this pipe, it sucked air through the crack at the top, although the float compartment was full of water.

I spent the afternoon in a feverish rush, stowing my gear, fuelling, collecting mail, and making myself a fresh chart for a direct flight to Sydney. I had made what now seems a crazy decision to fly direct to Sydney, 483 miles across water, whereas by increasing the flight by eighty miles I could have flown to Macquarie, the nearest place on the mainland, thereby cutting down the flight over water to 365 miles.

Just before midnight I went for my last run along the beach. I used to enjoy my two-mile barefooted sprint every night before turning in. Often, when the moon made the stars pale in a clear sky, I yearned to be up there flying again. It was the yearning which a frustrated airman will pay any price to satisfy – health, life, fortune. But that night I felt sad. My stay on the island was nearing its end. It had been the happiest nine weeks of my life, perhaps because I knew it was a crazy, dangerous flight which I had to face, the most foolhardy I had ever attempted; to fly across 483 miles of ocean, with a seaplane and engine which had spent a night bumping on the bottom of the sea. I dreaded the idea of the flight.

On waking in the morning I was surprised to find that I had slept all night without a stir or a dream. I felt that I was in the hands of fate, and that nothing I could do would affect the issue. But that was absurd; success would depend solely on my own efforts, on my flying, navigating, reasoning, and on my efforts in rebuilding the seaplane. I went outside, and looked at the pale flawless dawn above the edge of palm tops. My heart ached at the thought of all the wonderful things on the island, the charm of its simple, healthy life, Auntie's calm outlook, and her cooking, those grilled bluie fish which melted in one's mouth when dipped in butter with a dash of salt and pepper. Padding along the sandy pathway, the palm crests were silhouetted against the pale-blue sky. There was something young and tenderly virginal about the still air in the wood. Heavens! What a paradise. I overtook Charlie Innes, pushing a fixed-wheel bicycle. I borrowed it and had a mad ride, twisting and turning and doing tight figures of eight round the trees. I went down a hill at full pelt, and banked steeply to slow up, because the bicycle had no brakes. I turned a complete circle, and finished up in front of the boat shed, where the waiting people looked strangely at me. I did not care; I had squeezed a little more fun out of life.

Gower drew the dinghy under the propeller, and I broke the bottle of brandy on the propeller-boss. I had ordered the bottle from Australia with the materials. The mooring-bridle was cast off, the engine started and I was in the cockpit.

There was no dashboard clock; I should miss that. And the various tables used for reducing sun-sights had all been soaked off the side of the cockpit; I should miss those too. There was no wireless transmitter, but I had a pair of homing pigeons in a basket which Frank's uncle had given me.

A breeze was blowing away from the island to the reef, so I tried to taxi down wind to the reef. To my surprise I could not turn the sea plane. The stiff south-easterly blowing had a strong 'weathercocking' effect, but surely not enough to prevent a turn down wind. She would make a half turn, until broadside on, and stubbornly refuse to turn down wind. When I tried full throttle the leeward wing dipped into the sea, and threatened to capsize the seaplane. At each engine burst the new propeller cut into heavy spray. I gave up trying to turn, and set off across wind down the lagoon until in the end I reached the reef down by Goat Island. I swung into wind and opened up. As the seaplane gathered speed I felt her slew hard to starboard, and begin to trip over the float. Instantly, I throttled back. Would she recover without overturning? She settled back. But it had been a near go.

It is hard to understand why I did not realize that the starboard float was nearly full of water, and that a few more gallons would have sunk it. The fact that I had pumped all the float compartments dry, as I thought, had bemused my power to perceive this. It is amazing that the seaplane did not capsize while turning, and theoretically it was impossible to take off. I restarted the engine, headed into wind and tried once more. The seaplane ploughed through the water, throwing up a deluge of spray, but soddenly refused to leave the surface. I throttled back, and tried to turn down wind, but it was hopeless. Every time I loosed the full blast of the slipstream on to the rudder to swing the tail round, the off wing tipped into the surface, and the seaplane began to capsize. Drifting back was the only alternative. I was mildly surprised that she drifted so slowly with the wind driving her back. What did it matter? How crude was this struggle with all the superb beauty of nature around? I sat on the leading edge of a wing root, one arm on a bracing wire, and sat absorbed in the exquisite beauty of the sparkle and dazzle of the wavelets tossing their crests in little showers of spray. A piece of coral would appear at my feet, and I would slowly lift my eyes to follow the inricate clump of dark brown and purple while it receded, growing less distinct until it disappeared for good as I thought, only to be reflected again in distorted form by a wave surface.

The pounding roar of surf broke into my trance. The seaplane was nearly on the reef, where the surf breakers thundered on the coral, charging it in lines of seething white. I slipped off my seat and swung the propeller, then clambered back into the cockpit. The seaplane thrashed its way across the lagoon, and I feared for the engine running so long at full throttle under strain. The beach loomed ahead, and I switched off. The beach was spotlessly clean, washed yellow below high-water mark, bleached white by the sun above. The two mountains had doffed their heads of cloud; that must be an omen that I should leave, for they nearly always brooded in cloud.

I reached up and opened the top tank cock. The wind blew the stream of petrol, and it pattered on the taut wing surface. I also began syphoning petrol from the back tank to lessen the load. I saw one of the luscious island oranges under the cockpit seat, fished it out, and let it drop into the sea from my finger and thumb. Another? No, no, not food yet! But I jettisoned thirty-five pounds' weight of petrol, which left me nine hours' fuel. I sat on the cockpit edge, legs dangling over the water, watching the breakers appear larger as the seaplane drifted to the reef. This time I tried rocking the seaplane on to her bow waves, at each rock mounting a little higher, as I could tell by the lessened drag. I jumped her off the water, but it was no good, back she sank again. I determined to go on dumping gear and petrol until the plane did leave. I opened the cock again. Gower and Roley, who had been chasing me in a dinghy from one side of the lagoon to the other, at last caught me up. Gower stepped aboard, and suggested that I leave my kit of spare parts behind. I agreed reluctantly. After disturbing the tightly packed cockpit, there was some trouble in restowing the pigeon hutch. I let Gower do it; he was there, and after all, I felt indolent. I had only eight hours' fuel left, which would not be enough if I met an adverse wind.

I changed my tactics, keeping the seaplane down until she had long outrun the distance usually sufficient. Off? Yes! No, touched again. I held her down for another cable's length. Now, back with the stick. Would she hold off? Yes – no – yes. She was off. It had been a horrible take-off, but I determined to stay up. The seaplane had no flying speed, and I had little control over it; it was quite unresponsive. Slowly it righted, and lurched heavily. I pushed the stick hard over, and it righted to an even keel. Suddenly the port wing was struck down by an air bump, and the seaplane seemed to collapse on its side. I struck the control-stick hard over. It had no bite, and the ailerons flopped. The seaplane continued its slither to the sea. 'That's the finish of it!' I thought. My anxiety ceased and I felt resigned. Then the wings seemed to cushion on a layer of air a few inches from the water, and the seaplane slowly righted. Only the slots hanging out like tongues of dead-beat dogs gave me the least control. The wall of palms ahead blocked my path, and it was impossible to turn right or left. The only chance was to keep down in the thicker surface air to gain enough speed to jump the palms. They rushed at me. Every nerve rebelled, urging me to rise now. But too soon meant certain destruction. At the last moment I jumped the seaplane as high as possible. I knew that the jump would lose me all the flying speed gained, and I knew that the seaplane must drop after the jump. Could it get flying speed before striking the trees? The foliage came up at me, but suddenly a strong gust of wind reached the plane. I could see its blast spread on the tree-tops; it gave the wings lift, and the controls grip. It saved us.

Then I had the saddle to mount. I dared not turn. The slots were still out, and the seaplane laboured heavily up the slope. I thought that the engine must be defective, but a glance at the revolution indicator showed it reading 1,800. (The uncontrollability must have been partly due to the rush of water in the float as the seaplane changed tilt.) But once over the saddle the downwash of air helped; the slots quavered, then shut. I had control at last.

CHAPTER SIXTEEN

RETURN TO AUSTRALIA

IT was 9.30 AM local time. I could not get back to salute the people on the jetty – I just felt burnt out. A stiff breeze chased the seaplane along, and the sea glittered in the sunlight coming from behind my right shoulder. The sun seemed too far north for so early in the day: was my compass wrong? I uncased the slide rule, and computed the sun's true bearing. Of course, I had forgotten that it was nearly mid-winter, and the sun at its farthest north; the compass was all right. As the tailwind was drifting the seaplane slightly off course to the north, I changed direction ten degrees to the south. Observing for drift was an irksome fatigue; I wanted only to sit and muse. It seemed to me that with Australia presenting a face nearly 2,000 miles long it did not much matter whether I made a bull's-eye of Sydney or not. My wits were certainly bemused, otherwise I would have realized that this Australian coastline had a receding chin, and that every degree I flew south of the course rapidly increased the distance to land which might soon become greater than my range, whereas every degree north of the course would have shortened the flight over the sea.

Fifty-five minutes out, the mountains were still visible 100 miles astern, like two tiny warts on the face of the ocean. It seemed perfect weather, with a tailwind of forty mph I was nearly a quarter of the way across in one hour. But the wind had backed, and I was ten miles off course to the south as a result. At 160 miles out I had a shock: the engine backfired with a report loud above the roar – a thing it had never done before in full flight. Was there another piece of skin in the carburettor? I sat utterly still, waiting for the final splutter and choke. The engine continued firing. I reached up and tried the starboard magneto; it was all right. I tried the port, and the engine dropped fifty revs, firing roughly and harshly. A defective magneto – the only parts I had not repaired myself!

The engine ran harshly for two minutes while I listened intently, then suddenly it broke into an even smooth roar again. Thank God it was not the carburettor! And I did have two magnetos.

By the end of the second hour the wind had backed still more to the north, but still was driving the plane onwards. I had covered 217 miles, nearly half-way, in two hours. Again through the change of wind I had not corrected enough for drift, and was now twenty-five miles off course to the south. Every mile to the south added length to the flight, but it did not seem to make much odds in such perfect conditions. I changed course another ten degrees to northward.

Then came clouds, and I could see that I might be unable to get a sextant shot. I did not worry much at first – there did not seem much to worry about with a target 2,000 miles wide ahead. But the wind was increasing, and backing persistently. At 250 miles out the sky was completely shut off by dull grey, threatening cloud. I spurred myself to make some hurried drift observations; the wind had increased to fifty mph from the north-east, and the seaplane was forty-three miles off course to the south. With the drift, we were heading obliquely for the receding part of Australia. Forty-three miles off course seemed a lot, and I wished that I had not allowed it to build up so much. I changed course another ten degrees northwards.

At three hours out heavy rain stung my face. The drift to the south was becoming alarming; the wind had backed till it was now right in the north. I changed course another ten degrees to the north, which put the wind dead abeam. I dared not correct the drift more than that, or I should have made a head wind of the gale, which I sensed would destroy my chance of reaching the mainland. The seaplane was drifting forty degrees to the south, and moving half sideways over the water, like a crab. The rain became a downpour – I had forgotten that it could rain so heavily. I kept my head down as much as possible, but the water caught the top of my helmet, streamed down my face and poured down my neck. We seemed to strike a solid wall of water with a crash. I ducked my head, and from the corner of my eye I could see water leaving the trailing edge of the wings in a sheet, to be shattered instantly by the air blast. On either side of my head the water poured into the cockpit in two streams, which were scattered like windblown waterfalls and blew into my face. I was flying blind, as if in a dense cloud of smoke. I throttled back, and began a slanting dive for the water. Panic clutched me: if I got out of control, I would be too low to recover. But panic meant dying like a paralysed rabbit. I remember saying out loud, 'Keep cool! Keep cool! K-e-e-p c-o-o-l!' The seaplane passed through small sudden bumps, which shook it violently. I looked over at the airspeed indicator on the strut, but I could not see either the pointer or the figures in the smother of water. I had to make do with the rev indicator; if the revs increased, the dive was steepening. I felt that I had to find the surface of the sea, for I dared not try to climb blind. If I lost control and tried to spin out, the sea would not show up quickly enough to level off. I sat dead still, moving only my eyes from compass to rev indicator to vertically downwards over the cockpit edge. When the engine speed increased, I used the control-stick lightly with finger and thumb to ease up the plane's nose. There was more chance of the seaplane's flying itself level than of my keeping it level, flying blind. Thank God it was rigged true.

At last I saw a dull patch of water below the lower wing rushing up at me. I pushed the throttle, the engine misfired, and failed to pick up. I thrust the lever wide open as I flattened the seaplane out above the water; the engine spluttered, broke into an uneven rattle and back-fired intermittently; its roughness shaking the whole plane. But the plane kept up, and lumbered on. I concentrated on flying. The engine continued with an uneven tearing noise. The sea was only visible a plane's length ahead, where it merged in the grey wall of rainwater. I was flying in the centre of a hollow grey globe, with nothing to help me to keep level except the small patch where the globe rested on the sea. I hugged every wave, rising or falling with it, and the seaplane jerked its way along. The water poured over my goggles, distorting my sight; it ran down my face and neck, and streams of it trickled down my chest, stomach and back. I dared not take my eyes off the water to look at the compass or the rev indicator. One thing helped me – the violence of the gale itself. Although the seaplane headed in one direction, it was being blown sideways, so that it crabbed along half left, and I could see the next wave between the wings instead of its being hidden by the fuselage. I steered by the drift, keeping the angle of it constant. Otherwise I should have wandered aimlessly about the sea. There was a furious cross sea. Waves shot upward, to lick at the machine, but were slashed away bodily southwards by the wind. The tails of spume streaking south across the wave troughs enabled me to steer a straight course. I knew that I was flying as I had never flown before, but I also knew that I could not last long at that pace. At any moment I expected a muscle to lag, and the seaplane to strike a wavecrest. Suddenly I found myself flying straight into the water, and snatched back the stick to jump the seaplane's nose up, thinking my eye and hand had at last failed me. Then I realized that the rainfall had eased while I was in the trough between two rollers, and that the crest of the swell ahead had unshrouded above me. Next instant the seaplane shot into the open air. I rose 30 feet, and snatched the goggles up to my forehead. It seemed like 3,000 feet.

The compass showed that I was fifty-five degrees off course, headed to miss even Tasmania. That seemed strange, for I thought that I could fly accurately by the drift. I soon saw what had happened – the wind had backed another forty-five degrees, and was now north-west. I had to think hard. I picked up the chart case on which my chart was rolled, but the soaked chart was useless. Before the storm I had been drifted so far south that I was right on the edge of the chart; during the storm I was blown farther south at the rate of a mile a minute, and was now far off it. I had a small map of Australia torn from a school atlas on the island. There was not enough sea area on it to show Lord Howe Island's position, but it was the only thing to use. Where was I before the storm? The position on the school map came right in the midde of a city plan of Sydney in the corner.

I flew up to another line squall ahead, parallel to the

previous storm, and stretching from horizon to horizon, but I could see the water on the other side, as through a gauzy curtain. The rain was heavy, but the engine still carried on. We flew through the curtain of rain into an immense cavern of space between the illimitable vault of dull sky above, and the immeasurable floor of dull water below. It was solitary in that great space. Some slanting pillars of rain leaned against the wind, trailing across the dull floor of water like spirits of the dead drifting from the infernal regions. The vastness lent it all a nightmare air. In one place the vaulted ceiling bulged downwards with two black-cored squall clouds, each linked to the sea by a column of waterspout. Between the two columns another waterspout, a slender grey-white pillar was rising from the sea's surface. At a good height it burst at the top, like smoke expanding after an explosion. I flew straight towards it, fascinated. Suddenly the engine burst into a rough clatter again, and I realized that I must not fly near that thing; the disturbance capable of twisting it from the sea must be terrific.

I thought I saw land away to the north-west, purple foothills with a mountain range behind, but when I looked for it again later it had disappeared; land was still 160 miles away. At the foot of a great storm-cloud I saw smoke – a ship. It offered me a new lease of life, and I immediately turned towards it. It lay at the edge of the storm like a duck at the foot of a black cliff. I swooped down and read the name *Kurow* on the stern. It was an awesome sight. The bows slid out of one comber, and crashed into the next, to churn up a huge patch of seething water. When a cross swell struck her, she lurched heavily, slid into a trough and sank, decks awash, as if waterlogged; but wallowed out, rolling first on one beam and then the other, discharging water from her decks as though over a weir. There was no sign of life on board, and I could not imagine anything less capable of helping me. I felt as if a door had been slammed in my face, turned and made off north-west to round the storm. I felt that I would rather go fifty miles out of my way than face another storm. I had been only four hours thirty-five minutes in the air: it seemed a lifetime.

Round the storm we flew into calm air under a weak hazy

sun. I took out the sextant and got two shots. It took me thirty minutes to work them out, for the engine kept backfiring, and my attention wandered every time it did so. The sight in the end was not much use; the sun was too far west, but I got some self-respect from doing the job.

Suddenly, ahead and thirty degrees to the left, there were bright flashes in several places, like the dazzle of a heliograph. I saw a dull grey-white airship coming towards me. It seemed impossible, but I could have sworn that it *was* an airship, nosing towards me like an oblong pearl. Except for a cloud or two, there was nothing else in the sky. I looked around, sometimes catching a flash or a glint, and turning again to look at the airship I found that it had disappeared. I screwed up my eyes, unable to believe them, and twisted the seaplane this way and that, thinking that the airship must be hidden by a blind spot. Dazzling flashes continued in four or five different places, but I still could not pick out any planes. Then, out of some clouds to my right front, I saw another, or the same, airship advancing. I watched it intently, determined not to look away for a fraction of a second: I'd see what happened to this one, if I had to chase it. It drew steadily closer, until perhaps a mile away, when suddenly it vanished. Then it reappeared, close to where it had vanished: I watched with angry intentness. It drew closer, and I could see the dull gleam of light on its nose and back. It came on, but instead of increasing in size, it diminished as it approached. When quite near, it suddenly became its own ghost – one second I could see through it, and the next it had vanished. I decided that it could only be a diminutive cloud, perfectly shaped like an airship and then dissolving, but it was uncanny that it should exactly resume the same shape after it had once vanished. I turned towards the flashes, but those too had vanished. All this was many years before anyone spoke of flying saucers. Whatever it was I saw, it seems to have been very much like what people have since claimed to be flying saucers.

I felt intensely lonely, and the feeling of solitude intensified at every fresh sight of 'land', which turned out to be yet one more illusion or delusion by cloud. After six hours and five minutes in the air I saw land again, and it was still there ten minutes later. I still did not quite believe it, but three minutes later I was almost on top of a river winding towards me through dark country. A single hill rose from low land ahead, and a high, black, unfriendly-looking mountain range formed the background. A heavy bank of clouds on top hid the sun, which was about to set.

Well, this was Australia. Away to the south lay a great bay, and at the far side I spotted five ships anchored. They were warships. I flew south, and crossed the bay. Flying low between the two lines of ships I read HMAS *Australia*, HMAS *Canberra*. On the other side there appeared to be an aircraft-carrier. My heart warmed at the thought of getting sanctuary there, but all the ships had a cold, lifeless air about them. I supposed that I must fly on to Sydney. I flew over an artificial breakwater near a suburb of red-bricked, red-tiled, bungalows and houses like a small suburb in a dull-brown desert, with only a few sparse trees of drab green. There was not a sign of life, and not a wisp of smoke from the chimneys. Had the world died in my absence? If there was anyone left alive, there would surely be a watchman on one of the warships. I turned and alighted beside the *Australia*, its huge bulk towering above me. The seaplane drifted past and away from it, bobbing about on the cockling water. There was dead silence except for the soft *chop chop chop* against the float. I felt a fool to drop into this nest of disdainful battleships. I stood on the cockpit edge, and began morsing to the *Canberra* with my handkerchief. An Aldis lamp at once flashed back at me from the interior of the bridge. A motor-launch shot round the bows of the warship. I cancelled my signal, and stood waiting.

'How far is Sydney?'

'Eighty miles.'

I dreaded the thought of Sydney, and its crowds, but my job was to reach it. The launch was crowded with sailors, and at 20 yards their robust personalities gave me a feeling of inferiority. I felt that I had to get away quickly. I asked the launch to tow me to the shelter of the breakwater, and a sailor slipped me a tow rope efficiently. I climbed out on to the float to swing the propeller, and as I swung it I noticed mare's tails of sticky black soot on the cowling, due to the backfires. I wondered if the engine still had enough kick to get me away, but as soon as the seaplane started moving forward and pounding the swells, the futility of trying to take off was obvious. That settled it; I had to ask for help. The launch approached again. 'We'll tow you to *Albatross*,' an officer said. I made fast the tow line and I was towed up to the aircraft carrier, where I made fast to a rope dangling from the end of a long boom. I released the pigeons, feeling sorry for them, and they took off flapping and fluttering, presumably for their home loft near Sydney. A sailor let down a rope ladder from the boom, and I grappled clumsily up it, my feet often swinging out higher than my head. I made my way along the boom to the deck where a commanding figure, with much gold braid, was waiting for me. 'Doctor Livingstone, I assume,' he said, looking hard at me. 'At any rate, you have managed to discover the only aircraft carrier in the Southern Hemisphere. Come along to my cabin.'

I felt like a new boy in front of the headmaster. 'Did I say, when you came aboard, "Doctor Livingstone, I *assume*?" Of course, I meant, "Doctor Livingstone, I *presume*?".' But Captain Feakes of the Royal Australian Navy was a great host. He gave me a whisky and soda and made me feel like a long-expected, favourite guest. Yet I felt isolated, and drained of personality, horribly cut off from other people by some queer gulf of loneliness. I had achieved my great ambition, to fly across the Tasman Sea alone, I had found the islands by my own system of navigation which depended on accurate sun-sights worked out while flying alone, something which no one had ever done before and perhaps no one ever would do in similar circumstances. I had not then learned that I would feel an intense depression every time I achieved a great ambition; I had not then discovered that the joy of living comes from action, from making the attempt, from the effort, not from success.

Squadron-Leader Hewitt of the Australian Air Force arrived and offered to lift the seaplane on board *Albatross*. I asked him to let me do the job of hooking on. It was dark when

187

I went on deck. An arc-lamp shed a brilliance high up but only a dim light reached the seaplane as she was towed slowly under the lowered crane-hook. Standing on the top of the engine of the bobbing seaplane I tried to catch the ponderous hook; it was a giant compared with the one at Norfolk Island, with a great iron hoop round it, probably a help in hooking on big flying-boats, but only adding to my difficulties. I had to duck the hoop to catch the hook with one hand, and reach under it with the other to keep the two sling wires taut with the spreaders in place and the middle points of the wires ready for the hook. The hook itself was so heavy that I could not lift it with my arm out-stretched. The seaplane was rolling, and also there was a slight movement of the aircraft carrier, sufficient to tear the hook from my grasp, however tightly I clung with my knees jockeywise to the engine cowling. At last I had the wires taut and the hook in place under them, when either the seaplane dropped or the aircraft carrier rolled unexpectedly. The hook snatched and lifted the seaplane with my fingers between the hook and the wires. The pain was excruciating, as the wires bit through my fingers. I shrieked. I felt ashamed; but I knew that my cry was the quickest signal I could give the winchman. The hook lowered, and I sat on the engine top, knees doubled up, lean-ing against the petrol tank. I could not bear to look at my hand. The hook swung like a huge pendulum above me. I felt, well, I had bragged of my skill at this job; I should just have to get on with it. I cuddled the round of the iron hook in the palm of my right hand, and rested the wires in the crook of my thumb of the other hand. Everything went easily. 'Lift!' I said. The water fell away, and at last the seaplane swung inboard, stop-ped swinging, and dropped softly on to padded mats. I said to a man standing by, 'Help me down, will you? I am going to faint.'

When I came to I was in the ship's hospital. My right hand was crushed, but I lost only the top of one finger. The surgeon cut off the crushed bone and sewed up the flesh. I then became the guest of the wardroom officers as well as of Captain Feakes, and it is hard to recount such marvellous hospitality. It was like staying in the best club with the mysterious fascination of naval life added.

PART THREE

CHAPTER SEVENTEEN

FIRST STAGE TO JAPAN

THE Australian Navy took me into Sydney Harbour, and then I had to set about finding refuelling places and the necessary permits for the second half of my flight round the world. With the Gipsy Moth's range as a seaplane reduced to 600 miles, I had to find a sheltered river or inlet every 500 miles or so where the half-ton seaplane could ride out the night at a mooring, and where there was someone who could understand my talk or signs, and where I could get some petrol.

The first 2,000 miles up the coast of Australia was easy enough; the difficulties started with New Guinea. Merauke sounded all right; a steamer called there once a month. But where could I find a spot within range after that? The Admiralty Sailing Directions were the only guide I had at first:

'Frederik Hendrik Island . . . about 100 miles long . . . everywhere covered with dense forest and so marshy as to be almost inaccessible.'

'The Digul River . . . the natives were hostile, the boats and bivouacs being repeatedly shot at.'

'The Inggivake . . . twice shot arrows at the boats.'

Kaimana Bay seemed my best hope, it had several houses with corrugated iron roofs, but it was 600 miles from Merauke. Fortunately I met a Dutch skipper who knew the Arafura Sea well, and he told me that the settlement at Kaimana had been withdrawn and that Fakfak, 700 miles away, was the nearest place to Merauke. So the only hope seemed to be for me to dump some petrol myself in a creek, and return to Merauke to fill up again. My Dutch skipper said that if I alighted alone at 10 o'clock, I should be in the stewpot by 12; he said, 'Why not fly from Merauke to Dobo, the pearling centre in the Aru Islands 480 miles west of Merauke?'

The Dutch Government refused me permission to fly over New Guinea unless I guaranteed myself to repay any expenses incurred in looking for me. I imagined myself working for the rest of my life to pay for a week's cruise of the Dutch fleet. Later, they allowed me to fly to the East Indies if I signed a form absolving them from any responsibility. I was happy to do this, for I did not want anybody to go searching for me if I got into a mess. What I did not know was that the Dutch had cabled to New Zealand, and two of my friends, Eric Riddiford and Grant-Dalton, had guaranteed payment of any expenses incurred without saying anything to me about it.

While I wrestled with consuls to get permits, de Havillands gave my engine a complete overhaul. Some of the pistons were cracked, and the crank-shaft was full of sludge. One of the worst mistakes I had made in reassembling the engine was to screw up the propeller-shaft thrust-race too tight, and only a shimmy of it still remained when I reached Australia. Nothing could be found wrong with the magneto which had cut so mysteriously over the Tasman Sea, but the other one, which had kept spluttering and misfiring, had the distributor cracked, and they showed me a long blue spark jumping the terminals when it was tested. Major Hereward de Havilland, known to everybody in Sydney as D.H., red-faced with a deep slow voice, was an interesting friend. He liked to probe everything until he found the reason for it. Why was I attempting this flight which he considered impossible? Why did I not buy a yacht and sail round the world instead of flying? It was more comfortable, cheaper, safer and healthier. After a fortnight of wrestling with people and difficulties it did seem to me like paradise to be sunbathing on the deck of a yacht. Thirty years on, now that I am a sailing man, this idea seems a great joke; I get far more sunbathing in the middle of London in a month than I ever have on a yacht! Hereward had one theory which, I believe, was valuable and true; the only way for a flying man to keep alive was to be apprehensive.

Captain Feakes had allowed me to leave the seaplane in

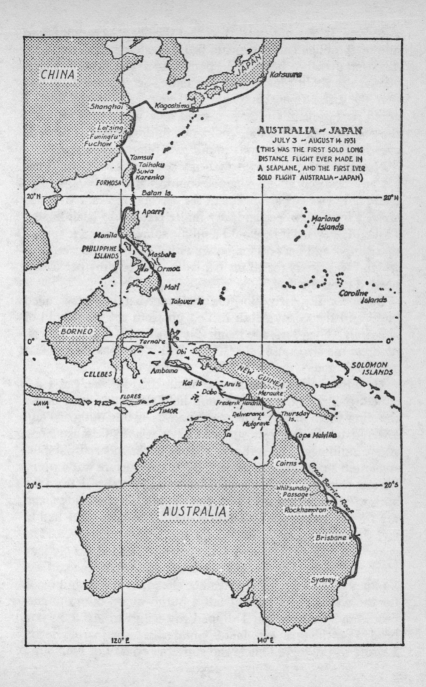

CHINA

JAPAN

Katsuura

Shanghai

Kagoshima

Lotsing
Funingfu
Fuchow

Tamsui
Taihoku
Suwa
Karenko

FORMOSA

20°N — Batan Is.

Aparri

Manila

PHILIPPINE
ISLANDS

Masbate

Ormoc

Mati

Talauer Is

Ternate

Obi

Amboina

BORNEO

CELEBES

Kei Is

Dobo

Aru Is

NEW GUINEA

Merauke

Frederik Hendrik

Deliverance

Mulgrave

Thursday
Is.

JAVA

FLORES

TIMOR

Cape Melville

Cairns

Whitsunday
Passage

Rockhampton

Brisbane

Sydney

AUSTRALIA

Great Barrier Reef

Mariana
Islands

Caroline
Islands

SOLOMON
ISLANDS

AUSTRALIA ~ JAPAN
JULY 3 ~ AUGUST 14 1931
(THIS WAS THE FIRST SOLO LONG
DISTANCE FLIGHT EVER MADE IN
A SEAPLANE, AND THE FIRST EVER
SOLO FLIGHT AUSTRALIA ~ JAPAN)

20°N

0°

20°S

120°E   140°E

Albatross. It was not until then that the flight-sergeant found one of the bilge compartments full of water; it had not been discovered before because a chock under the float had prevented the drain plugs being opened. The strange thing was that the aircraftman could not find any leaks in the float. I asked de Havillands to have a good look when they replaced the engine, but they, too, could not find anything wrong. If ever fate wove a web it was round that bilge compartment.

Nothing was going right with my preparations. I could not get any decision about where I could alight *en route*, and so could not make any arrangement for petrol supplies. No money arrived from New Zealand; my finger refused to heal; finally, I asked Hereward if he would lend me some money. He turned up trumps, and I set off for Japan with £44 in my pocket, with which I was to pay for all my expenses, and buy my petrol as I needed it on the way.

So one chilly early morning the great hatches were rolled back, and the Gipsy Moth hauled up from the giant hold of *Albatross.* When I tried to thank Captain Feakes and the others, he drew me aside and said 'If you find it's impossible, give it up, won't you?'

He offered to have the seaplane launched for me, but I declined, mounted the cowling, and held the crane hook under the sling wires myself. The seaplane was swung outboard and lowered to the harbour surface. Lazy wisps of smoke hung about buildings. The soft grey shapes of the moored warships suggested a peaceful existence. That glassy surface was a worry for me, though. The floats would not be able to break from the suction of smooth water; with the Captain on the bridge, and my friends watching, I should be unable to take off. I had to try, though, so first I headed for the harbour entrance. The water felt like treacle, and I turned and headed for Sydney Harbour bridge, but I could not break the grip of the surface. Suddenly I spotted a ferry steamer ahead, swerved, and made for the waves of its wash. I felt a bump-bump-bump underneath, and we were off. I dipped my wings to *Albatross* and headed for the open sea. It was wonderful to be soaring north. I wrote in my log, 'This is the supreme ecstasy of life.'

Three hundred miles later I was skimming the surface a foot or two above a waterway parallel with the coast. It was wild, rough country, with dark-green feathery-leaved trees overhanging the water's edge. I put up two big flapping birds, like flamingos, only white. I followed one close behind, and it could keep ahead at seventy mph, flying frantically with its great spread of jagged-edged white wings and its long pinkish legs streaming behind it. Suddenly it checked itself, its legs dangled limply, as if broken, and it crumpled and dropped as if shot. I expected it to hit the water in a burst of feather, but it suddenly took flying shape again and made off in another direction.

The Brisbane River was puckered and wrinkled by a breeze. I flew up-river to the bridge and alighted there. When I came to take off next morning it was foggy, with a light rain. There was not a breath of wind and the muddy water was as smooth as glass. I tried taking off up-river and down-river, I tried every trick I knew, rocking, jumping and porpoising, but I could not unstick the floats. It was nervy work, for I could not see far ahead in the mist, and there were ferry-boats, steamers, rowing-boats, buoys and moorings to be avoided. After repeated failures to get off, I tried up-river again, for the full length of the straight. I reached a right-angled bend and, although it had been drummed into me that a seaplane must be kept dead straight in taking off, I swerved slightly to obtain a few more yards' run. My hands were on the throttle to shut off when I thought that the floats rode a little easier. That was tantalizing – just at the bend where I must stop. I had a wild feeling, and I swerved hard to starboard. I could feel the port float lift; for an instant I straightened out, and then swerved hard again to starboard. As I straightened again I could feel that the starboard float had risen a little in the water. While still rounding the bend I lifted her off the surface. She was heavily stalled, but she was in the air, and stealing up-river. I learned something new about seaplane flying that morning.

I swung round, and flew the length of the river to the sea, then skimmed the passage between the mainland and Great Sandy Island. There were a lot of little flat islets, and I enjoyed jumping them. Then the screw-cap of the front cockpit petrol tank flew off the filler-pipe, which projected through the fuselage. A little safety chain held it, but I was afraid that this might break, and that the cap, hurtling back in the slipstream, might smash the tailplane. I had to come down, so I turned into wind above a stretch of water I thought suitable, and I was just about to settle when I noticed a snag sticking out of the water. I dodged it with a hurried swerve and came down on a narrow strip of shallow water between the mainland and a long sand-spit. There was a light breeze of eight mph from the south. There was no trace of man; alighting there was an indescribable thrill, and the silence and solitude were a balm. I screwed the cap on and let the seaplane drift sternwards until about to ground on a sand-bank before swinging the propeller and taking off again. Some hours later I flew up the Fitzroy River to alight just below the bridge at Rockhampton.

Rockhampton was a queer place, though full of character. There were a lot of odd-looking boats in the river and I had difficulty in persuading boatloads of youths not to jab at the floats with their oars, or grab the wings to hold themselves against the current. In the afternoon I worked on the motor and refuelled, finding it awkward with my bandaged finger. This seemed to hit everything, and dip alternately in oil, petrol and the muddy river.

There were steam trams in Rockhampton puffing about the streets, and everyone there seemed to spend a lot of time in asserting the equality of man. In the evening I was driven out to a pub, given a glass of beer, and set on a beer barrel to answer countless questions. When at last I got to bed I found that I had left behind the copy of Homer's *Odyssey* which I was reading.

In the morning I succeeded in taking off from the river, but I had hard work through sixty miles of heavy rain before flying into fine weather. I was then inside the Great Barrier Reef, though the reef itself was still 150 miles to seawards. At noon I reached the Whitsunday Passage, which stirred a romantic feeling at the thought of Cook's discovering it. I wanted to come down there myself, but with a fresh breeze blowing from the East it was difficult to find a suitable spot. If the water was sheltered there was not enough take-off run to clear the land ahead or else there was a sea running or reefs showed their dirty brown teeth. After passing one of the bays I decided that it would have suited me, but I would not turn back to it. I was getting hungry and impatient, but at last I reached Gloucester Island and came down on the passage between it and the mainland. The seaplane, once down, drifted back fast, and I could see a seething tide-rip which had looked negligible from the air. I hurriedly threw out my anchor, and although it jerked and bumped a bit, it held in time. It was lovely and peaceful there, and all the land in sight seemed uninhabited. I sat on the front wing edge, dangling my feet, and eating. Then I smoked a pipe and lazed – this was what I had dreamed about, complete solitude in the sunshine, and silence except for the friendly slip-slap of wavelets against the floats. But I had hundreds of miles to go before nightfall, so I had to tear myself away. I expected an easy take-off with the loppy sea and a good breeze, but to my surprise the seaplane stayed heavy in the water and when she struck the open seas beyond the island she suddenly swung to starboard. I thought that she was going to capsize and jammed on full opposite rudder. She righted, and finally bumped into the air. I wrote in my log, 'Horrible! Cannot understand it, I must have been flying atrociously, yet did not think so.'

After 450 miles I had the greatest difficulty in keeping awake, and I was tempted to alight at a beautiful little settlement on Palm Island. But I had to get on to Cairns to refuel, so I made myself go on. With thirty miles yet to go the petrol gauge showed empty. I knew that there was still some left, but to be on the safe side I began climbing so as to have a glide in hand in case of need. I flew over a watershed to see Cairns River within gliding range, four miles ahead. It had taken eight hours' flying to cover the 623 miles.

Cairns was a surprise to me in more than one way. From the air it looked beautiful, lying in a horseshoe basin split by the river, and almost encircled by ranges with a dark-purple bloom. But as soon as I alighted a launch rushed up. It was loaded with tourists clicking cameras. They stopped dead in my lee, and the seaplane promptly began drifting on to the launch. I jumped for the wing root, switched on, sprang to the float and began frantically swinging the propeller. Fortunately they could not hear my swearing at them. I started the motor just in time, and taxied away. As I was rigging my anchor at a fresh spot the launch came up again. Then the petrol agent arrived, and told me that I could not anchor there; I had been ordered to moor on the other side of the estuary, almost out of sight of the town. I asked with wasted irony if they suspected the Gipsy Moth of being loaded with dynamite. Next, I had to go with the agent to the storage tanks for petrol, so that I finished emptying ten 4-gallon tins of petrol into the tanks by torchlight. Finally, when I did reach the town, the petrol agent told me that I would not get a bed. I thought he was joking with Australia then in the middle of a slump, but I was turned away by the first three hotels. When at last a kindly Mrs McManus squeezed me into what I think must have been a housemaid's cupboard, I was grateful. Further, she fossicked some food from the kitchen, and Australian tea which makes one's hair curl. Apparently anyone in those parts who expected food after 6.30 PM was regarded as crazy.

I had to be off early again next morning, and my hostess generously got up to cook me breakfast, and she gave me a tin of sweetcorn, some bread, butter and jam and a magazine to take with me. Soon I was roaring north. The Great Barrier Reef was now within twenty or thirty miles of the coast, and there were detached reefs everywhere. The water over them was dark blue or pure green, and the sun struck through to the reef as if through plate glass. I flew eighty miles across Princess Charlotte Bay, out of sight of land for part of the crossing. Near the mainland I noticed a school of sharks in the lee of Cape Sidmouth, swirled round and alighted on top of where I had seen them, then cast anchor. It was so hot it made my eyes lazy. I took off my clothes and lolled about the seaplane. I was disappointed not to see any sharks, though splashes I heard showed they were still near. From above I had seen through the water as clearly as if it did not exist, but on the surface I could see only the bottom immediately below me. After eating and smoking I finally tore myself away, for I had to reach Thursday Island before dark. For hundreds of miles it was like flying along the coast of a desert. Once I spotted a wretched kind of shelter with the thatch beginning to collapse, and once I saw a group of horsemen on the beach. I came upon a lugger with sails drooping limply in the hot still air. It seemed black from a distance, and when I flew up to it I found it was covered with black natives. They were a strange sight, dotting the deck, and leaning over the bulwarks, with a string of them twisted up the mast, feet to woolly pate. They all kept utterly still as I flew up to them, and only twisted their heads to look at me as I flashed past.

I headed out to sea from Cape York, the northernmost point of the continent, for the group of islands fourteen miles off. Thursday Island was not marked on my chart, but the whole group was only twenty miles across, so I did not expect difficulty in finding it. And sure enough I recognized the island at once by the mass of luggers alongside it. As soon as I alighted near the jetty and cast anchor, a dinghy put off with two aboard. One was a man called Vidgen, who turned out to be a pearl merchant. He said that he had a mooring buoy ready for me in the lee of the jetty. He gave me confidence, and I liked him. I hauled in my anchor and stowed it, restarted the motor, and taxied slowly against the strong current to within a few feet of the buoy. I switched off, hopped quickly out of the cockpit and caught the rope thrown to me by Vidgen before the tide bore the seaplane out of reach. Soon we were fast to a proper mooring in a few seconds without any shouting, swearing or fuss. It was a pleasant change. People came down to the jetty to look. The Australian aborigines fascinated me with the absolute blackness of their skins, and their hair like thick black mats. I dropped one of my watches from my breast pocket and its pale face reproached me through the green water as it sank. The previous day I had lost the oil dip-stick. While changing the oil I was scared of dropping the sump-plug into the sea.

Vidgen invited me to spend the night with him. He had a dinner party for a Dutch captain from the Aru Islands. The manners of the party were gentle and punctilious, after the Dutch style. We had a huge, excellently cooked dinner, the sort of feast that one had fifty years ago in an English country house in the middle of winter. They asked me what I proposed doing if I came down in the head hunter country. I said that I had a .410 double-barrelled pistol, and had made the shot solid with candle grease. 'What range would it kill at?' 'Ten yards,' I said. This caused a general laugh. I asked what the joke was. I was told I would never see any Papuans, who kept behind the trees; they would shoot poisoned arrows at me from 200 yards, and would not approach until I was dead. Further, the Papuans used arrows both ways, so they could not be pushed through or pulled out. They seemed a nice bunch.

There was a small wooden bank building on Thursday Island and I walked through the heated air to it full of hope. But no money had come for me, and I had to leave with only £18 to see me through to Manila. Vidgen collected some mail for me to take to Japan, and I was asked to keep a look-out for a lugger which had been stolen from Thursday Island. I said I guessed that none of them had ever tried to identify a stolen lugger from an aeroplane. Oh, but it would be quite simple, they said, and to help me they gave me a photograph of another lugger which was like it, but had a mast two feet longer.

I said good-bye to Vidgen the pearl merchant with regret and left Thursday Island soon after noon to cross the Torres Straits. My first water hop was to Deliverance Island, fifty miles. The seaplane was awkward to trim which I think was because I had loaded her nose-heavy, filling the front petrol tank full, and leaving the rear tank empty. I thought that she might take off better with the weight forward, and I believe she did, but in the air she was so nose-heavy that I had to use three fingers to keep the control-stick back while I held the log-book between my finger and thumb. Deliverance Island was an atoll with smooth water inside the ring, and it was soon passed. I flew on, and rather suddenly realized that there was land below me; I had seen it for some time, but thought it a cloud shadow. Soon I was flying along a broad, shallow, muddy shore and I shall never forget the fantastic sight below.

Hundreds of crocodiles basking in the shallows went crazy with fear as I flew over, and sheets of liquid mud flew wide into the air to right and left as they lashed their tails with great writhing strokes until they reached deep water. Some of them by my float shadow were 15 feet long. I always thought that crocodiles lived in fresh water, but this must have been a sort of crocodiles' Brighton beach. Flying over one little sandy cove I saw a sailing boat drawn up on the beach, which looked like the stolen lugger. It would have been the perfect hide-out if a small seaplane had not happened to be flying through that part of the world. I reported it, and it turned out that it was the stolen lugger, and a police patrol recovered it as a result of my report.

Merauke was a tightly packed settlement in a space cleared from dense tropical growth. The river flowed in front of it, wide, smooth and muddy. Studying the layout as I flew overhead, I could see natives pouring on to the jetty and river bank, some white figures embarking in a launch, and I presently picked out the bright tricolour of the Dutch flag nodding from a drum buoy. I came down, and I think that there must have been 2,000 Papuans on the jetty and river bank. All the white men of the settlement were there too; three missionaries with long beards straggling to their waists, who seemed glad to see a stranger, although none could speak English or French; the *gesaghebber*, or Dutch official, and the doctor, who could speak a little English. It was an exotic place, packed tight with flimsy wooden or bamboo structures crowding narrow streets. There were one or two Chinese stores, surprisingly well stocked. I bought some petrol from one in unbranded tins, but I could not get any suitable oil, and was glad that I had brought a spare gallon tin with me. I had no map or chart for the next 1,000 miles of my route, expecting to have been able to get one at Merauke. But there was no map to be had. I should have been badly placed if the *gesaghebber* had not generously given me his own map.

I was taken to the stone guest-house where I stayed the night alone. I tried to ask about buying food, but our language was not equal to it, and presently a meal arrived, which I think the doctor or *gesaghebber* had sent, though I was never able to find out. The guest-house was in front of a prison guarded by four native sentries who each sounded a bell one after the other at every quarter-hour. Judging by the effect on me I should think it was an excellent way of keeping them from sleeping at their posts. On my way to the jetty next morning I met the prisoners going off to work on the roads. The Dutch official drew my attention to two husky prisoners with beaming faces laughing away and chattering rapidly at each other as they padded along the road. They looked ideal husbands. They were hill men who had formed a habit of coming down to the town periodically, selecting a fat town boy and treating him to a meal of drugged sago before they dragged him back to the hills where they cooked and ate him. The Dutch thought that it was not right to execute them for doing what they had been brought up to believe was the right thing, and so set them to road making for a few years, which they liked, the Dutch official said, because it gave them regular food without the trouble of finding it. It must be remembered that all this was thirty years ago.

Time after time I tried to get off the glassy surface of the river in the hot sticky air, and when at last I managed it, it felt like flying a mud-clogged old wheelbarrow with wings. Before I left that sea of tufted palm-tops I was sick to death of them, and my clothes were soaking wet.

I flew along the south coast of New Guinea and then made a seventy-mile flight across the middle of Frederik Hendrik Island. No white man had ever seen the interior of this island. All that was known was that natives attacked any ship becalmed near the coast.

Blotchy cloud shadows gliding over the ground were overtaken by the seaplane shadow flitting at an uncanny pace across tall reeds like corn or skimming up a wall of forest trees and rushing over the dense tops. In the middle of the island the swamp took on a definite pattern of stripes and cross stripes. I felt sure it must have been cultivated thousands of years ago, though now there was not a sign of man. Later I saw two tiny planted patches.

The air was uncomfortable, not with vicious bumps but as if pitching into lively short waves. At every pitch my face was showered with petrol from the air vent. By 10 o'clock I completed the traverse of the island and flew over the sea again. I had to navigate the 260-mile sea crossing to the Aru Islands with care, although they were a comparatively wide target. I had flown on a careful compass course for the last 100 miles and found that I had drifted fourteen degrees to starboard. I therefore changed fourteen degrees to port. After New Guinea the sea felt safe and friendly. I felt hungry, ate a good meal, and then sat musing or writing in my log. It did not seem long before I reached my target, and at 12.43 I entered the channel between the main islands Wokam and Kobroor. It seemed full of war canoes with high stems and stern-posts. Some fled, furiously paddled. On either side of the passage was magnificent forest, with tall trees festooned with pink, rose and red creepers. A frightful bump drove the thought of beauty from my mind and I hurriedly fastened my belt for fear of being tossed out.

I came down on sparkling dark-blue water off the small island of Dobo, which faces Wokam across a narrow passage. I had taken five hours and ten minutes over the 472-mile flight.

A launch put off with four Englishmen or Australians aboard, and chugged round the seaplane. Hearing English again made me feel like a boy home from school. They shouted jokes, but every time I suggested that they should come nearer, they seemed to be deaf. Presently a launch flying the Dutch flag came up. The Dutch official was exceedingly polite to the Australians, and spoke to me through them, and the Government launch took me to the jetty to get my petrol. A tremendous press of natives, thousands of them, suddenly burst into a shout, a thrilling sound which would have raised the sky. On the jetty the Dutch official proudly showed me the fuel he had had the kindness to prepare for me – a formidable array of big drums, which must have totalled five times the weight of my Gipsy Moth. Unfortunately, they were diesel oil, not petrol. I managed to get some petrol, however, and I spent a delightful evening with the three bachelor pearlers, who lived together in an airy ramshackle old structure of two storeys with wide verandas and hanging rattan curtains instead of doors. Next morning, as well as the pearlers, a Malay Rajah and his princess came to see me off. The Rajah was small, quiet, delicate and aristocratic, and he wore white flannels with a Savile Row cut. His wife was perfectly charming with tiny feet and hands, a perfect little figure.

The flight of 450 miles from Dobo to Amboina was uneventful. There were islands at intervals for stepping stones, and the longest water flight was only 110 miles. One thing which I recorded in my log has been strongly disputed by aerodynamic experts – I knew that the favourable trade wind had died away because the throbbing roar of the engine suddenly changed its note. Although I have been assured since that it is theoretically impossible, I could tell if I was flying up wind or down wind in a fresh breeze by the note of the engine; I think it may well have been due to a Doppler effect when flying low down. Naturally, flying for such long periods on the same course and at the same engine speed, I became extremely sensitive to the slightest change in note of the engine noises.

I had left the Aru Islands that morning in the middle of the dry season and reached Amboina in the middle of the rainy season. All evening the clouds dropped down, discharged their load of rain and lifted. There was not a breath of wind next morning and my attempts to get off never had the slightest hope of succeeding. I gave up trying for the day and went ashore. Next day I left ashore all the clothes, tools, sailing directions and papers that I possibly could spare, amounting to 19 lb., and jettisoned petrol until I only had six hours' fuel. I had intended to make Menado, in the Celebes, my next halt, but switched to Ternate in the Moluccas to give me a shorter flight. I raced to and fro across the water opposite the town. It was sprinkled with praus, and it was nervy work dodging them, as well as keeping a constant watch for fishing stakes. Finally I told the officials in the launch that my only chance of taking off was from the broken surface of the open sea; would they tow me out? The young assistant *gesaghebber* was troubled; it was a long way. Volumes of Dutch were poured out. In the end we started off with the seaplane in tow. Five or six miles down the inlet there was a slight swell; I cast off the tow and bounced into the air at the second attempt.

At the mouth of the Amboina inlet I flew into clear bright weather over a sparkling blue sea. I waggled the wings with joy, but it was premature. Thinking only of escape from Amboina, I had discarded every possible ounce of weight, including the map given me by the Dutchman, at Merauke. So I had a 140-mile sea crossing to make without a map, before I got back on to my own chart. I had taken a look at the big map in the Resident's office, read off the bearing of the first landfall, which was uninhabited Ombira Island 150 miles to the north, and thought that nothing could be simpler than to fly on this one bearing until I reached the island. But on turning the corner of Amboina Island I flew up against the tail of a big island right in the middle of my route – and which I could not remember having seen on the map. The east side ran more nearly in the right direction, so I followed that. It was black-looking country with high, densely forested, slopes, rising several thousand feet in dark-bluish haze before disappearing into cloud. When I had flown along it for twenty miles and saw no end to it I grew anxious, and a few minutes later I was dismayed to see land loom up ahead of me through the haze. Soon I found that I was blocked by a massive range of mountains, black and threatening, with the tops hidden in cloud, and stretching away to the east as far as I could see. This put me in a fix, for if I went back to try the other side of the land I should use up my reserve of fuel and would have to return to Amboina for more, a horrid thought. I had no idea how high the mountains were, so dared not attempt to cross them flying blind through the clouds. My only chance seemed to be to climb to the cloud ceiling and fly along beside the mountains to the head of the bay, hoping to find a gap. If I failed, I should have to return to Amboina.

As I flew on, slowly climbing, I was tempted to try crossing the mountains blind, but I was afraid. Then, turning a headland, I came on a saddle between two mountains on my left, with a rain squall above it. I was below the level of the saddle, and could not see if there was a passage through. I opened up the throttle. My climbing pace seemed deadly slow, as I watched the squall dropping down to the pass. Suddenly I got a glimpse of blue water over the saddle, and putting down the nose of the seaplane I scuttled for it at full throttle. The dropping rain caught me, but in a few seconds I was through, and out in the sunlight again. I made allowance for the distance I thought I had been deflected to the east of my route, and headed for where I now thought Ombira to lie. I felt hungry and fossicked out the remains of the excellent jam and egg sandwiches given me at Dobo. Alas! they had fermented. I tried the tin of biscuits, but the contents were saturated with petrol. I found some mouldy bread, age unknown, and ate it with butter. I longed for a smoke, but my pipe was broken, and the cigars were in the front cockpit. When eventually I sighted Ombira right ahead, I wondered how I could ever have worried about not finding it, it looked so huge. It was twenty-five miles wide, well watered, fertile and healthy, but it was uninhabited because it was said to be haunted.

At 3 o'clock I reached Gilolo, the largest of the spice islands after Ceram. I saw few signs of habitation, and the steep hills were smothered in jungle. Flying only a wing-span from the hillside, I disturbed countless snowy white doves. Their wings beat the air, but they never seemed to get anywhere. On the other hand the birds of paradise, black-coated with long tails like Court trains trailing behind, glided gracefully and without any hurry, but always managed to be out of sight by the time I drew level with them. I never caught more than glimpses of their sheeny black spread sailing through the trees.

Here I had trouble with a tropical rain-storm which lasted for forty-five miles, and when I flew out of it I thought I was looking at the twin islands of Ternate and Tidore. But I could not see any sign of Ternate town. This made me anxious, as I had only an hour's petrol left. The truth was that Tidore's volcano was in cloud or smoke. This had flowed down to the sea in the middle of the island, so that really I was looking only at the one island of Tidore, divided in two by smoke. As soon as I reached the north-east point of Tidore I could see Ternate plainly ahead, and flew over to it.

I had no diplomatic standing here, because Ternate was not one of the halting places I had nominated. At the other places, instructions had been received from the Governor-General of the East Indies to lay down moorings for me. Here there was nothing, but I managed to anchor, and was conducted to the hotel by a thousand yelling children and the Captain of Police. He spoke no English; no one at the hotel spoke English. In the morning, with 35 gallons on board – five more than the day before – I taxied to the windward side of the island and took off from lively blue water there. Ahead of me was a water-jump of 175 miles to the Talauer Islands. When I tried to test my magnetos I found that both the switches were stuck, and later, as I was writing up my log, the engine cut out for a fraction of a second. After I had been in the air for nearly three hours, I was attacked by sleepiness, and I decided to come down on the open sea. For 1,500 miles my curiosity had been growing to see whether I could come down on the open Pacific, and get away afterwards. I felt sure I could do it on that day. The danger was in swell which might make it impossible to rise again, but I felt confident that I could detect a swell if there was one. I headed the seaplane into wind, and watched the surface intently as I glided down. There was no drift, so I was dead into wind, no swell, an ideal sea with short choppy waves. When the seaplane came to rest I could not stop the engine, because the magneto-switches were stuck. I had to turn off the petrol, and wait until the carburettor ran dry. There was more sea than I had expected, and the Gipsy Moth rolled heavily. I logged, 'Funny how she always rides beam to wind', then lit a cigar, and took the magneto-switch to pieces. The tiny springs had corroded, and the make and break had jammed. I fixed it as well as I could.

We bumped the waves hard taking off, and every impact shocked the whole seaplane from end to end. It was an anxious time, but at last she rose. I had misjudged that sea; it was too deep for safety. (I think it would have been safe enough if the bilge compartment in the starboard float had not been full of water.)

As I left the Talauers astern, I logged, 'Can see water running from the tail of the starboard float all the time; so evidently it empties in the air from the same leak.' I thought that it came from the bilge compartment which I pumped dry every morning, and I did not then realize that it came from a compartment which was full up. Sixty miles north of the Talauers, I was writing in my log when suddenly the engine cut out. I was jerked instantly from a tolerant philosopher into a primitive animal. As I began turning into wind to alight, the engine cut in again, and I slowly settled after the shock. After I was on course again, the engine cut out briefly several more times. I tried the switches, but they were functioning perfectly. I thought that it must be due to the carburettor. After a while in the drowsy sticky heat I forgot about it.

I made a bull's-eye landfall of Cape St Augustine in the Philippines, and full of the joy of living I switched off the engine and circled the lighthouse in a steep spiralling glide. When level with the lighthouse I switched on the engine again. Nothing happened: the shock was like a stab from a red hot wire. I took in the lie of the water under me, and started manoeuvring to avoid the cliff beside me and to alight into wind. Then I looked at the switches and saw why the engine had cut; both switches were down, which meant that they were switched off. They must have dropped again as soon as my finger left them after switching on. I strapped them in the up position with the garter I used to hold the log-book on my knee, and flew on to Mati, my next port at the south-east corner of Mindanao.

Time after time I circled the town or village, as it appeared to be, but could not see any buoy or launch, or even a boat. I was about to alight in the lee of the pier, when I jibbed, thinking that there was no water there at all. So I alighted well out in the channel and taxied in slowly, expecting to run aground, but was surprised to find when I anchored that there was 40 feet under me. A light breeze was blowing, but the heat in the hot sunshine was like the radiation from a red hot stove. There was a steamer tied up to the jetty unloading cargo. After an age a ship's boat approached me from the side of the ship, sculled by a little brown man standing in the stern with a big oar. When only 10 yards off he was still coming down at full speed, in spite of my frantic shouts. I leant far out and caught the stem with both hands, and only then did he stop sculling and try to back paddle. I held off the bows and the stern swung to one side, when, catching the wind, it began swinging round fast to the wing. The trailing edge of the wing was too low for the boat to pass under. I waited until the boat was lined up with the wing's leading edge, when I gave it a mighty shove. I only just saved myself from falling in after it, but the boat shot off under the wing, with the brown man ducking his head. He came alongside again more carefully and landed me at the pier steps. There was such a crowd of Filipinos that I could not make a passage through them. I stood helpless, until a handsome young Filipino dug a passage through the mob with his elbows and said breathlessly, 'I am Chief Postmaster. When you leave? Doctor X wants you to take mail bag.' I thought, 'Damn Doctor X!' but said, 'I must get some petrol first.'

'Petrol?' he said as we swayed to and fro, jostled by the surging crowd. 'There is no petrol here.' I felt desperate; I knew Mati was cut off from the rest of the island except by steamer, but here was the steamer. It seemed incredible that there was no petrol. I asked again, 'Have you no petrol at all?'

'No, no petrol here.'

'But your radio station! How do you work that?'

'Press a key, just the same as for telegram.' Just then three more Filipinos forced a passage through the crowd and strutted up. The Postmaster said quickly, 'I introduce you to Chief of Public Works, to President-elect and to Chief of Police.'

Public Works – petrol. I asked him about it, but the Chief Postmaster translated his reply, 'No, no petrol here.' I thought of trying the steamer, but it was impossible to force a passage, so I asked the Chief of Public Works to make an inquiry on board. I watched a man mount the gangway and speak to a brown officer. I said, 'Where are the American officers of the ship?'

'No American in Mati; all Filipino in Mati; Philippine island for Filipino.'

The messenger returned; the officer regretted that he had no petrol; could I not use gasoline instead?

CHAPTER EIGHTEEN

GASOLINE AND TROUBLE

I TOOK the Postmaster by the arm and asked him if he could find me a cup of tea. A new arrival said, 'I am Commandant of Military here.' He added, 'The Governor-General has wired to me about you. You will stay at my house. Do you carry passengers? Do you know that the President-elect likes flying? It is possible that the President-elect might find you some gasoline.' It soon became plain that the Public Works Department, the Police and the Army all thought that they would like flying. By the time I got to the house hints were being hurled at me till I felt like an Aunt Sally. I began to fear that they would be offended when at last the Army said, 'What would happen if Governor-General Davis, Governor-General of the Philippine Islands wanted a ride in your plane?'

'He couldn't have one,' I said promptly and firmly. It was a merciful reply, for if I refused the Governor-General they need not feel insulted. Tea, cigars and brandy were served on the veranda. The matter of gasoline? It was a matter that could be gone into presently, very soon. There was something queer about the business; I decided to shut up and wait.

The PWD invited me to ride in an automobile to see the President. I said that I would rather eat and sleep, but they hinted, 'No President, no gas.' We started on a long drive along a narrow, washed-out road. Every now and then we met and forced aside a bullock and cart driven by a Filipino boy in a large, floppy, straw-plaited hat smoking a fat cigar. Every time I asked who owned the coconut grove or banana plantation we were passing through I was told, 'This belongs to President Lopez.'

We drove up with terrific hornblowing to a two-storeyed

house where many people were lined up outside. The President took me upstairs to a wide veranda. He was dressed in expensive golf trousers of pepper and salt flannel, black silk stockings, and white kid shoes. A handsome .32 calibre automatic with a mother-of-pearl handle made his cartridge belt sag at one hip. I was allowed to handle it, but not to fire it. He gave me a superb cigar, the best I have ever smoked. After dark, fireflies spangled the darkness, like twitching stars. The tropical night was cool and scented. The President took me off to see his crocodile. He shone his torch on a tough leathery brute about 9 feet long lying beside a concrete pool against some wire netting 12 inches high. It had a merciless unwinking stare. Then the President shone his torch round the wall of the snake house. I said, 'Where are the snakes?' He flashed his torch round again, but all I could see was a thick brown beam under the rafters on top of the wall. Did I not see it? It had dined on a cat the other day and was sleeping it off. Surely I could see the cat? Then I noticed that the thick bar all round the hut on top of the wall was mottled, and I saw a bulge in it like a football.

We went back to the veranda and sat there for ever. My last meal and the Sultan of Ternate seemed a long time away. In the end, after I had given up all hope, dinner arrived. We sat round a circular table, and a raised centre-piece was loaded with dishes. We spun this round and stabbed whatever we fancied. No one said a word; the only noise was the clatter of knives and forks, and the creak of the revolving table. It was quick work while it lasted. One after another the guests finished abruptly and moved away, to let the women have an innings. I was desperately tired, and every few seconds my eyes closed, and I angled for an invitation to sleep there. 'Sleep?' they said. 'Oh, no, no, no. The Postmaster has arranged a dance, and we must return to Mati.' So off we went again, after the President had presented me in front of his lined-up household with three tins of gasoline, some marvellous cigars, and a freshly salted wild cat skin. He had shot it himself the day before.

We returned to the military commander's house to find the vast central room clear of furniture. I woke up a little at the prospect of a lively evening among the maidens of Mati. But although some coy maidens did drift in from the darkness, they were tightly cased in Spanish-looking dresses of stiff brocade, and each was guarded by a chaperone with the eye of a bird of prey. I was led round and introduced to everyone, one by one, with a long speech in each case. I tried to smile without looking silly, and I danced once or twice with girls who kept as far away from me as possible while every step was watched by the chaperone. At last I had to waylay my Army host, thank him for his great kindness, and regret that as I was falling asleep on my feet, I must beg to retire. The poor fellow was much put out and thought me a dreadful boor, I fear. I remember being shown a bunk and estimating that the big drum of the dance band was about four feet from my ear through the thin partition; then I was asleep.

Next morning, in spite of the sultry heat, there was a good breeze and I took off at the first try, after a long run. I reached Ormoc, in Leyte, after a flight of only 300 miles. Again I was the guest of the local President. This one was a manual labourer. I had appalling trouble taking off again. The surface of Ormoc Bay was glassy smooth, and by 2 o'clock in the afternoon I had been five hours on the bay trying to get off. Each time I could get the seaplane very near to taking off, but she jibbed at the final lift. The suction of the smooth water seemed to hold the heels of the float firmly. I had pumped the bilges, and had found them in a good state, so I thought. I kept on trying to take off in the same direction round the headland, instead of returning over the same water: at least I was taxiing towards Manila in that way! After each failure I opened the petrol cock and let the reeking spirit patter on the wing surface. I was determined to get into the air in the end, even if I might have only enough petrol left to fly back to Ormoc. After struggling I was fifteen miles across the bay from Ormoc. I managed to take off at last in heavy rain; I think the rain-drops must have broken the smooth surface just enough to reduce the suction. I only had three and a half hours' fuel left, and searched my chart for some place within two hours' flight. I decided on Masbate.

On arrival at the Governor's house I noticed several large poles rising through the floor in the middle of the big room of the upper storey. They were evidently part of the structure of the house, and coils of stout rope round a piano bound it to one of the poles. I thought this was odd until I was woken up in the night by an earthquake. It seized the house and shook it violently until it rattled. I counted eleven earthquakes during the night, and each shake was weird and uncanny. The next morning was a terrible one. Before I started out on the hunt for petrol I felt feverish and dull-witted from my six hours in Ormoc Bay the day before, followed by the earthquakes through the night. I had no breakfast, and my head ached, and I went round asking, 'Where can I buy ten gallons of gasoline?' countless times. A motor-car took me to the Government offices, where the Governor, whose name was Cordova, introduced me to treasurers, attorneys, and many other kinds of official, all working in a big room in clean whites at schoolboy-type desks. After hours of discussion the town presented me with 12 gallons of petrol, for which I was most grateful. We then left on a hunt for oil, visiting shop after shop. I think the Governor started on the least likely ones; he was enjoying putting on an act in each shop, unbending affably and at great length to his people. After I had bought some of the most suitable oil I could find, it was difficult to find anything to put it in. The Chinese storekeeper was hurt at my noticing the dirt in the bottom of a tin he produced. I was quite firm that I did not want it in the engine, and finally he produced his handkerchief and wiped the tin clean with that.

If my difficulties in Ormoc Bay the day before had made me sorry for myself, I should have saved my self-pity for today. I had only 18 gallons of fuel on board, and a brisk 7-knot breeze to help me. At each attempt to take off, the motor vibrated horribly. One propeller tip had a piece bitten out of the edge where it had evidently struck a piece of floating wood or coconut, and the gap gradually widened as the propeller flogged the spray. The heat sucked my energy from me. Waiting for the engine to cool, I squatted on a float in the shade of a wing and wrote in my notebook, 'It would break your heart, this game; I have been out here three and a half hours now.' At my next attempt, when I opened up the motor, the starboard float buried itself in the water like a submarine submerging. For some distance I could not get it above the surface. At first I thought the float must have been holed by one of the many waterlogged coconuts drifting about. I tried all the bilges again, but they only held the usual quart or so. Then I thought that the starboard wings must have become waterlogged, and looking closely I found that the little drain holes along the trailing edge had never been punched through the fabric. I opened the nearest one with my knife, and some water ran out. In my rubber shoes, carefully balancing, I walked along the rear wing spar, pricking the holes open, but no more water ran out, so I decided that it must be the bottom wing at fault. For twenty minutes I tried to attract one of the canoes drifting round the shore, and at last one came up, the little man and his family in it watching me open-mouthed. I climbed in and manoeuvred the craft under the lower wings, so that I could prick each drain hole. There was a cupful of water in the wing, but no more. Next time I started taxiing, the seaplane went round in a circle as soon as I opened up. I kicked on full opposite rudder and pushed the throttle wide open, but the only result was that the starboard float drove under water and went on submerging until the wing also dipped in. I switched off before the seaplane capsized.

Next I tried streaming my drogue, like a canvas bucket with a hole in it, from the outer strut of the opposite wing, but it had no effect whatever. I seemed well and truly stuck. A motor-boat approached, which the Governor had sent to find out what was wrong. I asked for a tow, and threw out a line, but they missed it four times, the man at the wheel going full speed ahead each time he drew near the rope. When they did pick it up, they made it fast to their bow instead of the stern and proceeded to cross ahead of the seaplane at full speed. A pull from the side on a seaplane only makes it glide forwards or backwards, and as soon as the rope from the floats to the bow of the motor-boat took the strain, the motor-boat was pulled right round like a toy, and made straight for the seaplane's tail at full speed. I shouted at them to cast off the rope, but either they were taken by surprise, or else expected the seaplane to follow the motor-boat, because they held on, and I waited for them to crash into the tail. Then someone acted on the motor-boat and cast off the rope, and the boat just missed us. At last the tow rope was secured properly to the stern of the boat, and the seaplane was towed safely across the bay.

I walked up to the Governor's house. The heat seemed to let me through reluctantly, and everything seemed dreamlike. The Governor ordered a meal to be produced while I had a bath in a room with the floor joists open to let the water fall through 20 feet to the ground below.

I felt better after something to eat, and motored round the harbour with the Governor to find somewhere to beach the seaplane. When we returned to the wharf to fetch the plane, I had an impulse to open up one of the float compartments. The sea was dead smooth, and I opened up the front hatch without dropping a single screw in the water. The bilge was perfectly dry. I set to work on the second opening of the large middle compartment; when I saw what was inside I just stayed on one knee, staring into it, until the Governor called out, 'What is it?' This middle compartment, about 6-feet long, was half full of water; there must have been 50 gallons in it, equal to nearly half the weight of the whole seaplane. At last I knew what had been the cause of all my near disasters, the seaplane's nearly capsizing at Lord Howe Island, and trouble in taking off at Whitsunday Passage, Rockhampton, Merauke, Amboina, Ternate, Ormoc. To think of my pumping the bilge day after day and always finding it dry, while the main float compartment itself was flooded! I could see where the metal bilge pipe had been rammed by the keel when the float had been dropped on the deck of the cruiser; I could see where it had kinked and cracked at the top, so that I always sucked air instead of water through the crack. In a sort of apathy I pumped until dark, and lowered the level considerably. When I left off for the night I kept on muttering, 'Well, I'm damned,' till the Governor began to look sideways at me. To think of all my disgust and despair and raging at the antics of the seaplane on the water, and the difficulty of getting it into the air: now that I had discovered it, it was too late – the propeller was ruined. I seemed likely to be stuck in Masbate for months, a horrible prospect.

During the night I wondered if I could mend that propeller in some way. The difficulty was that I knew nothing about propeller construction, and I had been told that an unbalanced propeller would vibrate the engine clean out of the fuselage. Then I had an inspiration: why not try mending it with a piece of petrol tin? With that I went to sleep so soundly that I must have fed all the mosquitoes of Masbate. The net I had was too small to cover both my head and my feet. I had covered my head to keep the buzz away, and left my feet under the sheet. The mosquitoes must have bitten through this, because in the morning my flesh felt solid with bites.

After pumping the float dry, simple enough when I knew where to pump, I started work on removing the propeller. To do this I had to stand on the tip of one float and lean away from the seaplane, holding on to the propeller-boss with one hand, to keep myself from falling while I unscrewed the bolts with the other. Each bolt was held by a lock washer, and there were about a dozen bolts. I soon lost one spanner, and when a Filipino dived for it, he could not find it. I tied a second one to my wrist, and I tied a handkerchief round my forehead to keep the sweat out of my eyes. There was no breeze, and with the sun striking up from the water as well as down from above it was like working before an open furnace.

When I had the propeller on shore I cut a piece out of a petrol tin and worked it into a sheath for the tip. I asked the Governor to buy some shoe tacks for me. He produced some drawing-pins, which I thought hardly the thing for an aeroplane propeller, so he went off again and returned with tacks. After I had finished the damaged blade I bound insulation tape round the other blade, partly because it had been damaged too, partly to balance the tin, and partly out of curiosity.

It was more difficult to put on the propeller, because one blade must exactly track the other. I replaced the cover of the float hatch; the leak had been making a third of a gallon an hour. I swung the propeller, the engine started, and the propeller seemed all right. I was delighted, and opened the throttle wide. The Gipsy Moth took off like a bird. Suddenly there was a terrific din, flap! flap! flap! flap! I thought a blade had broken off, switched off instantly, and alighted on the spot. But it was only the tape which had started to unwind, and was whipping the float at each revolution. What I could not understand was that the tape, which had been thrashing round at 400 or 500 miles an hour, was quite undamaged. I took it off altogether. As soon as I opened up, the whole seaplane vibrated violently, and I could hardly hold the throttle. I expected the engine to be wrenched from its bed, and though I closed the throttle instantly, it seemed an age before the engine stopped.

This time I took the propeller to the Governor's house, sheathed the other tip with tin, and then threaded the propeller on my walking stick between two chairs and drove in tacks until it balanced, exactly horizontal. When I tried it out again the seaplane flew perfectly. The Governor had been such a willing helper that I offered him a flight. His personality was more developed than that of the other Filipinos I had met. I fitted him into the front cockpit among the gear. I knew that the seaplane would not rise from the glassy surface of the harbour with the extra weight, so I taxied out to the open sea. There I found a good breeze and just the right sea running. We were about to take off, and I could see the Governor laughing with exhilaration (there was no windshield to his cockpit, so the 100-mph slipstream driving straight into his face produced a sensation of great speed), when I felt a jar; the port float had struck. Looking straight down I saw to my dismay that we were in the middle of a coral reef. I switched off at once, and alternately looked at the float to see if it was filling up and at the reef astern of us. The seaplane was drifting sternwards fast before the breeze. The coral was alive, and the many branched shrubs of it had varying tints of red. Suddenly I noticed a broad clump of seaweed on the surface straight in our line of drift. I jumped out of the cockpit, landed on the float, slid into the water up to my waist, and held on waiting for my feet to touch. The seaplane was drifting fast, and at first its weight ran me off my feet. But I could feel the coral harsh and jagged through my rubber soles, and at last I secured a good footing, stopped the seaplane, and fended her off sideways. Then I went on, feeling for a foothold under water at each step, sometimes finding no bottom and falling in before pulling myself back on to the float, but every now and then getting a good push at what seemed a running pace under water until I had passed the seaplane round the outside of the clump. Then I jumped for the float and landed with my body across it. Next moment my feet touched again, and so I jumped from clump to clump with wild scrambles back on to the float until I had guided the seaplane back into the channel. From down in the water I could see the Governor still bubbling with glee, wrapped up in his own experience. He seemed to think it was all part of the game for me in my soft shoes to be pushing him round a coral reef in a seaplane. When we were safe, I told him about the float having struck the coral, and that I must get back as soon as possible to inspect it. He was quite satisfied, wanting no more thrill than that of taxiing at 40 or 50 mph. I was surprised and delighted to find the port float intact; it showed how sensitive I had become about anything touching the floats, because it must have been the lightest of scratches not to have ripped open the thin duralumin shell.

Next day I took off for Manila and was met by three United States Army fighters, fifty miles south of the city. They flew above me in formation and I was excited; I had reached Manila and it was thrilling to look up in the hot sunlight to see those fighter pilots above my head in formation, and sometimes waving at me. When I alighted at Cavite outside Manila, they swooped like three roaring hawks before zooming off.

At Manila I ran into terrific hospitality. After satisfying the US quarantine officer, I was driven to the Manila Hotel by Bagtas, the President of the Governor's Aviation Committee, and led to a man in a large wicker chair close to the entrance archway. This was Nicol Williamson, to whom I had a letter of introduction from someone in Sydney. He invited me to stay with him, and it would be hard to come across a more efficiently hospitable man.

Manila's society gave me a good time; lunch with the Governor-General's Aviation Committee, out to dinner, to a boxing match, to the English Club, to the swimming-pool where I watched the attractive women and girls bathing. The more functions and parties I went to, the more lonely I felt. I realized that I was little more than an abstract idea; I was the character responsible for a seaplane's having flown up from New Zealand to Manila. The more people I met, and the more friendliness, the more I longed for intimacy, the sharing of thoughts and feelings with one sympathetic person. Sometimes I day-dreamed of being alone on a yacht, lying on the deck and doing nothing but lazily sail it across the Pacific. Then I began to long for a wild party, but that would be a crime in such a friendly bastion of good behaviour. If I was madly attracted by someone, it was better to avoid her, because I would have to leave in a day or two. I became profoundly depressed.

A company owning a seaplane had lent me shelter in their hangar for my Gipsy Moth, which had been wheeled in on an axle. The floats were in a bad way; I could see daylight through the keel of the starboard one, and the port float had a bad bump. Long scores could be seen inside, caused by the coral reef. The first thing to do was to detach the floats. This company had two pilots, and the one on duty that morning was a bony-faced German with a sloping forehead and thin hair brushed back from it, who talked abrupt sentences of run-together words. I thought the obvious way to remove the floats was to sling the seaplane from the principal beam of the triangulated frame-work supporting the roof. The German came out of his office and refused to let me do it. I suggested something else, but he would not have that, either. I decided that he just plainly loathed the sight of me, and I could understand his viewpoint; why should an amateur be the spoilt pet of Manila when there were far more deserving veterans of aviation? I went into his office to talk to him and was astounded at his flying experience; he had flown nearly every type of machine, had flown right through the First World War. 'What squadron was he with?' I asked. 'Was it the American Lafayette?'

'I wasn't fighting for you, I was fighting against you,' he said.

I was full of interest and wonder at his experiences. What he did not know about aeroplanes was not worth knowing. I asked what he thought would be the best way to lift my sea-plane: he suggested tilting it up on to one wing-tip. I observed that perhaps the Gipsy Moth was flimsy compared with the important types he was used to handling, but he retorted briskly that he had handled dozens of them in China. We talked on without actually doing anything, and it was a de-pressed and baffled amateur pilot whom Williamson's boy fetched for lunch. After lunch the company's other pilot, Mac-Ilroy, an American, was on duty. We had the seaplane sus-pended from the roof in about thirty minutes, and both the floats and the propeller off soon afterwards.

The floats were in a bad way; in places only Roley Wilson's paint was keeping the water out. I decided that my only hope was the US Air Corps. But had their offer of assistance been merely a conventional politeness? I rang up Nichol's Field, and it was at once clear that the US Air Corps meant what it said. Major Duty, the officer in charge of Ordnance, came round at once. He was extremely efficient, and next morning at 7 AM an army lorry took the floats away. I set to work on the engine, wearing overalls only (I found them cooler than shorts) and a handkerchief round my elbows. An English engineer lent me an excellent mechanic to grind the valves, a job I detested. The exhaust valve in No. 3 cylinder was so pitted that we threw it out.

Major Duty invited me out to Nichol's Field. They had made a splendid job of the propeller by splicing in a piece of wood, and then sheathing the tips in copper. This made the propeller heavier, but by now it was obvious that only metal would stand up to the constant slashing through spray and wave crests. The propeller was on a spindle, and it was so well balanced that when I breathed on one tip it began to revolve. I was delighted. The floats would take some days; on their turning a hose into one, the water had gone straight through. The riveter wanted to cut a hatch in the top of the float in order to drive home the last rivets, but to avoid this it was finally agreed that he should screw the last plates home to a block inside the float, instead of riveting it. If only I could have foreseen the consequences of this petty detail!

CHAPTER NINETEEN

JAPANESE ENCOUNTERS

IT WAS five and a half months since I left Wellington, if I included the time spent at Auckland. I wrote, 'Five and a half months alone on a ship would be less lonely than this flying game. On a ship one would at least become used to the craft and all the parts of it, the sails, the ropes, the cabin, the decks, but with flying one is no sooner acquainted with any place or person than one must leave them and fly on again.' These were ground thoughts; life in the plane, in the air, was a life apart, strange, secret and thrilling, not to be thought of in the midst of materialism. I was a third of the way to England, with another 12,800 miles to fly.

One Sunday Mrs McCoy invited me to dinner. Her husband had commanded an American regiment at the capture of Manila in the Spanish-American war of 1898. My uncle had commanded the British ships sent to Manila to watch our interests. The Germans, who were looking for chances of colonial expansion, had sent a squadron under Admiral von Diedrich. Uncle Edward moved his ship between the American and German fleets, and indicated to von Diedrich that he would be up against the British if he made any move. The American Governor-General Davis was at the dinner; his name is widely known because he presented the Davis Cup for tennis.

I was fretting to leave. The charming Father Miguel Selga, Director of the Weather Bureau, used to visit me every day while I was working on the seaplane, to tell me with a kind of satisfaction how a depression was slowly forming east of the Philippines which he considered would turn into a typhoon. One day it had formed, and the next it was intensifying.

Finally, on July 30th, he called it a typhoon. On 31 July he handed me a typewritten notice, 'Typhoon warning. The Pacific depression or typhoon was situated at 10 AM today to the east of Northern Luzon, 17° N., 126° E. moving probably north-west.' That day began my strange race with the typhoon which, a few days later, was to destroy 2,000 homes in the Ryukyu Islands near Formosa, and which the *Asahi Mainichi* was to describe as the worst typhoon of the century.

Ever since I had arrived in Manila people had been asking, 'When is the typhoon coming?' This was not so that they could flee from it; they were complaining because there was no typhoon. The sultry heat was more oppressive every day, and the typhoon would clear the air. Typhoons rarely hit Manila itself, but were diverted north or south by the mountains, which typhoons usually preferred to go round rather than to climb. The Manila people had not long to wait; within a fortnight three-quarters of Manila City would be under water, and the only transport along the main streets would be bankas and canoes paddling.

A typhoon would be more dangerous for a seaplane than for a ship, but I was not seriously worried at that time because I thought that I could easily turn round and flee from a typhoon if I could not fly ahead of it. However, I had to reach Formosa before the typhoon got there. Formosa was my only possible route from the Philippines, and Father Selga was almost certain that this typhoon would make for Formosa.

The day the floats and propeller were returned, everything seemed to go wrong; spanners slipped, nuts cross-threaded, and people interrupted me continually. I was driven nearly mad by prickly heat, I had a wretched cold as well, and my decapitated finger throbbed. The climax came when the motor refused to start; I swung the propeller until I could not see for sweat in my eyes, and I felt like seizing a sledge hammer and smashing the whole machine. Suddenly I saw myself as a stupid little insect making infinitesimally small struggles. I laughed, returned to the house and went to sleep for a few minutes. When I got back to the seaplane I found that it was child's play to take all the electrical connections to pieces, clean them with petrol and replace them. The engine started at once. The whole seaplane and the floats were in excellent condition; the sun shone, and the sea sparkled. The motor had a harsh, full-throated bark that was music in my ears. The seaplane rose as lightly as a snipe, and skimmed to and fro over the surface trying out her paces.

Next morning there was no breeze whatever, and the seaplane was heavily loaded. I tried to take off two or three times without success, but the sea gradually calmed my angry impatience—I felt that I might be worse off. I took my kapok jacket, intended to keep a pilot afloat for three days, made a pillow of it on the wing and went to sleep. I woke to find a ten-mile breeze blowing. I tried twice more, and then pumped forward some of the petrol in the back tank. The seaplane seemed nearer taking off, so I opened the cock and ran off petrol till the back tank was empty. This left me with only five hours and twenty minutes' fuel supply for a five hours and twenty minutes' flight, but I thought that there would probably be some place where I could come down if I did run out of petrol. I got off at the next attempt. I flew back to Williamson's house and he waved to me from between two of his typhoon shutters. That cost me twenty miles, but I could not have left without doing it. Exactly five hours and twenty minutes later I came down on the Aparri River, which was my next stop. When I came to take off in the morning I stepped on to the float and it went straight under water; it was the same old bilge. I pumped for ten minutes, but the water was gaining, so I had the plane towed to shallow water close inshore. Slithering about on slime an inch thick, and standing up to my waist in water, I removed the manhole; the float compartment was about two-thirds full. I baled it out with the largest tin which I could pass through the hole at the top—a tobacco tin. When only a few inches of water remained I could see more water flowing in like a welling spring, but an A-shaped girder laid at the bottom of the float made it impossible to see the actual leak. I tried to think of some way to stop a leak which I could neither see nor feel, and which was under water. With some kindly helpers, I pulled the seaplane up the slimy bank and rocked the floats on to a bedding of coconut husks, but when I washed the mud off the keel bottom there was no sign of any hole underneath. I filled the float with water, and there was no sign of any leak. Finally we slid the seaplane off the mud into the river, and I peered into the float; there was no sign of any leak. It then was too late for me to start that day, so I took one of my helpers for a short flight up the river, and afterwards there was still no sign of any leak. Next morning, when I stepped on the float, it sank again, exactly as it had done the day before. Again I tried to find the hole, and failed. 'For heaven's sake,' I thought, 'I must do something.' But all that I could think of doing was to stuff a rag under the girder above the leak. With that I clapped on the hatch cover and took off for Formosa.

Flying north, I passed over Babuyan Island, and over Autau Su, the first Japanese island, which was forty miles east of the south end of Formosa. The Japanese had forbidden me to come near the coast of Formosa for another sixty-five miles, and when I did reach my permitted bit of the Formosan coast I found rock cliffs sheer enough for a stone to be thrown into the sea from 2,000 feet up. The Japanese had marked a big area at the north end of the island where I was prohibited from flying. I had no map of the land, but only a chart, which showed nothing from coast to coast except a few spot heights. These were of 11,490 feet south-west of my route, 8,887 feet to the west of it, and another of 3,480 feet just to the north, but this one was in the prohibited area.

I thought that my only problem would be to climb high enough to slip over a saddle; I thought the Gipsy Moth would struggle up to 5,000 feet, possibly flounder up to 6,000 feet, but certainly no higher. I fastened my safety-belt and climbed steadily. I crossed a saddle with plenty of height to spare, but instead of the plain I expected to find on the other side, I could see nothing but mountains and cloud in every direction. I was in a long, narrow-gutted ravine with a mountain torrent below, and ahead was a black-hearted rain-cloud, blocking my path. I hesitated but didn't want to turn back. If I went round to the north of the prohibited area out to sea, I should have had to alight and get more petrol first. Under the cloud, I could see a stretch of the river bed, with some rocky half-forested sides, which looked a bright watery green. This showed, I thought, that it must be clear of cloud on the other side. I decided to risk sacrificing my height, closed the throttle and dived under the cloud. I came out on the other side in a precipitous gorge with a turbulent torrent below, and completely sealed off with cloud 2,000 feet above my head. What awaited me I could not tell, because the gorge made a sharp turn to the right and I could see only a bleak V-section of mountain facing me. The seaplane whizzed up and down as it was buffeted by different air currents. I turned the big bend to find myself in another reach of ravine, completely filled by a thunderstorm. I hated the implacable Japanese officialdom which had forced me into this. It was as dark as twilight, and the rocks were black, with wisps of steam rising here and there. Each flash of lightning lit everything brilliantly, but afterwards it seemed darker still. The black cloud was not raining, and I sacrificed yet more height and flew under it. I cleared the storm and flew round a bend to find myself in another gorge. This seemed completely blocked; ahead of me a dense foggy white cloud, wedged between the sides near the bottom with an opaque curtain of rain, in which the river faded and disappeared. I felt paralysed with fright; I was trapped, because I had no hope of flying blind in a narrow gorge. I could not decide what to do; I began to turn, but hesitated because I was afraid, and I swung back on course again. But to go on seemed certain death; I had to turn, and I whirred round in a vertically banked turn. A picture of the whole ravine was sharply etched on my brain, with every tree standing out clearly, the falls and boulders in the river, the strange brighter green up the sides, the cloud ceiling overhead, and a little branch coming in from the north. That 'little branch valley', or side gulley, seemed to offer a chance, so I turned again vertically banked, and climbed at full throttle. When I reached the gulley it was clear, but sloped up to the clouds. I kept the seaplane climbing as steeply as possible at full throttle. Then, close under the cloud ceiling stretched across the top, I got a clear view far to the north, as though looking through a narrow slit. It showed me my escape. It led straight through the middle of the forbidden area, but I felt, to hell with the Japanese and their forbidden area – that seemed a minor hazard compared with the rocks of the gorge. But as I went on a saddle opened up on my left, and through it I saw a flooded plain. I turned sharply again, and shot through. As soon as I was safe I felt exhausted. I flew straight over the middle of Taihoku, the capital, towards Tamsui, on one side of a wide river, full of mud banks. I flew low down, and hundreds of Japanese children in school grounds stopped playing and stared up at me with a sea of brown faces.

I was astonished to see a lot of Japanese flags, spiky red suns on a white field, and flying along the stone-faced river bank I saw that it was crowded with people. Then I spotted three launches in the river, each flying a Japanese flag and full of white-uniformed officials. Somehow the thought of a ceremonious Japanese welcome had never occurred to me. I circled the water, and alighted outside one of the launches. There was a strong current, and the seaplane at once began drifting seawards.

Remembering how fast the water had rushed into my float at Aparri I felt flustered. 'I must anchor in shallow water,' I shouted. The officials in the launches chattered among themselves, and when I repeated my shout, they seemed undecided. The current carried me over a mud bank where the water seemed fairly shallow, and I thought that I had better anchor there in case the seaplane sank quickly. I extracted and rigged my anchor, which seemed to excite the officials. There were cries from them, and they talked rapidly among themselves. No one understood my need for shallow water, and although the sight of my anchor was obviously upsetting them, I let it go, and it held with a strong tide rip at the rope and floats. A launch of officials came up, and a man on board began introducing them to me one by one, as if I were holding a levee. One can lead a rational, orderly existence for month after month, but suddenly a fantastic ridiculous situation may occur which upsets all one's values and seems simply incredible. This was it. While official after official stood up in the launch, was introduced in English I could not understand, and bowed three times with most punctilious ceremony, I was in a fever of impatience at the thought of my float filling under me. Already I could feel the float losing its buoyancy. To make the scene more farcical, the Japanese were all dressed in spotless whites with smart uniform caps, and I must have looked like a disreputable tramp; from head to foot I was filthy with smears of Aparri mud and grease. My kapok life jacket, which never had an elegant shape at the best of times, bulged with cord and rags in the pockets; my soft rubber shoes were dirty and shapeless; my shirt was dirty and without a collar; my hair and beard were tousled, and my fingernails showed rims of black mud. But once the introductions had started I could not interrupt: a nation trained to *hara-kiri* (I thought) would expect me to continue bowing if the float disappeared under my feet. I seethed with suppressed fret as a second launchful of introductions was completed. As soon as I could I shouted again that I must get the seaplane into shallow water before it sank.

'You will tie up to mooring arranged for you, yes?' asked the English-speaking Japanese.

'My plane is sinking, my plane is sinking,' and so on, time after time.

'The Customs officer will come to your seaplane now.'

'I tell you that I am sinking.' I could feel the float under my feet steadily losing buoyancy. A third crowded launch arrived, and this one had the British Consul, Ovens, on board. Again I had to wait for the introductions to end before I cried out to Ovens, 'My seaplane is sinking.'

Ovens was a tall Englishman in a tropical suit of yellow-tinted white and a pith helmet. He had a long chin, a clipped moustache and scanty hair. He had difficulty in raising his voice loud enough to be heard, and he looked self-conscious, even sheepish. Everything about me and my seaplane was very unfortunate for him, and he seemed quite unable to grasp that I needed help urgently. He said the Customs man wanted to inspect my seaplane, and that I had better let him. I said it was ridiculous to insist on this immediately when it could be done just as well after I had been towed into shallow water. This caused a long discussion, which ended in his saying he thought it would be advisable for me to let the Customs official board the seaplane there. I said, 'Then they must send a sampan; that launch will only smash up the plane.'

In due course a sampan arrived, sculled by a small Japanese in a sailor suit, with a whistle cord and a round unpeaked cap with ribbons streaming from the back. He manoeuvred his flat-bottomed sampan with great skill, using a scull like Father Time's scythe attached to a blade at the stern. When the Japanese came alongside I gave them my journey log-book, sealed camera, double-barrelled pistol and ammunition. 'My seaplane has a hole in the bottom, you understand, and is sinking, sinking. I must get it ashore at once.' There was another long discussion, and then the interpreter said, 'They will inspect your baggage now.'

'They can inspect my baggage when my seaplane is on shore and not before,' I said desperately, 'I tell you my seaplane is sinking.'

After another long conference, they threw me a line from the launch, and towed the seaplane to a mooring above the pier. A worse situation could not be imagined; the current was so strong that the launch could barely make headway against it, and any mistake would mean my plane's being swept right into the piles of the pier. When they reached the mooring the float upon which I was standing went under water. I jumped across to the other float, and shouted to the launch to tow the seaplane to the beach immediately. They could not, or would not, understand; I could not land until the quarantine officer had been on board. A fourth launch arrived, with another Englishman on board. He was McKay, the Shell representative. When I told him what was wrong he understood at once, and tried to explain to the Japanese. Ten of them talked together very rapidly. At last I burst out to the Shell man, 'For God's sake, throw me a line yourself, man, and tow me in. I tell you the seaplane is going to sink at any moment.' He looked scared,

'No, no. I couldn't do that.' However, he redoubled his efforts with the Japanese, and his soft, almost timid, manner with them was successful; the launch towed me in close to the mud shore, a line was thrown and the seaplane secured in shallow water. McKay undertook to have the seaplane carried ashore on bamboo poles. He gave me complete confidence, and he put the operation in hand while I surrendered to the Japanese officials. First, I was shepherded through the crowd to the Customs House, to a long bare wooden table with wine glasses and a bottle of port on it. Standing round, they drank a toast to the foreign aviator. Then they got down to the real business of the meeting. Why had I not alighted at Karenko where I was supposed to? What route had I followed from Aparri? What was the horsepower of my engine? They surrounded me, hissing these questions and many others at the interpreter, not just two or three times each question, but dozens of times. One of the most repeated was, 'At what hour had I left Aparri?' I could seldom remember details about time immediately after a flight, and said, 'Five or six hours ago.' This really stirred them up.

'The telegram said you left Aparri yesterday.'

'I can't help what the telegram says.'

'You flew over Basco at 11.5 today, the telegram says. Is that so?'

'I dare say.'

'You left Aparri yesterday; you flew over Basco today. Where were you in the interval?'

'At Aparri, I suppose, since I left Aparri today, and not yesterday.'

'At what hour did you leave Aparri?'

They asked it twenty times, with a different selection of silly questions in between. It seemed incredibly stupid, because in the first place, had I spent the night photographing fortifications in south Formosa, the last thing I should do would be to lie about the time I left Aparri, which could easily be checked. Secondly, if there was anything worth spying on, surely there would have been a guard there capable of detecting the presence of an aeroplane.

Then they started on my route through the mountains. I became uneasy. Had they been leading up to this all the time? I said I had flown as straight as I could across the island as ordered, and I stuck to this right through. I had resented their having pushed me into the mountains so unnecessarily, and as the questioning went on for hour after hour, and seemed to be developing into a 'third degree' interrogation, I hardened up inside. In fact, the very minute of my leaving Aparri was marked on the chart and staring me in the eye, but by then I would not say it, and I stuck to my 'five or six hours'. I felt that they were repeating this same question endlessly, to make me break down and confess that I had been spying. A sort of cold rage took me, childish, perhaps, but I had had a gruelling day, apart from the 500-mile flight. Next time they asked me what the horsepower of my motor was, after I had been repeating 100 hp until I was sick of it, I replied 20 hp for a change. Then I said 25, and every time they asked me I added 5 horsepower, curious to see how high I would get. Actually, the horsepower varied with the revolutions, minimum 20 and maximum 100. Presently I began pulling their legs and making poor jokes. In the end they handed me over to Ovens, who took me home; he told me I had done a very risky thing in making fun of the Japanese, but they had made me bloody minded.

McKay came up to tell me about the float. The drain plug had been fastened to a plate. Screws used to fix the plate to the hull had not drawn tight, and when the float was in the water, the water pressed the plate away from the hull and rushed in. As soon as the float came out of the water, the water inside pressed the plate against the hull and stopped the leak. I asked McKay if he could get it mended for me, and he said he could, but that he would have to use steel, as he had no duralumin. I asked him to go ahead, and said that I would have to leave tomorrow because of the typhoon. Ovens said he knew nothing of any typhoon and went off for a forecast. It said, 'No low pressure in the neighbourhood of Formosa or Shanghai. Fine weather expected between them.'

'That typhoon,' I thought, 'must be a myth. How could

228

Father Selga have known about it in July without the Japanese knowing anything about it on August 5th?' So I decided to stay at Tamsui another day.

CHAPTER TWENTY

EN ROUTE FOR CHINA

IN the morning Ovens motored me to Taihoku where I had been 'commanded' to meet the Governor-General. At his palace we were ushered into a high room with a row of pillars down the middle, the walls hung with long black tapestries. The Governor sat at a square table, and watched me for a long time without the least sign of any feeling. After a long silence he spoke without taking his eyes off me, and the interpreter said, 'His Excellency says that he is pleased you reached his country of Formosa with success.'

I also waited before answering, 'You will please thank His Excellency for the honour he does me?'

His Excellency grunted and there was another long silence before he spoke again. In this manner the conversation had not got very far at the end of a quarter of an hour, but my opinion of the Governor changed. Although both his eyes and features remained completely blank of expression I seemed to become aware of his thoughts. I do not think they were complimentary, though I believe he had a feeling of bored weariness with his office and faintly envied me my bit of fun and freedom. At the end there was a bad moment when the interpreter said, 'His Excellency desires to know the horse-power of your motor,' and I only just managed to suppress a laugh before I answered, 'You will tell His Excellency that the horsepower of my motor is 80' – that being the figure I had now reached with five horsepower rises. His Excellency clapped his hands and a bottle of sweet champagne suddenly arrived, of which a single glass was formally drunk.

Ovens then took me to the Chinese Consul to whom the British Ambassador at Peking had cabled his permission for me to visit China. The amiable Chinese asked me where I proposed touching the Chinese coast, and when I replied 'Funingfu' he warned me not on any account to have a forced landing or alight anywhere along the section of coast north of it. It was infested with pirates, and every man there was apparently a potential pirate of a valuable looking seaplane with only one man to guard it.

The rest of that day was a holiday. I discovered at last why my finger had been hurting and irritating so much; the stitched up flesh had healed but a piece of fingernail had grown inside it, and could not get out. I cut open a gap for it with a razor blade. Next morning Ovens hummed and hawed about the work he ought to do and said that he could not come down to the seaplane. In the end I persuaded him to come. The seaplane still rested on empty petrol cases in the mud, and after I had refuelled and stowed my gear, police officials ceremoniously returned me my camera and my thirteen cartridges, solemnly counting them into my hand one by one. I was then led to a kitchen table planted in the mud on which stood the same twelve wine glasses as before. (Ovens told me that they were his, borrowed for the occasion.) Across the wide muddy river the sunburnt mountainside rose abruptly; the river flowed a few yards from our feet. Iron stakes had been driven into the mud with a dirty rope stretched between them to keep a square patch select, and here we stood round the table in the hazy sunlight, drinking port wine. I felt friendly towards my inquisitors. A squad of coolies lifted the seaplane by means of bamboo poles under the floats. The foreman snatched off one coolie's conical straw hat which threatened to puncture a wing, and then, sounding their cries like a lot of human swans, the coolies sloshed over the mud and set down their load in the water. They were a good-humoured, easygoing, practical lot, I think Formosans and not Japanese. Several were holding the floats when I started the engine, and the slipstream catching one of the enormous round hats sent it bowling over the mud, which drew a roar of applause from the onlookers. The owner of the hat was laughing as much as anybody.

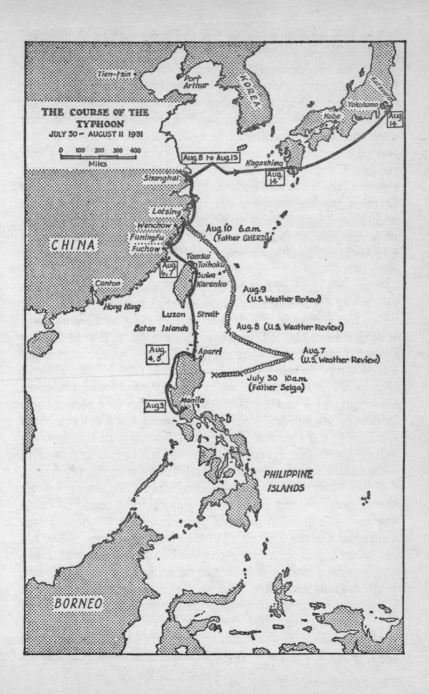

THE COURSE OF THE
TYPHOON
JULY 30 – AUGUST 11 1931

0   100   200   300   400
Miles

The current was running fast the same way as the breeze, and I could not get off. One of the launches came up and an official, picking up a rope, offered me a tow to the sea. I would have preferred to drift down, but could not refuse his kindly offer. A mile short of the bar we entered a small tide rip, where the broken water was ideal. I shouted and cast off the rope, and at that moment there came a waft of sea breeze. I started the engine, jumped in, and opened right up at one stroke. The Gipsy Moth rose from the waves easily, and I swept round in a wide arc and flew up-river. I saluted the Ovenses waving on their flat roof, then dived to the water and saluted each launch as I flashed past. I could see belches of white steam at the sirens of the ships and steam launches as I passed, but could hear no noise above the roar of my own engine.

That day the sun was behind me; I had overtaken it, so to speak, and I was leaving it to the south. I was soon out of sight of land, and the sea, which used to give me a cold feeling, was now like an old friend, restful and soothing. A hundred miles from Formosa I flew over the first Chinese territory, a small island forty-five miles from the mainland called Tung Yung. I shot past the lighthouse, where five Chinese stood intent on something in a small walled-in yard at the foot of the lamp buildings. As I drew alongside they broke out a red and black Chinese flag at the foot of the mast. The sight of that bunting warmed me, and I regretted having no flag of my own to return their salute. The best I could do was to dip my wings.

Soon I was over the mainland of China. The moist hot air was oppressive, and I was so drowsy that my head nodded. I started looking for a suitable bay on which to come down. One after another I rejected Funingfu, Tehinkoen, Namkwan Harbour, and Tanue Bay – they were all crowded with junks and sampans with black or brown sails, or white sails with black battens like ribs. The whole coast was infested with junks, and it seemed incredible that a single fish could survive so many fishermen. By the time I reached Lotsing Bay I decided to come down, junks or no junks. I chose the southern end, where I could see only one junk for several miles, and I decided that if I kept an eye on that one it should be at least an hour before any of the others could reach me. I shut off, twisted down steeply, skimmed the water to inspect it closely for fishing stakes or flotsam, circled and bounced before settling. That bump humbled my pride in my flying skill, but on coming to rest I found that I had bumped a smooth swell which was invisible from above. Every junk in the bay immediately set sail for the seaplane – except the one close behind me to the south, which continued on its course. I lit a pipe and stood on a float, idly watching the water lap at my feet. It was soothing to be close to the water in a heat so sweltering. Suddenly I spotted a sampan with five or six Chinese on board within 100 yards of the seaplane's tail. Nothing could have cured my drowsiness more effectively; that sampan must have been quietly dropped off the far side of the junk as it sailed past. I threw my coat into the cockpit, jumped across to the other float, switched on, and began swinging the propeller, wondering if the motor would jib. At the fourth swing it started, and I taxied off seawards. As I rose from the bay I roared with laughter, the slipstream catching me in my teeth. The heat was nearly overpowering, and when I spotted a black rain squall to the east I changed course and flew into it. At first it was delicious, but within a few seconds the sea was beaten flat and covered with a layer of spray indistinguishable from the grey downpour. I turned round and bolted back the way I had come. For ten or fifteen miles I had to fly over the sea, dodging small islands and junks that suddenly loomed up in the murk. After the squall I flew over a hilly coast with a solid little village on every other hill-top, looking like a grey roofed nest of pirates. All the hills were spotted with tombs like cathedral doors fallen flat in stone-faced niches in the hillsides. When I reached the city of Shanghai I flew down the Wusung River beside a cliff of solid buildings. A strong wind blowing across river was broken up by the mass of buildings, and the heat rising from the streets. The seaplane, slapped and buffeted by the gusts, rocked and lurched and bumped down the river, crabbing along half sideways in the cross wind. This drift did give me an unobstructed view to one side of the engine, of the fairway and the ship masts in it. The river was swarming with junks and sampans, but seemed even more crowded with steamers and warships, mostly gunboats, strung together stem to stern between great iron buoys. The neat little warships in grey or pale blue looked tiny beside the steamers. I bumped along ten miles to Wusung at the mouth of the river, where the wind blowing across the river was strong enough to raise a sea. We were tossed about like a leaf as I circled the mouth of the river looking for a flagged buoy. I could not see one, and flew back to the first bend, where a fleet of junks was anchored; still I could see nothing. Then I noticed a dribble of steam at the siren of a launch, and I dived towards it, and saw someone wave. I circled again, and with a firm hand put the seaplane down near the launch. Drifting rapidly, I was some distance down wind of the launch before I got my anchor down. The launch, or small tug, came at me. Shouting as hard as I could I persuaded them to hold off, and to send me a sampan. 'He wants a sampan,' someone said in an ordinary voice, which I could hear quite plainly coming down wind. They drew off, and beckoned a big sampan to them. It was a wooden antique, like the hull of Noah's Ark with a high raised platform at the square stern. It looked more suitable for ferrying elephants than boarding my seaplane, and the entire crew was one old woman with wisps of hair streaming in the wind. She stood on the stern platform, wielding a heavy bent scull. A thickset white man, with a mop of long black hair, jumped into this craft, and encouraged the old woman to make for me with dramatic excited gestures as if I were drowning. The sampan came straight down wind for the seaplane, driven by the old woman's oar plus a thirty-mile wind. Taking him for a high official in the Chinese Government I was as polite as possible when I shouted that the sampan was too big to come down wind. Every time I shouted he urged the old woman on more excitedly. The sampan struck the float tip end on with a bang; the stem scraped past, and in spite of my pushing against it with all my strength, fetched up against the wing. A coolie who had jumped into the sampan with the white man seized a boat hook, and jabbed at the leading edge of the wing – mercifully, I was able to strike it aside before it penetrated. Then the wind caught the stern of the sampan, and swung it round broadside on to the wing. The old woman's cheery smile had not changed, and her steady efforts with the big scull had not ceased; the coolie pushed off the wing, and the sampan drifted past and astern. It had been a lucky escape, and I felt sure that the man would realize that he must come up from astern. To my dismay he returned to the position up wind of the seaplane as fast as he could. 'Can't stay here,' he shouted so dictatorially that I assumed that he was a white mandarin. 'You are right in the way of shipping; have to move you.'

Taking not the slightest notice of what I said, he directed the old woman to work the sampan across my anchor rope, which the coolie fished up with his boat hook. Then they lifted my anchor. How that old woman had handled the sampan by herself in that wind had been a marvel to me; now she had the seaplane as well, and it takes a man's utmost strength to hold the seaplane in a strong wind. She stuck grimly to her scull, but we drifted back steadily, right into the middle of the shipping fairway. I implored the white man to drop my anchor, but he jumped about excitedly, waving his arms and ignoring me. He did at last realize that we were going to end up on the opposite shore, and then he did drop my anchor, and returned to the launch, leaving me right in the fairway, with large steamers passing one after the other making a strong wash. Presently he came back, again from the side. I could do nothing; with all my shouting in the strong wind, my voice had died away to a whisper. There was a tearing noise as the stem of the sampan penetrated the fabric of the wing tip. 'Can't stay here,' he cried, 'shipping – dangerous – not allowed.' The coolie picked up my anchor rope again with his boat hook, the launch backed down to the sampan, and passed a line to it which the mandarin fastened to my anchor rope with a number of granny knots. The launch moved off at full speed across wind. The seaplane, when pulled from the side, glided forward in the strong wind just as a kite rises into the air when the string is pulled, and was soon broadside on to the wake of the launch. The end of the float began to twitch under the strain, and I expected to see it pulled off. I rallied my voice for some last desperate yells, but no one took the slightest notice. Fortunately the anchor rope snapped, and I drifted sternwards without an anchor. The launch chased me and threw a line. With the mandarin absent on the sampan, they listened to me, and everything was arranged in a few moments. We began crabbing across the wind, dead slow, towards the fleet of junks. Every time the wing started to lift at a gust, I ran out along the spar to keep it down with my weight. At last, when we were out of the fairway, and somewhat sheltered among the junks, they shouted to me to come aboard. But the white mandarin had arrived in the sampan, and with flamboyant gestures, his hair streaming in the wind, he exhorted the old lady to bear down once more on the seaplane, down wind. With the hole in the fabric, the wing tip buckled, and several ribs in the leading edge smashed, besides one or two lucky escapes, I had had enough of him, mandarin or no mandarin. When he came close enough, 'You bloody bastard,' I said shaking my fist, 'if you barge into me again, I'll wring your neck!' This he listened to. 'What do you want, then?' he demanded.

'Come up from astern, you bloody fool,' I said as the sampan struck. Fortunately the old woman's skill was marvellous, and with my frantic shove from the float the sampan passed round the wing with only slight damage to the tip. In the flurry my hat blew off, and went bowling over the water. At last he came up from astern where, of course, the old woman brought up the sampan with the greatest of ease. 'And now,' I said, 'perhaps you will tell me who I have had the honour of dealing with all this time?'

'I represent the *North China Daily News*. I am a South African and a globe-trotter like yourself and a keen airman like yourself.'

On board the launch I met Colonel Thoms, who was a big, tall New Zealander in command of the Shanghai Volunteer Corps, Palmer, the Shell man, and a China Police officer. We debated what to do with the seaplane. Palmer said that it would be difficult to guard it there, and that it would take one and a half hours to get down the river by launch. I asked why he did not come down by motor-car. Thoms said, 'You can't motor anywhere here. There are no motor roads, and it is not safe to leave the town.' Here the old woman, her withered face wreathed in a friendly smile, manoeuvred her sampan alongside and returned my hat. She had gone off by herself and rescued it while we talked.

It was decided that I should fly up river to the Shell (Asiatic Petroleum Company) store and jetty, half-way back to Shanghai. Before getting into the sampan to return to the seaplane, I drew Palmer aside. 'Can't you come in the sampan instead of that chap?' I asked. 'It's pure luck that my plane is still intact; why didn't you come in the first place?'

'I didn't like to, because he is a flying man, and knows all about it.'

Palmer talked Chinese fluently and I was quickly back in the seaplane without any trouble. When I opened the throttle to take off I was only 170 yards from the river bank ahead of me, but the seaplane took off easily enough some thirty yards short of the bank. I circled to have a good look at the take-off scene, recalling all the long hair-raising attempts to get off during the voyage before the floats were mended. I came down by the Shell jetty and the seaplane was hauled up a grass bank beside it, with each wing tied down to oil drums full of water. By the time all this had been done it was dark, and we trod across a number of sampans to a jetty where the shadows were pitch black. 'Keep together,' said Thoms, 'they have a habit of sticking a knife into people here, and holding the body under water until all is quiet.' After a long wait beside a road while I tried to keep the reporter from sitting on the bundle containing my one suit, Palmer at last secured a car, and Thoms took me to stay at his house.

In the morning, my first concern was to find out about the weather over the Yellow Sea between China and Japan. The sea crossing was 538 miles, and if I should meet a head wind of 20 mph I should be forced down short of Japan. The only way to get a weather report was to go to the Observatory of the

Jesuit convent at Siccawei. This was outside the International Settlement, and I spent the whole of the next day travelling. First we hooted our way yard by yard through narrow alleys barely wide enough for the car, with cries from coolies, jingling of rickshaw bells and Chinese chatter continually in our ears. Thoms's Chinese chauffeur was lucky to run 10 yards without the human swarm closing round us and forcing the car to stop with a jerk. At last we reached the convent, which stood in a deserted old-world garden, with mossy stone flags. I waited in a cool, silent, stone hall, while a priest went to find Father Gherzi. He was a thin tall man with a slender high-browed head, and a narrow black beard. He wore a long black robe, under which appeared two enormous black boots. He was impatient, impetuous and clever. In a rapid, emphatic way, he said that there was a typhoon centred east of Formosa, that it was travelling fast straight for Shanghai, that it was impossible for me to leave for Japan because of a 35-mph head wind, and that I must secure my seaplane at once. After my experience the day before with the emphatic reporter in the sampan, I started cross-examining Father Gherzi about this weather. He showed clearly that he resented this, and that he thought me a fool.

Scared for the survival of the seaplane, I returned to Thoms's office as soon as possible to find the best shelter for my Gipsy Moth. Looking for the RAF Intelligence Officer, we visited the long narrow bar of the Shanghai Club, which ran deep into a building like a straight high passage. It was full, and I received a number of remarkable suggestions for saving the seaplane. On looking back, the best would have been to fly west-north-west away from the typhoon to Peking – a suggestion which came from Paddy Fowlds, an ex-RAF pilot, now with Shell in China. But I didn't want to go so far inland, and at last we located the RAF Intelligence Officer, who said, 'Had I tried the seaplane hangar?'

'What seaplane hangar?'

'The North China Aviation Company has a big hangar beside the river with a concrete slipway.'

We could get no answer on the telephone, so Palmer took

me up to the hangar in a launch. The slipway was on a lee shore with a strong wind blowing on to it at an angle. The hangar was also closed up and locked, but in any case it would have been impossible to get the seaplane to it in that wind. I had to leave her where she was that night.

Next morning Father Gherzi looked worried. The typhoon had destroyed 2,000 houses in the Ryukyus, the string of islands between Formosa and Japan. The Japanese had refused me permission to fly near these, and it was because of this that I was now in Shanghai facing the sea crossing to Japan. Father Gherzi told me that it looked as if the typhoon was going to curve and pass close to Shanghai to the east; that it was gathering speed; and that I must make my aeroplane secure. How was I to do that? In this whole vast city I could not find anywhere to shelter one small seaplane.

I went down to my Gipsy Moth, pulled her farther up the mud, and raised the float heels so that the wind would press the wings down instead of lifting them up. Next morning (10 August) Father Gherzi said that the typhoon was centred at 27° N., 123° E., which was 150 miles south-east of the bay where I had alighted when on the way up from Formosa. It appeared to be curving towards the coast, to pass inland, but that was unusual in August, and it seemed more likely to recurve itself and make directly for Shanghai. That day the steamer *Waishing* was wrecked in Namkwan Harbour, and the *Kwongsang* went down with all hands at Funingfu, my landfall on arriving from Formosa. The typhoon had travelled 360 miles in a day. Father Gherzi expected the wind to increase to 50 mph that afternoon.

At 4.30 PM the typhoon gun was fired, and I went off down the river in a launch to stand by the seaplane through the night. I had one hope. The seaplane would be quite safe in a 100-m.p.h. wind if it was facing into it in a flying position. Such a wind would give the seaplane a lift equal to a ton's weight, so that if I could face the seaplane into the wind, and weight it down with a ton, it should ride out the typhoon. Filling the floats with water, as I knew from bitter experience, was the best way to weight it down, but it would not be possible after that to change its heading if the wind changed direction. I had the seaplane moved to the lee of a wall and the eyebolts in the wings secured to four oil drums. Then I removed all the bilge plugs, so that when the tide rose the floats would fill with water. The caretaker put me up for the night in the houseboat in which he lived. Every time I woke during the night the wind was blowing unchanged in strength, and in the morning it was still the same. Suddenly I thought, 'What a weak fool I am to be sitting here like a paralysed rabbit!' I went back to Shanghai by the first launch that passed, and sought out Father Gherzi. The typhoon had struck the coast at the bay where I had alighted among the junks, and was moving inland, but was expected to curve northwards for Shanghai. I told him that I was going to leave Shanghai next morning, typhoon or not typhoon. A wind which would prevent my reaching Japan, would be favourable for a flight to Korea. If, after five hours over the sea, I took a sextant shot and found that I had not enough petrol to reach Japan, I would turn north and fly with the wind. I could do this even if the wind was 60 mph. I expected him to tell me curtly not to leave, but he said only, 'Very well.' Then he begged me not to leave until he had reports from Korea and Japan in the morning. But I could not wait for these reports. I had to leave Thoms's house at dawn if I was to reach the seaplane by 7 AM and take off by 9 AM. There were no telephones, or roads to the seaplane. Then I had an idea, and Paddy fell in with it. This was that I would take off, and fly *back* up the river; Paddy would get the latest report from Father Gherzi, and signal to me with a flag from the top of the Shell building as I flew past. If the wind was more favourable below 5,000 feet one flag; above 5,000 feet two flags; too dangerous for me to leave, three flags.

When I got back to Thoms's house I was told by Daly that I had been taken to the wrong hangar on Saturday; that one belonged to the Chinese army; the American Company's hangar was farther upstream, and they had waited for me there with a skilled launching crew.

In the morning, after the comprador of the petrol depot had

painted 'A fair wind and an easy voyage' on the fuselage in Chinese characters, I let the seaplane drift fast across the river, and took off with the greatest ease. I had 48 gallons on board, and regretted not having filled right up with 60 gallons which I could certainly have lifted.

At first I could not pick out the Shell building from the great row all so much alike. Then I spotted the semaphore tower like a tall pillar on the riverside, and worked along from there. There seemed to be flags on every building for miles. Then I spotted three flags in a triangle – three flags after taking off so easily with a full load. I was disgusted at everything. I flew on up river and easily located the company's hangar where it was kid's stuff taxiing up to a proper cradle with an expert crew and then drawing the seaplane up the smooth concrete. The Americans had a telephone into the city and I spoke to Paddy. I told him what I thought of his stopping me. He said, 'Quite impossible, my dear chap, quite impossible. Father Gherzi said there was a sixty- to seventy-mile wind against you. Sheer suicide.' I took the opportunity with the seaplane on firm land of inspecting the fuselage closely. The fabric was peeling off the underside of the fuselage, and the exposed plywood looked sodden. That glued plywood gave the seaplane its strength; if the glue had its life taken out by the sea water, the tail would break off in a gust. The Gipsy Moth was not built as a sea-plane, and it was not built to stand up to sea water. As I ripped off the useless fabric and covered the three ply with black bituminous paint I wished I had a parachute.

In the afternoon Father Gherzi said that I must not leave before he had the Japanese reports at 8.30 in the morning. That meant a 9.30 start, which was later than I liked, but what could I say to a man who was taking so much trouble for my safety? There was something fine about that dark impatient man, and he was good: each time I parted from him, I had an impulse to live a better life.

In the morning I set off again. It was the 13th of the month, and I was worried about the superstition that it might be un-lucky. But, 'Rubbish!' I told myself. 'Thirteen is my lucky number, not unlucky; I first flew solo on a 13th, left Wellington on a 13th, arrived in Sydney on a 13th, and today I am leaving Shanghai on a 13th.' Another part of me said, 'These 13s are repeated omens of disaster.' But I didn't care what they were; all I wanted was to fly the Yellow Sea on that day.

Father Gherzi said that I could leave, but that the conditions were not favourable. There would be a head wind for a considerable distance, Force 6 or so, but near Kagoshima the wind could be expected to calm. As I taxied up-river to warm up, I checked that everything was at hand in the cockpit; sextant, slide rule, nautical almanac, log-tables, watch, barometer, log-book, charts, dividers. There was still a high wind, and we slipped off the water easily. As soon as I had enough height above the river I turned and headed for Japan.

CHAPTER TWENTY-ONE

TRIUMPH AND DISASTER

I WAS in a strong south-easterly, and the seaplane was drifting 30 degrees to the north. At that height, for every mile I flew towards Kagoshima, I was being drifted half a mile away to the north; I decided to climb to see if I could find the westerly air stream which Father Gherzi had thought possible. At 3,000 feet the drift was still 25 degrees, but I climbed on, always hoping to reach a favourable wind just above. At 4,000 feet I checked my drift carefully, and found that it was still 25 degrees. At 5,000 feet I levelled off. The last 1,000 feet had taken thirty minutes to climb; the drift had not decreased, so that so far I had gained nothing by climbing. I flew on, hoping that I should soon pick up a strong westerly. I was happy to be flying again, and contented to be over the sea far from land. I feasted on a cold chicken which Thoms had given me. The sea beneath had been a dirty yellow for the first eighty miles, probably because of the muddy waters coming down the Yangtse Kiang. Now the colour had changed to a dull dark blue.

Two and a half hours out from China the seaplane was no longer drifting off course. The wind no longer had a south-easterly component, and I thought that I was probably in a slight westerly. In this case I reckoned that I could reach Japan, and as I hated the idea of going to Korea or anywhere else, I changed course 26 degrees to the right to get back on to my original route. At three hours ten minutes out I estimated that I had five and three-quarter hours' petrol left. With the dashboard speed-indicator broken, and the crude auxiliary one on the outboard strut unreliable, to say nothing of the uncertainty of the wind speed at 5,000 feet, I could not tell how far I had flown. If the strut indicator, which had been reading 60 mph all the time, should happen to be right, and if there should have been a thirty-mile wind against me from the start, I should be only one-third of the way across, and Japan would be out of reach. I had to get a sextant shot of the sun to find out exactly how far I had flown, so that if necessary I could alter course for Korea while I still had enough petrol to get there. I felt drowsy, my charts were awkward to handle in the cockpit, and neither of them included all three countries China, Korea, and Japan. It was difficult to plot on the loose windblown sheet, so I decided to descend to the surface, take a sun sight to find the distance flown, and determine the speed and direction of the wind accurately down there. I had a panicky urge to shut off the engine and dive down as fast as I could, but it would have been silly to sacrifice my hard won height. I pressed the control-stick gently forward till the speed rose to 100 mph on the indicator, and the spare height enabled me to keep up that speed for the next half-hour. I flew under a lake of cloud into a belt of close hot air, and levelled off at 800 feet. At that height I could make no mistake in reading the ocean surface; there was not a breath of wind there, and the rough water was only the lashed-up sea of some distant wind. Therefore, unless I flew into another head wind, I had enough petrol to fly 340 miles.

It had been hard to think up above but here in this sultry air it was a dreadful labour. I was afraid that I might have forgotten how to use a sextant but as soon as I brought the sun down to touch the horizon in the sextant I became absorbed and I remembered my sextant drill in a flash. They were excellent sights, and I twisted the results out of the slide rule. Then I plotted my position line on the chart, and found I had 270 miles yet to fly. I could reach Japan if there was no head wind for the rest of the way. Should I risk it, or bolt for Korea? I held to the same course, and half an hour later changed direction 26 degrees to the left again. I reckoned that I had regained the direct line between Shanghai and Kagoshima.

Every minute the sea quietened, and soon I was flitting in a dead calm over a dull glassy surface, with a faint tinge of burnished copper. A low gauzy ceiling obscured the sun, and increased the oppressiveness of the air. Doubts began to press on me, and tried to panic me; doubts about the accuracy of my drift reading, about the sextant work, about my compass. My neck ached with twisting, as I searched the horizon. My chart ended a few miles south of Kagoshima, and I was attacked by crazy suggestions, one after the other, to change course and fly north or north-east, or south-east. For each of these in turn there was some queer reason why it was my only hope. Then I saw land 10 degrees to the left of dead ahead. It was an island, but which one?

I identified it as Udsi Sima, two islands and a chimney rock. So thus far my navigation had been all right, and I was only 1½ degrees out on the whole flight. I poured myself a brandy, added water from a separate bottle and drank to celebrate the occasion. I lit a cigar, and in ten minutes had forgotten all my worries. On reaching the mainland, I skimmed a densely forested ridge of little hills, smothered in Christmas trees. On the other side I came upon Kagoshima in the dusk, at the edge of a purple-tinted flat beside a smooth expanse of inland water. The beauty of it all made me draw in my breath sharply; then I began searching the busy waterfront for a safe place to land. Launches and motor-boats were crawling everywhere, and after my experience at Formosa I had determined to alight somewhere where I could not be reached by a Japanese launch for twenty minutes.

I spotted a flagged buoy with two men on it, who appeared to be waving flags. I dived to fly close above them, for the twilight was making it difficult to see from any height. I found that it was an area buoyed off for swimming, and teeming with bathers. Near by was a small reef-enclosed lagoon, and I banked to alight, but as I was about to settle the floor of the lagoon appeared quite bare of water and scared me off. I had to be extra careful, because it was ten times harder to alight without any error of judgment after a long sea flight. At last I found a small creek entering the sea at right-angles. I swooped down, inspected it closely, circled and settled softly on the calm water, stopping fifty yards below a small bridge that spanned it. I looked at my watch, 9.55; I had taken eight hours and forty minutes. I looked at the petrol gauge; it showed empty, but I knew from previous experience that it held twenty minutes' flight after it showed empty. I taxied a few yards to the side of the creek to a small shallow, which I reckoned was too shallow for the launches, so that I could be approached only by sampans. By the time three launches packed with Japanese officials, reporters and photographers came swishing into the creek, I had all my gear on a wing root, with the seaplane ready to moor for the night. I was transferred to a launch from a sampan without a single shout needed.

After I had been introduced to all the officials the questioning began at once. Hayashi Sun was the interpreter, and they all fired questions at him rapidly.

'What iss first land of Japan you come, pliz?' I think every one of them asked me what land I had first sighted, my exact course from there to Kagoshima, and then wanted me to show it all to him on the chart. At first I thought this was only a matter of every official having to ask this in order to save his face before the others, but each asked it all a second time, a third, a fourth, and a fifth. Presently Hayashi introduced a new question, 'What iss your trade, pliz?'

'I am a company director.'

'Ah, so, but you are a young man?'

'They are young companies.'

They worked this line of questioning for a long time, a police official and Hayashi firing rapid talk at each other with frequent hisses indrawn through their teeth and short sharp 'ha's!', the police officer fanning himself rapidly as he talked. At last it came out, what they had been working up to. 'Your trade is, you are officer in army, iss not?'

'No, I am not an officer in the army.'

'You are a government fly.'

'No, I am a private fly.'

I got bored with this line of questioning after a while and, to liven the party up, said I was in the Territorial Air Force. The party was electrified. 'So you *are* officer in army? Pliz explain, pliz!' It was impossible for them to understand this, and in the end I said, stupidly I suppose, 'Reserve, I am in the Reserve.'

'Then you *are* officer in army, yess?'

'Yes, no, yes, damn it!' Later they started on my aeroplane engine and gear, but even a worm will turn, and I refused to go on answering silly questions about the length of my aeroplane. All my equipment was fully described in my registration and airworthiness certificates, my flying licence, my engine, aircraft and journey log-books which they could study all night while I had some sleep. Then they asked me to open up my baggage in front of them on all the launch.

'Look,' I said, 'as soon as we get ashore you can inspect my baggage to your hearts' content and not before.'

On shore this was done while the cross-examination continued unflagging. There was a lull then when I was conducted to a large schoolroom where a long table was set up with plates of sandwiches. It was like a summer storm indoors, with continuous flashes as the table was photographed, then the Mayor, the Chief of Police, and all the officials one by one. At last a loud pop cheered me a little and we sat down to drink some sweet champagne. Every time we drank, a flashlight went off. I toasted the Japanese people, the country, the city, etc, until the champagne gave out. Perhaps it was just as well that it did, for a glass is as good as a bottle to a tired aviator.

For a long time Hayashi had been noting down my answers by the flickering of a lantern, but the day was far from ended. I was handed over to a police officer. He was affable, easy going, smooth mannered and pleasant and it was just incredible that any human being could be so polite. With Hayashi, we motored along interminable narrow ways through a densely settled area. Each time I dozed off I would be jerked awake by another polite question. We arrived at an hotel in state. As we entered, a row of smiling girls knelt on the raised floor before us, bowed till their foreheads and palms touched the floor, then settled back on their heels repeating it all time after time. I had an impression of flowing kimonos, sleeves on the floor and voluminous *coiffeurs* of jet-black upswept hair. Hayashi and the policeman bowed profoundly in response; I did an Englishman's best. My shoes were removed by dainty fingers, after which I felt clumsy and flat-footed in my stockings on the padded floors. They tried to fit me with a pair of slippers from a row of them on the ground, but the largest only just admitted the tip of my toes, with the heel biting into my instep. I heartily agreed with Hayashi's suggestion of a bath, and a delicious little maiden led me into an empty room. I turned round to find a policeman behind me, and when I undressed it was the policeman who wound me into a kimono with a long wide sash, and led me into the bathroom. There was a square-tiled well about 3 feet deep in one corner full of water with bowls, basins and dippers lying about. I waited, but the policeman did not go. Ignorant of Japanese customs, I felt acutely self-conscious. In the end I slipped off the kimono, and sank into the tiled well up to my neck. The policeman immediately uttered a sharp cry, which brought in another Japanese, who seized me by the shoulder and began scrubbing my back with an instrument like a hedgehog on a stick. When I got out, the policeman seized my body, rubbed it furiously with a towel like a doormat, and wrapped up the remains in a kimono. Outside, I found the row of maidens waiting, and again bowing to the ground. I was now led to a stunted table, six inches high, and sat cross-legged on a cushion before it. A beautiful and polite little Japanese girl with her charming smile and dazzling white teeth squatted on a cushion beside me, and with a small porcelain jar kept on filling a tiny bowl of *sake*, which needed delicate holding between finger and thumb. She showed me how to use chopsticks, and I was faced with a tray full of formidable dishes. Under the first cover was a bowl of rice which gave me a false sense of security, but the second held chunks of raw fish with a clammy taste. It made me hurriedly drain the cup of *sake*, which had a less bizarre taste – it was rather like tepid sherry mixed with methylated spirits. I prodded the contents of the next dish with a chopstick, but it baffled me.

'Fish with many arm,' Hayashi waved his arms about in the air. Octopus! I thought it was like tough rubber. The girl seemed delighted with all this, and even Hayashi's look of a harassed father was occasionally lightened by a lukewarm smile. The last two dishes were eel and little cylinders of rice wrapped in seaweed, which were delicious.

After this the policeman and Hayashi started cross-examining me again, with their unfailing politeness, of course. After repeating several times all the old questions about where I had crossed the hills, etc, they wanted to know where my next halt was. I asked for my chart. (I could not help thinking that dressing me in a kimono did effectively detach me from my clothes with my pocket books, as well as my logs and papers.) I measured off the distance of my next day's flight, and said that I would alight at Kochi.

'But it is not permit to go to Kochi.'

'Oh, but it is; I have permission.'

I hunted through my papers and produced a letter from the British Consul-General saying that the Japanese permitted me to alight at Kochi. I might have saved myself the trouble, the police had instructions that I was not to approach Japan anywhere between Kagoshima and Tokyo, except for one place, Katsuura.

At last I was allowed to go to bed. I found it hard to stifle my yawns but Hayashi, I thought, had stood up remarkably well to the ordeal of five hours of nearly continuous questioning. I followed the lovely little Japanese maiden up the stairs into a bedroom. A faint rustle made me turn round – the policeman was fanning himself at my elbow. The walls of my room were all thin sliding panels; I slid one to find a Japanese couple asleep in the middle of the floor in another room. My room had a bed in it which the Japanese no doubt thought a prize exhibit of occidental furniture, a hideous cumbersome old-fashioned double bedstead with brass knobs. But I slept in it well enough. Next morning when I awoke, I groaned. I wished that I could rest for a day, but what chance would I have of rest? The Japanese would never believe that I could be subject to fatigue, they would be doubly suspicious, and every official in the district would come in smiling to hiss questions at me. How I longed for an uninhabited island, or uninhabited sea.

However, on looking out of the window, I found that it was a glorious still day of late summer, the smoke from one or two tall chimneys too lazy to rise. The sun shed an air of serenity on everything. To be flying round the world on such a day was the perfect adventure. After my camera and pistol had been ceremoniously returned to me, and the thirteen cartridges solemnly counted into my hand one by one, the seaplane was brought in to the beach for me to refuel it. The sunlight was balm; the water sparkled, the wavelets lapped the beach, and gently rolled the shingle. I felt happily lazy as I filled up with tin after tin of petrol.

On leaving land I had a 300-mile sea flight in front of me. I felt soothed and contented to be out of sight of land. The Pacific Ocean was friendly, and I skimmed the surface to be close to it. It seemed to give me strength. Life was grand; flying had become an art, and that morning I felt that I was master of it.

When I reached the mainland again I flew into a patch of dark windy weather, and in it came upon a rusty old tub of a steamer wallowing in the seas. She was the *Bellerophon* of Liverpool, and she seemed like a close friend in those foreign seas. The log line ran out a considerable distance from the high stern before it entered the water and the sea-plane, coming round the stern banked steeply, nearly caught it with the lower wing. I saw it only just in time, for I was watching the ship's cook in his white cap who had stepped on to the stern and was waving a frying-pan at me.

I flew round a headland, and began looking for Katsuura. It had not been on my chart, but the policeman had marked it in, telling me that it was a small fishing town, with a natural harbour. The whole coast seemed to be honeycombed with natural harbours, but at the spot marked on my map, I found a perfect harbour and town, an ideal place for a seaplane, but I thought it strange that I could see no sign of any launches. So I decided to fly on farther before coming down, and it was as well, because the policeman had marked a spot six miles south of the real Katsuura. There was no mistaking the launch party when I got there for one man was waving a small flag at me, and another an umbrella.

Katsuura was a beautiful place like a partly submerged crater on the edge of the coast with the ocean entering through a gap at the south end, and a jagged rim of precipitous rock separating the harbour from the open sea. I came down in an inlet like a fjord adjoining the harbour.

The launches came after me and detached a sampan to approach me. The man with the umbrella had lived in the United States for twenty years, and spoke an English which I could understand most of the time. His name was Suzuki, and he was most efficient. He invited me to stay with him, and I gratefully accepted. Suzuki's wife cooked us a meal on a little brazier, and after dinner he dressed me in a kimono and a pair of wooden sandals – because I attracted too much attention in European clothes, he said – and I clogged down the street with him to be shown the town. Suzuki wanted me to fly him to Tokyo next day but I refused; I told him that if there was a crash the person in the front cockpit was almost sure to be killed, though the man behind often escaped, and that I would not take the responsibility of putting him in front.

In the morning the launch picked up my anchor and towed the seaplane through the gap to the inlet adjoining the harbour.

'Will you make circles round the town?' shouted Suzuki, 'the peoples would like to see your aeroplane.'

The seaplane smacked the swell tops, and was soon off. I headed through the gap between the inlet and the harbour, still low over the water gathering speed. I decided to circle the village, as Suzuki had asked, but I could not do so without more height, so I reckoned to fly on through the north gap in the harbour rim to gain the necessary height outside, and then to return and circle. All the way across the harbour the seaplane was gathering speed; I preferred to gain speed rather than height until I was flying fast enough to make manoeuvring easy. When I was between the highest point of the rock peak on the outer rim of the harbour and the hill beyond the township, I pulled back the control-stick, and the seaplane began to climb sharply. I was looking at the township below me on my left, thinking what a pretty sight it was with the cluster of roofs at the base of the hill and the sunshine strong on the green harbour water beneath me, when there was a dreadful shock, and I felt a terrific impact.

My sight was a blank. Slowly, a small aperture cleared, a hole for sight, and through it, far away, I saw a patch of bright green scrub on a hillside. But it was a long way off, like a tiny glimpse seen through a red telescope. Now it was a round sight, half of sparkling water and half of rooftops, straight before me. I was diving at it vertically, already doing 90 mph. I remember thinking, 'Well, this is the end,' and feeling intense loneliness, a vague sense of loss – of life, of friends. Then, 'I'd better try for the water.' I was vaguely aware of lifeless controls, but suddenly all fear was gone.

The next thing I knew was a brightness above me and in front of me. On the way down I was so certain that I would be killed that when I came to and saw the brightness above and in front of me I thought it was a spiritual experience, and that I was in Heaven. Dozens of hands were clutching at me. Next time I came round I had a glimpse through dull red of people pressing round, of a man bending over me with his back close. There was a dreadful pain. Someone was stitching me up, and sometimes I counted the stitches. From the pain I had a terrible fear that I was a eunuch, and then I felt that there was nothing to live for, gave up resisting the pain and slid into unconsciousness. Presently I was back again and once more counting stitches, in, across, out. I was groaning with pain, felt that I was behaving badly, and was angry. After the man had finished he gave me morphia. At nightfall I was still alive. When I came to I was concerned only with one thing and terribly afraid. I dared not ask what state I was in. Presently a faint humour stirred, and when I spoke I wondered if my voice was squeaky.

Suzuki had stayed by me all night, and in the morning he came over to me.

'Suzuki, my eye – about my eye——'

'The doctor say he think you save that.'

Then I came to the only question that mattered to me at that moment; was I a eunuch?

'He say he think you save everything.'

That was one of the greatest moments of my life, and I put everything I could into the effort to get well again quickly. Now I wanted to know what had happened, for I had absolutely no idea of what had hit me or what I had hit.

What had happened was this: there were seven steel telephone wires stretched from the highest point on the outer rim of the harbour to the top of the hill behind the township. This was a long span, of perhaps half a mile. It is almost impossible to spot wires in the air when moving fast towards them, and the longer their span the less chance there is of seeing them. In this case I had no information that the wires were there, and I had no thought of wires so high up right across the harbour. I had flown straight into those wires. They had stopped the seaplane in flight, and catapulted it back. One or more of the float struts or booms had been cut through. The seaplane was shot back until the wires were at full stretch, and then the wires, hooked up behind the cut boom and struts, catapulted the seaplane forward again. Next, the wires cut through all the booms, struts and rigging stays of one float. It was cut away in mid-air, and fell apart from the seaplane. I think that this must have occurred when the seaplane was stopped again, after being catapulted forward. Then it somersaulted, and shot straight to the ground. I must have been already badly bashed, and I wonder if my attempt to deflect the seaplane into the water had any effect. Whether I was responsible or not, the seaplane *was* deflected, and hit the sloping wall at the edge of the harbour. It piled up at the foot of the wall.

Seen from the ground, this must have been a most fantastic accident to watch; a seaplane stopped in mid-air, catapulted back, then forward, torn apart in the air, then catapulted vertically down to the ground. I am only sorry that I could not have been on the ground myself to watch it! I wish I knew how long the whole accident had taken, for I should like to know how long was the period during which the scenes, the feelings and thoughts flashed on to my brain.

Suzuki's account of things ran like this:

'You have wonderful good luck. Nobody understands. They rush to pull you out before the fire catches. You must be dead. Great is their wonder to find you still alive. It was terrible a sight. I am nearly sick. Everybodies is so sorry for you. Everybodies prays to God for you. The doctor thinks you do not live for ten, twenty minutes.'

They decided to send me to Dr Hama's hospital at Shingu ten miles away. Suzuki continued, 'All young men carry you to train, very careful. They carry you all way one hour train journey.'

This crash took the form of the nightmare I had had perhaps fifty times – that my sight went black while I was flying, and left me waiting for the inevitable crash.

Although I had had a terrific impact with the ground, and could count thirteen broken bones or wounds, I was not seriously hurt. Things like a broken arm and crushed ankle seemed minor troubles. I suppose my damaged back was the worst thing, probably because with the language difficulty the doctor was not aware of it. It was ten years before I was completely recovered from that. Hama was a brilliant doctor; I had a slash in my leg about a foot long, and he used to dress this with some ointment, and I marvelled at how fast it healed.

The customs of a foreign country, though, can be hard to bear, and sometimes I feared that the Japanese kindness would make me mad. They were immensely sorry about the accident, and sympathetic with the foreign birdman who had come to grief. Thousands came from near and far to visit me. All day they passed through my room at the end of my bed. They walked in, dressed in robes of ceremony, black kimonos, with an unusual black skirt suspended outside by two black bands from the shoulders. Often I would come out of the doze I seemed to drift into against my will, to find them within the doorway or at the end of my bed, bowing silently, or perhaps with a faint hiss of indrawn breath, standing in black silk stockings with the big toes separate. They always carried fans; their straw hats they usually left outside.

If Suzuki were there he would introduce them to me:

'This is directors of the ice factory at Katsuura; they pray to God for you, and send you ice every day.' A 2 cwt. block of ice would arrive every morning, sometimes with a message in Japanese inside, or a bunch of flowers or some reeds and a fish frozen in. When there was a fish in the ice I waited patiently for it to melt out, hoping every time that it would come to life, but it never did.

'This is lady who has hotel outside where you fall.'

'Tell her that next time I hope I shall arrive without messing up the pavement.'

This was a stock joke always sure to bring down the house.

'Here is a priest of Buddha; they pray to God for you that you get well soon.'

Many of the people brought me presents of fruit or fans, dolls, photographs or *sake*. I always tried to make them a little speech of thanks, but sometimes I am sorry to say that a wild unreasonable mad fury possessed me, and I felt I was being tortured. Any other personality near me was like a concrete thing, an actual weight pressing on me. Hot fire would rush through my nerves until I was scared of breaking out into violent speech, and I would say, 'Please ask everyone to leave, I am tired and must sleep.' I knew that the people there were sometimes deeply offended. The Japanese could not understand that nerves could be so on edge as to drive a person crazy. Mine were; I sweated in an agony of fear if the nurse dressing my wounds twitched a single hair. I offended them, too, when I asked visitors to leave me alone when I was having my wounds dressed. Some of these wounds were in quaint places and I was at first embarrassed when women and young girls at the end of the bed watched them being dressed. Later I grew used to being watched as I grew used to other Japanese customs, and to Japanese food.

There was one visitor I was always glad to see. She was a Shintoist disciple, perhaps a missionary, because she left me Shinto tracts with an English translation headed 'Foreign Missions'. This amused me because 'foreign missions' conjured up for me a picture of a didactic intense white man making Polynesian natives wear Mother Hubbards, and converting people like the Japanese. The reason why I was always glad to see her – for this Shintoist disciple was a charming old wizened-up lady – was that she radiated goodness, and also did physical good each time. She prayed with a long droning incantation, and all the time she glided her hands over my body always in the same way until I felt soothed, then drowsy, and afterwards would drop into a heavy sleep, no matter how many visitors were in the room. Also, she gave me rice-charms to swallow, but I do not know if they had any effect.

I had a special nurse, who was a Christian Japanese. Afterwards I found out that she was employed by the police. She was quite unlike any other Japanese girl I met, and much of the time she spent sleeping loudly. Between whiles she showered me with glasses of water, medicine, ice and knocks. She was very clever at one thing, catching mosquitoes.

I thought the Japanese women I met were ideal with their happiness, desire to please, fondness of a joke, and their polite manners. They were small, with perfect figures, soft skinned, with plump firm flesh, doll's eyelashes, with soft, dark, slanting eyes, and jet black hair. They were the most charming and delightful women. The Japanese men seemed to treat them roughly, but they were extremely happy. I never could form a clear opinion of Japanese men. They were so intensely foreign to an Englishman that it was difficult to find a standard by which to measure them. They could be insensitive and cruel; they could be intensely kind. Here is a letter I had from Hayashi Sun, the interpreter at Kagoshima:

Sir, receiving the report of the mishap I have profound regret which never could be forgotten. I expected you will success as I said you, I hope you will success, when bid farewell on the beach. I hope you will buy fresh eggs with money that I present to you (I enclose a money order, ten yen, which you must ask for post office) and take them to make you healthy.

Yours truly,
M. Hayashi.

One of the Japanese newspapers, the *Nichi Nichi Shimbun* with a nine million circulation, published an extra about my crash. They printed a letter from a lieutenant of the Naval Air Force which said, 'We had been hoping that he would not encounter an accident when taking off at Katsuura. Kitsugura Bay is about 2,000 metres in diameter, flanked by rocks 100 metres high. The outlet of the bay is narrow, and just in front of it is an island. It is an ideal port of refuge, but a very dangerous place for seaplanes to come and go.'

Two days after the crash I began to wonder if I could write a book and get enough money by it to buy a fishing-boat. I wrote, 'I'm going to inspect a fishing-boat here as soon as I can walk. Doesn't seem to be much chance of ever getting a plane to finish my flight.' In Suzuki's house I wrote left-handed (it was my right arm which was broken), 'Every flight is moulded into a perfect short story; for you begin, and are bound to lead up to a climax.'

Apprehension and sympathy at Katsuura

Four of the contestants in the 1960 Transatlantic Race –
Chichester, Hasler, Howells, Lewis

Gipsy Moth III nearing the finishing line, New York, 1960

The Navigator

Chichester at
work in part of
Gipsy Moth's
cabin, showing
the Kestrel
transmitter

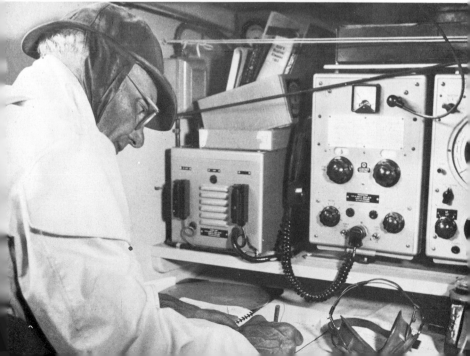

PART FOUR

CHAPTER TWENTY-TWO

BACK TO ENGLAND

WHEN I recovered enough to get out of bed I had to realize that action of any kind was going to be out of the question for a long time. I gave the remains of the Gipsy Moth to the local grammar school, and moved to Kobe in a small passenger steamer. I had a nightmare while on the way, and ended on the floor of the cabin. I think I had somehow jumped clean out of the bunk while lying full length there. I was immensely grateful that it caused me no more damage, especially as my face must have passed close to the sharp corner of a table beside the bunk.

From Kobe, I took a berth in a P and O steamer to England. In the east China Sea we passed through a typhoon, which was awe-inspiring. For a long time during that night I stood on deck at the stern, watching. The seas were not so impressive as in the small storm I flew through in the Tasman Sea, but they were more powerful. They looked immensely powerful as they swept past with long troughs; they would stand for no resistance by anything. There were no crests; these all flew off horizontally. The high-pitched scream of the wind in the rigging and passing over the steamer was the most thrilling feature. It was not a bad typhoon, and the steamer rode it well. On this voyage I found that one of the ship's engineers had been in the *Bremen* on my voyage out to New Zealand in 1919, and he told me the fate of my fellow trimmers.

When I got back to England I visited my family in North Devon, and stayed with them. This visit was a failure; I was a misfit in their way of life. They had a settled existence, with due importance attached to various happenings; for example, how many people were in church, and who they were, each

Sunday, and I represented a way of life outside their circle of interests. Also I was a different person since they had previously seen me. My personality seemed to have been shattered or weakened; I was a poor thing. My nerves were in a bad state, as shown by the torture I suffered if I went for a train journey; I had constantly to look out backwards, terrified that another train would run into us from behind. Going through any tunnel I just sweated with fear until we emerged again. I think that it is much more difficult to be kind and friendly to someone who has lost his strength and personality. Unconsciously, the herd instinct is at work which will cause a school of fish or even a flock of rooks to attack an injured fish or bird. I expect that my change in fortunes had made me irritable and difficult to live with. The atmosphere indoors, which my family seemed to enjoy, was cold and damp to me, and I was critical of the way they met the change in social conditions which had occurred in England. I particularly disapproved of their breakfasting by the light of an ugly paraffin wall lamp from the scullery, now perched on an old biscuit tin on the table.

Happily, my cousins from Instow invited me to visit them. They were daughters of the Admiral of Manila Bay fame, and were amusing, interesting and immensely kind. Mary Renshaw found me a lodging with a sporting farmer behind Instow, where I stayed for nine months while I wrote a book about my flight over the Tasman Sea. I tried hard to make a good job of this book, *Seaplane Solo*, and I wanted the reader to feel the emotions that I had felt. I wrote some parts of it many times, until they made me feel exactly as I had felt during the flight. Reading this book now, however, it seems laboured. I tried too hard. I tried to force myself to become an artist, which I was not. Some of the things I wrote were perfectly true but they sound silly, like this about flying: 'The thrill of life. Ha! ha! ha! Flying through space, devouring distance like gods – speed – up in the clouds, with life force dominant and throbbing in heart and veins.'

One day when I was working in Farmer West's front parlour I had a visit from Lord Charles Kennedy. He asked me if

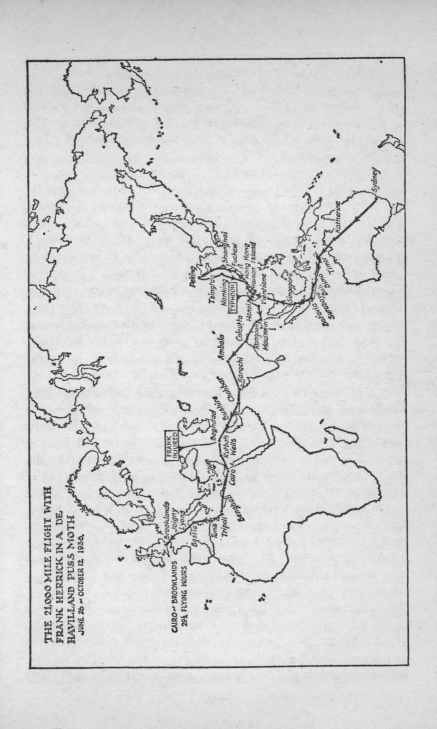

THE 21,000 MILE FLIGHT WITH
FRANK HERRICK IN A DE
HAVILLAND PUSS MOTH
JUNE 26 ~ OCTOBER 12, 1936.

CAIRO ~ BROOKLANDS
29¼ FLYING HOURS

Brooklands
Joigny
Lyons
Bastia
Tunis
Tripoli
Benghazi
Cairo
Es Soum
FRANK INJURED
Rutbah Wells
Baghdad
Bushire
Chahbar
Karachi
Ambala
Calcutta
Rangoon
Moulmein
Vientiane
TYPHOON
Hanoi
Hainan Island
Hong Kong
Fuchow
Shanghai
Nanking
Tsingtao
Peking
Singapore
Batavia
Surabaya
Bima
Timor
Katharine
Sydney

I would crew for him in the club races of the Tor and Torridge Sailing Club. 'Had I any experience?' 'Of course.' (I was careful not to say how little this experience was.) He said that we would go out for a trial sail, and as we got into his sailing dinghy he said, 'You take the tiller.' We cast off, hoisted the sail and he said, 'Luff!' As the tiller was the only thing I had in hand, I pushed it.

'I said "luff" damn you!' I pushed it the other way, and learned what luff was. Charles Kennedy had a personality; he was 6 feet 7 inches tall, with a rather untidy old-fashioned greyish pointed beard, and a slow deep gruff voice. He always wore socks with each toe separately knitted, like a glove. I crewed for him in one or two races which were good sport, but we rubbed each other up the wrong way though I respected him and liked him when we were not in the same boat. Finally he gave me the sack, and to make it worse gave my job to my young seventeen-year-old cousin, Judy Renshaw, a charming and most attractive girl. I managed to get one of the club boats for the next race, and asked Lois to crew for me; everyone loved Lois, and she was efficient, too. With her support, and by taking a risky short cut over a sandbank, I managed to beat Charlie. He kept quiet until the next race, when Bay Wyndham was crewing for me. There was a stiff breeze. Our yacht was a tangle of sheets and halyard falls and we were last, except for one boat which had lost its mast. As Bay grabbed the mooring buoy with the boat hook, I let run the mainsail halyard, but it jammed at the top of the mast. There was a wild flap and flutter while Bay held on to the mooring by brute force until I had the sail down. When we reached the club house it was packed with racing crews and Charlie, who was Commodore, shut up a telescope, and said in a loud voice, so that everyone in the club would hear, 'I would like to congratulate you, Chichester, on having the strongest crew in the club.'

It was through him that I had my first solo sail. I borrowed his dinghy, and sailed down to the junction of the Torridge and Tor rivers, then up the Tor to Barnstaple Bridge and back to Instow. This voyage introduced me to the thrill of single-handed sailing. It was only about six and a half miles each way, but I still think with keen enjoyment of the sport I had scanning the current to decide the best route and looking for a channel deep enough to carry the dinghy. In places I sounded with a bamboo pole as I sailed along over the mud-bank watersheds.

While I was in England the Guild of Air Pilots and Air Navigators of the British Empire presented for the first time the Johnston Memorial Trophy, awarded for the best feat of air navigation in the British Empire. This trophy was in memory of the navigator of the airship R101 destroyed over France. I became the first to receive this coveted trophy – for my navigation over the Tasman Sea. I doubt if I would have had it but for Geoffrey Goodwin, my partner in New Zealand, reading about it and proposing me. At that time few people in Britain knew of the Tasman Sea, and certainly no one had much interest in it. In those days, if I mentioned at a dinner that I was living in New Zealand, my neighbour would immediately lose interest in me. Later the pendulum swung, and British people began taking great interest in New Zealanders and Australians, but by then Britain had missed the bus, the Empire had turned into a Commonwealth, and the Commonwealth was already breaking up.

The Johnston Memorial Trophy was presented to me by the Prince of Wales, who became Edward VIII. Later it was awarded to Hinkler, Kingsford-Smith, Mollison and Don Bennett. Since then the terms of award have changed. First it became increasingly difficult to name a single navigator for it, and later it was difficult to name a single act of navigation by a team.

In 1932 I went back to New Zealand after finishing my book. I looked after the business while Geoffrey was away but we were still suffering from the effects of the slump, and there was not much doing, apart from some more planting, and a few land sales going through. I had changed, and had lost a good deal of my desire for action and adventure. I read a lot, and became a fanatical fisherman.

I was introduced to trout fishing by an Englishman. He showed me what to do and I went off by myself for the day. On the first day I caught no fish. My friend who was an experienced old hand and was not unhappy at my failure, had some good fish. The next day I went out by myself. I began to catch some rainbow trout but they were only two-pounders and I returned them to the river, rather ashamed. Then I came to a big pool where another river joined, a wonderful place, a great pool of dark water overhung by the evergreen forest trees, with a white rush of water where the rivers fed into it; a mysterious beautiful solitary spot. Here I caught three fish which totalled $14\frac{3}{4}$ lb. I carried home those fish somewhat diffidently, because my friend was such a tremendous expert and knew such an awe-inspiring amount about fishing. Now it seemed easy. I had no idea that I would never again in one morning meet three fighting trout like those, and have such thrill and excitement as I did on the day I caught them.

For four years I led an easy life. In the fishing season, I used to go off every evening after work to fish dry-fly for brown trout. I suppose it was some of the best trout fishing in the world. Part of the attraction was the wild, lovely, country that the fishing took me to. Once I joined an expedition to an uninhabited island. A distinguished geologist, Professor Marshall, had discovered a new rock-forming mineral, and the expedition was to look for the parent reef. Having no technical value I joined as cook. I had to use an open fireplace between some boulders on the beach, and I fear the culinary standard was not high. One day I grilled some steaks from a 150-lb. swordfish; I must admit that they were pretty tough. We had two professors in the party, and they had a dispute; one of them got so angry that he picked up a loaf of bread to hurl it at the other. He was so furious that when he drew back his hand to throw the loaf, it flew out backwards; when his hand came forward there was nothing in it. I thought this was the funniest thing I had seen for years, and doubled up with laughing. Whereupon they both turned on me, and said that it was entirely my fault; that my bad cooking had upset their livers. Apart from this the expedition was a great success. The parent reef was located at the bottom of the extinct crater which the island was.

In England, Hamish Hamilton, the publishers, offered a prize for a new book. David Garnett was to be one of the judges, and as I had had my best review of *Seaplane Solo* from him, and as I admired his writing, I got the idea of competing. I built a one-roomed hut at the top of the hill on our property, about 900 feet above sea-level, and retired there to write my masterpiece. *Seaplane Solo* had not sold many copies, so I thought that this new book must be made more attractive, like putting ordinary old chocolates in a gorgeous box with satin ribbon. As literary adviser I enrolled Marjorie Tweed, who had an impressive artistic bent. The first thing we did was to put the end of the book, the crash in Japan, at the beginning; there was a vogue for this kind of thing at the time. Then the book had to have an inspiring title; the final choice was *Ride on the Wind*. Not only did this book not get a prize, but even some of my best friends admitted that they could not read it.

One day I was visiting Flora and Frank Herrick, some friends of mine who lived on their sheep station on the east coast of North Island, and I persuaded Frank that it would be great sport to fly home to England across Siberia. He agreed enthusiastically, and it was arranged that he should provide the aeroplane, and that I should pilot it. We bought a second-hand Puss Moth, a high-winged monoplane, with a Gipsy Major engine. It was nearly five years since I had flown, and I started off with several hours of solid landing practice. The Puss Moth was a delightful aeroplane in many ways. It had a comfortable cabin with a splendid view under the wing in level flight. It cruised at around 100 mph and did twenty miles to the gallon. Its only drawbacks were that anything circled was hidden by the tilted wing, and it had a bad reputation for tearing off its wings, which had led to several fatal accidents. I accidentally discovered the cause of this. I was flying in to Rotorua at dusk and, having no lighted or even luminous instruments, was anxious to land before dark. Within ten miles of the airfield I put the nose down, shut off the motor, and started a fast glide. The Puss Moth was well streamlined, and quickly gained speed in a glide. When the time came to level off, I pulled back the stick – but it would not move. I had no parachute, and even if I had I could not have got out of the cabin at that speed, because the cabin door opened forwards. It was a paralysing prospect.

If I applied full force to the control-stick, either something would break, or the aeroplane would suddenly shoot upwards and pull the wings off. Feeling that I must do something, I opened the throttle wide. I do not know what made me do this, because the aeroplane was already near its maximum speed, but as I opened the throttle I immediately regained control. The elevators had been blanketed when gliding fast with the engine off. It was easy to see how an accident would occur; if the Puss Moth had glided out of thunder-cloud to find the ground close below it would be natural to wrench back the stick, whereupon the aeroplane would stand on its tail and pull the wings off.

The Puss Moth was shipped across the Tasman Sea to Sydney, where Frank and I met it, and we set off on a sporting tour by air, visiting various friends of his at cattle stations in Australia. We left Australia from Katherine, on the railway south of Darwin – a very different place from the Katherine I had last flown over in 1930. Now it was on the Imperial Airways airline route.

We had an uneventful but extremely interesting flight through the East Indies, calling at Timor, Bima, Bali, Surabaya and Batavia before reaching Singapore. Then we went on, touching at various places in Siam and Indo-China, to Hong Kong where we stayed at the (then) new Kowloon Hotel. After this we spent nights at Fuchow, Shanghai and Kiaochow, which is the airfield of Tsingtao, before landing at Peking. I found Peking much the most attractive and romantic city I had been to. I felt marvellously well and vitalized there. This may have been due to the dry, high-pressured atmosphere, charged with electricity – I gave off sparks freely! We were entertained by a Chinese family to a delicious dinner in their house, enjoying traditional delicacies such as bird's-nest soup and 100-year-old eggs.

I had a charming and delightful Chinese friend whom I used to visit in the old walled city, although I was told that I was taking a big risk travelling through it at night by myself in a rickshaw. This enchanting young lady was so small that my two hands could meet round her waist.

We waited for some time in Peking, trying to get permission from the USSR to enter Siberia by way of Mongolia if not through Manchukuo. Peking was a disturbed city, and uneasy with the Japanese infiltration to the east. There were shootings nearly every night, and armed guards were to be seen at nearly every establishment. I became friendly with the British Military Attaché at the Embassy, Colonel Lovat-Fraser. One day I flew him out to the Ming tombs, scuttling across the country at hedge-hop height, and inspecting each tomb closely from a few feet above it. Another day we had a flight to the Great Wall, and flew along this a wingspan from it. I was thrilled to see this great work of earth and stone, but I could not understand how it could have been effective; it looked as if it would be easy for a regiment of bowmen with plenty of arrows to keep the guards on top of the wall under cover while some ladders were brought up to scale the wall.

Our flight to England did not make much progress. One suggested route after another was turned down, and finally we were refused entry via Paotao and the Gobi Desert. This was disappointing, but why worry? The whole flight was a lark, and we turned round to recross China and get back on to the ordinary air route to England.

On the way south we had to visit Nanking to obtain some more permits for crossing China, etc, and then we flew on to Hong Kong. Next, we landed at Hainan Island to refuel, and I got a weather report from the Jesuit priest who operated a meteorological station there. He spoke very fast French, and I misunderstood what he said about a typhoon. We flew on in fine weather until near the coast of Indo-China where the route was barred by a huge snow-white cloud. It looked innocent and I flew into it, but we were soon in trouble; it was a small typhoon. We were in strong gusty winds, which whizzed us up and down. Rain fell like solid water, and it became increasingly dark. I was soon sweating, thinking fearfully of Puss Moths which had had their wings pulled off, for the buffeting we were getting was terrifying. To ease the strain on the wings as much as possible I set the aeroplane to its maximum climbing angle, until it was almost hanging on the propeller. We climbed steadily, 8,000, 9,000, 10,000 feet. At last I surrendered, turned round and worked my way back over our tracks. When we got to the edge of the cloud and flew out into the clear, I turned round to look at Frank. He was huddled up in the rear seat of the cabin, with his raincoat over his head. During the buffeting, the sliding window at the side of the cabin had worked open a quarter of an inch, and the rain had shot in as through a hosepipe, straight on to Frank. Later, when we landed at Hanoi and I studied the plot of the typhoon's track, I found that we had turned at the very centre of it, and I recalled how the turbulence had seemed a shade easier as we were turning.

On leaving Hanoi, we crossed the mountains of Laos to reach Vientiane, on the Mekong River, at dusk. When we arrived at the dot on my War Office map which marked the position of the town, I looked everywhere, circled and searched in vain for any sign of it. This was a serious business, with night about to fall, and no suitable place to land. I studied the map, bamboozled, but could not detect what had gone wrong. Then I remembered that at breakfast that morning I had been looking at a French magazine with a map of Indo-China in it. I have always loved maps, and I asked permission to tear this out and keep it. I asked Frank to dig it out of my bag, and when he handed it to me I could see at once what had happened. The dot representing Vientiane on my map was at the wrong end of the name, and at that scale it represented a distance of forty-five miles. So I headed west, pushed the throttle full open and raced across to the other end of the name. There we found the town all right and were able to land before dark.

From Vientiane we cut across the north of Siam to land at Moulmein, in Burma, and from there proceeded to Rangoon. Now we were on the regular Europe to Australia air route, and it seemed tame after our journeys in China and the East. I got some interest out of flying low along the coast of Burma, but we were nearly brought down by a boy on the beach who threw up a hunk of timber which passed between the main wing and tailplane.

When I was flying high over India, I read a book. We had no

266

permits from the countries ahead of us on this route and had been advised to go to Simla in the hills, where the Government had retired in the hot season. We landed the Puss Moth at Ambala and hired a car to climb the 6,000 or 7,000 feet into the hills to Simla. When we reached a point half a mile below the Hotel Cecil, where we were staying, the car driver refused to go any farther. He proposed to dump our baggage there. I was so outspoken about this that he finally put the baggage back and drove up to the hotel. The next thing I heard was that he had been arrested – only the Viceroy and the Governor of the Punjab were allowed to drive up to the hotel! After living in a modern young country, New Zealand, this looked like a piece of archaism specially designed to antagonize Commonwealth people. I went along to the Chief of Police and said if anybody was to be punished for the driver's offence it was me, because I had forced him to drive up to the hotel. In India then, nothing counted but appearance, and no value seemed to be attached to people's actions. The British officials whom we liked best in India were the forestry men; they were efficient, quiet and interesting, whereas some of the army officers and administrative civil servants were sickening snobs. Dealing with them I sometimes squirmed like Stalky at Westward Ho!

The Persian Embassy in India refused to allow me entry with my existing passport because when I visited Chahbar in 1930 it had been signed by my host, 'In political charge, Chahbar.' To overcome that difficulty I was issued with an Indian passport. But when we reached Bushire in Persia the Puss Moth was arrested, and guarded by soldiers with fixed bayonets. We could not understand this until we learned that they thought I was Lawrence of Arabia disguised with a beard, and proposing to proceed up-country to start a revolt. (I suppose they thought that Lawrence's reported death was simply an astute piece of camouflage.) It was intensely hot at Bushire; Frank was very irritated by the heat and hated it. His irritation was aggravated by being shut up and surrounded by foreigners who could speak no English. After five days word came through from Tehran that we were to be released. On walking over to the aeroplane I slipped my watch between my belt and shorts instead of into the pocket, and it fell on the ground and broke. I took this for a bad omen, and considering that it was already 1.30, and that we had a 500-mile flight to Baghdad, I told Frank that I thought we ought to put off the flight until next morning. Frank said, 'Let's get out of this hell-hole at any cost.' The cost was nearly his life. We took off, and proceeded to the head of the Gulf, plugging into a steady head wind of 20 mph. I expected the wind to die away with evening, but the light began fading when we were half-way between Basra and Baghdad, and the head wind showed no signs of dying down. We had now been five hours in the air, and I said to Frank, 'We have not enough petrol to reach Baghdad unless this wind drops. What about landing somewhere for the night?' 'Oh, let's press on to Baghdad,' said Frank. Night fell, it was dark, and there were no lights in the cabin; nor were any of the dashboard instruments luminous. I hung a torch round my neck and shone it periodically at the compass, the speed indicator and the revolution counter. Before we reached Baghdad the petrol gauge showed empty and I incessantly searched the ground below us for the best place to land if the motor cut. It was possible only to guess at the nature of the surface in the dark, but it is surprising how much one can deduce through experience.

But we did reach Baghdad, and I located the unlit aerodrome. I did not wait for any airfield lights to be switched on, for I was expecting the motor to die at any moment. I did not even circle the airfield, but changed my approach into a glide and landed directly. The Puss Moth rolled smoothly to a halt, and I said to Frank, 'Take a torch, Frank, and walk ahead of the plane towards the hangar, so that I don't taxi into anything in the dark.' Frank stepped out of the cabin, and I called, 'Look out for the prop.' The cabin door opened forward, coming up against the strut between the bottom of the fuselage and the wing. Frank walked round the cabin door into the arc of the propeller. To do this he had to turn sharply round the end of the door, and had it been daylight it could only have been done by a deliberate manoeuvre. I heard a sickening noise, and saw Frank stagger away to the right. I thought that he had been killed, and I had a desolate feeling of misery and despair. When

I got to him, he was sitting on the ground holding his arm. His left forearm seemed nearly cut through, and I could see the bone ends. In due course a car arrived and he was driven off to a hospital.

When I went round to the hospital first thing in the morning, I was utterly miserable: if the injury itself had not killed Frank, then the shock would probably do so. Not only was he an old man, but both blades of the propeller had been broken off in hitting him. But as I walked up to his bed, and before I could begin to say anything, he said, 'Where's that propeller? Make sure you keep it – I want it for a souvenir.' What a man!

Frank did not get well quickly. The heat was the obstacle – when it was 95° F. they told us that it was cool for Baghdad! The RAF station at Ramadi found us a metal propeller. It was not quite right for the Gipsy Major engine, but we managed to fit it.

I flew Frank to Cairo, with one stop at Rutbah Wells, and a halt in the desert for lunch during the six and a quarter hour flight from Rutbah.

In Cairo, Frank went into hospital, but he still could not get his arm healed. Again, he could not stand up to the great heat. We finally decided to make a fast passage home in the Puss Moth, and this we did, landing en route at Es Sollum, Benghazi, Tripoli, Tunis, Bastia, Lyons, Joigny and St Inglevert. It took us twenty-nine and a half hours flying from Cairo to Brooklands.

I am glad to say that Frank recovered completely and returned to his station homestead at Tautane with his propeller. I believe that his life had been saved by the fact that he always carried a silver cigarette case in his outside breast pocket. I think that the first blade, cutting down, had struck this cigarette case a glancing blow, and halted Frank, otherwise the next stroke would have cut down on his shoulder instead of hitting his forearm.

CHAPTER TWENTY-THREE

SHEILA AND THE WAR

IT WAS autumn when we arrived, and I went down to Devon to visit my family. My father had retired, and was living in South Devon. Then I went to see my cousins in North Devon, and had a happy time at Instow and Westward Ho. I was much intrigued by the talk about the impending visit of a girl called Sheila Craven. She was due to visit North Devon after a dance in Wiltshire, and instead of motoring down, she put her car on a train, an unusual move which interested me. I asked her why she had done this, and she said that she thought she would be tired after the dance, but wanted to arrive as fresh as possible so as to enjoy her Devonshire visit.

She liked comfort, and appeared rather languid. I felt that she should have a black boy following her with cushions, a rug and a parasol over her head. Time seemed to have little importance for her. But she was always interesting to listen to, and often had original views. And I was surprised when I discovered that this languid personality had just returned from a voyage alone to India and Abyssinia. I could better understand that having embarked on this voyage she should have become a guest of the Viceroy in India, and of the British Minister in Addis Ababa. She said that she had always wanted to go exploring. I thought that this was just an airy bit of verbal thistledown; if it had been revealed to me then that she would one day sail across the Atlantic with me, just the two of us, and a second time sail across it with our son as crew, just the three of us, I would have laughed at the joke. Anyway, the upshot was that I fell in love with her, we married, and went out to New Zealand by steamer. Sheila says that I boarded her London train at the next station and said, 'I have £100 in money, £14,000 overdraft and some trees, will you marry me?'

That New Zealand visit in 1937 was not a success. I could only afford a suburban villa, and there were various little things Sheila could not reconcile herself to, such as having to fetch the milk at the gate down the road because the milkman would not bring it up to the house; having to manage with little help in the house; and being unable to dine later than 6.30 in the best hotel in New Zealand. I tried to convince her that New Zealand led the world in social revolution, and had pioneered things like women's voting and baby care, also a National Health Service and State Insurance. I tried to explain that what was happening in New Zealand then would take place in England in twenty years; I said that if I was running a country like Britain or America I would place an astute observer in New Zealand, because world trends and development were apparent there, whereas they would be disguised by prejudice and proximity in the principal countries concerned with them. It was no good. Sheila detested the life we had to lead in New Zealand. Apart from that, I found myself in a difficult position, because there was not enough income from our business to justify my staying there without another job. Considering that war with Germany was looming in Europe, and that I would be taking part in it, we decided to move back to England. I made an arrangement with Geoffrey to look after our business, and we returned to England in the *Christian Huyghens*, via the Dutch East Indies.

On board the *Christian Huyghens* was Field-Marshal von Blomberg, who had been until recently the Minister of War in Germany. He became friendly to me, and we spent many hours talking: I have a snapshot which shows him bringing his fist down on the table between us to illustrate some point he was making. During the voyage he oulined to me the future history of Europe for the next ten years, and I do not think that he made a mistake. The chief point that impressed itself on me was that if we did not make friends with Germany, the German scientists and inventors would be absorbed by Russia, which would make Russia an overwhelming world power. One interesting thing he told me was that in the First World War, the British invented tanks and tried out three in the front line. These got stuck in the mud, and were captured by the Germans. He, Blomberg, was one of three German generals who had to decide whether to make these tanks themselves. He said that Germany had not enough steel to make all the shells they needed, as well as tanks, and it was his vote which was responsible for the tanks not being made at the time. Maybe he made a mistake there.

When I reached England, I applied to join the RAF as a fighter pilot. I thought that my flying experience, combined with my capability at shooting, would be just what they wanted. I was surprised and chagrined to be told that I was too old. I was thirty-seven, and the idea of being too old for anything had just not occurred to me. So I set about job-hunting. I felt that life was too precious to be used up for the sole aim of making money, and I wanted something creative or congenial, something, if possible, to do with instruments, or navigation. I tried to form a company for making instruments with Paul Goudime, Henry de Laszlo and Douglas Johnson, but we could not raise the necessary capital. Later, Paul started Electronic Instruments on his own, which he recently sold to Cambridge Instruments for three quarters of a million pounds.

I went on looking for a job, but could find no opening. There were not many jobs available in England then, and I think I did not fit into the English pattern. It was six months before Arthur J. Hughes made a post for me in Henry Hughes and Son, as a navigation specialist. One of my jobs was to help with the development of the bubble sextant. This involved many hours in the air taking sights, and on the ground checking instruments. One day I was taking off on a flight in Canopus with Don Bennett, the Australian pilot of Imperial Airways whom I regarded as one of the world's finest navigators. We were walking down to the hard at Hythe on Southampton Water to board Canopus for a long experimental flight. There was a fuelling launch alongside the flying-boat, and as I looked I saw a flame run along the hosepipe to the hull of the flying-boat. A tongue of flame licked the air from the nose of the flying-boat, and in a few seconds she was burning fiercely. That was the end of that flight.

I found it strange to be an employee of an English firm after having been a boss of my own business since I was twenty-one.

My salary was £8 13s. od. a week, which did not pay the rent of our flat in Chelsea. I found it a strain to defer to the opinions of my seniors, and not to be emphatic about my own. The jockeying for power and precedence in the big English firms was a surprise to me. Men were apt to be jealous if their colleagues were successful, and resentful if a junior showed more ability, skill, or enterprise than themselves. I had expected to find more teamwork, everybody trying to hurry work on, and to improve methods. I found my life restricted, and pondered how I could break through into a bigger life. There seemed to be no possibility of doing this. I was also restricted physically. In New Zealand I was used to open-air sport being easily available; in England, the countryside seemed crowded, even the roads seemed narrow and tortuous. I became so desperate for some outdoor activity that during one week-end spent with friends on their half an acre of land, I stood all morning in a deserted tennis-court among some trees waiting hopefully for a pigeon to fly over and give me a shot which I never got.

I started writing on navigation. *Flight* published a set of articles describing a system of navigation I evolved for bombing pinpoint targets by star navigation. I used to get up at 5 AM and write hard until I had to leave the house to get to my office at 9 AM. I wrote four small volumes on astro-navigation. These were instructions on how to navigate by the sun and stars. I tried again to get into the Air Force, but was turned down once more.

War came in 1939. Sheila and I were motoring across country, and when all the sirens wailed we decamped from our car and crouched in a ditch while three puny biplanes of our own Air Force came in to land at Hendon.

With another man in the Royal Aero Club, I tried to form a squadron of experienced pilots who were considered unacceptable to the Air Force because of lacking a leg, or for some similar reason. The object of this squadron would be to bomb valuable pinpoint targets in enemy country, flying in alone by precise navigation. The idea was turned down. I believe that this would have shown the value of a pathfinder force, and brought it forward by a year or two. I was disgusted at the turning down of my third attempt to do something with the RAF, and said, 'If they want me after this they can damn well come and get me.'

Factories had been asked to work long hours seven days a week, and at the Hughes factory at Barkingside production was gradually slowing down in consequence of this silly and hysterical demand. On a hot sunny Saturday afternoon that autumn, I went out into some neighbouring fields with my gun after a pheasant. There was a big German bombing raid, and our fighter pilots were attacking overhead. Cartridge cases and bullets were falling near me, and I sat in a ditch watching the battle overhead. Several pilots who had baled out were on their way down, their parachutes gleaming white in the sunshine. This was the first time I had seen a successful parachute jump. I had seen three jumps made in New Zealand and America, and in each case the parachutist had been killed. In New Zealand the man had gone into the sea with his parachute unopened, and a single column of water had shot up which looked 100 feet high.

I wrote a book called *The Spotter's Handbook*, which, although it contained a good deal of nonsense, was a best seller. And it may have helped to cut down the time wasted through stopping work unnecessarily when enemy bombers were on their way. I think that the book did something to give people confidence to go on working until it was really necessary to take cover. I need hardly say that I was an active member of the Home Guard squad of our factory.

I used to visit Philip Unwin to discuss the publication of the books I was producing, and it was a stock joke whenever an air-raid warning sounded while we were at lunch. 'Good for business!' we would laugh. I followed *The Spotter's Handbook* with another one, *Night and Fire Spotting*, which also contained a lot of boloney. I remember being at the bottom end of Bond Street at 11 o'clock one morning, and hearing the clop, clop, clop of a milk van horse, up at the far end of the street. It was in the dead silence preceding an air raid. This was at the beginning of the war, and I wondered if in a few years' time there would be grass growing the length of Bond Street.

My books, I think, got me into the RAF. Air Vice-Marshal Cochrane, director of navigation training at the Air Ministry, sent for me to write navigation notes for instructors and students. I was commissioned as a Flying Officer, and told to report to the Deputy Director who would be my chief.

I had once heard a wonderful story about an Air Force navigator, and had used it as the plot for a short story – the only work of fiction I have ever published – writing fiction has always seemed to me paltry compared with real life. This story was called 'Curly the Navigator', and described how the navigator had told the captain of the flying-boat that he was on the wrong course, which must result in the flying-boat's being lost at sea. An argument resulted in the navigator's knocking out his superior officer, and bringing the seaplane safely back to base. When I reported for duty at the Air Ministry, I found that my boss was Group Captain Kelly Barnes, a big red-faced character who looked and acted exactly like the traditional John Bull. He had been the flying-boat navigator whose story I had dished up. I was decidedly uneasy as to what sort of reception I should get. He called me into his office and, as I did my best to stand smartly at attention, he said, 'You know, you got the end of that story wrong; what actually happened was that I was court martialled in the morning, and called up before the Air Council in the afternoon to be awarded the MBE.' Kelly Barnes never liked me, and my two years in the Air Ministry was a frustrated, unhappy period. Kelly B. had been a navigator all his career; he was not only brilliant with the theory of it – he had revised the *Advanced Navigation Manual* – but he had sound, advanced views on navigation practice. For example, he devised a simple grouping of the stars which would make them much easier to recognize than those connected with mythology. I felt he resented my being brought in, an amateur, civilian navigator.

About the time I was brought into the Air Force, I produced a game, 'Pinpoint the Bomber', for teaching navigation. This was published by Allen and Unwin, and considering the limited market which any navigational work must have, it was a great success. I also brought out a sun compass which enabled you to tell the direction by the sun if you knew the time, or to tell the time if you knew the direction of the sun. This, in turn, was followed by a star compass made of cardboard and transparent plastic which sold for 5s., and a 2s. 6d. Planisphere of Navigation Stars. Another publication of mine was a big star chart designed for teaching star identification.

At the Air Ministry I worked for some time in the same room as Dicky Richardson, then a Wing-Commander who was re-writing the Standard *Manual of Air Navigation*, A.P. 1234. He made a fine job of it. Dicky was one of those sterling, stalwart citizens who make a country great if there are enough of them. He left the Air Ministry to become Chief Navigation Officer of Coastal Command, where he introduced a navigation drill which helped raise the standard of navigation and with it the standard of safety. Dicky's navigation drill was almost precisely the same as the system I had worked out for navigating to Lord Howe Island and Norfolk Island.

Convoy escorts and anti-submarine patrols were out for long flights with continuous manoeuvring, such as square searches to be plotted. I took part in one sortie, in a Liberator which was eleven hours and forty minutes out. We proceeded to 25° W. in the Atlantic, and after an oblong search for ships' boats, picked up a convoy on the return. Another day I joined a Fortress, for an eight-hour thirty-five minutes' flight into the Atlantic. I got into hot water with the captain of the aircraft for firing a burst from a .5 machine-gun I was interested in just as a corvette was passing below.

By the middle of 1943 I reckoned that I had written 500,000 words on navigation, and was becoming difficult to live or work with. I was offered a post at the Empire Central Flying School, with no official status and the rank of Flying Officer, the lowest commissioned rank except Pilot Officer. I accepted what looked like an interesting job. I was not allowed to do the sort of job I wanted, such as Navigating Officer at an operational station, because of my bad eyesight; and for the same reason I was not permitted to hold a General Duties post. I could have only an administrative job. I was not officially allowed to fly, not officially allowed to navigate, and I was not permitted to wear pilot's or navigator's wings on my tunic. One of the results of this was that whenever I visited an operational mess, unless I knew one of the members of the mess personally, I would soon be quietly edged out of any group of operational pilots talking at the bar. For my job at the Air Ministry I had been upgraded to the rank of Flight Lieutenant, but that was as high as I could rise.

I arrived at Hullavington where the Empire Central Flying School was stationed feeling like a new boy at a public school. The standard procedure for anyone coming into the Air Force was to do an Officers' Training Course. I had been moved straight into a uniform and into an office, and I knew little about the drill, customs and procedure. Hullavington was a big station – we had thirty-seven different types of aircraft there alone – and taking the parade as Duty Officer when the ensign was lowered at 6 o'clock was a formidable ordeal when my turn came. The last squad I had drilled was at my preparatory school in 1914. Naturally, I watched what the preceding Duty Officer did, but it was a very different thing to shout all the same commands in a parade ground voice to troops who were experts. It was a great relief to me when I found that I could get through it all right.

The Commandant at the Empire Central Flying School was a regular RAF Officer called Oddie, a stalwart character. He got himself into trouble with the Air Council because he believed in getting on with the war in the best possible way, and that regulations ought to be made to fit this purpose. After I had been there for ten days he put me into the Navigation Officer's post to succeed Wing-Commander Edwards, who was leaving for an operational tour. The ECFS ran courses for officers such as Chief Flying Instructors with ranks from Flight Lieutenant to Group Captain. They were mostly pilots drawn from every arm of the Service and from every ally. In one course we might have Fleet Air Arm, Army and RAF officers, together with Australians, New Zealanders, South Africans, Poles, Frenchmen, Norwegians and Americans. (But we never

277

had US Air Force and US Navy pilots at the same time, because they did not mix well.)

My job, principally, was to brief them on the navigation of their flights, and to devise navigation exercises for them. At the end of each course we used to have a navigation race with twelve light two-seater Magister training planes in it. This was fine training for the sort of navigation that is really valuable to a pilot. We made it a kind of treasure hunt. For instance, in one race they had to fly to Stowe, the public school, and count the number of tennis-courts there, multiply the number by x, and then fly in that direction for five miles to find another clue. These races were immense sport, and very popular. I acted as pilot in one of them to Group Captain Teddy Donaldson, who at that time held the world record for high speed flights. He had to do all the navigating, and I simply acted as chauffeur. He swore afterwards that I had made him airsick for the first time in his life, but I think the truth was that it was the first time he had ever put his head down to look at a map in a cockpit.

Another of my jobs at Hullavington was to devise methods for teaching 'nought feet' navigation to pilots intruding into enemy territory when they would be unable to take their eye off the ground ahead, and must be jinking all the time to avoid anti-aircraft fire. It amounted to map reading without maps, in other words all the map reading had to be done on the ground before taking off. It sounds an impossible requirement but, with the right methods, and plenty of drill, pilots could find a haystack fifty miles off while dodging about all the way to it. Oddie reasoned that it was impossible for me to do this sort of work if I was not allowed to fly or, for that matter, navigate. As a result, I was not only navigating continuously in the various types of aircraft at the station, but also had a light plane for solo flying and experimental work whenever I wanted it. This enabled me to prepare the flight tracks for the instructional films we were making, work up interesting exercises, and also to fly myself home occasionally at the week-end.

I used to land at Fairlop, a mile from our house at Chigwell Row. One morning, just before I took off, a cryptic message came through from Air Traffic Control London saying that I must take great care while flying and look out for anything strange. I usually flew low, because it was more interesting, and I was surprised to see all the children dash across a playground and take cover as I flew over. When this happened a second time, I realized that they were taking cover from me, and when it happened a third time, I wondered what it was all about. On this occasion I landed at the Fighter Station at Hornchurch. As I stepped out of the plane, I saw one of our fighters tip a doodlebug over with its wing tip, and send it crashing into the ground where it exploded with a mighty bang. The schools had mistaken my little monoplane for a doodlebug. When I got home I found that one of the first three of these infernal machines had flown low over our house where Sheila was living alone. Our house was slightly damaged many times (I gave up counting after it had been repaired nine times), and naturally it was a great worry to me leaving Sheila there. I tried to persuade her to come down to Wiltshire, but the only accommodation I could find was a room in a house which she would have to share with several others. She said that she preferred living in her own house with the bombs. One day I returned to find that a doodlebug had exploded nearby, and blown every leaf off the big lime tree next door. The completely bare tree looked strange in the middle of summer. Some weeks later I came home and was delighted to see a new crop of leaves appearing on the tree, just as if it was at the beginning of spring.

I tried to console Sheila by telling her that the bomb risk in London was nothing like the risk from flying accidents at the ECFS. Most of our students had been doing administrative office jobs before coming on the course, and when they were expected to fly every one of our thirty-seven different types of aircraft while undergoing an intensive course of lectures, it was not surprising that we had a high casualty rate. The chief safety factor when flying is thorough drill in handling the aircraft. It was thought, however, that we could not win the war if we played for safety.

It is an ill wind that blows no good, and if any of my students were lost on a navigational exercise I used to spend many hours in my light aeroplane searching where I estimated them to be. Two South African majors were lost on one exercise, and I hunted for days among the Welsh hills. Three months later when we had given up all hope for them, word came through that they were prisoners of war. They had flown the reciprocal heading of their compass, south-east instead of north-west. When they crossed the English Channel they thought it was the Bristol Channel. They were grateful when an airfield put up a cone of searchlights for them, and it was not until they had finished their landing run on the airstrip and a German soldier poked a tommy-gun into the cockpit that they realized that they were not on an English airfield.

I often used to make solo flights to operational stations to find out if there were any developments in navigation and, I must admit, to try for a job as navigator on a raid. When I climbed to the control tower after landing on a strange airfield the duty officer would look at my wingless tunic and say, 'Where's the pilot?' I enjoyed this, and regarded it as some consolation (childish, perhaps) for the indignity and disregard the non-flying man had to put up with from operational pilots.

At the end of the war I wanted to get into business on my own again, and decided to become a maker of air games and toys. I visualized toy jets. I dare say 10 per cent of the RAF had a similar idea. I also wanted to get into the air travel business. When on leave I marked off an area in the West End of London where I thought the air travel business would be centred after the war. This was a rectangle, with Piccadilly in the centre. I hired a taxi and drove through every street in the area noting down all the houses for sale. In the end we bought one in St James's Place where my business now is. My forecast of air travel has turned out to be right, because nearly every airline and major air travel firm has an office in this area now. But it was all wasted for me, because I never got into that business.

The first thing I found on being demobilized was that I could not get any materials to make my toys. A friend – or was it an enemy ? – suggested that I should make jig-saw puzzles. There were 15,000 maps left over from my 'Pinpoint the

Bomber' game. I bought a ton or so of cardboard, designed some cutters, and turned these maps into map jig-saws. I set off on a sales campaign and sold the first 5,000 to big stores and other shops. I came back elated thinking, 'Hurrah! I'm in business,' and promptly made 10,000 more. On my next sales round the buyers told me that the puzzles had not sold as well as they had hoped. I decided that this was due to using an old map, so I designed a new one. Several times when the sales lagged I produced a better map to help to sell the old ones. Then one day a man walked into my office and said, 'This picture map of London is the best I've seen; if you will take it off this lousy piece of cardboard I'll order 5,000.' And so I became a map publisher by accident.

CHAPTER TWENTY-FOUR

BACK TO SEA

AT THIS time, besides being the designer, producer and salesman, I typed all the letters, did the book-keeping, invoiced the goods, parcelled them up and delivered them – it was very much a one-man firm. I think map publishing was the right business for me, for I had been involved with maps ever since I made my first chart for my Tasman flight. My adventures with faulty maps when flying, the game 'Pinpoint the Bomber' which I had devised for teaching map reading, and my search for methods of teaching fighter pilots how to map read at nought feet without using a map, had left me with strong views on what should be put into a map and, equally important, what should be left out of it. My map of the Heart of London was different from a flying map, but I worked in a number of my ideas. For example I pictured prominent buildings; the eye would go straight to one of these, which would make it easier to find a near-by street; and I tried to keep the map clear, by not overcrowding it, and by keeping out unnecessary features. Gradually I made bigger and better maps, but it was a struggle for financial survival. At one time we kept only one room of our house in St James's Place, and I not only worked in it, but slept and lived there as well. Sheila was living in a week-end cottage on the banks of the Kennet in Wiltshire with our young son Giles, and I joined them at week-ends.

This Fisherman's Cottage was also an accident, like my map publishing business. After the war I tried once more to switch from flying to sailing, and looked for a cottage at various places near the sea. However, a friend offered us the Fisherman's Cottage with a length of the Kennet for trout fishing, and the north half of Savernake Forest, 750 acres, for rough shooting. I thought that if there was another war I should at least have fish to eat in summer and game in winter. However, shortly afterwards my family turned vegetarian, and when I did the same, I was left literally with the bag. I had had gallstone trouble. I have been told this is the greatest pain known to man; I believe it. Fortunately, a man can stand only a certain amount of pain, and then passes out. The doctor wanted to operate on me, but my wife refused to let him. I was introduced to a nature cure doctor, Gordon Latto, who said that he would stop the stones forming, but that I must go on a strict vegetarian diet for a year, besides knocking off drink and smoking, which he said was worse than drink. This was a tough régime; the gallstones gave up, but I survived. I found that I was cured of smoking, too. And I have preferred vegetarian food since then.

My New Zealand partner, Geoffrey, visited England and suggested that I should produce my picture map of London in pocket book form. Our Pocket Map and Guide of London was the result, but for two years it did not sell, and at one time I thought about dropping it. Then it started to sell, and in 1963 we produced our half millionth copy.

I fondly imagined that I had settled into a comfortable office chair and had finished with all the difficulties, discomforts and dangers of flying and suchlike adventures. But seven years after the war I was attacked by an overpowering urge for some practical navigation. The map business was growing slowly, but would not run to a twin-engined jet, which I should need for the sort of private flying that would interest me. So I decided to'go in for sailing or gliding, and plumped for sailing, because it was more sociable; the family could week-end in a yacht, but hardly in a glider.

My first sail was to the Baltic as crew for a friend. I accepted the invitation with the keenest anticipation of cruising over the waters made famous by Erskine Childers's *Riddle of the Sands*, which I had re-read time after time since leaving my first school. That cruise was not a success, but it did result in my becoming an ocean racer. Rationing was still in force in England, and things like butter and cheese were scarce. After my gallstone trouble I found that the vegetarian diet had agreed with me so well that I now preferred it. However, man cannot live by bread alone. My skipper had a fine hunk of cheese, but said he wanted it to last him his whole voyage, and he used to watch me like a cat whenever I nibbled at it like a mouse. One day he took umbrage at my scraping the mildew off the surface. (I think it was due to his having spent his life in the Merchant Navy.) When we reached Holland I bought some more cheese, which I thought was the solution, but when he found out he took greater umbrage. In the end we never reached the famous sands of the 'Riddle'. I suspected that he had never intended to go farther than Terschelling, and that the Baltic had been bait to get me to sign on.

At the end of that voyage I decided that sailing would be a misery for me if I was going to worry about the weather all the time, about getting caught out in a gale and being fearful of my gear in a blow. If I was going to sail, I must learn to do it properly. I thought that the Royal Ocean Racing Club sailors would be the ones to learn from, because they raced in all weathers. I advertised my services as a navigator in an ocean race, but nobody seemed interested in an air navigator who knew nothing of the sea. So I was forced to buy a yacht of my own in order to learn. I said nothing to Sheila about this, because I felt sure that she would disapprove when we were so hard up, but I was determined to get a yacht. I went round looking at various likely yachts for sale, and finally bought a day sailer with the horrible name of *Florence Edith*. She was fitted with two comfortable seats on each side of the doghouse, where the owner and his wife could sit while out for a day's fishing. I paid £1,150 for this yacht in September 1953, and started sailing her immediately to get in as much time as possible before the end of the year, to decide how best to convert her for ocean racing.

Then I had to break the news to Sheila, expecting a terrific rocket for my extravagance. Imagine my astonishment when she said, 'Oh, I always wanted to sail. What an excellent idea!' I had no time to spend on navigating, charged sandbank after sandbank on the east coast, and when Sheila came up to have her first sail from Brightlingsea no one had seen or heard of the *Florence Edith*. At last an old fisherman said to her, 'Oh, you mean that there yellow boat? She be lying on Buxey Sands, and it's lucky 'tis fine weather, otherwise she'd be sunk when t'sea rises. What's more, there be thick fog coming up, and if she do get off the sands, it'll be a long time before you see her in Brightlingsea.' My wife was urged by the friend she was staying with to go home and get a divorce, but she decided to defer that, and left a message in case I should turn up. The fog did come up, as the fisherman forecast, but I had an amusing bit of navigation feeling the way along the channel into Brightlingsea by means of the hand lead. Sheila had her sail next morning, and enjoyed it. She joined in enthusiastically in redesigning the interior of the yacht. We rebuilt the cabin, making berths for six, which cost as much as the boat.

Next spring I entered for the North Sea race, 220 miles from Harwich to Rotterdam round the North Sea. I had been in only one race before, and was the only member of the crew who had been in any. Sheila had so much faith in me as a navigator that she expected me to win, and was most disappointed when I telephoned from Rotterdam to say that we had come nearly last. Before the start I had run aground off the River Crouch, losing my kedge anchor in the process of getting off.

We renamed the yacht *Gipsy Moth II*. I changed her from sloop to cutter rig. With her mainsail, staysail and yankee she carried 540 square feet of sail. She was 8 tons, Thames measurement, and 24 feet on the waterline, the minimum length permitted to enter for RORC races. I had one brilliant idea after another for speeding her up. For example at great trouble and expense I streamlined her sharp-edged iron keel with a false wooden keel, bolted on below. It made not the slightest difference to her performance.

My next race was from Cowes to Corunna. Unfortunately there was a weakness in the new masthead fitting which had been specially designed for her, and the top of the mast snapped off in the middle of the night in some dirty weather west of the Channel Islands. From the cabin it sounded like the crack of doom, and when I darted up into the cockpit there was a tangle of shrouds, halyards and wires wherever I shone the torch over the boat or in the water. Then one of the crew dropped the torch overboard with the light still shining, and as it sank getting fainter and fainter, it looked like a ghost leaving us for a better world. One of the crew evidently thought that we might be doing the same, and wanted to signal to a steamer whose lights were visible some distance off for help. I squashed that, perhaps more roughly than I need have, and told everyone to turn in except for one man to keep watch. When I awoke and went on deck I found our watchman fast asleep in the cockpit. Next morning we cleared up the tangle of gear, set a small staysail, and headed for Guernsey. There was a strong current as we approached the island, and it looked as if we were going to be carried on to the rocks. One of the crew was a very devout Roman Catholic, and I noticed his lips praying nervously as we were being carried towards the rocks. We cleared the point, sailed into St Peter Port and tacked up to a mooring buoy by carrying from one side of the deck to the other the boom to which the staysail was attached.

In my first season I sailed that boat 2,510 miles, including three races. Our racing record was one of the worst in the club, but I was learning.

Next season in the North Sea Race one of *Gipsy Moth II*'s crew was an ex-wartime naval commander, who claimed to have sailed a lot. He had been maddening the rest of the crew throughout the race across the North Sea. We crossed the finishing line in the dark, running down wind with spinnaker set in a fresh breeze. Two of the crew were lowering the spinnaker, I was at the helm, and I asked the fourth man of the crew, my naval friend, to take in the rotating log trailing astern. When he said he must have someone to help him do it I was so enraged that I felt a hot flood in my belly as if something had burst inside me.

On the way back from Rotterdam to the Solent I began to feel ill. Sailing down channel I asked this same man to pump the bilge, but he refused. I pumped it myself, but shortly afterwards was in agonies. Later in the season, before the start of my first Fastnet Race, I was becoming a sick man. The race took us six days, and before it ended, I had to be helped out of my bunk to the cockpit, and had difficulty in holding on while navigating. I went off to a hospital where a specialist, after examining the X-ray, said that I was a typical case of chronic arthritis. I certainly was in a bad way; I could not open a door without great difficulty, even using two hands, and once I dropped a full plate of soup over myself because I was unable to grasp the plate. I started visiting the hospital regularly for treatment. One day my nature cure family doctor said to me, 'Ask your fellow patients how long they have been receiving this treatment, and then decide for yourself whether it seems likely to cure you.' This made me think hard, and as a result I underwent a severe course of nature cure treatment at Edstone. Shortly after I arrived there I sat down on the ground on a fine autumn day and was unable to get to my feet again. I had to wait there until someone happened along who could pull me up. Fortunately the treatment succeeded; it seemed to take a long time, but by next spring I was a fit man and started a hard season's racing in *Gipsy Moth II*.

The first race of the season was the 220 miles race from Southsea to Harwich by way of the Hinder Lightship in the North Sea. *Gipsy Moth II* won this race outright, and it sounds terrific, but the truth is that the going was very slow in light airs as far as the Dover Straits, and many of the other competitors gave up. One of our own crew said we must stop racing and put him ashore. I said, 'There's the shore; you can swim for it if you wish, but *Gipsy Moth* is racing on.' Perhaps the real reason why we won was because we had Marston Tickell, a Sapper Colonel, on board, who is one of the best ocean racers that I know. The way he made *Gipsy Moth* sail was a revelation to me. When we reached our mooring at Harwich at the end of the race we found the *Ann Speed* not only moored up but with all her crew away ashore. We were much depressed to think of one of our competitors having got in so far ahead of us. It seems extraordinary how this deep depression can go with success; our rival had given up the race at Dover, and cut across the Thames Estuary to shorten the distance by forty-five miles.

The next year we raced hard again. The Cowes-Dinard Race was interesting. Sheila sailed in it, and two other members of the crew were Martin Jones and Michael Jones. Martin had crewed for me in a number of races, and I regarded him as hard to beat as a deckhand and helmsman. Michael was a lieutenant in the Navy, and later became the Queen's Sailing Master skippering *Bloodhound*, the Duke of Edinburgh's 34-ton yacht, and a very different proposition from *Gipsy Moth II*. There was a fresh wind with a choppy sea, and I was cutting the corner fine at Guernsey, standing in as close to the rocks as I dared in the hope of avoiding a tack and the loss of time that it would cost. Mike did not like being in so close, because he had been wrecked on these rocks in another boat, and Sheila was gossiping with him below about social nothings because, she told me afterwards, she thought the atmosphere was too tense. I barked harshly at them (a sure sign that the skipper is too tense himself) because I wanted to be ready to tack at a second's notice. At that moment I saw a column of water shoot 20 feet straight into the air, where a wave had hit a submerged rock a cable's length (200 yards) on the beam. I said nothing to Mike, because I thought he would have a fit, but I laughed to myself and carried on – if the rocks were going to show up as clearly as that, I need not worry. We managed to scratch past without having to tack. Sheila was presented with a cup by the handsome commodore of the Dinard Yacht Club, and I think nothing could have given her more pleasure.

At the end of *Gipsy Moth*'s fourth racing season she had started in sixteen RORC races and I had learned a lot about sailing; perhaps more important, I was aware how much more there was to learn.

CHAPTER TWENTY-FIVE

CANCER OF THE LUNG

I FIND it difficult to think about my whole lung cancer story. It was so dreadful for me that for a long time I could bear to think only of a small bit of the story at a time; sometimes I could talk about a part of it to a friend if I felt strong sympathy with him. Recently, however, Tubby Clayton, of Toc H, pressed me to tell the story; he said it was my duty to do it for the good of other sufferers. I shrank from it, but came to realize that since I was the only person who *could* tell the story, I must face up to it. It was really this decision that made me write the whole of this book.

In 1957 I had a tough year in the office, with a lot of worry, and also a hard season's sailing. I raced my own *Gipsy Moth II* in three RORC events, and at the end of the English Channel race in my own yacht, jumped aboard *Figaro*, the crack American yacht, to navigate it for the owner, Bill Snaith, in a series of races for the Admiral's Cup. This cup was presented by the Admiral of the RORC for international competition by teams of three yachts. *Figaro* had a crack crew; Bill Snaith was a first-class sailor, and an excellent, hard-driving skipper, but fair; Bobby Simonette had been acclaimed one of the world's best foredeck hands; Ed Raymond was one of America's best sail makers and a real old salt; Kanud Reimers, the Swedish yacht architect, told me that he had designed more yachts than he could remember; young Buckie was a first-class deck hand. Buckie had served in the Korean war, and now acted as permanent crew for Bill, looking after the yacht for him. They were a fine crowd to sail with. I enjoyed studying

288

the famous American out-to-win methods, and I learned a lot from them. Also the differences between the American and British viewpoint amused me continuously; little things like eating marmalade *on* bacon. I don't know what they thought of me.

Our first race was for the Britannia Cup, and I felt really tense. If we lost, the Americans could blame their British navigator; if we won, the British team could accuse me of being a renegade. Either way I was due to get the stick, and as a result I was, perhaps, over-keen to win. My first suggestion in tactics put us in the lead of the fleet. I was thrilled. Unfortunately my next stroke of genius turned out a flop, and cost us the race which we had had in our pocket.

In our next race, for the New York Yacht Club Cup, an unusual bit of navigation for a big yacht played an important part. In light airs we tacked into the mainland coast of the Solent, bucking a foul tide stream. Our depth steadily decreased as we neared the shore, till it looked as if we were about to ground and Bill called out, 'Tack.' I said, 'Hold on, hold on!' I had bathed from this beach, and remembered a long mud bank with a shallow channel inshore of it. We hauled up the centre board, and kept on inshore. I held my breath 'as the depths decreased. Then they began to increase again and I sighed with relief. We had crossed the mud bank. Now we worked our way up close inshore, where the current against us was least. At one time we were becalmed, and dropped the kedge anchor. I took the opportunity of dropping over-board myself for a swim. I think my American friends were horrified at my treating a race so flippantly, but at that time were too polite to say anything. Presently we were leading the fleet and won the race.

I had high hopes of *Figaro*'s winning the Fastnet, which is the finest of all races from the navigator's viewpoint. Nearly every mile of the 600-mile long course requires careful navigation, and the conditions are changing all the way along the route. This Fastnet was considered a rough weather race, and only twelve out of the forty-five starters finished the course. Afterwards I was surprised to read about the stormy weather. *Figaro* seemed so steady and comfortable after my 8-ton *Gipsy Moth II*, that I had not noticed anything out of the ordinary about the weather.

It is easy to be wise after the event, but here are some of the things which slowed us down. Firstly, I believe that Bill and his crew had been celebrating the winning of the New York Yacht Club Cup on their last night in Cowes. We were late over the starting line, and when on leaving the Needles I asked for the starboard tack to take us out into the Channel, Bill said, 'Can't we sail the other tack (towards Swanage) which looks less rough?' The navigating instinct is a very tenuous affair, and I could not give a good reason why the Swanage tack should not have been equally good. So we took it, but as it turned out it cost us many hours of racing time.

American yachts favour 'points' reefing, which undoubtedly sets the sail better than roller reefing. *Figaro*, however, had a big pram hood over the companion way, and it was difficult to get at the main-sail boom to reach the sail; the hood was not substantial enough to stand on. As a result, we were reluctant to reef, reefed too late, and later, when the wind abated, we were equally reluctant to unreef, and unreefed too late. Another drawback was that the yacht was stuffed with experts. Everyone tended to exercise his own special expertise. Bobby wanted to demonstrate his latest methods of gybing, which cost us time unsnarling the spinnaker and repairing the damage. Ed liked to harden in the foresails, unconsciously demonstrating how strong they were. He had five men hardening in the jib sheet, using two big winches. They were marvellous sails, but often hardened in too flat for the best speed. Of course, this is only my opinion; no doubt I was doing the same sort of thing with the navigation. I do not want to give a wrong impression; on the whole, that yacht was sailed really well. We only lost one sail, a spinnaker was blown out when we were running down from the Fastnet Rock to Land's End – only a few ribbons of it were left. Bill was eating his breakfast at the time, when someone poked his head in the hatchway and said, 'Spinnaker's gone.' Bill went on eating, unmoved, and said, 'Tell Ed that's his bad luck; I haven't paid for it yet.'

It was a great race, and I enjoyed it from start to finish. We ended up third in Class II. John Illingworth was first in that class, and *Figaro*'s sister ship *White Mist* second. After the race, Bill asked me to navigate *Figaro* from Plymouth to the Port of London for shipping back to the United States. I said, 'Yes, if Sheila can sail with us.' I wanted her to experience a good yacht. The crew consisted of young Buckie and Teddy Robins who was an American University student of nineteen.

Two better deckhands could not be found. We had a fast run up from Plymouth to the Isle of Wight, where I wanted to dodge into the Solent and anchor for the night. The boys then did not like this idea, so I agreed to press on. As we passed St Catherine's Point it began to blow up. I gave a course to steer and retired for a sleep, because I could see we were in for a dirty night. The boys asked Sheila if she thought I knew where we were. Soon after dark, Buckie called me out to take the helm while they hauled down the mainsail. As they hauled up the trisail, I could see that we did not need any sail at all, but Buckie was determined to have it. We were now running dead before a gale, and the trisail periodically gybed with a report like a gun's being fired. It was a mistake for all of us to stay on watch getting tired, and as soon as Buckie turned in, I told Teddy to haul down the trisail. It was a thrilling ride. All night we averaged $5\frac{1}{2}$ knots, running dead up Channel under bare poles. It would have been most uncomfortable if the wind had been even 5 degrees different in direction, but as long as *Figaro* was pointing dead down wind, the cockpit was comparatively sheltered. If I let the head swing only 5 degrees either way, the din of the wind made it hard to hear anything else. The Met. reported gusts of 90 mph at Brighton, which we passed in the night, but I reckoned we were not in more than 75 mph. Usually I would be worried about a wind of this strength on a dark night in the Channel, with the shore close alongside; but in this case I reckoned that if the gale blew up into a storm, and it became impossible to enter Dover Harbour, or turn the Goodwins, we could safely run straight through the Dover Straits into the North Sea. My only uneasiness was due to our being bang in the middle of the shipping lane, where a thousand ships pass to and fro during a day. At one time there seemed to be ships' lights round us in every quarter, and it was hard to keep track of them, because they disappeared every time we were in the trough of a wave.

Sheila had turned in happily, because the bunks were fitted out with a luxurious comfort which she had never experienced in *Gipsy Moth II*. As the sky lightened for daybreak, she heard me say that we ought to be sighting Beachy Head soon. She popped out her head and said, 'I never knew the cliffs at Beachy Head were green.' The fact was that the sea looked pale green in the faint dawn light. Sheila can always be relied on to say something which will stop me from taking life too seriously.

Once round Dungeness, we got into sheltered water, and as we ran up to Dover the storm abated. We hoisted some sail, and entered Dover Harbour to anchor in the submarine pen.

Early in the year, Sheila had said, 'It's time you had a new boat,' just as she might have said, 'It's time you have a new suit.' She said, 'If you can win prizes with your old boat, you ought to do well with a new one.' 'We haven't got the money to pay for it.' 'I'm sure something will turn up if you order it. Have faith, and go ahead.' I sketched on the back of an envelope the hull that I should like to have. This was passed to Robert Clark, who designed *Gipsy Moth III* for us. Jack Tyrrell's boatyard in Arklow, Ireland, started building it. Throughout the year, worried about my business, I alternated between bouts of despair at the liability of the new boat, and waves of enthusiasm for it.

After the last sail in *Figaro*, I had a desperate attack of worry. I was struggling hard to make my map business pay. It was not big enough to pay for the new talent it needed in both the sales and the production departments, but it was too big for me to provide all the new ideas as well as the sales drive needed. Now I had this ghastly load of a new boat added, with all the extra work of planning it, and visiting it in Ireland. I had a nightmare fear of not being able to sell *Gipsy Moth II*, and of being landed with two yachts. It was all too much to bear. The trouble was that by the end of the Fastnet I was tired out. If only I had laid off everything for a week, I should have regained the strength to cope with things.

Every week-end I went down to the Beaulieu River, and worked on *Gipsy Moth II*, trying to tidy up the mess after the season's racing. I worked feverishly by myself, feeling that I could not afford to pay a boatyard to do the work. Sheila said this was nonsense. Bitterly, I accused her of failing to help me, and came down by myself. I worked furiously while the yacht swung to her mooring in the grey swirls of autumn mist on the glassy water. There always seemed so little time for work on the yacht, after I had cooked my meals and done the boat's housekeeping.

One of my jobs was to remove some old paint on the forecastle sole (floor). To do this, I used a strong chemical paint-remover, to dissolve the old paint. I worked on my knees, doubled up over the stuff on the floor, and the forehatch was closed above my head, because of the cold. I believe that the fumes burnt my lungs, and that my lung trouble started then. I was in bad condition, run down, and flooding my body with poisons distilled from negative feelings – despair, resentment, bitterness, fear, worry, exhaustion. I began to cough. I retired to bed in my little room at the top of No. 9 (St James's Place) with a 'cold on the chest'. I got better, and went to Ireland with Robert Clark to see the frame of *Gipsy Moth III*, and to discuss the building. When I got home, I went to bed with pleurisy. I got better again, and my nature cure doctor said that I should have as much fresh air as I could get. I went out in a cold wind, and retired to bed with pneumonia, it was said. Again I improved, again did the same silly thing of going out in cold air, and again was back in bed, this time with an abscess in my lung. Three or four months after I first got ill I improved, and went down to Brighton for a weekend. Here we ran into an ocean racing skipper acquaintance; he was a doctor and implored us to have my lungs X-rayed.

My own doctor wanted this too, so I turned up at a famous London hospital, where I waited on a bench for six hours while X-rays were taken and discussed. The radiologist asked me a curious question, 'Had I ever breathed in a feather into my lungs?' The surgeons wanted to discuss the X-ray pictures, and I had to go back some days later. I began to feel much worse, due (I thought) to the travelling to and from the hospital, to the waiting about, and making efforts. I was interviewed by the chief surgeon, one of the leading lung and heart men in Britain. To my surprise a door opened, and in filed a dozen young student surgeons, and the big chief proceeded to use me for a demonstration. He said, 'This is a typical case of an advanced carcinoma. Now breathe out. No, not into my face. Here are all the usual symptoms.' He discussed my breathing, prodded the base of my neck with his finger, and picked up my fingers to show something in the fingernails, but flung them aside.

I came away feeling degraded, defiled and deeply depressed. I did not know, however, that carcinoma was cancer; I thought it was a lump, or something like a mastoid.

When I got home, I found Tom Killefer there from America, with his young wife Isabel. I was very fond of Tom; I suppose everybody must be. As a lieutenant of the United States Navy Air Force he had done a course at the Empire Central Flying School, while I was Navigation Officer there. I did my best to entertain Tom and Isabel and took them to Wiltons for dinner, but I felt ghastly. I could not suppress my coughing bouts, and the party was not a great success.

I had been told to go back to the hospital some days later, so that a bronchoscopy could be carried out. This was a simple operation; a surgeon pushed a lighted periscope down my throat to examine my lungs. Foolishly, I declined to have a general anaesthetic, because of the old, unpleasant recollection of being chloroformed after my snake bite. It was a rough and most unpleasant performance, during which a piece was broken off one of my back teeth. I seemed to be sinking steadily deeper into physical and spiritual degradation.

Before I left the hospital the next day I cornered the surgeon who had done the bronchoscope deed. At first he refused to tell me the result. But he was an Australian; I understand Australians, and finally persuaded him to talk. 'Cancer,' he said. 'You can't be sure, can you?' 'We are making these examinations all the time, and cannot possibly be mistaken.' 'I don't believe it; how can you tell?' 'I not only saw it, but cut off a piece and sent it off to the laboratory to be examined.' 'What can be done?' 'I think it's already too late to operate.' I took this to mean that the cancer was straddling both lungs. 'Your only possible hope is to remove one lung immediately.'

Half a year had passed since I was first ill, and when I emerged from the hospital it was a fine spring morning in April. As I walked along, the sun shone in my face. I heard the gay spring-song of birds. Young pale-green leaves were beginning to tint the trees. Life had never seemed more wonderful – a priceless, desirable thing to lose. My body seemed empty, my bones full of water. It was like a nightmare where I was in a bottomless space of loneliness. I had read about this sort of thing happening to other people; somehow I had never imagined that it would happen to me. I walked along slowly, wondering how long I had got before I was snuffed out from this lovely fresh spring of life.

By the time I got home, I had decided that it would only make things worse to be weak, but I felt desolately sad while I told Sheila. Only then did I realize that she had known everything that was going on for weeks past and had been discussing every step with our family doctor, and others, for a long time. She said, 'What are you going to do?' I said I had done what they told me to do—booked a room for the operation next week. 'How can you be so feeble as to agree? It's the wrong thing to do.'

Sheila thought that I was so ill that I had weakly agreed to anything; that I was too ill to make a decision. 'Dammit,' I said, 'first of all the radiologist says he is examining pictures all the time, and can't possibly be mistaken. Then the surgeon says he has not only seen the cancer, but removed a piece of it. The chief surgeon said it was cancer. What else can I possibly do but agree to the operation?' Sheila said, 'It's wrong to operate; your lung is in such a state that you are bound to die if they operate.'

First she wanted me to have a totally separate examination by a lung specialist of great reputation. He said that it was the worst case of neglect he had ever seen, and that his diagnosis was the same as the hospital surgeon's. By now five different doctors, surgeons or radiologists had given the same opinion. A week later I set off for the hospital, as arranged. On leaving my house, I called in at the Royal Ocean Racing Club to have a farewell drink. Talking to some of my friends at the bar there, I felt intensely lonely. The thought of being cut off from my friends, added, I suppose, to fear and dread, turned my bones to water and already I seemed isolated in unbridgeable space. I did not say where I was going; no one wants a spectre at a feast.

CHAPTER TWENTY-SIX

DELIVERANCE

WHEN I was a boy at home, I used to hear my father pray every Sunday, 'From sudden death, good Lord deliver us.' This had always puzzled me; sudden death seemed a fine way to go out. Now the meaning seemed clear; the prayer should read, 'From death before we are ready to die, good Lord deliver us.'

On the way out of the club, I paused and glanced at the notice board in the lobby. I saw a notice proposing a single-handed race across the Atlantic, signed H. G. Hasler. I thought briefly, 'That would be a terrific race,' and passed on, thinking that the only other race I was likely to take part in was to race old Charon across the Styx.

I was resigned to my fate. Not so my wife; she was now really in a fighting mood, and went into action. She asked for an interview with the head surgeon. 'I don't interview the relatives of patients.'

'I want an interview. I will pay you for it as a patient.'

'Very well, then.'

I imagine that the surgeon was intrigued to know what sort of a woman this was. As she was waiting on a bench in the

296

gloomy corridor, he came out of his room, walked past, looked at her, and then came back.

'I don't believe an operation is the right thing in this case,' she said.

'You are wasting valuable time.'

'I'm sorry. I realize you are busy.'

'I mean the patient's time.'

'I want the opinion of another physician.'

'You are destroying his only chance of living by delaying the operation.'

'He is so ill, the shock of the operation would kill him.'

'Many people live with only one lung.'

'His lungs are in such a septic state that he is bound to die if you cut into them. I refuse to consent to the operation.'

The surgeon then spoke of certain neck symptoms, and said he would examine me again. I suppose that he, like me, had never met a woman like Sheila – someone who would carry the responsibility of refusing to allow an operation against the overwhelming weight of medical opinion.

As far as I was concerned, things moved slowly, and in somewhat of a dreary blur. Hospital routine; dreadful nights, lying for hour after hour unable to sleep, sometimes choking and gasping for breath; not allowed to switch on a light, because it would wake up other patients in the ward. Patients coming in, having a lung removed, suffering bravely, leaving. Every day the surgeon on his rounds poked my neck with his finger as if to see if I was ripe for the knife. The physician's report was the same as before. The laboratory report on the lung tissue came in. The surgeon told me about it.

'The report is negative.'

'Then it isn't cancer?'

'It's cancer all right; the negative report means only that it is not active at the moment. That often happens.'

Sheila persuaded the chief surgeon to carry out another bronchoscopy himself. The results were shrouded in haze for me; it seemed that 'it', whatever it was, had not increased in size. It was agreed not to operate. I was subjected to a series of treatments, the worst was a course of antibiotics.

After a few days I could not stand, and found coughing a serious strain. I thought, 'I'm damned if I'm going to be killed this way', and started hiding the pills. Sheila came every day to visit me. It was a great strain for her; there was a bus strike, and often she walked the whole way. My prolonged illness was not only a big expense itself but now my map publishing business was beginning to run down.

I was still on the Court of the Guild of Air Pilots and Air Navigators, and one day I had a state visit from the Master of the Guild, Sir Frederic Tymms. It did me good, because Freddie, who was extremely kind, obviously thought that I was shortly taking off for another world. This amused me, and put a little ginger into me. Many of my friends visited me too, but often I felt too ill to talk. I would make an effort, but felt I needed to conserve the vital spark, and not to fan it into flame. I wanted only to lie still in peace, and to defer the horrid moment when I would start coughing, and pass through the experience of feeling suffocated. There came a time when I said that suffocation had caused me to die a thousand deaths, but this was an exaggeration; perhaps it was a hundred, or even less. But it is what *seems* that counts, not what is. I had always heard that drowning was a pleasant death. I cannot understand this. Perhaps it is different to be choked by water from outside. I developed a terrified dread of that slow choking from within. I despised myself as I became an abject coward about dying that way. As each fresh crisis built up, I wanted to cry as if surrendering to that weakness would give me respite.

Then Sheila said that if only I could get together enough strength to stand moving, she would take me to a nature cure place in the country. I made a great effort. 'It' had not grown in size, according to the X-ray photographs, and after a month Sheila decided to risk a move. It was a bad journey in a motor-car, but I arrived. Enton Hall was heavenly after the hospital. After the standard hospital diet, I was grateful for vegetarian food, with fresh fruit, and raw grated vegetables. I found that when it became difficult to breathe, a complete fast for two or three days made breathing a little easier. As soon as I discovered this I played it time after time, whenever breathing was too difficult to bear. A strange situation now arose, for instead of being encouraged to fast, as is usual in a nature cure hydro, I was being advised either not to do it, or to cut it short because I had not the strength to stand it. My being there became a strain on the establishment, which was not intended for seriously ill people. My coughing disturbed others at night. They did not think that I could stay there much longer. Fortunately for me another patient was Ann Todd, the actress, famous for her part in the film *The Seventh Veil*. She had been coshed by a thug. The doctor suggested that she should go and talk to me. Hearing of her troubles did me good. She gave me a lift. She said afterwards that I showed her plans of *Gipsy Moth III*, and talked of sailing out to New Zealand, but I do not remember it. There came a night when everyone gave up hope for me. My own doctor had driven down from London. He told Sheila that my heart was giving out under the strain. The house doctor said that I must be taken away to a hospital. Sheila was there, and I was left on her hands; dumped on her, as it were. The building seemed strangely quiet that night, as she applied hot and cold compresses on my back. I knew that they had given me up that night, and somehow it did me good. It infused will to live in me. I think it was a crisis.

After surviving that night, I got a little better, and was able to shuffle into the grounds. It was a gorgeous summer. I loved the warm touch of the sun on my skin, the rising scent of the pine needles, the soothing green of juicy, young curled-up bracken fronds. I liked to watch a big ant-heap of large fierce black-red ants at work. It was fascinating to watch them bury a piece of branch or a stone, completely sinking an object the size of half a brick into their nest in a day and a night.

I was able to go home, to the only place where I wanted to be, to my room at the very top of the house, my cave, my kennel, where I could wrap a blanket round the remains of my shattered personality, and turn my face to the window. I could sleep only on one side, could breathe only propped on one elbow, but at least it was facing the window. My arm and shoulder joint began to change shape, and a muscle in my throat grew taut like a cord with the strain of staying in one position. Perhaps I suffered most at this period, and became most frightened with the suffocation attacks. I felt that I could not stand it, and was at just about as low an ebb as I could be. My personality had shrunk to almost nothing. This upsets people; they are used to someone's having a certain personality, and if that personality changes, the person feels among strangers. My nerves were in a shrinking, cringing state. Physically I was no better off; one day I found that I was sitting on something in my bath which was hurting me. Gingerly I moved to discover what it was. There was nothing; it was my skin being pinched between my bones and the bath. My skin hung in folds; my weight had dropped 40 lb. When I struggled for breath sometimes oxygen, always at hand, seemed to help, and at other times it seemed useless.

My map business had been running steadily downhill. Finally Sheila could not stand it any longer, entered the office and took charge. She had never had anything to do with business before, and on top of that she's artistic, with a slow casual approach to an issue which can be maddening to the business mentality. On the other hand, her perception is brilliantly acute, her judgement excellent for half the occasions, and her imagination amazingly fertile for new ideas. Her chief asset, however, is that if she makes up her mind to do something, she will do it. She overcame the inevitable frictions, introduced some new ideas, which, if not successful as money-spinners, infused some new life into the firm. The hive had a new queen, and came alive again.

Early in the spring of 1959 I screwed myself up to visit my mother in Devonshire. I felt that I must go to see her before it was too late. My mother and sister never seemed to feel the cold, or to have any idea of comfort, according to my standards, and unfortunately the weather was cold and damp. My sister did her best, and dug out some more blankets for my bed; I think they were the same that I had used as a boy, but now matted hard with fifty years of use. She also put an oil stove in my bedroom, given her, by, of all people, my girl friend of fifty years before, Nancy Platt. But the bad attack of bronchitis and asthma which I now had, really needed a dry, constant heat. I was in bed on the Sunday morning, feeling ill and miserable, while my family were away at church. My mother could not approve of staying away from church, whatever the cause. After church there was a commotion, a mix up of voices and steps, which permeated my semi-consciousness. Stumblings on the stairs brought me out of bed, to find that my mother was being carried up. I put on my clothes as fast as I could. My mother had failed to get up after praying in church. They carried her out, thinking that she was dead, but she came to in the churchyard. I did what I could to help, but it was a feeble effort. To make matters worse for my sister, who insisted on doing all the housework, I was a wreck. The doctor was called in, but he could not help me, and said to my sister, 'Does his wife know how seriously ill he is?'

'What with?'

'Cancer.'

When I heard this it cheered me up; in fact I laughed. I don't suppose many have laughed on hearing that dreadful verdict, but I reasoned that I must surely have been dead eighteen months ago if it had been a living cancer.

When I got back to London I felt more optimistic and got better. An X-ray was taken and it was OK. Suddenly I had a tremendous urge to go to the South of France. I asked Sheila to get two tickets on the Blue Train for the next day. It seemed an irresistible urge.

We left for St Paul de Vence as soon as it could be organized. I was all right when I arrived, but began to feel ill again. I did not like the place where we were, and moved up to the Hotel Falcoz in Vence. Here I got worse, and sent to the chemist for a cylinder of oxygen. It could not be supplied without a doctor's order. In England oxygen can be obtained at any time from a chemist, and I was annoyed, thinking it was a game to bring in a doctor unnecessarily. However, I grew worse, until I agreed that the doctor should be asked for the oxygen. He not only sent round his assistant to get the mask, etc, to the cylinder, but would not accept any payment.

When I grew worse, I finally said, 'Ask the doctor to come.' That was how I met Dr Jean Mattei, a remarkable man. He examined me, and said, '*Ce n'est rien*, and if you follow my treatment you will be climbing up those mountains in three days' time.' The fantastic thing is that I did, in fact, climb up the Baou Blanc in five days' time. At 2,200 feet it may not be much of a mountain, but it was the most wonderful climb I ever made.

What I regarded as a miraculous chain of events had started in London when I felt the urge to go to the South of France. There I reached a doctor who had been considered one of the cleverest lung physicians in Paris before he settled in Vence; also I had fetched up in a town which had been considered a health resort, with a magic quality of air for lungs, since the time of the Romans. How did this thing come about? Sheila said that the doctor gave me back my confidence, that my illness was already on its last legs. For myself, I think that some part of my body had ceased to function, that the doctor correctly diagnosed what this was, and supplied the deficiency. To me he was a wonderful man; short, nuggety, fit, with terrific energy exuding strength and activity. He never seemed to stop work, seeing thirty patients a day at times. I heard tales of his sitting up all night with a seriously ill patient, for two nights running.

It was April when I fell into the good doctor's hands. In June I accepted an offer to navigate *Pym* in the Cowes-Dinard race. *Pym* was a fast, racing eleven-tonner, a beauty to sail, designed by Robert Clark and excellently sailed by Derek Boyer, her owner. I was not supposed to do anything but navigate, but I forgot, and hauled on a rope which caused a commotion in my lung. I coughed, spluttered and gasped, and finally had to call in a local French doctor at St Malo to ginger me up. Derek said afterwards that he was worried stiff about me, but I was not worried about myself. By July I accepted an offer to navigate the crack Italian yacht *Mait II* in the Cowes Week Races, and in the Fastnet. This was great fun, with eleven Italians (seven of them Olympic helmsmen); none of them could speak English, and I could not speak any

Italian. We talked in slow French. At the end of this Fastnet race, as we turned the Lizard into Plymouth Bay on the last lap, the wind piped up to a near gale. The wind was on our starboard quarter, and we were running fast towards the lee shore. It was murky weather, and the visibility poor; at the cliffs for which we were headed it might be very poor. I pondered the situation. If I were 400 yards out in my navigation, we could come slap up against the rocks at the entrance to Plymouth Sound. This would require turning instantly, and coming up into wind. I thought of the Council of War that had been held every time that I had previously suggested fresh tactics. I also thought, perhaps basely, that we had not done well enough in this race for five minutes' extra sailing to entail the loss of it. I said, 'Alter course 10 degrees to starboard. We will make a landfall of the Eddystone Light before entering Plymouth Sound.'

My great friend Michael Richey was navigating the Swedish yacht *Anitra*. They had come along earlier in similar conditions, but with the visibility worse. Mike said to the owner, 'If my navigation is correct, we shall make Plymouth breakwater (the finishing line) and win the race, but if it isn't we shall pile up on the rocks outside. It's your yacht, you decide.' Sven Hanson, the owner, said, 'Carry on.' And so *Anitra* won the Fastnet race of 1959.

People criticized Sheila for letting me go ocean racing; they thought that I was still too ill because I coughed a lot, and had periodic attacks of bronchitis, asthma and other things. But Sheila staunchly stood up for her opinion that it was the best thing for me. She has a strange and amazing flair for health and healing. She believes most strongly in the power of prayer. When I was at my worst, she rallied many people to pray for me, my friends and others. Whether Protestants, Roman Catholics or Christian Scientists, she rallied them indefatigably to prayer. I feel shy about my troubles being imposed on others, but the power of prayer is miraculous. Hardly anyone would doubt its power for evil – for example the way the Australian aborigines can will a member of their tribe to death; so why should its power for good be doubted?

On the material side I believe that fasting is the strongest medicine available and that it played a very important part in my recovery. I believe that my being a vegetarian for preference helped a lot.

After the Fastnet race, when I entered the Royal Ocean Racing Club again, I spotted Blondie Hasler's notice about the proposed solo Atlantic race, still on the board. I thought, 'Good God! I believe I can go in for this race.' I regard it as miraculous that within thirty-two months of being first taken ill, and within fifteen months of my appealing to Dr Mattei for oxygen in Vence, I was able to cross the starting line for the toughest yacht race that has ever taken place, and able to finish it in forty and a half days. However, during the next eight months, it was touch and go whether the race would ever get organized, and touch and go whether the yacht and I could get to the starting line. It was formidable; the prospect of racing alone across the Atlantic, when I had never been alone in any boat larger than a 12-foot dinghy.

PART FIVE

CHAPTER TWENTY-SEVEN

TRANSATLANTIC SOLO

A SOLO race across the Atlantic from east to west was the greatest yacht race that I had ever heard of, and it fired my imagination. Three thousand miles, plugging into the prevailing Westerlies, probably strong, bucking the Gulf Stream current, crossing the Grand Banks off Newfoundland which were not only one of the densest fog areas of the world, but also stuffed with fishing trawlers. No wonder the Atlantic had only once before been raced across from east to west. That was in 1870, by two big schooners, the *Dauntless* and the *Cambria*. The *Dauntless*, 124 feet long with a crew of thirty-nine, and a potential speed of 14 knots, lost the race by one hour and thirty-seven minutes, due it was said to spending two hours looking for two of her crew washed overboard while changing a jib. Anything once lost sight of in a seaway is difficult to find again, so it is not surprising that they failed to recover the men overboard.

Sheila backed me in every way to get into this race. She was criticized for this because I was thought to be still a sick man, but she stuck to her view that it would complete my cure. I wrote to Colonel Hasler and disputed some of his proposed conditions for the race, particularly one that entrants must first qualify by a solo sail to the Fastnet Rock and back. This course requires constant accurate navigation throughout, because of the nearness of land and the shipping routes along it, and a single-hander would find it difficult to get any sleep during the six to ten days' sail. Blondie Hasler came to my office for a talk. He was a quiet-speaking, interesting man, short, round and bald-headed with a red face. He never seemed to move a muscle while speaking. He steadily and quietly pursued his affairs. He was a regular officer of Marines, retired with a total disability pension for a back injury, and famous for the expedition he thought up and led in the war which resulted in his being known as the Cockleshell Hero. Ten Marines in canoes made their way sixty miles up the Gironde River to Bordeaux, where they sank several steamers at the quayside. Only two of them returned alive. Blondie was also an expert ocean racer, and one year, with a novel type of boat for ocean racing, came top of the smallest class of the RORC for the season's racing.

Blondie's proposal was that this Atlantic solo race would encourage the development of suitable boats, gear and technique to simplify sailing. But the race had stuck; people were scared of it, saying that it was a dangerous hare-brained scheme. Sheila and I threw all our weight into the effort to get it going again. Blondie had first suggested the race to the Slocum Society of America, who seemed to me an amiable bunch of cranky American sailors quite different from what one would expect to find associated with the name of Slocum, who was an expert navigator as well as a fine sailor and a fine man. The Slocum Society had first praised the idea of such a race, later refused to support it, and now seemed to have lost all interest in it. Blondie had also enlisted the interest of the editor of *The Observer*, David Astor, a friend of his who had served with him in the Marines. It seemed at first that a starting line was the only thing needed for a race across the Atlantic, but the hard truth was that it also needed considerable money for a yacht in racing trim, with the special gear and six months' stores required for a double crossing of the Atlantic, apart from expenses while in America. During that half year a man would be away from his job, and probably receiving no income from it. At first *The Observer* offered a prize of £1,000 for the winner, and £250 for each yacht taking part. Then they shrank into their shell, warned that if the yachts were sunk, their rivals would tear them in pieces for luring the flower of young British manhood to its doom with offers of sordid gold. Fortunately they were a sporting lot, with Chris Brasher and Lindley Abbatt backing up the Editor, and finally they

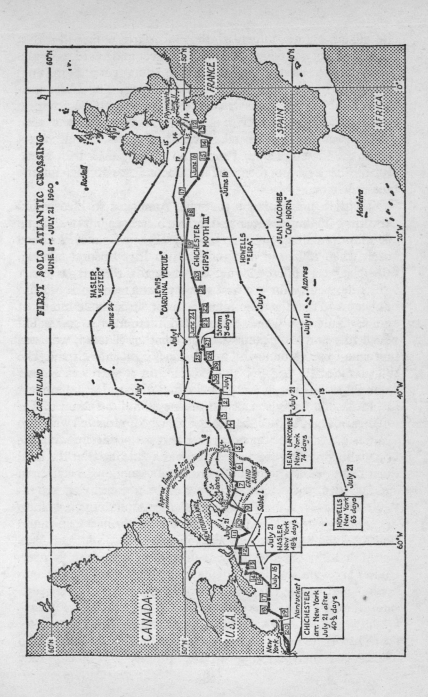

offered £250 each to any starter as option money for the winner's story, for which another £750 would be paid. Several good clubs were asked to start this race, but all turned it down. One of my friends, Bill Waleran, suggested the Royal Western Yacht Club of England. Of course! Plymouth was the traditional place from which to set sail for America, and the RWYC was the club to take over the race – it had sponsored the first Fastnet Race, and the ROAC had been founded in its club rooms. The Slocum Society agreed to finish the race.

The prize money may seem small compared with some of the prizes in horse races and other matches, but we were concerned only to be able to take part in such a race. At one stage, when it looked as if no one would sponsor, start or finish the race, I offered to race Blondie across for half a crown.

Blondie's entry for the race was a junk-rigged Folkboat. It has been said that the junk sail is the most efficient in existence, and certainly the Chinese have had thousands of years in which to perfect it. Joshua Slocum, that great sailor and the first man to sail around the world alone, built himself a junk-rigged canoe in the 1890's, and sailed in it with his family from Buenos Aires to New England, making a fast passage, including one day's run of 150 miles. Blondie was a canny, tough seadog, and with his yacht made a formidable rival.

I was going to race my new yacht *Gipsy Moth III* which had been launched the previous September. She had been built during my illness, and few new yachts can have been less supervised or visited by the owner. We saw her only twice while she was building. Once during a temporary improvement in my lung trouble I flew over to Dublin with Robert Clark and Sheila. While Robert and I walked down to the yard beside the river, the biting cold wind seemed to drive right through me. Robert grew more and more irritated at my stops for coughing bouts, and finally snapped, 'Stop coughing, now!' To my astonishment I did stop, and wondered if I must be a *malade imaginaire*. Fortunately for Robert this lull did not last long, otherwise I should have had to ask him to live with me until his new cure was complete.

When we visited the yacht, Sheila said that the seats in the main cabin were too low. Robert assured her that they were the standard height. Sheila, probably because she is a portrait painter, has an incredible eye for line and form. She was convinced that they were too low, and refused to budge in her opinion. They argued about it for hours on the way back to the hotel and throughout the evening, but Sheila, although she was opposing a famous architect who had been designing yachts all his life, refused to change her view. Before breakfast next morning Robert went down to the yacht and returned with this story: the water tanks under the cabin sole (floor) had been built the wrong shape, and were two inches higher than designed. Instead of re-making the tanks the yard had re-made the cabin sole two inches higher.

Several times when my illness was at its worst and seemed hopeless, I said, 'Sell the yacht, and let's be free of that worry at least.' Each time, however, I changed my mind and hung on. Jack Tyrrell and his firm were very good about my illness; they moved the half-built yacht to the side of the shed, and let it rest there until I was well enough to consider starting again.

In September 1959, after the Fastnet Race in *Mait II*, Sheila and I crossed to Arklow on a Monday morning to launch the yacht, which we found sitting in her cradle beside the river. The tides are erratic there, and we waited about all Tuesday for enough water to launch her. We had given up hope for the day, and were in the middle of our dinner at the hotel, when a boy came rushing up to say that the boat would be launched in ten minutes. We dropped our forks, grabbed a bottle of champagne, and rushed down to the yard. There were only a few people standing by when Sheila climbed on to the platform and well and truly crashed the champagne on the stem of the yacht, showering us with champagne and glass fragments as she named the yacht *Gipsy Moth III*. The yacht had looked powerful and tall standing on the hard of the river bank, and slid away quietly into the water.

Next morning Robert Clark arrived and rowed with me round the moored boat. 'What's wrong with the doghouse?' he asked. The doghouse is the raised part of the cabin roof at the aft end. I said, 'It seems all right to me; in fact Sheila and I were saying how attractive the yacht looked.' 'Oh well,' said Robert, 'if you are satisfied, that's all right.' It appeared that the Tyrrell family, who have been building boats for generations and have strong views of their own, had reversed the doghouse, so that it sloped down aft instead of up. This was a much better design, made the cabin roof stronger, and gave the whole line of the deck a more handsome look. The price we paid for it was countless cracks on the head when stepping too quickly from the cabin up to the cockpit outside.

I had often puzzled why a famously fast yacht or ship had never had an equally fast sister ship. Now I realized why. *Gipsy Moth*'s designed length was 38 ft 6 in overall. When launched she measured 39 ft 7 in, which is 13 inches longer. I mentioned this to Robert, and he said, 'If that's the only difference from the plan, you ought to be grateful,' implying that no wooden vessel can be built exactly as planned. The yacht suited me. She was staunchly built, and gave me confidence. She seemed so powerful that I felt at first like a small boy astride a tall, strong, broad-backed horse which would not stop. When we left for England on Saturday, four days after the launching, I think that there were several leprechauns still on board. One must have had his feet jammed in the rudder stock. By the time we reached the Solent I could only move the rudder by exerting my full strength with both hands on the tiller, and both feet on the cockpit seat opposite. However, *Gipsy Moth III* has always had a friendly atmosphere, as if she carried the goodwill of the craftsmen who built her, and I try to avoid strangers coming aboard for fear they might trample the Little People and drive them away.

The rudder stock tube could not be trued up until the yacht was hauled out, so that I had no chance to try out *Gipsy Moth*'s sailing qualities before she was laid up for the winter. As a result I had only ten weeks when she was launched in the spring, on April 3rd, until the start of the race on June 11th, in which to try her out for sailing qualities, to learn her tricks and foibles, and to improve my handling of her. I need two seasons of solid sailing to get anything like the best out of a boat, and would prefer to have three seasons. I think this might well apply to all yachts; certainly the last race for the America's Cup was won by a 12-metre which had been raced hard for three seasons.

Gipsy Moth III was a good deal bigger than my *Gipsy Moth II*, and I soon found that there were drawbacks as a result. She drew 6 ft 5 in and I went aground several times. With her high freeboard and 55-foot mast, the windage was considerable, and with her 13 tons she was likely to go aground good and hard. When I laid out a kedge anchor by myself to kedge her off mud it was desperately hard hauling without a winch.

The high freeboard made it more difficult to haul the dinghy on deck by myself, and because of this I lost the dinghy one day. I was sailing out through the Needles, towing it astern, when the painter snapped. There was a short, steep sea and a tide race, and although I sailed up to the dinghy several times, I could not get hold of it with the boathook while controlling the yacht at the same time. In the end I hauled down the sails to try approaching the dinghy under motor. While lowering the mainsail I lost sight of the dinghy, and was never able to locate it again. I spent my first night alone at sea looking for it. I carried out a square search, increasing the length of the sides each time. I had no self-steering device fitted then, the wind was unusually fickle, changing speed and direction every few minutes, and I could not make *Gipsy Moth* sail herself, though I kept on trimming and retrimming the sails. When I was not exhausted with the effort of handling the heavy gear, sweating with heat under my thick clothes, I was shivering in the cold wind. My 380-square foot mainsail, with its 18-foot boom, was awkward and heavy to handle. While lowering it, one of the runners (moveable stays bracing the mast) had to be slacked away, and its big blocks would be flying round, trying to dash my brains out as I gathered in the mainsail for furling. My main halyard carried away one of the main jumper struts at the top of the mast. I had no lifeline or harness, and nearly fell in.

When it was too dark to look for the dinghy any longer I

tried to make *Gipsy Moth* sail herself so that I could have some sleep. She pigheadedly refused to settle on any of the courses I chose. Finally I gave in to her, furled the mainsail, made the tiller fast and waited to see what she would do. She swung round on to a south-south-west heading and stayed on it, jilling along at half a knot. This was taking her right into the main shipping lane, but I switched on all my navigation lights and slept soundly till dawn. I had lost my dinghy, but I certainly gained plenty of experience that night.

I was hampered in my trials by having no self-steering gear until May 5th, only five weeks before the start of the race. It was clear that no yacht without a self-steering gear could have a chance against yachts equipped with them. One of the rules of the race was that no yacht could use an automatic pilot—or any other gear—driven by electricity or any other form of power. We were allowed only wind-powered or hand-operated gear.

I had been thinking about self-steering gear from the start, and I had talked it over with an old friend, Allen Wheeler, who was at school with me at The Old Ride, and who is now a celebrated boffin or aviation consultant. He said, 'You must have a modern self-steering device operated by an air-driven propeller.' This was to be like a windmill at the stern of the boat. It would be kept facing into wind by a wind vane, and it would wind up a cord attached to the tiller to pull it one way or the other if the boat's heading changed relative to the mind. This sounded marvellous, and I was stuffed full of hope. Presently Allen said that he had not enough time to make it work. By now I was so intrigued with the idea that I took it over myself. I niggled away at the design until I had a model in Meccano working satisfactorily. I showed this to another friend, Dingle Bell of the Sperry Gyroscope Company, and he was enthusiastic about it. He said that Sperry's would make it for me, and pay me a royalty if it turned out to be a popular design and suitable for all yachts. It was not until March that their engineers came to the conclusion that it would need a minimum of 7 mph of wind to actuate it. My hopes were shattered; half my sailing would be done with less than that wind strength. And so in March, after I returned from visiting Vence to get my lung checked up by Jean Mattei, I was stuck with the task of getting myself a self-steering gear with only three months in which to design, to build, and to practise sailing with it.

Every Sunday morning I took a bus to Kensington Gardens where I watched the model yachts being sailed across the Round Pond. I reckoned that if a model yacht can be sailed across the Round Pond without a helmsman, then my yacht could be sailed across the Atlantic in the same way. I bought an excellent book on model yacht sailing, and incidentally learned a lot about ocean racing from it though I dare say the author would be surprised to hear it. My new design was in principle a wind vane, which would always weathercock into wind. In fact it was a mast which could rotate in a socket at the stern of the yacht, with a flat sail instead of a metal vane. As soon as the yacht was sailing to my satisfaction I would lock the vane to the tiller. If the yacht came up into wind, the vane would be moved round with the yacht, and the wind would press on the side of it. This would pull on the tiller until the yacht had been steered back on to its original heading, when the vane would be weathercocked again, and do no work as long as the yacht kept on its original heading. The model yacht book told me that the area of the vane must be four and a half times that of the rudder, and so I designed my vane sail to be 45 square feet. The chief problem in design was to make all the parts, the stays, and the spars, strong enough to stand up to a gale, or even a storm, without being so heavy that it would require too much wind to weathercock the vane. I cannot describe how ugly it looked on the beautiful *Gipsy Moth*.

It was not till May 7th that the yard finished and installed the vane. I crossed the bar at the entrance to the Beaulieu River, headed the yacht across the Solent and locked the vane to the tiller. *Gipsy Moth* started tearing through the water, sailing herself entirely. Her wake was almost dead straight; it was fascinating to watch. That was one of the most thrilling moments of my life. Gradually I found out that Miranda, as I christened the self-steering device, required just as much skill to get the best out of her as does setting the sails of a yacht in a keen race. Also it gave me the same pleasure to succeed.

There were jobs like swinging the compass and calibrating the D/F loop to do, besides the sailing and self-steering experiments, and the sail handling drill. Sometimes I felt such despair, swamped by worry at the hopelessness of getting all the countless jobs done in time, that I longed to chuck up the whole project. My hands became so sore that I had to use my little fingers to pump water at the galley. Some of my swollen fingers would not close, and my fingernails were torn to the quick.

But sometimes when I had had a good day, and thought that I was getting ahead with my single-handed training, or beginning to master the tricks of the wind vane, Beaulieu River seemed to be a river in paradise. Gliding up to my mooring at dusk I would see the trees and clouds etched in the still surface of the river, and I would hear the occasional plop of a sea trout jumping. After dark the nightingales would start singing in the woods alongside the mooring, and in the morning the sun would light up the pale-green, tender, young, spring leaves on the trees.

At Sheila's invitation, Tubby Clayton came aboard with three disciples. He donned his robes in the fore-cabin and held an impressive service of blessing the ship. With Edward and Belinda Montagu there were ten of us standing in the cabin. When Tubby imperiously demanded to be disembarked, I found that Giles had gone off with the dinghy. So, somewhat fortified with 'Liffey Wather', I offered to motor the yacht down to the jetty at low water of a spring tide, with the mud banks showing horribly on each side. Turning 30 yards below the jetty we went on to the mud, where we were presently heeled over 43 degrees. To run aground within an hour of the ship's being blessed must be a record.

One night I wrote in my log, 'I feel very happy again to-night. I have not enjoyed myself so much since I was preparing to fly out alone to Australia in 1929. I was thinking the old query, "Is fate too strong for man's self will?" Am I so happy because I am doing the sort of thing I was destined for? How I enjoyed it – no, that's not right because I hated a lot of it, always scared stiff – my flying. No, I should say, how it satisfied me!

'Somehow I never seemed to enjoy so much doing things with other people. I know now I don't do a thing nearly as well when with someone. It makes me think I was cut out for solo jobs, and any attempt to diverge from that lot only makes me a half-person. It looks as if the only way to be happy is to do fully what you are destined for.'

The stores came abbard at Buckler's Hard. They were no trouble to me because Sheila had prepared a list of them. One hundred was my magic number; I had 100 lb. of potatoes, 100 fresh eggs, 100 apples, onions, carrots and oranges, and also 100 bottles of grog. (This last hundred was an exaggeration, because most of them were only cans of stout.)

On June 5th Sheila sailed down to Plymouth with me, and we tied up alongside the three other British entries for the race. We had four days of rushing about, Press and television interviews, visits and talks; it was all great sport. On the night before the race, Sheila and I decided to have a quiet dinner together with Giles at Pedro's. Lindley Abbatt of *The Observer* asked me if he and his wife could join us, and before we had finished it was a dinner party of seventy people. I always intend to start an ocean race with a clear head, after no drink taken. Perhaps one day I shall succeed, but that night I remember walking up to the Hoe after the party with Mike Richey, secretary of the Institute of Navigation, and a very experienced ocean racer. Sheila asserts that at 1 o'clock in the morning we were trying to get a star fix from a street lamp.

Dawn came cold, blustery and wet, and my spirits sank to their lowest ebb. Sheila and I went down early to move *Gipsy Moth* out of the tidal dock at high water. We tied up in a little basin outside, and I tried to eat something on board, but could not. My three rivals looked fairly bleak, too. They were Blondie in his junk-rigged *Jester*, David Lewis in *Cardinal Vertue*, and Val Howells in *Eira*.

Several owners who had intended to start in the race did not come up to scratch; one American in a handsome yacht was prevented by his young wife; another American, Piver, on his way over from America in his trimaran with a full crew, had not yet arrived, and when he did he found he lacked enough time to chase after us and take part in the race. I met one of his crew in New York afterwards who told me that nothing would have induced him to try sailing it across alone. Piver had done well to sail it with a crew from west to east. Humphrey Barton had intended to start in his 12-ton *Rose of York*, but withdrew because he could not make her sail herself. He had made a forty-seven-day crossing in *Vertue* with O'Riordan as crew.

In the tensed-up jockeying for position at the start I cursed one of my friends out alone in a yacht who baulked me. It was enough to keep clear of rivals, without having to dodge yachts, launches and a big trawler full of sightseers.

The starting gun was fired. We were off! What a race! Instructions read, 'Leave the Melampus Buoy to starboard and thence by any route to the Ambrose Light Vessel, New York'. The others got away ahead of me, but I began to catch them up as soon as I had set my big genoa. Then I slowed down as I pinched into the wind, to squeeze past the breakwater without tacking. As I drew away from the land the wind freshened and the seas got rougher, and I was soon wet through with sea water and sweat reefing the mainsail. The difficulty was to get the sail to roll easily on the boom without someone at the aft end to haul out the creases and folds. The last I saw of David Lewis, he had tacked inshore after the breakwater. He was well to windward of me, and not far behind. That must have been just before his mast broke in two; he rigged a jury sail and sailed back to Plymouth, where the Mashford brothers repaired his mast for him and got him away to sea again three days later. He is the only man I have heard of who has finished third in a race after breaking his mast at the start.

For the first three days the weather was rough with gales. Heavy seas burst on the deck, and I reckoned that it took thirty seconds after a sea had broken on deck before the water finished running out of the lee scuppers. I had considered *Gipsy Moth* a dry boat apart from one or two minor leaks, and I had pumped no water out of her during the three months she had been afloat. After the first three days, however, all the cabin walls were streaked as if they had been in a slanting shower of rain, and everything was damp or wet. I can only imagine that the tremendous weight of seas bursting on deck opened the planking or seams for an instant to shoot spray through. The terrific crash of a sea several times started me out of my berth, thinking that the yacht had been struck by a steamer, or that the mast had snapped. While I was asleep one sea shot me into the air off the heavy wooden settee I was sleeping on and jumped it out of its fitting. The clothes I got wet stayed wet, and I did not get a chance to dry them out until thirty-seven days later. At the end of the first three days I had had nothing to eat except a few biscuits; I had been feeling seasick or queasy all the time. Reading through my log gives me an impatient longing to sail the race again. I see the mistakes I could have avoided, and how I could have made a faster pace. This is nonsense really, for the mistakes and errors are the price for the great romance of doing something for the first time.

Miranda's antics cost me a lot of time. The lever which locked the wind vane to the tiller was periodically knocked free by the backstay, and I would be rousted out of my bunk to find the yacht headed the wrong way. I had a nightmare fear of the yacht's gybing herself to bring the wind vane against the backstay and snap its spars. Immediately I sensed the yacht's going off course – and I soon became sensitive to the least change in sailing conditions – I rushed out to the stern whatever I was doing, or however undressed.

Reefing the mainsail, lowering it, and hoisting the trysail in its place, with the frequent changing and handling of heavy Terylene foresails, exhausted me, and I was not sailing the yacht as she should be sailed. I envied my rivals the comparative ease with which they would be able to change the smaller sails of their boats, although I reckoned that their boats were too small, just as mine was too big; the best size for this race would be, I thought, a nine-tonner. In rough water my bigger boat should be better off, but I was losing too much valuable time over my sail changing. It took me up to one and a half hours to hoist the mainsail and to reef it in rough water. I know it sounds inefficient, but my 18-foot main boom was a brute to handle when reefing. I had to balance on the counter and slacken off the main sheet to the boom with one hand, while I hauled on the topping lift with the other hand to raise the boom. Meanwhile, it would be swinging to and fro, and I had to avoid being knocked out by it.

While hoisting the mainsail, I could not head into wind for fear of the yacht's tacking herself, and causing further chaos. As a result, the slides would jam in the track, the sail would foul the lee runner, and the battens would hook up behind the shroud as I tried to hoist the sail. All this time the boat would be rolling to drive one mad, and bucking. With heavy rain falling, and wave crests sluicing me, I would feel desperate until I got into the right mood, and told myself, 'Don't hurry! Take your time! You are bound to get it done in the end.' Once, after all this, I had just got the mainsail to the top of the mast when the flogging of the leech started one of the battens out of its pocket. So I had hurriedly to lower the sail and after saving the batten go through the whole procedure again.

At the end of this unpleasant three days I was only 186 miles south-west of Plymouth. My chest was hurting me on one side where I had been thrown across the yacht when a door burst open forward; on the other side it had been stabbed by a sharp corner when the cabin hatch, which I was leaning against, suddenly slipped forward a foot; a patch of my skin over my ribs had been caught in a doorway when the door slammed on it, and I had cut my scalp on the roof of the cabin. Then my seasickness ended, and it was not long before I was recording that I would not change places with anybody in the world.

I got steadily more skilful in handling the yacht. One night *Gipsy Moth* really began to show her paces. I was called on deck by the hull slamming, the sails banging and snapping. I had too much sail set for the rising wind, I thought, so I slacked off the genoa before lowering it, and the result was extraordinary. *Gipsy Moth* went quiet, and shot off in the dark and fog at speed. I imagined that she had smiled to herself and said, 'This is what I've been waiting for.' There was no fuss, no disturbed wake and almost no noise. It was awe-inspiring on deck, with a black Hades rushing past the bright light shining from the stern. There was a slight, snaffly, clinky jingle from the end of the main boom which, from the cabin, sounded like the bit in a horse's mouth. *Gipsy Moth* was going so fast that it was hard to stand up. She was like a horse flying over fallen logs on rough ground, haunches thrusting up with a wobbly movement, as if shaking her powerful stern in the air. The strange thing was that Miranda quietened too; she had a gentle weaving movement, instead of jigging and flapping and snapping as she had been doing before. *Gipsy Moth* cut out 8¼ knots for the next two hours. It was not comfortable, though; while getting dinner I was pitched into the galley stove, and knocked it clean off its frame.

Next morning I was woken up at 8 o'clock by the yacht's tacking herself. I felt her go upright and heel the other way. I was about to spring up and rush to the tiller, when I looked at the pendulum which measures the heel of the yacht and was astonished to see that we were still heeled over 25 degrees to starboard. She had simply eased up suddenly from a heel of 45 degrees, which had fooled my drowsy senses.

During that night *Gipsy Moth* had sailed 86 miles in 12¼ hours, 7 knots on the wind – wonderful sailing. That was what I had come for! By next night the going was beginning to get rougher. *Gipsy Moth* rushed at the waves and ski-jumped off the crests to land with a terrific splash. The noise below was appalling, and I marvelled at the strength of the boat to stand the bashing. It was hard to sleep for more than ten minutes at a time, and I woke feeling that the gear, mast and sails could not stand the strain, and that I must change down the headsail. Sheila had warned me that carrying too much sail would be my biggest risk, but I hated to slow down the yacht.

Then, an hour after midnight, an extra heavy sea came on board and I decided that the time had come. I rigged myself out in my full kit; oilskin trousers, long boots, long oilskin coat, cotton towel scarf, storm cap, knife, spanner and torch round my neck, with safety-belt over all to hook to the lifelines. But when I came on deck I found that *Gipsy Moth* was sailing as well as she possibly could. We must have sailed through a rough patch. It was thick fog on a black night, visibility 50 to 75 yards with plenty of wind and a rough sea. A steamer passed me, sounding her deep foghorn, and I answered with the right toots from my little mouth horn to show I was under sail on the port tack, though whether she could possibly hear anything I don't know. She seemed a big boat and fast, because I was doing 7 knots and she just swept by. I went back to my bunk and slept soundly for four hours, when I was woken by a calm. *Gipsy Moth* had had a sail which I felt that it would be hard for me to beat single-handed – 220 miles on the wind in 33¼ hours, an average of 6.6 knots.

Every day I tried to call up a ship or an aircraft on the radio telephone. Each of us in the race had been lent one, and we had had elaborate instructions on how to contact aircraft flying over, but the telephones were ship-to-shore sets for use only in coastal waters; also they had not been fitted until the afternoon before the start of the race. I spent hour after hour trying to raise a ship or an aircraft. Once I heard a Pan-American Clipper calling the yachts in the race, but it did not hear my reply. On June 17th I got a sun fix with the sextant, taking advantage of the fog's lifting enough to show a horizon and the sun visible through the mist. I was pleased to find that my dead reckoning was only fifteen miles out after six days. One could expect this if racing with a crew of good helmsmen. I always worked up the dead reckoning carefully, but I could only guess what course Miranda had been steering while I was asleep.

During the next week the main theme of my log was fatigue. I kept on complaining about the heavy gear and endless sail changing; the wind changed force and direction like an angry rattlesnake. Sometimes it swung right through to the opposite direction within a few hours. In spite of my troubles, I averaged 135½ miles a day for five consecutive days – distance sailed, that is, not distance made good in a straight line. On June 25th, after two weeks, I had made good a distance of 1,264 miles in a straight line from Plymouth. I knew nothing then about my rivals, but in those fourteen days Blondie had made good 1,038 miles. I had not feared Blondie as a rival, although I knew his Folkboat hull was fast and seaworthy, but I thought that his junk rig would not take him to windward well. The Amateur Yacht Research Society, however, considers that a junk sail, slightly modified, is the most efficient rig there is.

The rival I dreaded was Val Howells in a Folkboat with a boosted up sail area. She had looked a fast boat, driven by a formidable sailor. And this was a race of man and boat; both equally important. Val had served his time in the Merchant Navy, was extremely powerful, and had told us he did not know what fatigue was. Looking at him with his huge black beard I believed him. He had had much sailing experience with a voyage to Spain alone before the race. Also, he had on board a keg of his magic brew, raw eggs mixed with rum, which sounded a formidable weapon in his hands. Lastly he was a Welshman with a wonderful voice, so that whenever in trouble or unhappy he could practise for the next Eisteddfod. If I tried to sing the fishes would groan. Val after the fourteenth day was 900 miles from Plymouth. Lewis was 500 miles behind me; he had been delayed three days by his mast breaking, but had avoided that period of dirty head-on weather.

This was the state of the race when I ran into big trouble on June 25th.

CHAPTER TWENTY-EIGHT

THE STORM

I HAD turned in the night before with all sails set in light airs, ambling towards New York at 3 knots. I had a fine sleep from midnight to 5 o'clock local time, when I woke to find the yacht headed due south; the wind had backed steadily during the night, and was now east-south-east. I retrimmed the sails and Miranda before starting to prepare the twin headsails for running. It took me two and a quarter hours to get the twins rigged, and drawing on the right heading. I thought this was good going, because it was only the second time I had run with twins since the yacht was built, and there was a lot to do. On every trip from cockpit to foredeck I had to transfer the snaphook of my lifeline four times. I had to unlash the two spinnaker booms from the deck. Then each of them, $14\frac{1}{4}$ feet long and 18 inches in girth, had to be hooked to the gooseneck 7 feet up the mast at one end, and to a strop at the clew of the sail at the other end; then hoisted up by a topping lift, while two guys from the middle of the pole down to the deck kept it from swinging fore or aft. The tiller had to be freshly adjusted after each sail was hoisted, because the sailing balance was then changed. When both headsails were drawing, it took me a quarter of an hour for the final adjustment to the self-steering gear, and then *Gipsy Moth* sailed down wind at a quiet, silky 6 knots.

The bow waves rumbled with a hint of distant thunder, and in the cabin I could hear them breaking and rushing along the hull. It was a delightful change after days of plugging into wind.

My next entry in my notebook was twenty-two hours later, and in between so much happened, and I had had such strong sensations, that I could not recall them all.

I had been below for two hours after setting the twin head-sails, when I noticed by the telltale compass attached to the cabin table that the course was erratic. Occasionally a sail filled with a loud clap. I found that the clamp which locked Miranda to the tiller was slipping, and I knelt on the counter to begin fixing it. The boat was yawing to one side or the other, and each time one of the sails would crack with a loud report. I turned round and grabbed the tiller. We were going at a great pace, and the following seas would pick up the stern and slew it hard to one side. The yacht would start broaching-to with one headsail aback, promising serious trouble ahead if I did not check it. I could not leave the tiller, and wondered what I should do. It was, however, exhilarating, charging through the seas down wind, and if I took the tiller myself for four hours the thirty-six miles would be a valuable step towards New York. Fortunately I became so sleepy that I could not keep my eyes open, and realized that I must get the sails down. I thought hard for some time before making up my mind how to tackle the job. At a favourable moment I made a rush for the foredeck, after slacking off one sheet from the cockpit to let the spinnaker pole forward, and to decrease the area of sail offered to the wind. As soon as I stepped on the deck I realized that I was in for big trouble. I found a 60-mph wind, which I had not noticed in the shelter of the cockpit with the yacht bowling down wind. My sleepiness had been partly to blame, but the storm was blowing up fast. When I slacked away the halyard, the bellied-out sail flapped madly from side to side. The noise was terrific, and the boat began slewing wildly to port while the great genoa bellied out and flogged at the other sail with ponderous heavy blows. I was scared that the forestays would be carried away. I rushed back to the tiller and put the yacht back on course, and then forward again to grab some of the genoa in my arms and pass a sail tie round it to decrease the area. I had the 380-square-foot genoa on one side, and the 250-foot jib on the other. Next, I slacked away the halyard to let the lower half of the genoa drop into the sea, while I struggled with the spinnaker pole on that side. I had more trouble with the jib, because I could not get the sail clew free from the spinnaker pole; the sail was like a crazy giant out of control. In the end I twisted the foot of the sail round and round at the deck, and finally I got control. It was dangerous work, and I was grateful and relieved to find myself whole in limb and unsmashed at the end of it.

I realized that I had a serious storm on my hands. I spent five and a quarter hours on deck without a break, working hard. After lashing down the spinnaker poles, I next started on Miranda, who was already breaking up. The topping lift had parted, letting the spanker drop, and the halyard of the little topsail had gone. I could easily have got into a flap;

it was now blowing great guns, and I had to stand on the stern pulpit while I worked with my hands at full stretch above my head at the wet ropes jammed tight. Miranda's mast was 14 feet high, and free to rotate with the wind. I was standing with stays and wires all round me, and could have been swept off the pulpit horribly easily if the wind had suddenly changed direction. I told myself that it would be much worse if I had iced-up ropes to deal with; not to fuss; and to get on with the job. There seemed fifty jobs to do, but I did them all in time. I lowered the mainsail boom to the deck, and treble-lashed it there. It was only after I had finished that I became aware of the appalling uproar, with a high-pitched shriek or scream dominating. I managed to strip off both Miranda's sails, and secured her boom with sail ties. I reckoned that the wind was now 80 mph. (I still think of winds above 60 mph in terms of miles per hour instead of knots, because of getting used to the speeds of my seaplane propeller slipstream in mph.)

The seas had been moderate when the storm broke, and by the time I got below at 4 o'clock in the afternoon I was still able to cook myself a breakfast, a fry-up of potatoes, onions and three eggs. I reckoned that the wind was now 90 mph. I went to sleep reading Shakespeare's *Tempest*. At 8.30 in the evening I woke to find the sea getting up, and the ship taking an awful pounding. Some seas, like bombs exploding, made the ship jump and shake; she was lying beam-on to the blast, which was from the north-north-east and was moving pretty fast, about 3 knots. I knew that I must try to slow her down, so I dressed in my wet oilskins. First, I tried to head her into wind, but no matter where I set the tiller she refused to lie other than broadside to the wind. I had a big outer motor tyre for a sea anchor, and I shackled this on to the anchor chain, paying out 10 fathoms of $\frac{5}{16}$-inch chain over the stern; I also paid out 20 fathoms of $2\frac{1}{2}$-inch warp over the stern. It did not seem to make the least difference to the speed.

I put the wind speed now at 100 mph. The noise was terrifying, and it seemed impossible that any small ship could survive. I told myself not to be weak – what was a 90- or

100-mile wind to a man on Everest? I filled a punctured tin with oil, and hung it over the side amidships in a piece of canvas, but it had no effect at all – the oil was too thick, and we were moving too fast. In any case, it was soon carried away.

As night came on I tried to sleep, but waiting in the dark for the next crash made me tense, and I kept on bracing myself against being thrown out of the bunk. I was afraid; there was nothing I could do, and I think that the noise, the incredible din, was the chief cause of fear. The high-pitched shriek from the rigging was terrifying and uncanny. Two hours before midnight I came to think that we were headed into the eye of the storm. I dressed reluctantly, feeling dry in the mouth whenever I started to do anything, but better as soon as I began to do it. With difficulty, I climbed out into the cockpit. It took strength to hold the rudder full on, but slowly the ship gybed round. She seemed easier on the east-south-east tack.

When I went below again I could not help laughing; all the same books, clothes, cushions and papers were back on the floor. I dozed, but could not sleep. I lay tense and rigid, waiting for the next sea to hit. Nothing mattered to me now except survival. My main fear was that one of the spinnaker poles would break loose and hole the hull. I found that by shining a torch through the cabin ports I could see the poles where they lay on the deck, and I was relieved to find the lashings still holding. I decided then that I had made a blunder, and that the south-east heading would take me into the eye of the storm, not away from it. However, the ship seemed better off on this tack, and I left her.

But that tack was taking me away from New York, and four hours after midnight I could no longer bear it. I dressed and went on deck again. Some of the seas were breaking clear over the ship; one filled the ventilator and shot a jet into the cabin, but everything in it was already wet. I gybed round on to the west-north-west heading. I reckoned that the wind had dropped to 80 mph, but the seas were rougher and would be rougher still later on. The angle of heel indicator came up against the stop at 55 degrees, and I watched it do so time after time. It was difficult to stand up or to move about the cabin, but the queer thing was that the Aladdin heater went on burning steadily throughout; it just did not seem to care a damn for any storm, and was a great comfort. All night the ship ploughed ahead at 2 to 3 knots, towing the sea anchor and the warp.

Next morning the wind had dropped. It was still Force 9 but I went on deck relaxed and grateful to be alive. I climbed on the stern pulpit to try making some temporary repairs to Miranda, and looked round to survey the deck. It was incredible, but nothing much seemed to have happened. The dinghy was still on deck, lashed to the cabin top. (I had doubled all the lashings, of course.) Apart from Miranda's gear, which was in a mess, and her gaff gooseneck, which had sheared, the only damage was that the bolts fastening five stanchions had snapped, and a small section of bulwark carried away.

The wind was still north-north-east. The turbulent, impressive seas, like mountainous white-capped country, rode down on to the ship. The waves were not regular. Looking down from a crest to the trough below, I estimated the height at about 25 feet. With the wind abated, I could now hear the striker seas coming. There would be a lull as the ship was deep in the trough, and I would hear the sizzling sound from the comber before it struck. I wondered if I could set a spitfire jib aback to ease the deadly rolling which made it dangerous to move about below. I hoped that none of my rivals had been caught in this storm. They might well have escaped it if I was right in thinking that it was a small cyclonic eddy, a williwaw, of perhaps only fifty miles diameter between a high and a low pressure system. The calm preceding it, and the rapid decrease in wind strength afterwards, were evidence to support this.

By 8.45 PM the wind was down to Force 6, and I had a small jib set and drawing. I could not set any more until Miranda was in action again. She looked a forlorn wreck. While I was writing up my log a sea broke over the whole boat. I was driven nearly crazy by the rolling. I put one foot against the chart table so that I could peel some cooked potatoes, but the boat snapped over on to the other beam and the whole saucepanful of potatoes shot over the cabin floor.

Next day I worked for fourteen and a half hours non-stop, repairing the damage to Miranda. There was no wind, or very little, but the seas were 24 feet from crest to trough, and steep. The rolling was really nasty, back-snapping stuff. It was difficult to stand on deck, and even when I tried sitting on it I was suddenly slid from one side of the deck to the other. I wanted to reach the top of Miranda's mast, 14 feet above the deck, to replace a parted rope. I started climbing up, wriggling my way through the network of wires, stays and cordage. As I neared the top the yacht rolled, and I swung round with the rotating mast until I was clinging to the underside of it. I hung on tight, waiting for the yacht to roll back. She gave a kind of flick roll, which made the mast continue turning – with me clinging to it. The next roll caught it at exactly the right instant, and in a few seconds I was spinning round and round fast, clutching the mast like a scared mouse. After my first astonished fright I was not worried about myself, because the yacht was not moving, but I was scared stiff that Miranda would snap under the strain. Then it struck me what a fantastically comic sight it must appear from a fish's eye view – to see me spinning round like a monkey clinging to a pole. I burst out laughing. But I was relieved when I had succeeded in hooking the top of the pulpit with my instep, and managed to stop the spin.

One curious thing about the storm was that, although it blew the burgee to shreds, it left untouched a pair of underpants which I had buttoned round the handrail on the cabin top, hoping that they would dry in the calm spell before the storm started.

I interrupted my work twice to get sunshots when the sun appeared, but did not stop to work them out. Next day, however, I worked up my dead reckoning for 8 days to June 27th, allowing for every change of course and speed, and allowing for the speed and direction in which the yacht had moved during the storm. The lie of the anchor chain with its white wake had given me our line of travel. The sun fix showed that my DR position was ninety-eight miles too far west; I had forgotten to allow for the head-on Gulf Stream, which at half a knot would set me back ninety-six miles in the eight days.

On June 29th the *Mauretania* passed a mile away, looking vast, powerful and steady in the dirty-grey weather. I tried to signal with my Aldis lamp, but it would not work. With three blasts of her foghorn she was on her way, leaving me forlorn. This was only the third ship I had seen since the start, although I had heard two pass me in the fog.

During my third week I made good only 284 miles in a straight line. I lost two days in the storm, one day repairing the damage, and a fourth day when I was so exhausted that I sailed badly. The remaining three days of the week I was soused in fatigue, although I did not realize it at the time. The night of July 1st was a sample; the wind was dead in the eye lookind at New York, the sea was rough and nasty, and I could not get off to sleep until 1.30 AM. An hour later I was woken by the thunderous crash of a sea breaking on deck. I went on deck after donning my whole oilskin rig, but found nothing smashed or even displaced. I was overtired and jittery. I stayed on deck, trying to get more than the 2.8 knots *Gipsy Moth* was doing and which I thought not nearly enough, but I could not trim her to sail faster, however I tried. The truth was that she was being overpowered. It was a Force 7 wind, and I did not realize it; I was getting used to wind. At last it dawned on my dopey brain, and I tried to reef the mainsail. I began slacking away the mainsail to ease the pressure on it, which was jamming the reefing gears. The ship at once shot ahead into the night like a scalded cat, and the more I slacked away the mainsail the faster she went, until by the time the mainsail was practically weather cocking with the sail weaving in the wind, I reckoned our speed at 10 knots.

It was exhilarating sport, tearing through the black night with the seething, foaming bow waves dazzling white in the bright light from my pressure lamp rigged in the stern. When I moved forward to the mast I saw the fantastic sight of a huge black giant in the sky ahead moving as I moved. I thought I must have rubbed Aladdin's lamp and that here was the Genie of the lamp; it was my own huge shadow, projected on the fog ahead by the lamp in the stern. In the end I lowered the main-sail and, standing on top of the dinghy lashed to the cabin roof, I gathered in the madly flapping sail by armfuls until at last I had it subdued and furled. The speed was still 5 knots with only the working jib set, so I left it like that and finally got to sleep at 8 o'clock in the morning. I was up again at 11, feeling exhausted.

Everything seemed to go wrong in that week. I ended it up on the night of July 2nd by freeing Miranda and leaving the yacht to sail herself through the night. I refused to struggle any longer with one sail change after another. During my half sleep I could hear the yacht turning round in circles, and in the morning the log showed that she had moved only nine miles during the night. Wearily I struggled out of my blankets after five hours, when I longed for another twelve hours' sleep. As I was making some coffee I was thrown across the cabin, which not only caused great pain to the tail of my spine, the first part of my body to hit the other side, but shattered the Thermos flask I was holding, so that it took me ten minutes to sweep up the splinters scattered all over the cabin floor.

At the end of this third week Blondie, who had escaped the storm, had sailed farther in a straight line from Plymouth than I had. However, he had been bearing away to the north, passing within 300 miles of Greenland, and he was still eighty-five miles farther from New York than I was. Lewis had gained on me too, and was now only 350 miles astern.

During the next week's sailing I came to terms with life. I found that my sense of humour had returned; things which would have irritated me or maddened and infuriated me ashore made me laugh out loud, and I dealt with them steadily and efficiently. Rain, fog, gale, squalls and turbulent forceful seas under grey skies became merely obstacles. I seemed to have found the true values of life. The meals I cooked myself were feasts, and my noggins of whisky were nectar. A good sleep was as valuable to me as the Koh-i-noor diamond. All my senses seemed to be sharpened; I perceived and enjoyed the changing character of the sea, the colours of the sky, the slightest change in the noises of the sea and wind; even the differences between light and darkness were strong, and a joy. I was enjoying life, and treating it as it should be treated – lightly. Tackling tough jobs gave me a wonderful sense of achievement and pleasure.

For example, on July 5th I was fast asleep, snug among my blankets at 9.30 at night. I woke with a feeling of urgency and apprehension. A gale squall had hit the yacht, and I had to get out quickly on deck to drop sails. This is one of the toughest things about sailing alone – switching from fast sleep in snug warm blankets, to being dunked on the foredeck in the dirty black night a minute later. Conditions have to be at their worst to demand the urgency, and I had that dry feeling in my mouth as I dragged on my wet oilskins in the dim light. Then I was standing in the water in the cockpit, and from there pressing against the gale. I made my way to the mast, and wrestled with the mainsail halyard with one hand, slacking it away as I grabbed handfuls of mainsail with the other hand and hauled the sail down. The sail bound tight against the mast crosstree and shroud under the pressure of the wind, and the slides jammed in their tracks. The stem of the yacht was leaping 10 feet into the air and smacking down to dash solid crests over my back. The thick fog was luminous when the lightning flashed, but I heard no sound at all of thunder; it was drowned by the thunderclaps from the flogging sails. I scarcely noticed the deluge of rain among the solid masses of seawater hitting me.

When I got below, my oilskins off, sitting on the settee in glorious comfort sipping a bowl of tomato soup, I had a wonderful sense of achievement. It was a positive, but perhaps a simple thing, dealing with a difficult and tricky job in a thrilling, romantic setting. When next I left my blankets I found that *Gipsy Moth* had averaged 6.1 knots for the past four hours with only a storm jib set, which showed that there had been plenty of wind.

This was the sort of life I led day after day and night after night. Everything in the boat seemed to be wet. One morning I was delighted to see a dry patch on the cabin floor, only to find that it was a piece of light coloured material which had slipped out of a locker. I began to worry about a fuel shortage for the Aladdin heater, which was going day and night. Whenever I had the Primus stove alight I heated a big saucepanful of salt water, and wrapped clothes round it to dry them out a little.

By this time I was over the Grand Banks, and in fog nearly always, thin fog, thick fog or dense fog, always some kind of fog. Before I started I had intended to heave to and keep watch in fog, but in the event I never slowed down; I was racing, and what difference would it make if I was stopped anyway? I had expected 300 miles of fog, but actually I sailed through no less than 1,430 miles, equivalent to two and a third complete Fastnet Races. It did not slow me down directly, but indirectly it did, because sometimes I would lie in my bunk for hours before I got the necessary peace of mind to drop off to sleep. My reason told me the chance of being run down in the broad Atlantic was infinitesimally small, but my instinct said you must be a fool to believe that. There was something uncanny about charging at full speed through this dense impenetrable fog, especially on a dark night.

Then there was ice. I dreaded icebergs, though there were many times more trawlers on the banks than icebergs. I could not get any ice information with my radio, and could only guess at the ice area from the information got together before the race. Once a cold clammy air entered the cabin, and I thought there must be a big berg near. I climbed into the cockpit to keep watch, but found dense fog on a pitch black night. I could not see 25 yards ahead with a light. *Gipsy Moth* was sailing fast into the darkness. I decided that keeping watch was a waste of time, went below and mixed myself my anti-scorbutic. The lemon juice of this wonderful drink not only keeps physical scurvy away, but if enough of the right kind of whisky is added to it, mental scurvy as well. *Gipsy Moth* sailed on through the dark.

One day I had a surprise when I saw a long low island in the foggy mist. By my reckoning the nearest land was 360 miles away. Then it moved. The fog had thinned, and this was a big swell looming in the mist half a mile away. The Grand Banks seem wrapped in romance after the turbulent Atlantic. One night, sailing through a calm sea with the moon behind fine clouds, a bird flew overhead, making queer squeaky mewing sounds, as if it wanted to talk.

Once I was nearly becalmed, and thought that I would try for a fish, as I was on the greatest fishing grounds of the world. My line had not been down long and I was below, when I heard a sort of deep sigh, which brought me up into the cockpit. Four whales were just diving, their backs above the surface. I could have prodded the nearest with my boathook. They looked awfully black, sleek and powerful, and the thought flashed through my brain, 'Are you friendly?' When I looked round there were about 100 of them near. I hurriedly hauled in my log line, and then I took in my fishing line; those backs seemed a broad hint that I was poaching. As I watched, I got the impression that the whales were in a number of small groups which one after the other sent one whale to inspect *Gipsy Moth* until at the end after ten or fifteen minutes they all dived like one and vanished. I did not really wish to catch a fish after living alone for a month; I remember that Slocum could not shoot a duck in the Magellan Straits although he was short of food.

On July 8th, excitement; after twenty-seven days of calling in vain on my R/T, I had an answer! It is true that I closed the land to within forty miles of Cape Race, Newfoundland, but I got through a message to Chris Brasher in London. It was a Saturday morning and I felt that he would urgently need some news for the next day's *Observer*. I had an odd feeling of excitement in speaking to someone after four weeks' silence.

Next day ended the fourth week of the race. *Gipsy Moth* had sailed as she should, like a horse picking up its heels and going full stretch. During that week she had made good 690 miles towards New York, and as a result at the end of the fourth week I was only 865 miles from New York, whereas Blondie was 1,208 miles. My dreaded rival, the black-bearded Viking, because of his taking the longer route in the south, had still 2,190 miles to go, and barring accidents to Blondie and me, he was out of the race. Lewis was about 600 miles astern now. Of course I did not know any of this at the time.

After leaving Cape Race, which is the southernmost tip of Newfoundland, my next concern was Sable Island. This is a twenty-mile-long sand bank, ninety miles offshore from Nova Scotia. I have a chart of this island drawn up by a lighthouse keeper there, which shows 200 ships wrecked on it since 1800. In every account I had read of wrecks on Sable Island, the captain had thought himself a long way off when his ship struck. I was puzzled about this, and apprehensive.

I think I know now why many of these wrecks occurred. At first it looked as if I was going to pass south of the island. Then the wind changed, and I began heading north of it. I ought then to have been in the favourable Labrador current, a comparatively narrow stream wending its way south-westerly along the eastern seaboard of America. Flowing alongside it, in the opposite direction, is the Gulf Stream, with such a sharp division between the two that it is known as the Cold Wall. As I approached the rocky coast of Nova Scotia I reckoned that I was in the favourable Labrador current. I never saw anything of the 300-mile-long coast, although I tacked close to it on three occasions. I was in fog most of the time, and so cold that I was still wearing my long woollen underpants as well as thick clothes, with the Aladdin heater going day and night. Yet I heard a radio station reporting temperatures in the 80's only fifty miles away. On July 12th I got a good fix by bearings from radio beacons on Sable Island, Sambro Light Vessel and the north-east point of Nova Scotia, which showed that my dead reckoning position was twenty-two and a half miles in error, too far west. Three days later my DR was again too far west, this time twenty-eight miles. Here was a total error of fifty miles, which could easily have caused a wreck if I had not discovered it. I think my error could have been caused only by an eddy from the Gulf Stream invading the Labrador current, and reversing it. No wonder the sailing ships of 100 years ago were wrecked when they lacked my advantage of being able to take bearings of radio beacons on Sable Island and the mainland.

During this passage between Nova Scotia and Sable Island I had a narrow escape. I was sitting in the cabin with the last bottle of whisky aboard on the swinging table. *Gipsy Moth* suddenly performed one of her famous ski-jumps. She would sidle up the side of a wave and roll sharply at the top before taking off the other side, and landing a with terrific crash in the trough. This was more than the swinging table could cope with, the bottle of whisky shot up into the air, turned a somersault, and was headed for the cabin floor neck first. I was faced with tragedy – my last bottle of whisky. My hand shot out and I fielded it by the neck on the way down. I could not have been more pleased if I had brought off a brilliant catch in a Test Match. I was not so lucky next day, however, with a jug of tea which was shot up into the air in the same way. I could not help laughing; it was incredible that so many tea-leaves could come from one spoonful; the table, the seat opposite, the whole floor, and the side of my settee were all plastered with tea-leaves. There were even some in the dust-pan stowed away in the cubbyhole under the seat.

July 16th was a key day for me. It was the thirty-seventh day of the race and the first completely fine day so far. Also, it was a perfect sailing day, with a soldier's breeze from the north, not a cloud in the sky, big round sun, and a small crescent moon. I was bustling to and fro all day with clothes, bedding, mattresses, cushions, etc. My green velvet smoking jacket, which I had fondly hoped I should be changing into occasionally for a quiet dinner on board, was nearly solid with mildew, with parts worn through by chafing against the side of the ship. However, I put it to dry, and later, when I came to brush it, to my surprise the mildew came off, leaving that part spotlessly clean. Had I found a cheap rival to dry cleaning? By the end of that day there really were dry patches on the cabin floor. And at night the sky was clear with bright stars twinkling like diamonds, the first time I had seen them.

Next day I moved on to a chart with New York at the other end of it. I had sailed 3,516 miles, but had no idea of how I was placed in the race. How well I knew from previous races that heart-sink feeling on arriving to find my rivals already in!

But even if I were last, I should have had the romantic thrill which only a voyage like this can give.

I was approaching the Nantucket Shoals, which the Admiralty pilots describe as, 'These shoals extend forty miles south-east of Sankaty Head Lighthouse, and render this one of the most dangerous parts of the United States coast.' At first I hoped to sail round them to the south, without having to tack, but the wind veered, and headed me straight for the middle of the shoals. I was racing, and did not want to tack. I studied all the charts I had to see if I could thread a safe passage through them, bearing in mind that I had seen no landmark or seamark of any description since the Eddystone Rock 3,700 miles behind me. These shoals have affected American history; the *Mayflower*, with the Pilgrim Fathers on board, put about when she came upon them and headed north, to found their settlement at Plymouth, New England, instead of proceeding to New Jersey as they had intended. Later, Captain Hudson was diverted by the shoals, put out to sea and sailed on to New York, where the Hudson River is named after him.

A night of exciting navigation followed. I went to sleep an hour before midnight, headed for the middle of the shoals, and slept for two and a quarter hours, when I got up for a radio-beacon fix, then slept soundly again for an hour and a quarter. I woke with a start. The night was pitch black, and there were no lights to aid me. I could not get soundings, and radio-beacon bearings are unreliable at night. Yet I decided to get radio-beacon bearings at intervals; I thought I could see a way to make a safe passage, even if some of the bearings were inaccurate. None of the radio fixes I got agreed with one another, and the dead reckoning differed from them all. However, if one could rely on accurate information, navigation would be a simple science, whereas the art and great fascination of it lies in deducing correctly from uncertain clues.

I passed over one shoal, but I knew that there was enough depth and sailed on into a squall, which turned out to be a thunderstorm with a deluge of rain. My track should have taken me, by my reckoning, within two miles of a Texas radar tower built on legs on the shoals, but I never saw it, for as soon as I was near the middle of the shoals a thick fog rolled up. I did hear the tower foghorn from the direction where it ought to have been, giving two deep moos like a sick bull, but I could not tell how far off it was. Then it fell dead calm. I was not happy; I could not get a radio-beacon fix because the three usable beacons (Nantucket Light Vessel, Cape Cod and Pollock's Rip) were all in a line with *Gipsy Moth*. However, I kept on taking bearings from them and formed an impression of where I was. I set the ghosting genoa and tended it with great care all morning, trying to edge westwards, but there was seldom enough wind to move smoke. We were just moving, however, sailing slowly westwards at the edge of a tide-rip like a field of earthed-up potato rows. The forward half of *Gipsy Moth* was in smooth water, humping up as if about to break; the aft half was in the tide-rip, which advanced at exactly the same pace as the ship for what seemed a long time. The danger of these shoals is that a sea may break and dump the ship on the bottom, to be overwhelmed by the next comber. Since we *were* moving, I hoisted the mainsail, and our speed went up to 2 knots, but at the same time we were being carried north-wards towards the shoals at 2 knots. Three-quarters of an hour later we were still moving, but still had twenty miles of the shoals to cross. I could not think of anything else I could do, so I went below and turned in for a siesta. When I woke it was 9.10 and I found the ship going well at 5 knots. I felt that I had been lucky.

Next morning I sighted my first mark, Block Island at the north entrance to Long Island Sound. I embarked on an orgy of cleanliness. Sheila had made a strong statement that it was quite unnecessary for a single-handed sailor to turn up looking like a tramp with a dirty boat, so, after I had washed the cabin floor, the stove and everything washable including my shirts, I set to work on myself and threw in a haircut.

That night I had a grand sail along the 100-mile coastline of Long Island, averaging 7 knots for nine hours. But I could not relax, and had to keep awake, though at times I had diffi-culty in keeping my eyelids up. *Gipsy Moth* was close to the shore, and any change of wind could have run her aground. Also, the navigation was difficult at night; there were lights, but not close enough for two to be seen together to give a fix, and as a result I could not tell how far offshore I was in the dark.

At 9.30 next morning I logged, 'Twenty-four miles to go. Will that black-bearded Viking be in already?' But an hour later I was becalmed.

At 1.30 PM as I decided to eat lunch, a faint breeze livened up, and I did not get a meal till twelve and a half hours later, two hours after next midnight. As soon as *Gipsy Moth* began sailing, I tried to call up the New York coastguards. Suddenly a clear voice broke in, which sounded elusively familiar. 'This is the *Edith G.* at the Ambrose Light. Your wife is on board and wants to speak to you.' I could hear a word or two from her, but she was pressing the wrong button. Then the clear voice came back. 'What is your course?'

'270 degrees.'

'OK two-seven-zero. We will meet you.'

My lunch was off. I was out of sight of land crossing from Fire Island to the Ambrose Light, and I watched every launch excitedly. I took a set of radio bearings of Ambrose, Barnegat and Fire Island to check my position. At 3.50 PM I was met by a fishing-boat. Sheila waved to me, looking very smart in her Mirman hat. Great wavings from friends aboard. I thought to myself, 'This is very fine but what about the race? They know, I don't. How can I find out without appearing too pushing?' I thought of something. 'What news of the others?' I asked. Someone said, 'You are first,' and those words were honey sweet.

I crossed the finishing line at 5.30, 40 days 12 hours and 30 minutes after the starting gun, having sailed 4,004½ miles to make good 3,000 miles on the Great Circle Course. I had to sail sixteen miles up New York Harbour through the narrows to Staten Island, and no one was allowed aboard until I had been cleared by the health and immigration authorities. My clockwork seemed to have run down, and when I rounded up off Coney Island I lowered and handled my sails like a landlubber, until I seemed to have a tangle of sails, ropes, warps, fenders all over the deck. Every few seconds I had to stop to try to hear, try to answer, some question shouted at me. I was grateful for a tow for the rest of the way when it fell calm, and I was unable to start my motor.

CHAPTER TWENTY-NINE

NEW YORK – AND NEW PLANS

THE clear strong voice which had hailed me as I approached New York belonged to Captain Jim Percy, Senior Captain of BOAC, and I had last heard it at a meeting of the Court of the Guild of Air Pilots and Air Navigators. Jim had been asked by the Grand Master, Prince Philip, and the Master, K. G. Bergin, to welcome me on reaching New York. He donned his full robes of a Warden, together with the broad squashed cap, and we were photographed shaking hands. Someone had presented me with two brandies and sodas, and I thought it was because of them that I hit the doorway a solid thump when I tried to pass through it; actually, I had lost my sense of balance, and I realized then that I had lost it at sea days before, which explained why I had difficulty in doing any job which required two hands while standing up.

Bubbling with an excitement which could never be recaptured I went off with Sheila to her room in the New York Hotel, where Chris Brasher turned up with a marvellous feast. This was at 2 AM and I started to enjoy it, but Sheila and I both fell asleep in the middle, and Chris tiptoed out.

Hasler came in eight days later, and Lewis was third seven and a half days after Hasler. Howells, the black-bearded Viking, arrived sixty-three days after the start. His route was nearly a great circle till past the Azores, and from there he sailed to Bermuda, where he put in to have his watch repaired. Jean Lacombe in the small yacht *Cap Horn* started five days after the rest of us, and arrived on August 24th. Sheila and I

met him being towed in as we were leaving for Plymouth.
I lost 10 lb. during the race, because, I think, of the big
physical effort. Blondie, who said that he had done no work
at all with his big Chinese sail, also lost 10 lb. Lewis lost 20 lb.
and Howells 18 lb.

During my race I wrote 50,000 words of log, which were
formed into a book entitled, *Alone Across the Atlantic*. Every
day I used to look forward to writing in my blue book after
breakfast, when I had come through another night and was
feeling rather pleased and optimistic, with the next night out of
thought. I used to imagine that I was talking to Sheila or a
friend, and I think it kept me from being lonely. Chris spent
ninety minutes on the Transatlantic telephone one day
sending through an extract from this log for the *Observer*.

I stepped straight from forty days alone at sea into a high-
powered businessman's life, with hundreds of letters and tele-
grams to answer, newspaper and radio interviews, and one or
two pretty shady television appearances. Sheila brought about
a deal with *Sports Illustrated* for me to write them a long story,
and I found the staff delightful people to deal with. Percy
Knauth lent me one of their offices, where I worked on my
story.

The most interesting thing for me was Sheila's story; how
she had set sail in the French liner *Flandres* before she knew if
I had passed Land's End, and I do not think there would have
been much interest in the race in America if it had not been
for Sheila's flair for public relations; and I am sure that no
one would have come out to meet me if it had not been for her.

We had an invitation from an American cousin to visit her at
Cape Cod. We wanted to go, but there seemed an awful lot to
do in New York. A week later Cousin Dick or 'Grandick' as her
family called her, telephoned, asking us again. We wanted to
go, but it seemed a formidable undertaking to get out of all
the things we had to do in New York and sail to Cape Cod.
Then she telephoned to say, 'My son Felix is flying down in his
plane to pick you up, and he will fetch you from the hotel in a
car.' This was the start of the most delightful visit imaginable.
Cousin Dick, born a Chichester, had married Felix du Pont

Senior, and had bought a point of land, Indian Point, where she had her own summer house and several other houses for members of her family. What was so delightful about them was that they never showed what odd fish we must appear to them. 'Grandick', who was over eighty, wanted to take us out to a party to meet a host of people every day, or else to go to see some famous landmark like the Plymouth Rock, whereas all *we* wanted was to loll about on the beach, bathing and eating a wonderful beach lunch with lots of clams. Nothing could be more foreign to the American way of thinking than our attitude and desire to do nothing. Felix, Cousin Dick's son, had learned seaplane flying not long after I had, and as he too now had a yacht, we had much in common to discuss. Cousin Dick was an interesting benevolent autocrat, who enjoyed her swim every morning before lunch.

The time came when we had to leave this paradise. *Gipsy Moth* was at City Island, undergoing minor repairs. Sheila and I moved aboard to prepare for the return voyage. It was a hot August, and with *Gipsy Moth* tied up alongside the dock in 90°F., and no fan on board, Sheila found it an ordeal. Felix and his wife Marka flew down to help us. They tried to persuade Sheila to give up the sail home and fly back, but Sheila had made up her mind to sail with me, and would not give in.

On August 24th we left City Island to sail down the East River through New York City. Rosie (Morris Rosenfeld, the world-famous yacht photographer) tagged along in his Fotolaunch. I was really rather dreading the prospect of another Atlantic voyage, and although there was only a good breeze I reefed the mainsail, and set a smallish jib for fear of stronger wind giving me trouble among the skyscrapers. This must have been disappointing to Rosie. The weather steadily improved, and we had an interesting cruise through the city. My chief interest was Brooklyn Bridge; I remembered the picture postcard of the old bridge which my father had sent me when he visited New York when I was six. Sheila took fright that the bridge was going to snap off the mast, and I could not convince her that it was far above us.

After leaving New York I headed south-east to sail along the

39th parallel to the Azores. Ninety miles from land we passed close to Texas Tower Number 4, a fantastic-looking object in the middle of the sea, with three large white domes like a cluster of spider's eggs on top of a three-legged platform. When we were half-way to the Azores this tower was damaged by the hurricane 'Donna', and later it capsized in a storm with the loss of many lives.

We had lovely weather, though too calm to suit me, and too hot to suit Sheila. It was up to 98°F. in the cabin. I rigged an old sail in the cockpit, and filled it with Gulf Stream water, and we used to take turns to wallow in this several times a day.

I found only two flying fish on deck during this voyage. They were delicious, fried. One knocked some paint off the cabin top when it landed there. Perhaps more interesting were the small squid which flew aboard at night. The *Kon-Tiki* crew were the first to discover that squid flew when one hit a member of the crew in the face at night.

The weather and seas roughened as we approached the Azores. When we arrived towards the end of the day at the northern end of the channel between Fayal and Pico Islands we were faced with a beat into a head-on gale, under spitfire jib and trysail, in order to reach the port of Horta. There was a strong current against us, and we could not have arrived till the middle of the night. I decided to start the motor, but I could not get a kick out of it. This made me angry. The motor had been temperamental before I left England, and the boatyard at Buckler's Hard had put in a lot of time on it; then it jibbed in New York, and the City Island boatyard had worked on it. This time, I said, I would damn well find out for myself what was the matter with it. It was no picnic, with *Gipsy Moth* bucking about in the short steep sea kicked up by the gale, and presently I was lying at full length under the cockpit to get at the bottom of the petrol tank. Every few minutes I had to pop up and tack the ship. But I found the trouble: the petrol tank was made of iron, and there was $\frac{3}{4}$ inch of rust sludge at the bottom, which kept on choking the carburettor. After I cleaned the pipes I could get it to run only for a few minutes before the sludge chocked it again. Finally I said to Sheila,

'Do you mind if we heave to and wait outside the channel till dawn?' She was relieved. I backed the spitfire jib, and we jilled about in the lee of Fayal while I fished out a bottle of Californian wine and we had a good dinner. Next morning we beat up the channel against a Force 8 wind, but had a great welcome from the charming Portuguese people at Horta when we finally arrived.

We stayed there for two weeks while I had a new petrol tank made of copper. We enjoyed a lazy life; our only disappointment was being unable to get a bath. That, and a feast ashore, are the chief things a yachtsman looks forward to after a passage of twenty-six days. All the island's plumbing had been fractured by a big earthquake.

We left Horta on October 3rd. The locals were shaking their heads, and saying that it was too late in the year for a yacht. Sheila was apprehensive, and looked somewhat longingly at an island steamer which called in, but decided to stick to *Gipsy Moth* and see the voyage through. The Azores were a great disappointment to me; instead of the calm fine weather I had expected in the middle of the Azores high pressure system, it was always squally or bad weather, and there were strong currents, not shown on any of my charts. We left Horta in a dead calm, but within an hour it was blowing a Force 9 gale, with steep seas breaking on the counter. I felt ham-fisted with Miranda after my fortnight ashore, and asked Sheila to take the helm while I went below and cooked some breakfast. I should have liked to heave to, but we had an island in our lee which we had to clear. After breakfast I took over for an hour or two until we had cleared the point, when I gratefully lowered all sail and *Gipsy Moth* jilled along under bare poles while I went below, had a hot whisky, and a sleep for an hour and three-quarters. Then I set a spitfire jib, and by midnight we were clear of the last island, out in the open ocean and I could relax.

We were fifteen days on passage from the Azores to Plymouth, and on nine of them we were under storm sails, spitfire jib and trysail. There were impressive seas, magnificent and monumental, but not malicious. It was exhilarating to watch those mountains of water creeping up and passing. I spent hours on deck trying to get a good photograph of a big sea but found it difficult. The whole passage was a grand sail, and much more relaxing for me than the hot calms and light airs after leaving New York, when my temper and fingernails had been worn' to the quick by the incessant sail changing and trimming. As soon as it blew up to Force 7, I could set the storm rig and retire below to prepare a good feast with a bottle of excellent American wine. Sheila was now quite happy with big seas in a gale, and I was amused to recall her candid comments on navigation when we left New York if we were bumping somewhat at 6 knots in a fresh breeze.

I had lost both my log spinners. I rigged up an old-fashioned log, which worked by timing the run-out of a given length of line, but as time went on I found that the log was not really necessary, for I could judge the speed of the yacht to a quarter of a knot with fair accuracy.

On the way up from Plymouth to Buckler's Hard, on the last day's sailing after a wonderful voyage of 8,000 miles, I was seasick again in some nasty weather off Portland Bill.

Next spring – the spring of 1961 – I had intended racing *Gipsy Moth* in the ordinary RORC programme with a conventional full crew. At the start of the season I was alone on the Beaulieu River, checking the compass, when *Gipsy Moth* drifted aground, and I damaged my back hauling her off. I was flat on my back for ten days, and before I had recovered fully, I had a sharp attack of hepatitis. I had cancelled my own racing programme, but, having agreed to navigate for John Illingworth in Cowes Week and the Fastnet race, I did not like to back out at the last moment; so concealed the hepatitis, and joined John in *Stormvogel* for the Channel race. *Stormvogel* is a big 75-foot yacht of very light displacement. Caes Brynzeel (her owner) asked me to stay with him for the Fastnet and I was glad to do so. It was a good experience, sailing with Caes; a tough hard-driving Dutchman with a racing mentality. He had built several revolutionary yachts over the years, and had won the Fastnet Race in 1930. We missed an all-time record for the Fastnet course by only 100 minutes. This was comfortable racing, with seventeen on board, including a cook, but I could not take advantage of the good fare for the last three days – my hepatitis had got the upper hand again, and I navigated on hot water only.

All this time I had been pondering my 1960 race across the Atlantic. Before the start I had known that the rival yachts would never see each other, and I had set myself a target time to race against, thirty days. This was the time I reckoned that a winning yacht of *Gipsy Moth*'s class should take with a full crew of six, in an RORC race across the Atlantic from east to west. In 1962, for example, there were twelve RORC races in British and French waters. They averaged 250 miles apiece, so that the twelve totalled the same distance as the single-handed race, 3,000 miles. Adding the times taken by the winners of these twelve races for the same size class as *Gipsy Moth* gave an average speed of $107\frac{1}{2}$ miles per day. Allowing for the Gulf Stream's setting her back $9\frac{1}{2}$ miles a day for the first 2,000 miles, I reckoned that 100 miles per day throughout was the equivalent speed, and the best I could hope to do. When I took forty and a half days I was disappointed. I thought *Gipsy Moth* was too big, and her gear too heavy to handle for one man. By the end of the 8,000-mile voyage, I had thought up a number of different ways to make the gear-handling easier, and the yacht faster. I asked John Illingworth if he would redesign the mast and sail plan to my requirements – he is not only one of the most experienced and successful of ocean racers, but also an engineer who probably knows the stresses involved in tough ocean racing better than anyone. During the winter of 1961 a metal mast was built for *Gipsy Moth*. It was a little shorter, 53 feet instead of 55 feet. Some of the other changes I planned were:

A smaller mainsail, which would balance the headsails better, and be easier to handle.

The heavy main boom, which had caused me so much trouble, was cut down from 18 feet to 14 feet, and the lethal runners which had seemed animated by a mad lust to brain me were eliminated.

The headsails were bigger, to compensate for the smaller mainsail, and the sloop rig was changed to cutter rig.

Besides changing the sail plan, I had thought up a number of devices and methods for making the gear-handling easier.

As soon as all this was under way, I had a strong urge to try out *Gipsy Moth* in 1962, to see if my ideas were correct. I believe that this is the greatest urge to adventure for a man – to have an idea, an ideal or an ambition, and then to prove, at any cost, that the idea is *right*, or that the ambition can be fulfilled. At first I thought, 'What about a sail to the Azores and back?' Then I remembered our delightful visit to Indian Point, and thought, 'What fun it would be to nip across the Atlantic to see them again.' From here the next step was easy: 'Why not try for a record crossing? Air pilots and racing motorists are always trying for records; why not a sailing yacht for a change?'

My enthusiasm was dampened when I came to consider the cost of the double crossing, together with the cost of all the changes and improvements to *Gipsy Moth*.

'Why not send the story of my record attempt by radio-telephone every day?' A New Zealand magazine had bought a similar story from me on my 1936 flight.

I offered my story first to the *Observer*, because they had been so pleasant to deal with in the 1960 race; but a daily story was not really suitable for a Sunday paper.

Towards Christmas 1961 John Anderson of the *Guardian* asked me to present the annual prizes to a sailing association of which he was vice-commodre. I remembered a review he had written of my book, *Alone Across the Atlantic*, which had fascinated me by the writer's uncanny perception of the true values and spiritual issues involved in solo racing across an ocean. This seemed to me like fate, and at the prize-giving I offered him my story for the *Guardian*. The *Guardian* accepted and I declared that I would start at 11 AM on June 1st. This was a bold, rash statement; as a pioneer airman I remembered my dislike for stating a definite time of departure, which was thought to invite disaster. There is a similar feeling now about yachts, especially when a race is involved. In the 1960 solo Atlantic race, if one succeeded in crossing the starting line on time it was an act of good luck on the credit side; whereas this time I should have to turn up at the starting line on time, or else it would be a disastrous failure on the debit side.

The problem was how to transmit a story every day to the *Guardian*. With the help of friends I got in touch with Marconi, who thought they had a set which might carry my talk half-way across the Atlantic. The GPO was very ready to help; the Post Office people were keen to receive *Gipsy Moth* from farther than any small yacht had ever transmitted. No one, however, dared to hope that I might reach right across the ocean.

By the end of January I had finished designing a new Miranda. This was much simpler than Miranda I, and would have double the power, although the mast would be only 8 feet high instead of 14 feet. Yet there would be so little friction that she should work in the faintest zephyr. I made a full scale model in paper, which I pinned on the wall of my office. The top had to spread over the ceiling because her gaff was $10\frac{1}{2}$ feet long.

In February I went to Vence for a check up of my lung by Jean Mattie. Every day I timed myself up the Baou Blanc, 2,400 feet, as a measure of how fit I was getting. The complete break from office work was invaluable. I did practice transmitting Morse every day, but I had to stop this when I found that my set, which was designed to teach Morse to Boy Scouts, spoilt the hotel television picture downstairs.

At the beginning of March work started with a meeting of technicians on *Gipsy Moth* at Buckler's Hard. The cold wind in the bleak dim boatshed pierced one's spirit, and sent it chilled to one's boots. Place had to be found for four heavy banks of accumulators in acid-proof boxes, with Atlantic proof tops; also for a special charging motor, which might seem light to them, but was heavy to me; and for a radio-telephone of half a man's weight, which had to be high above the water line. All this weight would put the stern down, increase the rolling moment and decrease the sailing power, but the brilliant technical bandits were merciless to *Gipsy Moth*. My chart table and navigating department had to be partially wrecked to make room for the telephone. There followed trouble with the transmitting aerials, trouble with the receiving aerials, trouble with the earthing arrangements, trouble with electrolytic action, trouble with noxious fumes from the batteries being charged. Fortunately Marconi's were really keen that the R/T should transmit, and the GPO men were determined that it should be received. The boatyard was due to launch *Gipsy Moth* at the end of March, but she did not get into the water until the end of April, and then there was delay because the mast had to be stepped twice, the first time for measuring the length of the rigging. Unfortunately, there was only enough water beside the crane at certain times of the month. Once again the trials and sail drill which I had promised myself had to be mostly forgone.

I had only three weeks left before the start of my Atlantic crossing. I did manage to swing my compass, but had no opportunity to calibrate the D/F loop. I used to wonder why ships of the line took months to fit out; I wonder no longer. I believe that my 13-ton *Gipsy Moth* has just as many items of gear and stores to go aboard for an Atlantic crossing as had the *Agamemnon*, Nelson's favourite ship of the line, which was built at Buckler's Hard in 1781. The quantities are different – for instance, my armament is one Very signal pistol instead of sixty-four guns, with red and white flare cartridges, instead of ball, and grape shot; but I dare say I have more food items; I doubt if the *Agamemnon* carried tinned cods' roes or chinook salmon. Both ships carried sextants, but I have an echo sounder as well as a leadline, also a radio D/F set, an R/T and two engines to service, which the *Agamemnon* did not have.

The Shell Company made me some special cans for my petrol (needed for the charging motor), and for my paraffin, which helped with the stowage, but I should have been hard pressed if Sheila had not taken over the stores again. The stores list was much the same as in 1960, except for the liquids. In 1960 my chief drink had been whisky; I seemed to need it, as if it supplied an essential vitamin (I think that this must have been connected with my illness). Now I no longer needed it, and my favourite drink on board this time was Whitbread's pale ale, of which I carried several cases. (After all, we are always reading how ocean voyagers need to conserve their water supplies!) This time I did not intend to take an oven to bake bread, because on the last race my wholemeal loaves had lasted me until I reached Long Island. I did carry some flour and yeast, however, planning to bake in a saucepan in case of emergency.

On May 27th *Gipsy Moth* sailed for Plymouth.

CHAPTER THIRTY

ATLANTIC AGAIN

JUNE IST, 1962, was a fine day, with the sun shining in a blue sky, a calm sea, a light breeze and it was perfect for the start of a transatlantic race. I say 'race', because I was racing against my deadline of thirty days, just as much as if I had been racing against a crowd of competitors. I boarded *Gipsy Moth* at 9.0 AM, which I thought was in good time for an 11 o'clock start. I had nothing more to do; even the Customs clearance had been obtained the night before. How mistaken could I be! I was working away, getting my sails up and hanking them on, when a big launch came alongside, which disgorged two Customs men. They said that they had heard that the BBC had lent me a tape recorder, and they wanted to inspect it. They even cut open the battery box, and turned out all the batteries, looking at them one at a time. It appeared to me as a deliberate piece of obstructionism on somebody's part; they were so slow about every slightest movement they made. Unfortunately I could not find my clearance slip, but I do not believe it would have made any difference if I had. I was hopping mad at the thought of all the people down at the starting line waiting for me to appear at 11 o'clock. When I did finally get away, Sheila took the helm, while I worked like a beaver. Sid Mashford, the boat builder, was also on board to give me a hand. When we reached the starting line with Sheila and Sid still on board, I shouted to someone in a near-by yacht, 'Has the first gun been fired?' 'Yes,' he shouted back, as I frantically hoisted my mainsail and started sailing, while Sheila and Sid scrambled into the launch alongside and shoved off. In the end, I managed to cross the line only a few moments after the starting gun had fired.

What could be more thrilling than a 3,000-mile race across the Atlantic! It is true that the romance of doing something for the first time can never be equalled, but now I had not only the fascination of a 3,000-mile voyage, and the romance of heading into the adventures I could be sure of meeting, but also the thrill of sailing a yacht in first-class racing trim.

My first day was almost too fine. I seemed to be trimming or changing sails all day, and moving slowly. At one time, the wind swung from south-west to north-west within a minute. By the end of the day I was still not in a single-handed frame of mind; I could not stay below for more than a few minutes without popping up to see if there were any ships or land near. I knew that later I should be content to stay below, because I should hear or feel the slightest change of conditions around the yacht.

I planned a route farther north than my 1960 track. Every route across has its pros and cons; the amount of fog, strength of current, wind, weather and ice are everywhere different; in fact, no two square miles of Atlantic are the same. My route took me north of the Scillies and that clump of rocks known as the Seven Stones. So far I had fine weather; the sun shone out of a cloudless sky, and there was a lovely dark-blue sea. For a while I lay sunbathing on the cabin top, stretched out on a sail. I had never had a day's weather like this in the 1960 race. I was running before a gentle breeze and here was another contrast to 1960, when the biggest sail area I could set for running was 600 square feet, and that was soon out of control in the big storm which hit me. Now, with my new rig and self-steering gear, I set 1,100 square feet, and felt in control of it, so that I could sleep peacefully. And Miranda really was in control of the steering. I had no more fear of her being smashed in a gybe.

The second day out a great event occurred; I found a handsome homing pigeon with bold black bars slashed across its folded wings sheltering in the lee of a sail on the foredeck. Pidgy, as he was soon to be called, was shy and not to be caught.

349

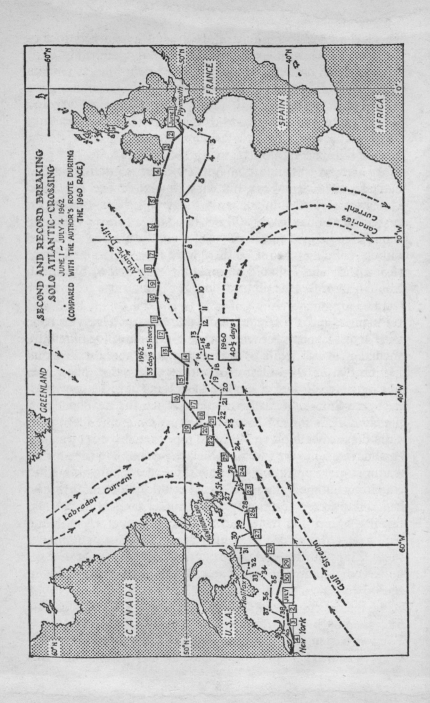

SECOND AND RECORD BREAKING
SOLO ATLANTIC-CROSSING
JUNE 1 – JULY 4 1962
(COMPARED WITH THE AUTHOR'S ROUTE DURING
THE 1960 RACE)

1962
33 days 15 hours

1960
40½ days

He was intensely curious, and as soon as we had met he followed me about the ship, watching closely everything I did, his head cocked slightly to one side, one bright round eye attentive. Each time I went below he perched on the companionway. As I was tuning up the radio for my daily talk to the *Guardian*, Billy Cotton suddenly came through with his wisecracking. This was too much for Pidgy, who promptly hopped on to the edge of the chart table, listening intently. Next morning I gave him some of my breakfast, muesli, a Swiss peasant dish made of oatmeal, raisins and nuts, but without a grated raw apple and honey which I added for myself. Pidgy enjoyed it, and sipped some water from a saucer. While I was sunbathing on the cabin top, Pidgy slipped inside the cabin, and by the time I found this out he had made the most frightful mess on the cabin floor (fortunately not on Sheila's new nylon carpet). I had to shush him out into the cockpit.

I had nightmare visions of what he could do to my bunk and the settees, and I had plenty of work without having to cope with that. I soon discovered that his personal habits were shocking; he was nearer to discovering the secret of a perpetual motion than any scientist ever will be – I had to follow him round the deck with a mop and bucket. Later, his loose behaviour was to be actually the cause of slowing up the ship. I prepared a box for him in the cockpit, and presented him with a wooden mallet and a small coil of rope to stand on. (I thought that maybe I should be able to sell the guano deposit on that mallet at great profit in America!) It was not long before I decided that Pidgy had a most stupid streak in his character; he kept on pecking frantically at a saucer, long after he had finished everything in it, and refused to look at another one with a new supply of food which I put in the box, although I showed it to him several times.

Just before midnight on June 3rd, a fine night with winking stars, I could see the Fastnet Light flashing to the north of me at the south-west tip of Ireland. In the morning the weather forecast was for a south-east wind, increasing perhaps to Gale Force 8. *Gipsy Moth* was running well, but it was a rolling twisting ride in the Atlantic. It made me feel queasy, and I was not the only one; Pidgy looked terrible, all fluffed up with his head tucked under his wing, and bleary eyed when he looked up at me. I feared that he was going to die. I had heard that birds are unable to be seasick, and are therefore worse off than humans. Next morning, however, he was still alive. He looked miserable and twice his size, a huge puffed out ball, with his head nearly sunk in his shoulders.

From below in the cabin I heard a loud bang and rushed on deck to find that the rope holding the big genoa to the spinnaker pole had parted in a gale puff. It took me seventy-five minutes to clear up the mess. After that I found that the breakband locking Miranda to the tiller was slipping. I fixed that, and had started taking a sextant shot at the sun when a steamer, the *Bristol Gift*, circled *Gipsy Moth*. By the time I had finished my observation and turned on the radio-telephone, I was just in time to hear GCN 2, the GPO station, signing off, having given up hope of contacting me. However, I got through to them all right at 10.30 that night.

I was woken during the night by the sails roaring, with *Gipsy Moth* rough-riding across the seas in a gale of wind. In the morning I had more trouble with the steering because Miranda was slipping badly. I fixed her as well as I could in a wind, gusting to a full gale.

Pidgy was squatting on the corner of the cockpit seat and took no notice when I stepped right alongside him. He must have been feeling awful. I too felt sick, and had some hot water and sugar, my latest seasickness cure.

June 5th. A squall gusting to 60 mph had me out on the foredeck setting a storm staysail and a spitfire jib. Several waves broke over me, and to my disgust water ran up inside my oilskin trouser legs and over the top of the long boots inside them. I then had to double-reef Miranda, which was a difficult and tricky job, with seas picking up the ship and throwing her down on her side, or slewing the stern round while I was standing on the counter using both hands above my shoulders to reef. Just as I got below and hung my wet scarf and boots above the Aladdin heater, an RAF Shackleton started buzzing me. Although it had done well to find me in that disturbed sea,

I did not feel hospitable. However, when it buzzed me a third time, I pushed back the hatch enough to poke half my head out. I promptly got a sea down my neck. Swearing, I put on an oil-skin coat and flashed my Aldis light at the aircraft. It started flashing a message at me, but it was coming at me from behind the trysail and I should have needed to chase out on deck to read the signals. I could not face a drenching below the waist, so merely flashed an acknowledgement.

Looking round, I could not find Pidgy, which made me sad; I thought that the swooping aeroplane must have frightened him, and made him take off, and I also feared that we were too far from land for him to make it. Two hours later I had good news; Pidge was back. He must have hidden away somewhere from the Shackleton. He looked all in, poor devil. But at least he could do something that I couldn't; he was standing on one leg on the cockpit seat, and swaying to the roll of the ship with-out looking. It was real Atlantic weather; grey mist, turbulent sea, moaning wind. It was not comfortable, but I had great satisfaction that *Gipsy Moth* was charging ahead at a steady 6 knots under her storm rig, and I felt in complete control.

June 6th. I was rousted out twice during the night when parts of Miranda's rigging gave way. The first time I found all the sails aback, and the yacht headed for England, which does not put up the average speed when racing towards New York.

I began to jib at calling up London on the R/T at a fixed time every morning. It was then my best chance of a sleep after the schemozzles of the night. I would be drowsy and snug in my blankets when the alarm went off, unwilling to get up, have no copy ready and be dozy-brained when I tried to think of some. On top of that, as soon as I did get up I would be sure to find that a sail change or a retrim was needed, and I would either regret losing racing speed if I telephoned, or regret missing the transmitting rendezvous if I changed a sail. I asked for the transmitting time to be switched to the evening, and promised better copy then.

Under the cockpit seat I found Pidgy, bedraggled and sick-looking. I feared for his life. I made him a hut under the seat with a transparent plastic covering, and gave him a dish of

Macvita and bread, with a bowl of fresh water, both of which he went for. Later he seemed better.

The battery-charging motor began to give trouble. It would stop every few minutes when the yacht rolled. I had to think of some way to get over this, for the batteries must be charged if I was to get my story through. I fashioned a piece of wood to plug the petrol tank opening and to raise the petrol level, but it did not work. The motor still petered out at each big roll.

When 600 miles out I had to reset the storm sails for a gale squall. It was rugged work; several seas broke over me on the foredeck, and once I was bucked clean into the air.

At the end of the day I had just got below and was sitting fagged out, when I was faced with getting on deck again for another schemozzle – the tell-tale compass showed that *Gipsy Moth* was away off course. I started pulling on my wet sea boots, mentally groaning and cursing, when I had an inspiration. I had been eating some shortbread, and the tin was on the end of the swinging table just above the tell-tale compass. I pushed the tin along the table, and the compass needle swung back to the right heading. Gratefully I hung up my boots again. Who would have thought that a tin could have been so highly magnetized!

June 7th. The charging motor spluttered and went dead with a squealing squeaking noise. I tried to turn the flywheel by hand but it was seized up solid. *Finis* the charging! And no charging, no transmitting.

The first thing I did was to dig out the cabin paraffin lamp, some candles, and the paraffin riding light. I must save every little watt of electricity for transmitting. When I next transmitted I described the disaster and asked for advice. I cannot describe the hours I spent during the next few days grovelling and fumbling in the bowels of the ship connecting and disconnecting wires and terminals, removing and refixing floorboards, engine covers, battery box lids, while kneeling on the cabin floor of a jumping, lurching, pitching, rolling and (I could well believe) laughing ship. In the end I had the 24-volt batteries of the radio-telephone wired up to the 12-volt dynamo of the auxiliary motor, but as soon as I started up the motor the propeller shaft began to turn. That was no good – I was out for a sailing record. I switched off hurriedly, and after failing in various different ways, I finally stopped the propeller shaft from turning by winding a length of cord round it and making the end fast. But after running the motor for sixteen minutes it was so hot that I had to stop.

June 9th. Big news! In the middle of the night Pidge gave tongue – *roucou! roucou!* Perhaps he was feeling better, or was it only a dream in the dark? No, in the daylight he suddenly began imitating an eagle! Standing head up, chest out, he spread his wings like the eagle of the old German flag and flapped them bravely, hopping on his toes. In the morning I made a tent for him with two thicknesses of old canvas which I stretched from the cockpit coaming to the edge of the seat. I provided him with a plastic bag for a ground sheet.

I worked hard on the engine, head down under the cockpit and arms at full stretch beside the engine. I had to work by feel, because my arms left no room to see. I only just escaped being seasick. The result was a failure.

On deck I found that I had lost my sense of balance, and could not walk along without holding on all the time. I had to sit down to change headsails when the job required both hands.

With Pidgy's tent at the forward end of the cockpit seat, I could not see him from below. I missed his beady eyes, so, after cleaning up after him in the cockpit, I made a new tent at the other end of the seat where he would stand in the entrance and, no doubt, laugh secretly at me as I cleaned up his mess.

Through London I got a message from Martin about the engine. He keeps the Buckler's Hard garage, and has a flair with engines. As a result I succeeded in pumping current into the batteries for half an hour, but the result was scarcely noticeable. I had a desperate feeling of futility when I thought how every hour's charging used a gallon of my precious petrol, and of the seemingly endless and tedious chores I had to perform every time I started or finished charging.

That afternoon my back went click. It was very painful to move about. I feared that it was the start of a disc breaking out as a result of struggling with the gear-lever bolts with my back arched under the cockpit. I decided that if I could avoid another sudden jerk or twist, it might get no worse.

That night was a rough one, and next morning I was tired. I looked up at the rigging and around the deck, and thought that this kind of sailing was becoming absurd. There were no fewer than thirty ropes of different kinds coiled up or in use for my sailing. It seemed mad not to have a simple rig like Blondie's one junk sail, and a few ropes to operate it. I went forward to change my working jib down to a spitfire jib and then in the middle of the operation changed my mind, and reset the working jib; that was a sure indication of fatigue. I only ate one meal all day, another sign. However, I had made good by that day over 1,000 miles from Plymouth on a Great Circle course from the Lizard, a third of the distance to New York. One thousand miles westwards in ten days was one ambition I had achieved. If only I could keep that rate up! Of course sailing conditions so far had been good for the Atlantic, but how ridiculous to be depressed or feel tired; especially with my back better, for which I was very grateful.

Pidgy looked disgusted; what a life for a bird! Streams of water were sluicing into the cockpit, the air was wet and windy. During the night he had moved from his new camp and stood on the seat beside the companionway, but I had to move him back for fear I should tread on him. He tried other spots, but he was in the way wherever he went, poor devil. I debated taking him into the cabin and putting up with his indescribable mess, but then I thought, 'Surely a bird is used to the open air', and contented myself with making his tent as snug as possible. I gave him a box full of muesli which was his favourite food (except for the raisins which he threw out, just as my son Giles does). A big sea gave his den a fair washout, and swamped the rest of the muesli. I gave him another plateful in the tent, but he just sat outside waiting till that too had got soaked. That night I was woken frequently by crashes and once wondered if something had broken or come adrift but all was well. *Gipsy Moth* was sailing at 6 knots through rough water. During the night Pidge seemed quite happy, squatting inside his wigwam facing the entrance. He chattered his beak silently at me when I spoke to him. I ate a handful of dates and an orange in my berth. My nails were worn too far down to peel the orange, but I managed by starting it with my teeth, and finishing with the ball of my thumb. On the whole I had an easy night, which did me good.

In the morning for some reason I laughed at Pidge. To my surprise he was sensitive about it, and much disliked it. He stamped to and fro, chattered his beak and gave me dirty looks.

June 12th. I woke at 5.30 in the morning to find the ship headed north, and cursed at having to get up. But I fell asleep again, and woke two hours later to find the heading east-north-east. Horror! I was headed for Iceland – not the way to increase the daily average run.

John Fairhall of the *Guardian* in London gave me the positions of the known icebergs which I had asked for. I wanted to know how far south they came, so that I could plan my route.

While charging the batteries I noticed that the motor's speed varied, suddenly running much faster, then slowing right down. After forty-eight minutes of charging there was a loud 'plonk', and the propeller slipped into gear. I switched off immediately. The cord holding the shaft had snapped. I found steam blowing through escape holes in the gearbox and the clutch. They were so hot that rain dropping on them sizzled. The clutch must have been partially engaged. The truth was that this engine was not built to freewheel for more than a minute or two after starting up.

The biggest penance I suffered through the failure of the charging motor was due to the paraffin riding light I used at night instead of electric light. Unfortunately my little Old Faithful of the 1960 race had been broken, and I bought what I was told was the best riding light to replace it. What I suffered through that lamp! Night after night I spent from half to one hour trying to get it into the rigging alight. In the cabin the slightest jerk put it out instantly. In the cockpit any sudden puff of wind extinguished it. If only I could get it fastened to the backstay in a steady wind before it went out it might survive for several hours. I tried warming it up in the cabin before venturing out, using a higher or lower flame and filling it only half full. How I cursed the makers of that lamp! How I damned the designer, and wished he could be brought into the Atlantic to try making it work.

June 13th. Great sailing! A rough breaking sea, with *Gipsy Moth* crashing through fast and strongly as if she loved it. Great sailing, but not for Pidge; I saw the look of disgust on his face when he caught a sea (I think he must have been a crabby old bachelor). Sometimes he seemed to give me a malicious look. Later when I went on deck I found that the log had stopped, and at first was puzzled why. Indirectly Pidge was responsible. I had given up stowing the coiled ends of the ropes in the lockers under the cockpit seats because Pidge fouled them up so horribly. I had left them coiled on the deck beside the cockpit coaming. The seas breaking on deck had washed them overboard, where they had tangled with the log line. Ropes trailing in the water are used to slow up a yacht, so that this schemozzle must have cost us speed. On top of that I spent hours untangling the log line with its thousands of tight twists. A lot of clear white sparkling sea was coming aboard as I did so; it was blowing a gale though the sun was shining. I could not be sure how long the log had been out of action.

June 15th. Pidge! Pidge! Pidge! He ruled my life then. Every morning I had to feed and water him as soon as I emerged, before I trimmed the sails and got the ship back on to her proper heading. I couldn't bear his forlorn beady look. Then I would notice the various messes on the cockpit seat, etc, which I'd tread in while handling the ropes, so I had to go round and clear all of them up before getting to work on the ship. During the night, even if I darted out in an emergency, I had to shine my torch round and locate Pidge before stepping into the cockpit for fear of treading on him. That morning when I fed him, and gave his tabernacle another covering, he let me stroke him, so I reckoned that he must be pretty fed up. He looked like a sick jackdaw.

I got another sun-shot when the sun half showed through the ragged stormy sky. I had to grab the chance, and though I only poked my nose out of the hatch, both the sextant and I got a thorough sea bath again. The seas were very rough, about 12 feet, and with a gale south-west by west.

June 16th. How that anchor light maddened me! Once it went out while hanging quietly on a hook in the cabin without being touched.

The battery charging on this day got the acid level up to 1,143. I was still getting my story through every day, and wondered if I could keep it going. Later, I had to stop charging, because the exhaust flames were blowing through the asbestos wrapping round the short exhaust pipe at the forward end of the motor. I could see the red hot gases flowing quickly, like a river. The pipe had been burnt away.

During the day the wind dropped to a zephyr, and in a short while veered through 225 degrees from north right round through east and south to south-west. Taking the opportunity to shave, I spotted that the barometer had dropped a millibar in the ten minutes while I was shaving. I went on deck at once, and changed the big genoa to the tiny spitfire jib. The genoa was already being overpowered. After midnight the ship was thrown about so badly that I had to change to a leeward berth for fear that I should be thrown right across the cabin into the pilot berth at the far side while asleep. (Apart from the effect of this on me, all the eggs were stowed in that berth!) As soon as I had settled into the new berth, *Gipsy Moth* tacked herself, and came up aback, headed north-east. All my oilies and boots had to go on, and I gybed her round. The anchor light went out, of course, and I could not get it out on the stay again alight until three attempts had failed. What a job in a gale! Nine hours later *Gipsy Moth* was becalmed again. What a life!

Pidge seemed to like bread chopped small better than anything else now. I had tried him with both cheese and sugar, but he turned them down. He had two red bands on his tough, scaly legs, and I passed his number to London. It turned out that he was a French aristocrat coming from a long-distance racing family and that he was racing from the Channel Islands to Preston, Lancashire, when he came down on *Gipsy Moth*. Perhaps the very old blood in his veins made his manners so peculiar! He never finished more than two-thirds of any dishful I gave him, and rejected any piece which was a fraction bigger than his maximum. I never understood this; if a pigeon can swallow a whole acorn, why can he not eat a piece of bread a fifth of the size?

Fog came, reducing visibility to half a mile. I was amazed at how little fog I had met so far; in 1960 I was in fog for more than a third of the voyage. My course to clear the icebergs was 247° True.

June 18th. I hit a head-on gale, a very different proposition from a gale on the beam. A modern yacht can make headway against a gale, provided that the sea is not too turbulent, but in a west Atlantic gale, the ship gets thrown about so much and its way is stopped so frequently that it cannot progress into wind, and every time its way is checked, the wind pushes the hull to leeward.

At 9 o'clock in the evening the jib sheet parted at the clew with a sharp twang. I rushed up to get in the sail before it flogged itself to bits. The stem I was standing on was jumping 15 feet above the water. My hands were so numb that I had trouble tying the knots of the sail ties. During the jib trouble, the halyard fouled up the forestays, locking them together, so that I could not set another headsail. It was all my fault, because I ought to have shortened sail long before. I had been repairing the motor exhaust and had wanted to finish that job before going on deck. I tried to get moving with a trysail and a staysail. As I was setting the trysail I was swung round the mast, and my head was knocked into the reefing gear of the boom. I was surprised that I was not knocked out. When I set the staysail as well as the trysail, the ship seemed to go mad, and I hurriedly dropped the staysail again.

The barometer had dropped nearly 20 millibars in a period of minutes, and a pinkish glow suffused the overcast. I expected hell to be let loose that night.

When I came aft from the jib picnic, Pidge was missing. My heart dropped; I thought that he must have been washed overboard. In the end I found him back in his locker under the cockpit seat, very forlorn, wet and bedraggled. I gave him one of Stalker's oat cakes; nothing but the best for him on such an occasion. He seemed to love it.

In the twilight before nightfall I set about reefing *Miranda*. I believed this to be the toughest job I have had to do at sea. First I lowered the gaff to the boom, and as they swung weather-cocking astern I slung a rope over them and managed to haul them round against the wind, to lash them to a backstay. Next, keeping my footing as best I could on the bucking, twisting counter, I worked away, mostly by feel, to find the reefing eyes in the folded sail, and pass a reefing cord through them. I had to use both hands on this job, working above shoulder height, and holding on by grabbing the head-high spars when neces-sary. I do not know how long it all took; I would estimate two and a half hours. I stopped in the middle and went below till I had some feeling again in numb fingers. I was being bull-minded, bloody-minded if you like, but I had made up my mind to reef that sail. I had ceased to consider whether, with the gale increasing, I should be able to use it when it was reefed. In the end I finished the job, and somehow felt in better spirits for having done it.

CHAPTER THIRTY-ONE

BACK TO NEW YORK

DURING the next nine hours *Gipsy Moth* only moved ten miles to the north-west. Even so, I reckoned that I was working too far north, and would soon be north-east of the icebergs, so that they lay between me and New York. I dreaded those bergs, though the chance of hitting one of them was minute com-pared with the risk of steamers – but icebergs take no notice of the international regulations that a yacht has right of way! I decided to change tacks and head south. I had difficulty in get-ting the ship to tack without a headsail in the gale, with big tur-bulent seas. With dawn I set to work on untangling the fore-stays, but it took me more than two hours before I had the spitfire set; and after that the spitfire was not enough to keep the ship's head up to the wind in the wild sea running.

Poor Pidge. The cockpit was half full of water, and I could see his skin as if his bedraggled feathers did not exist. He looked so miserable that I took him below and tried to settle him in a large biscuit tin. Unfortunately I had nothing really suitable. He would not stay in the tin, so I took him back to his cubbyhole. I supposed that a pigeon was used to roosting out in anything, but it was bitingly cold.

By noon I had made good only nine miles towards New York, although I had sailed seventy miles. My hands were numb after only twenty minutes of handling ropes in the cockpit. The gale had now backed, and I was headed east of south. I decided to hold on to the southerly course, however, to get clear of the icebergs. I had made a blunder heading north-west the day before. The sea was very rough, with plenty of surf from the combers, and the breakers twisting in all directions. I could not keep warm, though I had on my long woollen underpants, a thick knitted ski-sweater and a padded nylon jacket, with the heater going full blast. Every time I came below I propped my sea boots upside down on top of the heater, and hung my scarf and storm stalker on a hook above it. The storm stalker was saturated, but I put it back on wet and clammy each time because it was invaluable for protecting my eyes against flogging ropes. The most I could hope for was that the stove heat would warm it, and dry it a little each time.

I finished repairing the burst exhaust pipe, and started charging, but there was no oil pressure until I added another pint to the engine. I was amazed that I succeeded in transmitting to London with green seas catching the aerial. I lowered Miranda's gaff, furled her sail, and secured the whole to a backstay. I thought *Gipsy Moth* would sail herself in that gale without Miranda, but as soon as I got below and started cooking some vegetables, she tacked herself, putting the sails aback. I had to dress up again and gybe the ship back on to her old heading.

By 9 o'clock that night the gale had veered 45 degrees. The ship's heading had improved as a result, but she was taking a frightful bashing. I felt I should do something drastic before she was damaged. I tacked ship, leaving the sails aback. This slowed her up, but she was still being knocked over. Then I lowered the trysail, leaving only the tiny spitfire. I let this draw, and then tacked again, so that the spitfire would be aback on the southerly heading. This was an improvement below, except when green seas hit the deck. Once I was standing in the cabin facing forward when a big sea broke on top. A little cloud of fine spray shaped like a ball appeared in front of my eyes below the cabin roof. That cabin top is one solid piece of thick plywood, with no break in it anywhere, except where a ring bolt passes through. That was the only place where the spray could have been forced through, and showed the tremendous pressure which a big sea must exert.

An hour after midnight on 20 June I logged that I had spent nearly an hour trying to get the anchor light to stay alight. It went out in the calm of the cabin before it even met the gale. Finally I decided that I must sail without a light, or use electricity and be damned. In this rough weather the light was most needed, so I rigged the electric light.

At three in the morning I changed over to a leeward berth to avoid being thrown across the cabin. We were still going much too fast, although it was only 3 knots. I pondered how I could slow the ship up. I went on deck, and lashed the tiller hard alee. This headed the ship closer to the wind by 30 degrees and slowed the speed down to $1\frac{1}{2}$ knots. An occasional heavy sea came on board, and one put out the cabin light; I suppose the shock caused by the bang did it. I reckoned that the wind on deck was 60 knots.

At dawn I found that the log had stopped again. This time I could not blame Pidge; the burgee halyard had parted, and one part of it, with the burgee stick, had been washed into the sea, where the spinning log had twisted it hopelessly round the log line. I finished unravelling the log line – among other jobs – six hours later. By noon I had moved fifty-nine miles southwards in the past twenty-four hours, but because of the Gulf Stream and the leeway caused by the gale, I had been driven back twenty-five miles towards Europe.

By the evening, the wind had veered to north-west, and

decreased to Force 7. The seas, though less rough, were still turbulent. I was getting very worried about Pidgy. He looked bare, wet and cold, and had whitish scabs round his eyes. I could not bear to see him looking so miserable. I made him a dovecote out of a cardboard box which had originally held a Thermos jug, and had a circular hole in it. I secured this box to the cabin roof above the galley and placed Pidgy through the hole, after wrapping him in some old pyjamas. He pecked me when I picked him up. For a while he lay there, just looking, but later I saw that he had stood up. I feared that he was about to hand in his chips, but presently he started eating a Stalker oatcake in his eyrie. I felt that called for a celebration – a strong gin and lime.

Having settled Pidgy as well as I could, I got to work on the trysail, and finished setting it. The halyard kept getting tangled up in the strong wind. When at last I got below I was surprised to find it calm. On looking out, I was even more surprised to find that it was still blowing Force 7.

I worked up my dead reckoning for the past day, and found that the nearest iceberg was now ninety-three miles off to the west. I had to keep below west to avoid it. Then I started work on Miranda. Her gaff gooseneck, which had sheared off, I managed to replace with an old screw-eye, which I filed down to fit. This was an acrobatic effort, which involved hanging over the pulpit in the stern above the jumping Atlantic. I used shackles and lanyards to replace various bottlescrews and stays which had come apart or snapped. It was dreary, tedious, tricky, and depressing work, but before midnight *Gipsy Moth* had started sailing again in a modest sort of way. When I turned in at midnight Pidgy's tail was sticking out of the box above the galley and I think he was asleep.

When I woke at daybreak, 7 o'clock by my time, *Gipsy Moth* was becalmed, after sailing only twelve miles in seven hours. There was a shower of rain, but it looked as if it would be a fine morning later. The nearest berg was seventy miles to the west. I set a bigger headsail, and *Gipsy Moth* began moving to a light breeze. The sea had gone down.

I took Pidge (somewhat reluctantly on his part) from his

dovecote, and put him on the cockpit seat, as I thought that he ought to have some fresh air and movement. I then cleaned out his dovecote, and lined it with paper. When I stepped into the cockpit Pidge had moved on to the counter and made as if to fly off. He often flew off, and circled the ship once or twice before alighting again. 'Yes, go on,' I said and waved him off. He took off astern, but stalled into the water a few feet away. At first he flapped the water to try to take off, then turned round and started flapping frantically to catch up the ship. It was heart-rending to see his panic as the stern moved steadily away. I sprang to the cockpit, grabbed the tiller and, over-riding Miranda, brought the yacht round.

I aimed to arrive at the spot nearly dead into wind, so that the yacht would be moving slowly. I could not reduce sail, or do anything which would make me take my eye off the pigeon. I knew from the experience with my lost dinghy that I should never see him again if I once lost sight of him – and one tiny grey pigeon in the middle of the Atlantic was infinitely smaller than a dinghy. I had to come up to him, so that he would be within a foot of the side of the ship, otherwise I should not be able to reach him. It was not easy, because from where I stood in the cockpit the pigeon would be out of sight, hidden by the bows, for the last 50 feet of my approach. When I thought that it was the right moment I left the tiller, sprang forward to where the freeboard was lowest – the only place along the deck where it was low enough for me to reach the water with my hand – threw myself on the deck, and thrust my arm and shoulder under the bottom lifeline. Pidgy was right there, and I clutched at him with my hand. But when I pushed my arm down suddenly, as I had to do in a hurry, he must have thought I was going to strike him, for he flapped madly away from me as I touched him, and I missed my hold. I felt terrible, that he should take me for an enemy. I ran back to the tiller and slowly, as it seemed, came round again. I had to stay by the tiller till the last moment, and then make a rush and a grab. Once I slipped, but I had no time to clip on my safety-harness. The next three passes I made at him he eluded me. I could see that I would not get him that way, and tried to squeeze an idea out of my head. Could I throw him anything that he could climb on? I looked round. I could not get below. The only thing I could see was a piece of old sail I had used for Pidgy's tent. I threw this out, but he thought I was throwing it at him and moved away. Then it sank. The big red gash bucket was at hand, and I hurriedly fastened it to the end of the boathook. I think I made fourteen circuits and passes at Pidge. I had him in the bucket about four times, but unfortunately as I lifted the bucket out of the water the overflow from it washed the pigeon out. The last time he was washed out he was swamped by the water and lay inert, with only a little of his back at the surface of the water. Next time I came round I picked him out easily with my hand as he lay inert.

I felt cut up as I held his soaking body; I felt responsible for him, and somehow his mean crabbed nature and his dreadful habits made me feel worse. I squeezed his lungs and the water dribbled out of his beak. Then I went on squeezing regularly, trying to revive him by artificial respiration. I think I was doing it the right way, because I could see air bubbling through his nostrils. At one time I thought he made a sound. I kept at it for, I think, about twenty minutes; then I wrapped him in hot clothes warmed from water in the Thermos. I filled a hot water bottle, and wrapped him with it in paper. But it was no good; Pidgy's spirit had flown. It was pathetic to look at his poor, emaciated, sick-looking body, which seemed to have only a few feathers. He looked either very old or very sick. It was the breakdown in communication between a human being and an animal which was so distressing. If only he could have trusted me, could have understood that I was trying to help him, and not hurt him, he would have still been alive.

I gave him a sea burial in my best biscuit tin with holes punched in it so that it would sink. I watched it till I could see it no longer as *Gipsy Moth* sailed away.

I moped about that day. I had already been depressed, for the gale had cost me not only two and a half days but had set me back twenty miles. To say on June 18th that I had made good 560 miles during the past seven days was not bad; but to say three days later that I had made good only 540 miles during the past ten days was too bad. To achieve my ambition of a thirty-day crossing now entailed making good 1,400 miles in the next ten days, which was practically impossible.

That day I put my house in order; I filled the petrol tank, the paraffin storage tins and bottles, also the stove, the meths priming cans, swept the carpet, cleaned and dusted and tidied. At 4 o'clock in the afternoon *Gipsy Moth* began to sail, at first ghosting in light airs alternating with calm. She seemed to gather herself together, and began moving fast and efficiently in the little wind there was. There was much calm and fog, but she knocked off 100½ miles that day. Then she began sailing across the Grand Banks and down the eastern seaboard for the last 1,300 miles of the voyage as she had never sailed before.

I had one or two minor adventures. The night of 23rd-24th June I was fast asleep, with *Gipsy Moth* sailing at 4 knots through fog on a dark night. I woke up and stepped into the cockpit, rubbing my eyes, to see a huge fishing steamer across the bows. It was vague in the fog. I grabbed the tiller, over-rode Miranda, and pushed the tiller hard down to bring *Gipsy Moth* up into the wind to avoid the steamer. I reckoned that we were going to collide so I brought the tiller hard up the other way, to turn down wind and pass astern. Then I could see that I was going to hit her amidships. She was a blaze of lights there. The sleepy daze was clearing from my brain and I said to myself, 'I must be able to range alongside if I head up into wind,' and with that I pushed the tiller hard down again. Now I was close enough to see through the fog that the steamer was stationary. This was what had foxed me. I passed across her bows, and as I did so she sounded a foghorn.

I trimmed the sails to get back on course before going below and mixing myself a stiff hot grog. My hands were so cold that it was difficult to hold a pen to the log.

That day *Gipsy Moth* knocked off 131½ miles. I crossed the bows of another trawler 100 yards away; a third I heard, but did not see in the fog. There seemed to be fog all the time at this stage of the passage. Occasionally I could see the sun through the swirling mist overhead, but no horizon. I took a sun-shot with my bubble sextant, with its automatic

367

averaging device, but I do not think that I could have succeeded but for the thousands of shots I had taken when we were developing the bubble sextant for flying in the war.

During the night a bird kept circling the ship chittering and mewing and I wondered if it was the same one that I had heard on the Banks in 1960. On June 24th I wrote in my log, 'This is the sailing that sailors' dreams are made of, across the misty mysterious Grand Banks smooth as the Solent with water gliding along the hull gurgling and rumbling.' The magic of the voyage was in my blood. It was sheer joy to set or trim a sail to keep *Gipsy Moth* sailing at her best; it was sport getting over difficulties. I laughed at incidents like coming across that steamer on the Grand Banks. It began to seem as if life was a joke, and should be treated as one. I was bursting with fitness and *joie de vivre* that seemed to build up after a few weeks alone. Perhaps it had taken three weeks to shed the materialism of ordinary living. I had become twice as efficient as when with people; my sensations were all greater; excitement, fear, pleasure, achievement, all seemed sharper. My senses were much more acute, and everything was much more vivid – the shape and colour of sky and sea; feeling spray and wind, heat and cold; tasting food and drink; hearing the slightest change in the weather, the sea or the ship's gear. I have never enjoyed anything more than that marvellous last 1,000 miles sailing along the eastern seaboard of North America.

On June 27th the day's run was 132¼ miles. At 9 PM I turned in early; the wind was backing and I expected to be called out soon. At 11 PM I woke and lay listening to *Gipsy Moth* riding madly through the night. It was rough going, but also it was intensely exhilarating, and I lay for some time pondering whether I should let her carry on. I thought that the mast, sails and gear could stand the strain, but Miranda was the weak link I feared for. Finally I dragged myself out of my blankets and climbed into the cockpit. *Gipsy Moth* was on a reach under yankee and full main, with a Force 6 wind on the beam. She was rushing into the dark with apparently acres of white water from the bow waves

368

tearing past. I reckoned that we were doing 10 knots, faster than we had ever sailed before. Occasional combers rolled the boat over on to her beam, or slewed her stern or bows round. Regretfully, I lowered the big jib, and reefed two rolls of the mainsail. Still, *Gipsy Moth* was going faster than she had done before on the voyage. It was a rough night, but when I woke at 6.30 in the morning I found the sun streaming into the cabin out of a clear sky.

At noon that day *Gipsy Moth* had sailed 159½ miles in the previous twenty-four hours. If only she could have had a fresh breeze all the time since the end of that gale! But day after day brought hours of calm, and hours of light airs. The daily distances sailed showed how well *Gipsy Moth* was going; one day she logged 132 miles, in spite of four hours' calm and five hours of light airs. On three days after the gale she sailed more than 130 miles a day, and only on four days out of the thirteen sailed less than 100 miles. To have *Gipsy Moth* sailing well and under full control by Miranda in a zephyr gave me just as much pleasure as having her going well in a gale. Once in the middle of the night I woke up to find her becalmed. As I lay I pondered why the sails were asleep instead of flapping, and why the boom was not creaking as it swung to and fro. I went up into the cockpit and the first thing I noticed was a reflection of the planet Jupiter in the sea, something I have never seen before offshore. The sea could not have been calmer. To my surprise *Gipsy Moth* was ghosting along at 1½ knots in the right direction, with Miranda in control. It seemed hardly believable; I suspected that the log was reading wrongly, and out of curiosity I popped up again an hour later. I found that *Gipsy Moth* had sailed 2½ miles during the hour.

One day the wind pressed me out of the Labrador current into the Gulf Stream. This set *Gipsy Moth* back eighteen miles, the Gulf Stream averaging three-quarters of a knot. It was unfortunate from a racing sailor's point of view, but from a personal viewpoint it was wonderful – a perfect fine day, with pale-blue sky and deep-blue sea sparkling in the sun. Now and then *Gipsy Moth* sailed through a lane of dark yellow seaweed from the Sargasso Sea. I thought that here was the occasion to change for dinner, to put on my green velvet smoking jacket which I had hopefully carried from England hanging in the clothes locker, and to sit down to a royal feast of grapefruit; cold salmon, with fresh potatoes and onions; ginger nuts and Danish blue cheese (a *specialité de la maison*); almonds and raisins; coffee. But it was not to be; when the time came for dinner, I was too tired. All through this voyage I had been racing much harder than in 1960, changing the sails more often, and trimming them more frequently. Preparing my daily reports, making contact with London, and transmitting, used up about an hour a day, navigation filled up to two hours, and the antics necessary to charge the batteries used up between half an hour and three hours a day. Usually it was so late at night before I could sit down to my third meal that I wanted to drop down asleep immediately afterwards, with restless dreams to follow. When I cut down to two major meals a day I felt much fitter for it.

At 6 AM on July 1st (ship's time was now the same as New York time, five hours earlier than British Summer Time) I had been thirty days out from Plymouth. I was still 340 miles short of New York.

Shortly before this I sailed out of the Gulf Stream and back into the Labrador current again. I was now in fog, and the sea was greenish. A few hours earlier I had been on the foredeck in swimming shorts an hour before midnight; now I lit the Aladdin stove. Soon I was becalmed in thin fog on George's Shoal. Trawlers hooting in the fog were passing unseen to and fro all around. Trawlers presumably indicated fish, so I rousted out my line and streamed it overboard. When below again, I heard an uncanny quiet plunk! ending in a sigh. 'Aha,' I thought stepping into the cockpit, 'I know that sound.' I was in the middle of a large school of whales, and three of them were headed straight for the stern of the boat. Sensitive animals like whales, I thought, must know that the boat is there, but, as they came on unswerving, my confidence vanished. I believe that many small boat disappearances have been due to whales. Those charging *Gipsy Moth* were only small ones; 15 to 25 feet long, but they were big enough and I picked up my horn and blew the hardest blast I could. Twenty feet off they dived under the stern and came up 50 feet away on the other side. There were a lot – I thought about 100 – milling round at speed. Suddenly they all dashed off towards the west at full speed, leaving a seething white wake. Then I noticed an equally big school coming at full speed from the west. They met head on, and there seemed to be about an acre of seething boiling white water where they milled round madly. Then, as one, they all dived, the surface became smooth again, and I saw them no more. Were they meeting for love or for war, I wondered. Had those three rushing headlong at *Gipsy Moth* thought she was one of the other school? I hauled in my fishing line, taking it as a hint that my efforts were not approved of. I was grateful when a breeze crept in, and *Gipsy Moth* was able to steal away from the fogbound shoal.

That evening I had a fright. I had been charging the batteries and when I switched off to listen for trawlers I heard water running. I snatched up the trapdoor in the cabin floor, and found the bilge full of water. It was a blood-freezing sight. Where was the hole? Could I find it, and stop the inrush before the ship sank? These questions flashed on my brain as I started to search.

It was only the pipe bringing in seawater to the cooling jacket of the motor which had parted. The bilge was not full of water, it was only half full. Now I could laugh at the joke, but it called for a celebration that it was nothing worse. After due thought I set to work and made a do-it-yourself repair of the joint. I wondered what else could turn up to interfere with the battery charging.

On July 2nd at 2.20 PM I saw my first mark since the Eddystone Light – a whistle buoy abeam, and a few hours later the Texas Tower which I had hoped to see from the shoals in 1960. If I had only known it, Sheila was looking down at me. She was flying across, and Jim Percy, knowing my position from London, had diverted the plane a few miles to pass overhead. Sheila recognized *Gipsy Moth* five miles below her.

My repair to the water pipe seemed successful, but it was not long after I started charging again before an exhaust flame showed through my exhaust pipe repairs. Once more I donned the old black raincoat I kept for dirty work on the motor, and worked away in acute discomfort to botch up another repair.

When next I looked at the Texas Tower I saw the three white domes standing high above the horizon on long stilted legs – a mirage. I had a fascinating view through my binoculars of the sun setting. Because of the mirage, it looked like an untidy heap of red-hot metal dumped on the horizon. Gradually it flattened and widened and as it disappeared I was able to see the famous green flash magnified seven times.

Next day the American coast was undoubtedly close. I was surrounded by fishing launches, with high latticed towers, and as many as five men standing on them, one above the other, watching with fanatic intentness for signs of fish. This was my first day without bread, for I found my last loaf too mouldy to eat. At 7.45 in the evening I had my first sight of land for thirty-two days – Block Island.

That night I was sailing fast along the coast of Long Island, a few miles off shore. By midnight I was pushing my eyelids up to keep awake, and the frustrated longing to sleep was painful. The wind was slowly veering and heading me in towards the land and I dared not risk sleeping. Forty-five minutes after midnight the other tack, offshore, had become equally good. I tacked, and as I was now headed out to sea in the direction of the Bahamas I immediately flopped into my bunk and went to sleep. At 5.25 in the morning I woke and rolled my eye to the telltale compass beside my berth. What I saw was the letter N, for North. It meant that I was headed right for Long Island. I was out of my bunk and into the cockpit in record time. Day was breaking, and there was land dead ahead, but still two miles ahead, thank God. The wind had continued to veer through the night, and *Gipsy Moth*, keeping her same course relative to the wind, had veered with it, until she was pointing dead ashore. After I had calmed down, I pondered on why I had woken up then instead of thirty minutes later. I believe that the instinct for danger is latent in man, and becomes active as the senses sharpen during a long period alone. It was this same instinct which woke me when I was near the fishing steamer on the Grand Banks.

Later the wind backed, but not enough for me to clear the south coast of Long Island, and I was making short tacks off shore each time I sailed in too close to the beach. I was looking at the damsels sunbathing on the beach when I was intrigued to see a large Stars and Stripes run up the flagpole of a beach house. Not realizing, as an ignorant Englishman, that July 4th was Independence Day, I wondered if they were taking *Gipsy Moth* with her White Ensign flying for a British invasion.

At last I reached a point where *Gipsy Moth* would just clear the gently curving coast at the south end of Long Island. I studied the chart to make sure there were no obstructions ahead, and then set about preparing lunch before having a nap. By the grace of God I popped my head up through the hatch for a look round, and found that *Gipsy Moth* was headed for the middle of a great long line of poles emerging from the sea at all angles, and stretching half a mile off shore. When I came close I found that they were linked together by heavy cables, and had big nets suspended from them, which were presumably used as fish ponds. Had I relied on the chart I should have charged right into the middle of them.

As the daylight faded I could see the three flashes of the Ambrose Light Vessel, my finishing mark. I called up London and told John Fairhall that the Ambrose Light was in sight. This was 3,000 miles away and thinking of all the difficulties I had had to keep the transmitter going I had a surge of feeling with the thought, 'Well, that's finished!' Then John took me aback by saying, 'Please call me again when you have actually crossed the line.' After talking to him day after day, very often with an awkward situation at my end, there was something between us, and I reluctantly agreed.

I called up the Ambrose Light Vessel and asked the operator there to time my arrival. Two welcoming launches arrived, but the light was too dusky to see who was on board. The time of my finish was 9.07 PM. Then the fun began.

To reach the Ambrose Light I had been beating into a freshening wind. Immediately I turned the Light, I had to reset my sails, retrim Miranda and start running down wind for New York. It was nearly dark, and I had no idea where I was to go. I had assumed that someone on one of the launches would tell me, and I had not studied the charts. I thought that the bigger launch was Laurie Hamilton's; who had been so friendly to us at Indian Point in 1960. The launch took up a position astern, just out of hearing range, and resolutely kept position there, as if I had the plague. I was darting about, retrimming, trying to see ahead. In the dark I seemed to be surrounded by launches. I had promised to call up London again. I connected up the aerial and darted below to switch on the set and warm it up. I had a nightmare Alice-in-Wonderland feeling of charging into the unknown dark, surrounded by a circle of baleful red or green eyes, like wolves waiting to pounce on an exhausted prey. Immediately I got London I snapped that I was across the line and must close down, which I immediately did.

I dragged out a chart and tried to study it in the cockpit with a torch. Between whiles, I hurriedly scanned ahead, to see if I was on a collision course with any of the launches, or with the huge buoys lining the steamer lane into New York. I decided on a heading and stuck to it. I could see that I should need to keep a sharp look-out for buoys. I knew that I ought to lower my sails and get information, or reduce sail and speed, but *Gipsy Moth* was by now going like a bat in Hell, with a great sailing breeze, tearing up New York harbour in the dark. It was exhilarating and exciting. The pilotage was difficult, because of the countless lights all round; shore lights in the background, steamer lights, buoys winking red ahead, and navigation lights of smaller craft near me. One craft near abeam which I could see silhouetted against the shore lights appeared to be a powerful naval or Customs launch. To the north, hundreds of big fireworks were shooting into the air. I assumed that was a normal evening's performance at Coney Island, not connecting it with Independence Day. On reaching the narrows I kept on for Staten Island, sixteen miles from Ambrose Light. As I branched into the Hudson River, still at a grand pace, the pilotage became trickier still. There seemed to be lights not only in every direction, but also up in the air. Suddenly I spotted a small white light away to starboard, small and low-powered among the thousands of lights all round. Then I noticed a red navigation light away to port. Something puzzled me there, I don't know what. I stared intently. Then, out of the night, took shape the extra blackness of a long string of unlit barges, perhaps a quarter mile long, right across my path. I was headed straight for the middle of them. 'That's enough,' I said to myself, and rounded up into wind.

And so ended the thousand miles along the eastern seaboard, which may have been the most wonderful sail I shall ever have.

CHAPTER THIRTY-TWO

HOME AND AWAY

IN THE middle of the night I was in a dock at Staten Island, having a welcome from Sheila who, I now discovered, had been aboard Laurie's motor yacht all the time. Before I got off *Gipsy Moth*, Laurie said that he had an important telegram. Standing on the dark dockside above me, shining a torch and with Alistair Cooke, the writer, beside him, he read out a most complimentary telegram. 'I would like to extend my hearty congratulations to you on your successful new record-breaking crossing of the Atlantic Stop Your skill and gallantry as a sailor are already well known but this new achievement will certainly cap your career Stop And we are particularly pleased that you have arrived in the United States on July 4 the great historic day in United States history when we celebrate our independence = John F. Kennedy.'

It always abashes me if someone important in the world uses his valuable time and thought to send me a message. In the morning, when I woke up, Laurie produced another exciting telegram, this time from Prince Philip, which read, 'Delighted to see that you have achieved your ambition to beat your own record Stop All members of the Guild and millions of other admirers send their heartiest congratulations on a magnificent achievement = Philip.'

Later in the morning I was proceeding up East River under motor with Sheila and Laurie's skipper on board, when the exhaust pipe finally blew my repairs into asbestos smoke. The cabin was smothered in it, as if from a volcanic eruption. The Statue of Liberty was abeam, and at that critical moment the *Queen Elizabeth* passed close on her way out of New York Harbour. She saluted *Gipsy Moth* with three blasts, and that was one of the great moments of a lifetime.

Although I had failed to beat my 30-day target by 3 days, 15 hours, 7 minutes, at least I had knocked nearly a week off my 1960 time – 6 days, 21 hours, 3 minutes, to be exact. (And if I had succeeded in making a thirty-day crossing, as I had hoped, I should have been deprived of the immense sport, anticipation, hope and excitement of trying again!)

After getting the motor repaired by our old friends at Minneford's Boatyard, City Island, Sheila and I had a happy cruise down Long Island Sound to Cape Cod. Abreast of Fishers Island a small yacht came near as we were sailing, and the man at the helm said, 'Welcome. I am the temporary pastor at Fishers Island, and I am delighted to meet *Gipsy Moth*, because I used Miranda and her guidance as the text for my sermon last Sunday.'

Early one morning we left Stonington in a fresh breeze which steadily increased. There was a yacht on our starboard bow, and we kept together for hour after hour. As we approached Point Judith, and the area where the 12-metre races for the America's Cup are held, Sheila said, 'Do shorten sail. We are not racing, and it's getting much too bumpy.' I went on deck and reefed the mainsail. The yacht ahead reefed at the same time and, as we overtook her, I was surprised to see her name, *Carina*. Dick Nye's *Carina* had won two Fastnet Races, in which I had been taking part. When we reached Indian Point we tied up to the dock at the end of

Cousin Dick's garden, and next morning she said, 'Come for a ride in the automobile; I want to visit a very old friend of mine at Wood's Hole.' His name was van Alan Clark, and when Cousin Dick introduced me he said, '*Gipsy Moth!* Why, I was coming down from Long Island Sound on Saturday in my son's yacht *Carina* and had just said to him I must have someone relieve me at the helm, I can't take it any longer, when I'm damned if your *Gipsy Moth* didn't sail by with no one at the helm at all!' This had been Dick Nye's previous yacht.

We had a great welcome from Cousin Dick and her family, and stayed with them for three weeks. Giles flew out to join us as soon as his term ended at Westminster School. He arrived a few days after his sixteenth birthday, and we waited to let him have a week at Indian Point. My impression was that he filled every available minute of it. At one dance he was putting everything he knew into the twist. Cousin Dick was, or pretended to be, shocked. 'Well, to think that I should live to see that,' she said, 'and from an Englishman too.' I think Giles was laying it on. Afterwards I noticed Cousin Dick dancing with him, though not the twist.

What wonderful sailing water the Americans have! From our bedroom, where I could hear *Gipsy Moth*'s halyards rapping the metal mast where she lay at the end of Cousin Dick's jetty, I could also hear the sailing instructor coaching the boys and girls of the Wiano Yacht Club as they tacked and manoeuvred near the house.

Our American friends wanted us to leave from Plymouth, Massachusetts, for Plymouth, England, but we wriggled out of it, wishing for a quiet start from Indian Point. We left on August 13th.

As we cleared Pollock's Rip at the entrance to the North Channel through the Nantucket Shoals, it fell dead calm, dense fog rolled up, night fell and the tide turned, setting on the shoals south of the channel. We were not racing now, and I needed only to start the motor. But when I tried to, the exhaust pipe blew out clouds of asbestos, and the motor stopped dead. Nothing would induce it to go. I spent the night

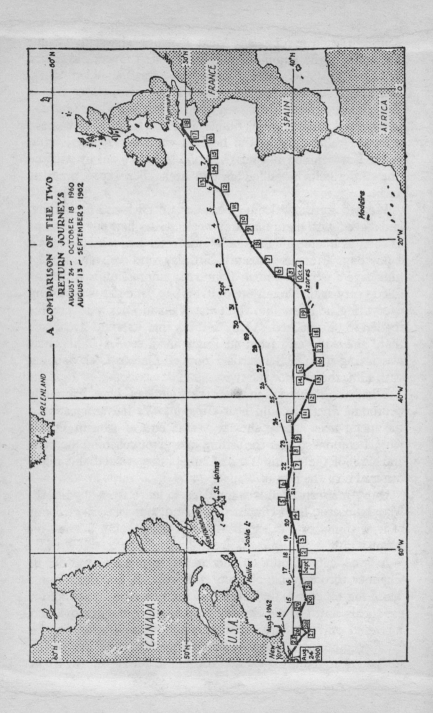

at the helm, coaxing *Gipsy Moth* to ghost eastward with any breath of wind I could detect. I did not like it, but managed to keep clear of the shoals until the tide turned at 3.25 in the morning, and I handed over the tiller to Sheila after twenty hours on the job.

Although we had some great sailing on this passage home, I was not happy. I did not like sailing with Sheila aboard without keeping a watch. When alone, I had only myself to consider. Now Sheila was not fit enough to take a watch, and in any case did not want to, and would not agree to Giles keeping watch on his own. For a lot of the time I was seriously worried. Sheila had sailed tired out from the efforts she had made with the map publishing business in my absence, and helping to organize my departure from England, as well as our arrangements in America. After flying out to America she had led a strenuous life in New York before sailing down to Cape Cod. Soon after we sailed she began getting severe headaches, and felt sick. We ran into rough seas and strong winds, and I think she was worrying about Giles, who was also in his berth with headaches, and felt sick for day after day. The voyage was a formidable enterprise for a boy of sixteen. The heat did not help. I had aimed for the centre of the Gulf Stream, and often the water was hotter than the air. On August 15, 16, 17, and 18 it was 80°. I used to sluice myself down with buckets of Gulf Stream in the cockpit, but Sheila was not well enough to do this. Day after day I logged winds of Force 6, with sometimes Force 8 or 9. We made good 750 miles in five days through rough seas. Even with the help of the Gulf Stream this was a good pace. Sheila could not rest because of the rough going, and after a fortnight I was getting seriously worried about her. On August 20th she had some brandy, and wrote in her diary that she felt well, but had no appetite. I could see no improvement. Giles continued to feel ill, and I suspected that his eyes were causing headache due to the strong light reflected from the sea. I feared that ocean sailing was not for him. Then, at the end of the third week, he made a big effort, came on deck, and began helping me with the sail changing. Every day after that he got stronger, and before the end of the voyage he was changing headsails by himself, working the foredeck alone. Before the end of the voyage he was a first-class foredeck hand.

For Sheila, I did not know whether it was better to sail on regardless of the rough going and reach England as soon as I could, or to halve the speed for easier going, and take much longer over the voyage. In the end I compromised, sailing fairly fast, but not at racing speed.

Had it not been for these worries it would have been an interesting voyage. I found it fascinating to plot the temperature of the Gulf Stream day by day, and also to compare my dead-reckoning position with my sextant fix, to get a rough idea of the meanderings of the Gulf Stream or Gulf River as it might well be called. The lanes of dark yellow sargasso seaweed, considered with the wind direction at the time, seemed related to the direction of the Stream, which sometimes flowed north or south, sometimes looped westwards, before continuing its easterly passage. This sargasso weed frequently stopped the log spinner several times a day. I used my long boathook to catch clumps of it as we sailed past, and when I examined them in a bucket they were full of tiny crabs and shrimps.

Several stormy petrels, Mother Carey's chickens, came on board. It is easy to understand how these birds have intrigued sailors through the ages. I used to watch them, fascinated, as they crossed and recrossed the logline with their fluttery, irregular wing beats, occasionally pecking at the line as it twisted after the yacht like a thin snake. Sailors have dreaded them as forerunners of storm, and when we saw so many on this voyage we certainly had rough weather, though no storm. The one that came aboard on August 24th I found later in the evening in one of the lockers under the cockpit seat, with its wings outstretched. It was a small bird, and fitted neatly in my hand, cool to the touch. Its long black legs had three long toes, webbed with a membrane like a bat's wings. Its curved beak was like a tiny parrot's. I held it pointing into wind in my hand, and it took off into the night. Then, when I was on the counter looking at Miranda, it flew back towards me, and came quite close, fluttering feebly as if wanting to alight again. When I went on deck two hours after midnight I nearly trod on it. We were having a rough ride on a starry night. At 3.20 AM when I next went on deck, the petrel was still there; and it took off from my hand like a black moth.

August 27th dawned with rain squalls in all quarters under dirty, stormy-looking skies, and I donned an oilskin coat for the first time with regret. Until then I had been doing fore-deck work in bathing shorts only.

Throughout the voyage Miranda gave trouble nearly every day and Sheila worried about it. On September 3rd Miranda lost her grip after *Gipsy Moth*'s stern had been slewed round by a big wave, and while Giles and I were trying to fix it up again, we were both well sluiced by a wave which pooped *Gipsy Moth*, and filled the cockpit. The two chief causes of Miranda's slipping were some self-tapping screws which kept on working loose and freeing the collar they were supposed to hold; secondly, a stainless steel band, doubled over to hold a bolt, was slowly being drawn open.

My anxiety about Sheila was at its height, and I was feeling sad and unhappy about her, when we sailed over the slope of the Continental Shelf into soundings. This was 150 miles south-west of Land's End, and here it was like sailing over a 7,000-foot cliff into the comparatively shallow water of 400 feet depth. This change in the ocean floor has always been important to sailors: west of it the oceanographers have recorded waves 70 feet high in the Atlantic, whereas on the Cornwall shores waves rarely exceed 20 feet.

As we sailed over the shelf a magical change took place in Sheila. She recovered so quickly that I could see a change every time I looked. The fact that it happened as we sailed out of deep water was no doubt only a coincidence, but it was odd that her ailing at the beginning of the voyage should have coincided with our sailing off the American Continental Shelf when the depth suddenly increased from 300 feet to 12,000 feet. I felt an immense surge of relief.

By my reckoning we were forty-eight miles from the Lizard when I had a blinding row with Sheila, though why I cannot remember. I turned in and slept without moving for twelve hours. Giles and Sheila kept watch, and Giles logged the Lizard light abeam at 3.10 in the morning. When I surfaced at 8 AM they said that they had had an exciting fast ride into Plymouth Bay.

As we sailed into Plymouth Sound on a fine sunny day with an ideal sailing breeze, I photographed Sheila sitting on the cabin top with her back against the mast, and Giles lolling with his hands on the spinnaker pole, and thought that I had never seen a happier, healthier-looking pair. Giles had started the voyage as a boy, but finished it a self-reliant man. As we crossed the line of Plymouth breakwater it was five seconds past noon GMT and we had made the passage from Pollock's Rip in 26 days, 12 hours 14 minutes. Even from west to east it was a fast passage short-handed.

During the winter of 1962–3 I planned a number of changes to rig, gear and methods, which I hope will speed up *Gipsy Moth* next year. Now I am impatient to return to the Beaulieu River and start my sailing trials. All my new ideas must be proved right or wrong before the spring of 1964. The single-handed race across the Atlantic starts on May 23rd, and I believe that there will be a formidable entry for it. It seems to have fired the imagination of many yachtsmen, and so it should, if it is the greatest of all yacht races. I feel sure that my rivals will all be out after my title. I believe that with luck *Gipsy Moth* can go a good deal faster yet, and I look forward to a thrilling, fascinating race. What is more, I shall take my green velvet smoking jacket again, hoping that my new handling methods will be efficient enough for me to dine in style one night while keeping *Gipsy Moth* racing at her full speed.

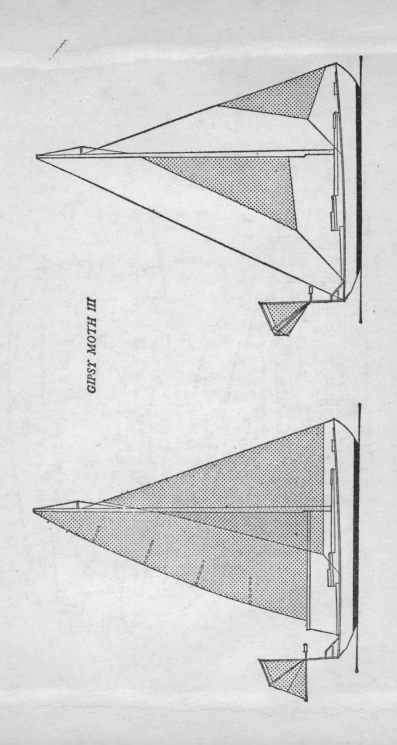

GIPSY MOTH III

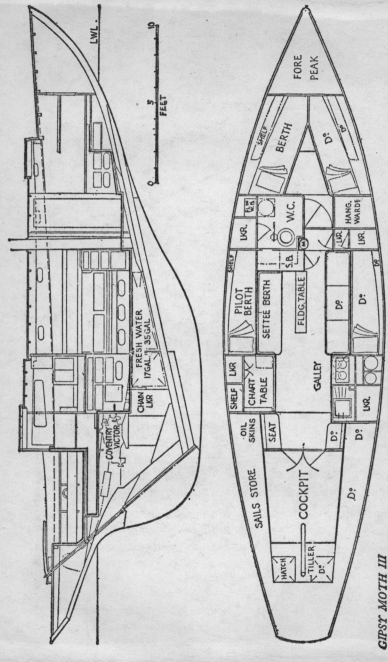

GIPSY MOTH III

SOLO ATLANTIC RACE 1960
Gipsy Moth III

SAIL CHANGES

	No. of times set	Total time set hrs. mins.	Average hrs. mins.
No. 1 jib (genoa)	17	398.58	23.28
No. 2 jib	11	246.00	22.22
No. 3 jib	7	144.45	20.41
No. 4 jib	1	24.00	24.00
No jib set	3	12.50	04.17
Ghoster jib	3	22.05	07.22
Full mainsail	23	418.00	18.10
Main with one reef	6	42.50	07.08
Main with two reefs	4	37.35	09.24
Main with three reefs	6	58.04	14.21
Trysail	7	79.15	11.19
No mainsail or trysail	25	186.56	07.29
No. 1 jib boomed out as spinnaker	2	35.22	17.41
No. 2 jib boomed out as spinnaker	2	33.22	16.41
Bare poles	5	47.50	09.34

WIND

On the wind	636.24 hrs. =	26 days 12 hrs. 24 mins.
Wind-free	288.16 hrs. =	12 days 00 hrs. 16 mins.
Bare poles	47.50 hrs. =	1 day 23 hrs. 50 mins.
Total	972.30 hrs. =	40 days 12 hrs. 30 mins.

FOG

16 times   345.02 hrs. = 14 days 09 hrs. 02 mins.
This amounts to over 1,430 miles of sailing.

INDEX

Avro (A. V. Roe), 64
Azores, 340–2

Babuyan Island, 222
Baghdad, 90, 92, 93
    accident to Herrick, 268–9
Bagtas, President of Aviation
    Committee, Manila, 216
Bali, 264
Baou Blanc, 302, 346
Barnes, Group Captain Kelly,
    275
Barnstaple Infirmary, 20
Barton, Humphrey, 316
Basco, Formosa, 227
Bastia, Corsica, 269
Batavia, 97, 100, 264
Bathurst Island, 104
Bay of Islands, New Zealand,
    56, 57
Bay of Plenty, New Zealand,
    56
Bazzan, Libyan farmer, 89
Beaulieu River, 313, 314, 343,
    382
Beaumont, Christopher, 115
Belgrade, 72
Bell, Wing-Cdr J. C. G., 312
Bellerophon, steamer, 249
Benghazi, 76, 89, 269
Bennett, Air Vice Marshal Don,
    261, 272
Bergin, Dr K. G., 338
Bima, Java, 79, 102–3, 264
birds-nesting, interest in, 29
Biscay, Bay of, 35
Black Forest, 74
Blackwater Gold Mine, New
    Zealand, 43
Blackwell, Charles, 66
Block Island, 336, 372
Bloodhound, Duke of
    Edinburgh's yacht, 287
Boldrewood, Ralph, 31
Bounty mutineers' descendants,
    140

Boyer, Derek, 302
Brasher, Chris, 306, 332, 338,
    339
Bremen, S.S., 35, 40, 257
    ship's fireman on, 36–7
Brent, mechanic at Norfolk Is.,
    144, 145, 146, 147
Brightlingsea, 284
Brisbane River, 193
Bristol Gift, steamer, 352
Britannia Cup, 289
British Broadcasting
    Corporation, 348
Brooklands, 66, 68, 77, 269
Brooklyn Bridge, 340
Brunette Downs Homestead,
    Australia, 106, 107, 108
Brynzeel, Caes, 343
Bucharest, 73
Buckie (Riordan), deckhand on
    Figaro, 288, 291
Buckler's Hard, 315, 341, 343,
    347
Bunderberg, Australia, 71
Burma, 266
Burton-on-Trent, 33
Bushire, Persia, 94, 267
Bygrave slide rule, 134

Cairns, Queensland, 195–6
Cairo, 90, 269
Calcutta, repairs at, 95
Cambria, schooner, 305
Cambridge Instruments, Ltd,
    272
Camooweal, Australia, 105, 107,
    108, 109, 111, 112, 113
Canberra, HMAS, 186
Cancer of the lung, 288,
    293–302
    decision not to operate, 295,
    296, 297
    Dr Mattei, 302
    nature treatment, 298–9
    power of prayer, 303

388

389

Chris Bonington
Quest for Adventure £4.95

'Adventure involves a journey, or a sustained endeavour, in which there are the elements of risk and of the unknown, which have to be overcome by the physical skills of the individual' – Chris Bonington

'Himself a famous adventurer, Bonington has assembled stories of modern adventure and tries to discover their common factors ... Thesiger whose journeys across the Empty Quarter were an experience of deep personal impulse, and Armstrong, whose moon-steps were controlled by computer and watched by 500 million people ... the yachtsman Moitessier ... Fuchs and Hillary' OBSERVER

Adrian Vaughan
Signalman's Morning
and Signalman's Twilight £2.95

Adrian Vaughan's two chronicles of the signalman's life through the last years of steam are certain to become classics of railway writing. When he became a signalman he witnessed the swift sweep of change over the iron way. First as the Great Western became British Railways Western Region and then as the Beeching Axe dealt the final blow to a way of working life unchanged for a hundred years.